# STREETLIFE CHINA

In this extraordinary collection, Michael Dutton offers both a lively reader and a unified theoretical argument about contemporary Chinese streetlife. The pieces—drawn from newspapers, government documents, academic writing and interviews—build a vivid picture of everyday life in China. Dutton's editorial hand and incisive commentary on these pieces form a rigorous discussion around current theory. Streetlife is shown to be a creative, dynamic, dissenting, deviant and often compliant aspect of the economic, political and cultural face of China. Key themes are the emergence of a market-driven consumer culture, and how this intersects with social outsiders; state strategies and the street's response. Underlying this narrative is the theme of human rights. There is no better introduction to contemporary China, and few more entertaining, vivid and stimulating accounts of shifts in cultural life and politics.

MICHAEL DUTTON teaches in the Department of Political Science at the University of Melbourne, and is also the Co-Director of the Institute of Postcolonial Studies in Melbourne. He has held three visiting research fellowships in China. He is co-editor of the journal *Postcolonial Studies* and author of *Policing and Punishment in China*, published by Cambridge in 1992.

**Cambridge Modern China Series**

Edited by William Kirby, Harvard University

Other titles in the series:

Warren I. Cohen and Li Zhao, eds. *Hong Kong Under Chinese Rule: The Economic and Political Implications of Reversion*
    0 521 62158 5 hardback, 0 521 62761 3 *paperback*

Tamara Jacka *Women's Work in Rural China: Change and Continuity in an Era of Reform*
    0 521 56225 2 hardback, 0 521 59928 8 paperback

Shiping Zheng *Party vs. State in Post-1949 China: The Institutional Dilemma*
    0 521 58205 9 hardback, 0 521 58819 7 paperback

Edward S. Steinfeld *Forging Reform in China: The Fate of State-Owned Industry*
    0 521 63335 4 hardback, 0 521 77861 1 paperback

'Movement on a Clear Morning', Lu Ren
《清晨的活动》鲁人

# STREETLIFE CHINA

## MICHAEL DUTTON

CAMBRIDGE
UNIVERSITY PRESS

PUBLISHED BY THE PRESS SYNDICATE OF THE UNIVERSITY OF CAMBRIDGE
The Pitt Building, Trumpington Street, Cambridge, United Kingdom

CAMBRIDGE UNIVERSITY PRESS
The Edinburgh Building, Cambridge CB2 2RU, UK
40 West 20th Street, New York, NY 10011–4211, USA
10 Stamford Road, Oakleigh, Melbourne 3166, Australia

www.cambridge.org
Information on this title: www.cambridge.org/9780521631419

First published 1998
Reprinted 1999, 2000

Typeset in Adobe Frutiger 10 pt, Adobe Garamond 11 pt

*A catalogue record for this book is available from the British Library*

*Library of Congress Cataloguing in Publication data*

Streetlife China/Michael Dutton.
p.   cm. – (Cambridge modern China series)
Collection of articles by various Chinese writers about the life in
contemporary China. Includes bibliographical references and index.

ISBN 0-521-63141-6 (alk. paper).
ISBN 0-521-63719-8 (pbk.  : alk. paper)

1. China – Social life and customs – 1976–
2. China – Social conditions – 1976–
I. Dutton, Michael Robert. II. Series.

DS779.23.S75  1998
951.05' 7 – dc21
98-8136
CIP

ISBN-13  978-0-521-63141-9 hardback
ISBN-10  0-521-63141-6 hardback

ISBN-13  978-0-521-63719-0 paperback
ISBN-10  0-521-63719-8 paperback


Transferred to digital printing 2005

# CONTENTS

| | | |
|---|---|---:|
| Illustrations | | x |
| Preface | | xii |
| Timeline on Chinese History | | xv |
| Streetlife Subalterns | | 1 |

### Part I: Rights, Traditions, Daily Life and Deviance — 16

| | | |
|---|---|---:|
| 1 | RIGHTS AND TRADITIONS | 23 |
| | Human Rights and Chinese Tradition *Xia Yong* | 23 |
| | The Traditional Chinese View of the Cosmos and the Practices of Daily Life *Li Yiyuan* | 31 |
| | The Gift of Self | 39 |
| | The 'Gift' and the Confucian Notion of Propriety, *Li* *Xu Ping* | 40 |
| 2 | DAILY LIFE IN THE WORK UNIT | 42 |
| | People of the Work Unit *He Xinghan* | 42 |
| | The Work Unit: A Unique Form of Social Organisation *Lu Feng* | 53 |
| | The Work Unit: 'Face' and Place *Yi Zhongtian* | 58 |
| 3 | DEFINING 'OUTSIDERS', LABELLING *LIUMANG* | 62 |
| | To be Defined a *Liumang* *Chen Baoliang* | 63 |
| | Second-class Citizen *Ge Fei* | 65 |
| | Homosexuals in Beijing *Jin Ren* | 70 |

### Part II: The 'Strategies' of Government and 'Tactics' of the Subaltern — 76

| | | |
|---|---|---:|
| 1 | ANALYSIS | 81 |
| | Household Registration and the Caste-like Quality of Peasant Life *Gong Xikui* | 81 |
| | From Caste to Class: A Brief Introduction to *A Third Eye* | 85 |
| | A Third Eye on China's Living Volcano *Leuninger* | 87 |
| | Peasant Movement: A Police Perspective *Yang Wenzhong and Wang Gongfan* | 89 |
| 2 | GOVERNMENT STRATEGIES (1) | 93 |
| | The Resident Identity Card and the Household Register *Zhang Qingwu* | 94 |
| | Registration Files, Registration Cards *Yu Lei* | 97 |
| | Beijing's Fee for Residency Scheme | 99 |
| | User Pays Beijing *Zhou Daping* | 100 |

The 'Bill' of Beef Street                                        103
Mass-line Policing: Weikeng Public Security Committee,
   Beijing   *Feng Rui*                           107

3  GOVERNMENT STRATEGIES (2)                                     112
The Special Professions   *Yu Lei*                               113
The Special Population   *Yu Lei*                                115
Beggars, Prostitutes and Undesirables: The Internal Rules of the State   118
Transient Beggars in the City                                   120
Prostitution                                                    125
Female Education and Fostering Centre                           128

4  SUBALTERN TACTICS, GOVERNMENT RESPONSE                       130
Nursing Change                                                  131
Beijing *Baomu*: Taking Beijing People's Money and
   Doing Beijingers' work   *Sun Xiaomei*        132
'*Baomu* Blues'                                                 140
'Life on the Outside'                                           144
Zhejiang Village, Beijing: A Visit                              147
Zhejiang Village: A Government Tale                             152

*Part III: Naming, Framing, Marking*                            160

1  NAMING                                                       165
Revolutionary Culture   *Yang Dongping*                         165
What's in a Name: Revolutionary China and the New Cosmology
   of the Name   *Yang Dongping*                 169
What's in a Name: Traditional Chinese Cosmology
   and Naming   *Li Yiyuan*                      171

2  FRAMING                                                      172
The Body According to the Acupuncturist                         173
Mao's Body as Acupunctural Art                                  174
Male Body Parts                                                 175
Female Body Parts                                               178
Slang Relating to Police                                        179

3  MARKING                                                      180
The World of the Tattoo   *Xu Yiqing and Zhang Hexian*          181
Tattoos: A Revival   *Gao Jian*                                 182
The Tattoo of the Criminal   *Jiang Fuyuan*                     187

*Part IV: The Architecture of Life*                             192

1  CITY SPACE                                                   196
Traditional Chinese Architecture and Hierarchy   *Zhao Dongri* 196
On Beijing   *Yang Dongping*                                    197
Beijing: The City as Compound   *Zhao Dongri*                   200

2 SOCIAL RELATIONS AND THE ARCHITECTURE OF LIFE 203
Clans, Gifts, Architecture  *Xu Ping* 204
Traditional Chinese Architecture as Symbolic Hierarchy  *Wang Shiren* 207
Changing Compounds: From Compound Household
  to Work Unit  *Yang Dongping* 208

3 OUT OF THE WORK UNIT 214
From a 'Person of the Work Unit' to a 'Social Person': Psychological
  Evolution Under the Impact of Reform  *Zhu Huaxin* 215
'One Family, Two Systems' 220

4 CHANGING LANDSCAPES, CHANGING MENTALITIES 222
High Risk, High Rise: Changes in Work Unit Accommodation
  and the Problem of Crime  *Xu Hanmin* 224
Compounds Old and New 228
Work Units and High Rise 229
Going Shopping 229
Buying Nation: Imperial and Commodified Renditions of Nationhood 231
Mapping Mao: From Cult to Commodity 232
From Mao Map to Tourist Trap 232
Mao Badges Enter the Market 235

*Part V: Stories of the Fetish: Tales of Chairman Mao* 238

1 THE BADGE AS BIOGRAPHY 242
Introduction to the Mao Badge (1)  *Wang Anting* 243
Introduction to the Mao Badge (2)  *Zhou Jihou* 244
Stories of 'Excess': Mao as Gift, Mao as Curse  *Zhou Jihou* 245
Buying Mao: Then and Now  *Liu Xin and Zhou Jihou* 249
An Introduction to Wang Anting: China's 'Badge Master'  *Zhou Jihou* 252
Interviews with the 'Badge Masters' Wang Anting and Dang Miao 253
The Story of Yan Xinlong  *Zhou Jihou* 258
My Story  *Zhou Jihou* 260
The Black Hole of Mao Zedong: The Art of Zhang Hongtu
  *Cao Zhangqing* 262
Chinese Culture Drawn into the Market  *Da Yang* 265
Mao and the Revolution Enter the Market 269

*Part VI: Market Trainings* 272

Tales of the Market, Tales of the Fetish: Stories from the Street 273

Select Bibliography 285
Index 290

# ILLUSTRATIONS

| | |
|---|---|
| Picture yourself in Beijing … | 2 |
| Tiananmen Square, June 1989 | 16 |
| Three levels of balance | 32 |
| The cover of Ge Fei's *Second-class Citizen* | 65 |
| A household registration booklet | 76 |
| The cover of Leuninger's *A Third Eye on China* | 86 |
| Codes used in resident identity cards | 96 |
| Scene from Beef Street | 104 |
| Special Population Form | 117 |
| Cultural Revolution nurse | 131 |
| 'Chinese' calendar girl | 131 |
| Poster advertising cures for sexual ailments | 131 |
| The '3.8 Family Services Company' sign | 135 |
| Li Ninlong | 140 |
| Lu Naihong | 144 |
| Scenes from Zhejiang village, Beijing | 148 |
| Beijing city map | 153 |
| Tattoo of Dragon | 160 |
| The body according to the acupuncturist | 173 |
| Mao's body as acupunctural art | 174 |
| The male body according to the thief | 175 |
| The female body according to the thief | 178 |
| Tattooing the body | 183 |
| The architecture of life | 192 |
| Inner and outer city of Beijing | 198 |
| The Forbidden City | 201 |
| Clan household | 205 |
| Compound household | 209 |
| A work unit in Beijing | 211 |
| Hu Lianpin | 220 |
| The character *chai* | 223 |
| Water tower | 223 |
| The work unit and compound household | 228 |
| Old-style work unit residences | 229 |
| New-style high-rise apartments | 229 |

An old-style Chinese store front                          230
Interior of an old-style department store                 230
The new shopping centre in Xidan district, Beijing        230
Inside the shopping pleasure dome                          230
Empire and nation                                         231
Commodification and nation                                231
Map of Mao badges                                         233
Yan'an Cave dwellings                                     234
Map of Mao Park                                           234
The 'long march' through the park                         234
Entry ticket to the park                                  234
Pure Mao                                                  235
Mao priced                                                236
Mao badges                                                238
Mao badge                                                 240
Mao badge as biography                                    243
Dang Miao                                                 253
Revolutionary cake                                        253
Wang Anting                                               254
The very small museum                                     255
The museum entrance                                       255
Wang in the museum                                        256
*Contemporary Cultural Relic*                             257
The Cultural Revolution alarm clock                       270
A Mao restaurant                                          271
The 'East is Red' double-cassette cover                   271
The Cultural Revolution alarm clock                       272
Cui Jian                                                  276
Chen Jing                                                 277
Monopoly (Entrepreneur)                                   279
A Mao watchface                                           281
A Mao lighter                                             281
Another face of Mao                                       281
A woman of the Chinese Revolution                         283
Bourgeois trappings                                       283

For me, this book is like a treasure box of possibilities. Possibilities both for Chinese society and for those of us in the business of making sense of it. While the diversity of this collection gives rise to its own heterogeneous possibilities all the pieces, in one way or another, build toward a picture of China in transition. In a funny and private way, this work also marks a very personal transition.

Any book with a readable title page is, to some extent, autobiographical, says Paul de Man, and this one is no exception. As I moved ground from researching a fairly empirical work on the Chinese police and toward a more cultural studies orientation, this collection took shape. This came about in part because of my growing interest in the work of Walter Benjamin, who spent many of his later years 'loitering', flâneur-like, in a study of the early commodity form in the West. This work not only helped frame many of the issues covered in this book but it also heavily influenced the form it would end up taking. It was Benjamin who wanted to 'write' using snip-bits of work stolen from the pens of others. Through these stolen lines he wanted to create his own mosaic of shock-like impressions about early capitalism. This idea enchanted me, but it proved hard to imagine how such a work could be organised and still be written in an accessible manner. Hard, that is, until I re-read Geremie Barmé and Linda Jaivin's *New Ghosts, Old Dreams*. Barmé and Jaivin arranged their collection of Chinese dissident writings in such a way as to produce a text that could be read as though it were a sustained piece rather than a collection of writings. *Streetlife China* became an attempt to build on Benjamin's radical insights by drawing on the architecture of Barmé and Jaivin. It was this desire to 'write' using other people's—Chinese people's—words that formed the contours along which the material now before you was collected, translated and arranged.

As this collection took shape friends, colleagues and students not only helped me carry the workload but pointed me in new directions. To those people I am eternally grateful. Foremost among them was Professor Xu Zhangrun. He not only collected and translated large parts of this volume but spent considerable time explaining to me the significance and depth of Chinese cultural difference. Kaz Ross tutored in the course in which much of this material came to life and she brought new and fresh ideas to the collection, pointing to possibilities I either didn't or couldn't see. The same was true of 'Waku Tongzhi', who read the manuscript in an earlier draft and offered some very useful suggestions. Then, there are my many friends and colleagues at the Institute of Postcolonial Studies. People like Phillip Darby, John Cash, Rob McQueen and Don Miller have had an ongoing and profound influence upon my thinking as have the co-editors of the journal *Postcolonial Studies,* Dipesh Chakarabarty, Leela Gandhi and Sanjay Seth. I should also mention my students, the postgraduates in particular, who have never really fitted into a politics department and therefore came to study with me. They brought a diversity of scholarly interests with them and that has left its mark on this volume. At a much more concrete level, there was an army of translators involved with what in China would no doubt be thought of as a 'campaign to produce a book'. David Bray, Sylvia Chan, Li Shaorong, Li Tianfu, Xu Zhangrun, Sun Xiaoli and Tom Clarke all contributed. The authors, artists, designers and photographers whose work has been used in this volume should also be thanked, as should Jiang Tingyao who helped me track all these people down. The Australian Research Council gave me money for research on Chinese policing and social control and, through this, I was able to produce a book that, if it tells us one thing, it is that China is quickly becoming a country so diverse that it is impossible to police.

At Cambridge University Press, a range of people are to be thanked. The anonymous reviews gave me heart and advice. Professor Bill Kirby, the editor of this Cambridge series, did likewise. Authors are usually quite egotistical about their work and I was no exception. In hindsight, however, I bow to the wisdom of those who had the temerity to criticise! On the production side of things this text has proven to be nothing short of a battlefield and it is Jane Farago and Rosemary Perkins who are on the frontline, negotiating the various financial and production problems. Ron Hampton, the designer, took my rough sketches and ideas and brought them to life while Foong Ling Kong transformed my purple prose into readable English and, along the way, picked up quite a number of errors of translation. Most of all, I should like to thank Phillipa McGuinness and her assistant Sharon Mullins. Throughout the entire process of submission, review and finally acceptance, they kept the faith. It is fair to say that without their advocacy, this book would never have seen the light of day. Lastly, and on a very personal note, I could not have done this had it not been for Deborah and Tavan. It is to them that I dedicate this book.

### Acknowledgements

The author and publisher would like to thank the following for permission to reproduce copyright material:

AAP Information Services for photo, p. 16; *Twenty First Century* for articles, pp. 31–9, 171; *Masses Press* for articles, pp. 94–7, 107–11, 120–9; *Women's Studies* for articles, pp. 132–40, 265–9; Shanghai Social Sciences Journal Publisher for article, pp. 81–5; The Architectural Society of China and Geological Press of China for articles, pp. 196–7, 200–2, 207–8, 211–12; also for maps, pp. 153, 198, 201; Chinese Political Science and Law Publishing House for article, pp. 23–31; *People's Daily* for article, pp. 215–20; Yang Dongping for articles, pp. 165–71, 197–200,

208–10, 212–13; Wang Anting for articles, pp. 243–4, 257; Zhang Hongtu for drawing, p. 174; Zhou Jihou for articles, pp. 244–53, 258–61.

Every effort has been made to obtain permission to use copyright material reproduced in this book. The author and publisher would be pleased to hear from copyright holders they have not been able to contact.

# Timeline on Chinese History

**Zhou Dynasty** (1100–221BC)
(including the Warring States Period 475–221BC)
**Qin Dynasty** (221–206 BC)
**Han Dynasty** (206BC–220)

Other dynasties

**Tang Dynasty** (618–907)
**Five Dynasties** (907–960)
**Song Dynasty** (960–1179)

Other dynasties

**Ming Dynasty** (1368–1644)
**Qing Dynasty** (1644–1911)
**Republican Period** (1912–1949)

| | |
|---|---|
| | Nationalist Party (Guomindang) Rule |
| 1927 | Communists purged. They flee first to Jiangxi and then later to Yan'an |
| 1937 | War against Japan led to a united front between Guomindang and Communists |
| | Yan'an Period—a Communist base area that was a rural model for the future People's Republic |
| 1946 | Civil war between Guomindang and Communists |

**People's Republic of China** (1949–today)

| | |
|---|---|
| 1950 | China enters Korean war |
| 1950–53 | Campaign to suppress counter revolutionaries, other campaigns follow |
| 1953 | First Five-Year Plan |
| 1956 | China declared socialist |
| 1957 | Great Leap Forward |
| 1966–1976 | Cultural Revolution |
| 1978 | Economic Reform Period, a period of unprecedented growth and material prosperity but also increasing disparities in wealth |
| 1989 | Beijing: Tiananmen Square Massacre—a cold chill descends politically but economic reform continues |
| 1997 | Deng Xiaoping dies but liberal economic reform programme continues |
| | Hong Kong returned to China |

**A Note on Method**

… the book is an obsolete mediation between two different card-filing systems. For everything essential is found in the note boxes of the researcher who writes it, and the reader who studies it assimilates it into his own file.

—Walter Benjamin (1928)

**A Note on Content**

To the ordinary man.

To a common hero, an ubiquitous character, walking in countless thousands of streets … The floodlights have moved away from the actors who possess proper names and social blazons, turning first toward the chorus of secondary characters, then settling on the mass of the audience … a multitude of qualified heroes who lose names and faces as they become the ciphered river of the streets, a mobile language of computations and rationalities that belong to no one.

—Michel de Certeau (1984)

**An Introduction**

This introduction is like a snapshot accompanying a tourist's tale. Like all snapshots, it needs explanation. The tales that accompany this snapshot lead from the life stories of ordinary people through to the rules, rituals and rationalities that govern their daily existence. This is a story that begins in a backstreet and never really leaves it. This book is a note box, a file, a dossier, a collection of stories of the streets, ordered in a way that excited and made sense to me. I hope these stories will do the same for you.

—Michael Dutton

## AN ALL-CONSUMING CHINA

Picture yourself in Beijing, in a city market, in a place called Qianmen. Picture yourself in one of the tiny little alleyways called *hutongs*, with their even tinier shops, stalls and benches, all of which nestle together at the back of Tiananmen Square and collectively make up the mercantile heart of this area. This is where the grandiose, expansive architecture of the Square, the Great Hall of the People, the Revolutionary Museum and the wide tree-lined boulevards of the Avenue of Eternal Peace (*chang'an jie*) seems to fall into a sea of cacophonous, chaotic people, alleyways and stalls which, before liberation, would have constituted the lifeblood of traditional city street life virtually anywhere in China.

Qianmen is, however, street life with a difference. Gone are the traditional traders of old—the shoe repairers, the ironmongers, the tin men—all of whom would have floated down these tiny backstreets in search of household consumers in need of their trade. These days, the flow of traffic in Qianmen is heading the other way. Consumers in their tens of thousands gravitate to Qianmen and its surrounds, and it is they who constitute the traffic in the busy and over-crowded streets. The traders no longer float by, but are now installed in an ever-changing but semi-permanent array of stalls which are tucked into virtually every nook and cranny. At the back of Tiananmen Square and, quite literally, behind the back of the late Chairman Mao, primitive capitalism is practised in all its exciting, chaotic, desperate, and exasperating glory.

As huge crowds push their way through what are apparently the backstreets of Beijing, the contrast with 'the front streets'—the regime's showpiece, Tiananmen Square—could not be put into sharper relief. Tiananmen, the 'people's square', the symbolic heart of Chinese Communist power, with its Haussmann-like expanses and clear open lines of vision, seems somewhat jaded and dead next to the bustle of Qianmen. This Square, which was once occupied by millions of Red Guards and, more recently, by tens of thousands of protesting students, appears more like an extension and 'socialist update' of the Palace Museum (which borders it immediately to the north) than it does a site of Communist power. With Mao at its centre, it has become, almost literally, the burial ground of socialism.

Despite this, it is Qianmen and not the Square that is currently under threat. While the bustle of these backstreets is not at all threatened by any extension of Tiananmen Square socialism, the bulldozer's blade, nevertheless, carves its way through these little streets, 'reorganising' them so that they become part of a more orderly way of life. Far more ornate and enduring structures are quickly

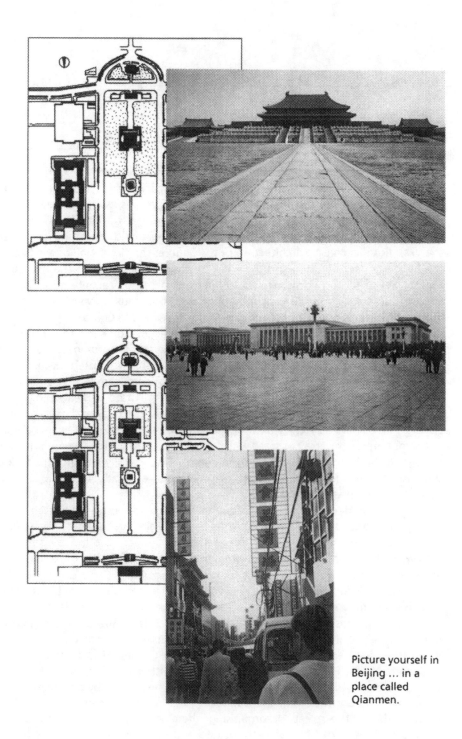

Picture yourself in Beijing ... in a place called Qianmen.

replacing the chaos of the little stalls and backstreet shops. The 'socialist shops' of old, the so-called 'one-hundred things department stores' (*baihuo dalou*) are under threat. Their factory-style layout—neon-strip lighting, assembly-line forms of shelf display—and abrasive staff attitudes are being replaced by a new consumer-friendly architecture and attitude.

The new structures and forms that are replacing the old are not, however, 'socialist' in nature but are more permanent and elaborate monuments to the consumerism practised 'daily, hourly and by the minute' (Lenin) on the backstreets of Qianmen. The stalls and old-style mercantile shops, like the socialist arcades of old, are being demolished to make way for the department stores and shopping centres of a new and 'more advanced form' of consumerism.

The haste with which this change is effected is at once a recognition of the speed and power of commercial development in China, and a tell-tale sign of the unease felt both by the Communist Party and the *nouveau riche* about this partic- ular form of small-scale and pre-reform 'socialist' trading. It is as though 'the successful' entrepreneurs wish to obliterate their more squalid or state-sponsored counterparts and, in so doing, cover up their own backstreet 'origins' such as might be found in places like Qianmen. For the wealthy merchants, it is as though these forms of trading, which constitute so much of their own 'history', are best forgotten. In China, where such 'histories' literally 'set up shop' on the walls of the 'present', the tainted and vulgar 'pasts' of the great entrepreneurs are on show for all to see. The story that this past tells is one of compromise, ambivalence and of 'making do'. It is one the current crop of rich merchants would rather forget or, at least, have the power to retell in their own way.

Why this urge to be remembered differently? Part of the reason may well be that theirs is not the story of legendary and gloriously independent capitalist trad- ers seeking economic freedom and individuality in the face of a totalitarian and unbending government. The story is not one of a 'class' that will one day end up translating its economic freedom into political democracy. Instead, it is the story of capital accumulation based upon, sponsored by, and growing out of the 'womb of socialism': the work unit system (see Part I, 2; Part IV, 3). It is the story of the emer- gence of class in China: not just the new mercantile class that has grown rich with reform, but also of the subaltern classes that have not.[1] It is a story made possible only by the positivist dreams that consumption promises—and all too often betrays—and a governmental policing strategy that enforces the limits of all such dreaming. Such dreams are given concrete form in the display windows of the

---

1   The term 'subaltern' is drawn from the work of a group of mainly Indian scholars known as the Subaltern Studies Group, who attempted to re-insert and broaden the voice of 'the people' into colonial narrative history. They employed the term 'subaltern' to capture the heterogeneity of the 'people's voice', and the vast and changing array of positions that came into being as effects of power relations (see Prakash 1990). While the attempt to enable the subaltern to speak is not without its problems it has, nevertheless, produced 'knowledge effects' that have complicated the unity of the historical narrative by producing and inserting 'murmurs' of other ways of writing and other historical objects. In the context of Chinese history writing official Party class discourse colonises the space available for a subaltern history. The 'effect' of the re- insertion of the term subaltern, which includes its propensity to heterology, leads to a non-linear historical account which, in turn, offers a dynamic rendition of classes that draw breath from the mercurial nature of China as it undergoes economic reform.

new shopping arcades: look, but don't touch, unless you pay. This is the new slogan of the shopping wonderworlds of China. Yet the display windows of this wonderworld are more than a physical manifestation of consumer dreams; they also constitute the 'technology' through which a veritable pedagogy of 'training in desiring' comes into effect. The old dreams of socialism, of a modern revolutionary China, pale before the windows of promise that the modern reifying form of consumption promotes. It is here, in these shop-window displays, that one begins to recognise the power of consumption. One realises how this power, beyond commitment to any single cause, beyond any simple-minded notion of 'ideology', is so voracious, so all-encompassing and so powerful. By evoking in the consumer the desire to consume, the consumers are themselves consumed.

The 'all-consuming' nature of this mode underlines the point I want to make here, that is, China's economic reform programme cannot be understood simply in conventional terms. The depth of change cannot be appreciated by the simple statement of economic facts. One cannot see the power of economic reform if one simply highlights the State's decision to shift from the production of capital to consumer goods. One cannot see the way it harnesses and remodels desire by noting the adoption of the economic contract system or in the responsibility system in agriculture. These 'techniques' to raise production become thinkable only when desire is silently factored into the calculations. Yet desire is not 'given', it is produced, or at least reproduced, in a particular way, such that time *does become* money and the more you work, the more you *will* get. What you get is an ability to move toward the dream by consuming, in part, what the display window has to offer. Herein lies the power of consumption and the reasons why Chinese economic reform is chaotically heading down this never-ending trail, buoyed by the dream that to consume is to be headed for a bright new future where, it is thought, dreams will be fulfilled in the purchases made at the new shopping malls. Yet such 'trainings' also have a secondary and, dare I say, subversive effect.

The power of the consumptive mode, while supplementing and promoting government initiatives and dreams of development in some ways, also undermines them in others. Consumerism transgresses the boundaries of government initiative, forcing the State itself to partake in 'market initiatives'. In other words, this mode consumes government too, as recent State initiatives in the market all too clearly demonstrate. Nowhere were these government initiatives at their clearest and yet most precarious than in relation to the Mao paraphernalia craze of the late 1980s and early 1990s.

## The Many Faces of Mao

Mao, this mammoth symbol of socialist China, is remembered on the centenary of his birth. Yet in the China of economic reform, this remembrance takes on a perverse form. Mao reappears, but as commodity and, along with the new consumer-friendly Canto-pop version of the 'East is Red', becomes a star reborn. Revolutionary memorabilia is commodified and becomes a 'big seller' in the new 'China market'. In the three-year period between 1990 and 1993, over 11 million posters of Chairman Mao were sold, while in the first two months of its release the disco cassette version of the 'East is Red' sold some 3.5 million copies (see Da

Yang's article, Part V). Along with other 'revolutionary' paraphernalia such as watches, double-sided Mao portraits designed to dangle like dice from car mirrors and lighters that play the 'East is Red', Mao's image is reproduced on an endless array of items for sale. All classes and tastes are catered for: from solid-gold embossed Mao watches for the *nouveau riche*, through to the simple and traditional wall poster. A new form of ubiquitous 'Mao imagery' re-emerges as government and trader alike recognise that 'Mao sells'. The question is, if Mao is being 'reborn' in this renewed process of edification, what is he being reborn as?

This contemporary reification of Mao actually eats away at the Mao of old to the point whereby the meaning of Mao is no longer anchored in the Party. The Party must now fight for ownership of his body and image so that it can have a chance of 'ownership' over the collective soul. But this new consumer Mao defies a single Party-designated form or expression. Instead, 'one hundred schools of thought' come into contention over his image. This plurality of meaning around his image leads to a panoply of symbolic forms: Mao as sage in a resurgent peasant messianic phase; Mao as 1950s leader, bringing stability and offering an exemplary alternative to the chaos of economic reform; Mao as young rebel leader standing against authority in a similar fashion to the images of the young Chinese punk rock heroes of today. This myriad of Maos comes to symbolise a new consumer-based pluralism that actually transgresses the limits of any attempt to 'inlay' a dominant ideology. Yet in this dispersal of readings one constant remains: the ever present appetites and desires produced by consumerism. The pluralism brought on by the competition over Mao's body comes out of the single shared desire to own the Mao image. Thus, this form of plurality of views itself comes to reinforce the power of the reifying gaze within this increasingly consumer-based society.

It is for this reason that Theodor Adorno and Max Horkheimer were so insistent that the consumptive mode is always responsible for the 'constant reproduction of the same thing'.[2] While Adorno and Horkheimer examined the emergence of consumption in the West, the point they make about it is no less valuable in relation to China today. In tracing the emergence of Western consumer-based society they insisted that individuality and creativity were the first casualties. This was because the individuality produced under consumption was 'mass produced like Yale locks, whose only difference can be measured in fractions of millimetres'.[3] Adorno maintains that the result is a kind of 'pseudo individuality' that reifies the new but which ends up reproducing it as 'always-the-same'.[4] In this respect, Chinese forms of commodification differ little, enabling the adroit observer of Chinese street life, Geremie Barmé, to comment that even dissent in China today has become a commodity with a niche-market value.[5]

2   Theodor Adorno and Max Horkheimer, *Dialectic of Enlightenment* [Trans. John Cumming] (London: Verso, 1979), 134.
3   Adorno and Horkheimer, 154.
4   Theodor Adorno, *The Culture Industry: Selected Essays on Mass Culture* [Edited and introduced by J. M. Bernstein] (London: Routledge, 1991), 35.
5   Geremie Barmé, 'Soft Porn, Packaged Dissent, and Nationalism: Notes on Chinese Culture in the 1990s', *Current History*, 93 (1994), 272.

Barmé points out that 'underground' art, novels, rock and roll and the 'alternative' film industry in China are all too aware of the appeal both at home and abroad of the Chinese rebel voice. This new and growing 'dissident genre' thrives on its ability to promote rebellion, but always operates within acceptable limits. The new cultural products mark out a tactic that actually works to annoy, but not infuriate, the State censor. Such works must attract a critical rebuke from the censor in order to qualify as 'dissident', but they must also get through the censor's office intact, otherwise there would be no dissident cultural product to sell. Having succeeded in getting their 'dissident' product onto the domestic and international market, they can then 'cash in' on the 'dissident label'.[6] Rebellion itself becomes a commodity with its own market niche, and its own very lucrative form of marketing. Dissent in China, to use Barmé's expression, is quickly becoming 'packaged dissent'—commodified, and sold like any other product. For him, this packaged dissent, if not quite equalling betrayal, nevertheless proves very 'disturbing'.[7] In Barmé's reading, packaged dissent seems to extinguish the very rebellious and individual voices that the process of commodification tries to celebrate and sell.

There is much of interest in Barmé's position. He is probably one of the best informed Western China scholars on dissident voices in China today and clearly has his finger on the pulse when analysing the predominant form that these sorts of cultural products take when confronted by the market. The problem with his analysis, however, is its under-theorised approach to commodification. For Barmé, commodification is to rebellion what the full stop is to the sentence: it marks an end. Yet commodification operates more like a syntactical structure, detailing the contoured forms available to rebellion and life rather than as a sign of its demise. The fact that we may not like the particular form dissent takes, or approve of it being offered for sale, does not alter the dissident nature of the act, nor the delegitimising effect it has upon government. In producing expressions of dissent that are marketable, popular and—let's face it—fun, the commodity process demonstrates an almost uncanny productivity. The process is productive in so far as it does not simply cater for a market, but actually produces it, by manufacturing desire. It is uncanny, in that this very act of market production also produces space for critique, enabling certain tactical responses. The existence of these various responses illustrates the folly of unifying consumption such that it appears as 'a thing' rather than 'a relation'.

To go beyond commodification as a 'thing', however, requires a prior mental move. This is the mental separation of consumption as a macro-level and generalised mode of life from the specific (micro-level) act of producing and consuming (that is, specific acts of 'doing'). While the former, in the language of Michel de Certeau, is akin to a 'strategic field', the latter is a tactical choice that offers within itself the possibility of a range of playful and mischievous acts of disruption. The tactical play on market forces to produce a market for dissident voices, no matter what the subjective and personal motives of these 'dissidents' are, cannot be

6   Barmé, 272–73.
7   Barmé, 270.

anything other than a tactical act of dissent. In adopting this approach, one can avoid contemporary variants on the traditional 'great man' approach to the question of dissent by decentring the dissident speaking subject while, nevertheless, valuing the message propounded. To value the tactical space commodification opens up, while simultaneously recognising the limits it imposes on acts, leads us away from the lionisation of the 'heroic subject' of dissent and toward an examination of the conditions under which the tactical act takes place. Moreover, in moving away from the 'heroic subjects' toward the micro-level act also shifts the focus onto the otherwise anonymous characters who are caught in the structural and systemic web of life in China. It is their lives that are currently being reconstituted by the process of commodification. Here again, it is the work of de Certeau that puts this in sharpest focus.

## Other Rebellions

> To a common hero, an ubiquitous character, walking in countless thousands on the streets ... This anonymous hero is very ancient. He is the murmuring voice of societies. He squats now at the center of our scientific stages. The floodlights have moved away from the actors who possess proper names and social blazons, turning first toward the chorus of secondary characters, then settling on the mass of the audience. The increasingly sociological and anthropological perspective of inquiry privileges the anonymous and the everyday in which zoom lenses cut out metonymic details—parts taken for the whole. Slowly the representatives that formerly symbolized families, groups, and orders disappear from the stage they dominated during the epoch of the name. We witness the advent of the number.[8]

In 1984, what was described as the first 'major reform' of household registration laws in post-liberation Chinese history effectively witnessed the advent of the number in China, in the form of the 'resident identity card' system. Here is the strategic field within which the anonymous, ubiquitous characters of China must operate. Under the unity established by the 'proper name'—both signed and printed on every card—there was a 'second kind' of (biographical) unity displayed, in the form of a number detailing the uniqueness of every card and its bearer. In the number, the unity of the proper name is tied to a (secondary) set of biographical details. The proper name and the coded number are the unities around which the card and the government functions (see Part II). Through the number, details of the name—its specific place of abode, gender and date of birth—are given. More than simply scant biographical details, these numbers operate like library catalogue codes, tying the 'proper name' back to a personnel file, to a record, and to a household register. With this catalogued code as the reference point, details of the life of the card-bearer can be further checked and elaborated upon. The number leads back to the file which, in turn, leads back to the lives, loves and indiscretions of the name. To go beyond the name and number, however, requires knowledge and access beyond that available to the ordinary person. These coded numbers operate within a very specific scriptural regime that offers access only to

---

8  Michel de Certeau, *The Practice of Everyday Life* [Trans. Steven Randall] (Berkeley: University of California Press, 1984), n.p.

those the authorities deem worthy. The codes on the card are not transparent and need to be decoded into a language that can be read by all. It is only through the codes and manuals of the security forces which are never made public, and therefore never seen, that the card offers access to the biographical life of the bearer.

Within this regime of codes and symbols, the bearer of the card cannot speak but is instead spoken of and spoken to. Such nameless numbers will tell of many things about the unspeaking subject. What they will also tell us, however, is about the way in which the government constitutes citizen subjectivity and within that, the way it separates the wanted and worthy from those who require more draconian forms of surveillance. What the card offers us is not only an example of the 'outer limits' of policing in China, but also a mechanism through which one can move the spotlight away from the stars of the human rights campaigns and onto the anonymous, ubiquitous characters de Certeau speaks of. Western critics of Chinese human rights have been slow to pick up on certain types of human rights abuses in China because they have all but ignored the overall anonymity of the process of abuse. It is anonymous because it is, in part, a structural feature of the very 'reform process' the West as a whole has embraced as the means by which China can economically and politically liberate itself.

Chinese human rights abuses today are, in the main, quite different to those which predominated in the Maoist era. At that time, there were no transient criminals, no vagrants, few prostitutes and virtually no drug addicts or triad gangs. These are the products of economic reform and it is these 'rebels' who are subject to the most numerous and most tragic human rights abuses among the Han Chinese community. To unearth their tales requires an enquiry beyond the fetishised goods of consumer China. It requires excavating the quarry that is economic reform. Laid out before you in *Streetlife China* are the fossil-documents that may be of help in piecing together at least part of this story. It is a part of the story characterised by the emergence of a definite murmur of 'subaltern voices' in China.

Human rights abuses in China are, in the main, less about heroic dissident voices being suppressed than about the desultory practices of the hooligans, pimps, prostitutes and unemployed being extinguished. Human rights abuse in China may be multifaceted, but the frequent and most serious cases invariably involve the stranger, the outsider, the vagrant or the wanderer. This is because the principal human rights story in China is a tale of movement: the movement of the society from one mode to another as it attempts to modernise, and the movement of the subalterns to the city as they attempt to gain a share of the wealth that modernisation brings.

In the new China of economic reform, this new subaltern group has a name and that name is all too often *mangliu*, meaning, quite literally, 'to blindly travel'. Yet there is nothing blind in the travels of these people. Migration in contemporary China is always undertaken 'tactically', that is, to make the best of a bad situation, to try and find work, get money, or if they are really lucky, make it rich. Migrants enter the cities and are distinguishable only by what they are not; their 'foreignness' is their only defining feature, and something they carry with them wherever they go. It is a foreignness to city life made evident by the way they speak, the way they dress, the dialect they speak, the way they walk and the way they address others. So visible and different are the *mangliu* of Chinese cities that their position is somewhat akin to migrant workers anywhere. It is their foreignness that marks them out not only as different but, all too often, as inferior. As Homi Bhabha points out, in relation to migrant labour in Europe, their presence signals a new 'imagined community' of nationhood.[9] They are the markers of a shifting boundary of nationhood. But is it possible to talk of shifting national boundaries when referring to ethnic Han in their own land? Perhaps ...

Paul Virilio, commenting on the postmodern American city, offers a useful insight. Virilio begins his book, *Lost Dimensions*, with a poignant quotation: 'At the beginning of the 60s, with black ghettoes rioting, the Mayor of Philadelphia announced: "From here on in, the frontiers of the State pass to the interior of the cities".'[10]

What Bhabha and the Mayor of Philadelphia miss in restricting the issue of the shifting national boundaries to race is the question of class. What both are discussing here is not just the break-up of an imagined national homogeneity because of racism and bigotry, what they are (re)telling is the story of subaltern labour exploited to breaking point. We could, in fact, retell these two stories in the language of Marx, in the story of the English peasants' movement to the city and the social panic this movement occasioned there. Alternatively, we could tell this story in terms of the Chinese peasants as they move in endless columns into the Chinese city in search of work and favours. In China, one may object that the story is different for, in this case, the subaltern is the same colour and of the same ethnic group. But again, to say this is to ignore the way in which difference operates as a floating signifier of the group named for its aimless 'floating' migration.

The subaltern of the Chinese city is always the stranger. She is the itinerant migrant worker who is as visible and identifiable to the local resident of a city like Beijing as an Afro-American is to the Caucasian in the cities of America, or the Turk is to the German. In China, however, the subalterns are diasporic in their own nation because, for them, the city is a foreign place, it is not their *laojia* (hometown). It is this connection to their *laojia*, to their *tongbao*, provincial county or village that unites them. From such marginalised unity in the foreign land of the city have grown some very powerful means of self-protection, promotion and, ultimately, exploitation: the dreaded triads or secret societies.

The Chinese peasant who is said to 'drift blindly' into the city does so with a single aim: to find work. The peasant takes up a diasporic position in the hope of occupying another position: that of city worker. Peasants migrate for work, but the work is limited, badly paid and often brief. Many fail to find work or refuse to accept the conditions. For them, it is either a return to the rural area from which they have fled or an attempt to eke out an existence on the margins, which sometimes means employment as beggars, prostitutes or thieves. All of these occupations, however, bring forth an erratic, arbitrary, but invariably harsh response

---

9  Homi Bhabha, *The Location of Culture* (London: Routledge, 1994), 164.
10 Paul Virilio, *The Lost Dimension* [Trans. Daniel Moshenburg] (New York: Semiotext[e], Autonomedia, 1991), 9.

from the police. As the peasants move, the technologies of surveillance over them increase and they are caught in a double bind. Move, but only within limits. Move, but only if you have money.

Two moves of government, two responses, two sets of regulation form the 'double pincer movement' through which this drama is played out. Peasants are offered to the market as 'free' labour (what Marx describes as the wage slave) and simultaneously disciplined into the language of the market by the harshness of the alternative (strict laws against vagrancy, prostitution, itinerant suspects etc.). This double move is a compact signed under two names: one signs 'freedom' (the freedom of movement to places of work, the freedom to buy and sell one's labour power, not to mention the freedom to trade), the other signs 'restriction' (restrictions upon those who can and cannot remain in the cities, restrictions upon acceptable and unacceptable forms of work: women can work as char-ladies—the so-called *baomu*—but not as sex workers). Clear divisions operate, but the market has its limits: one can sell labour power but not human flesh.

What is interesting about these 'two moves', what is described above as a 'pincer action', is how much this story has been told countless times before. In the past, and elsewhere, it is known as the process of capital accumulation leading not only to an extension of commodity relations but also to the creation of 'free prole-tarian labour' by 'the separation of agricultural workers from the land in such a way that they become "available" for industrial employment'.

By pointing out these twin legal moves—one to loosen the highly restrictive household registration laws so as to allow labour to be 'freed', the other to tighten the regulation of those who will, if properly policed, come to constitute the reserve army of unemployed—we are able to draw a close analogy with the legal processes discussed by Marx in *Capital*.[11] Moreover, the shift from a capital to consumer goods driven development, which is the hallmark of China's economic reform process, has created new needs and raised the price of indigenous prod-ucts in much the same way as Marx suggested early capitalism did in *Grundrisse*.[12] In both cases, they led to a speeding up of the transformation of money into capi-tal and, as a consequence, farm workers into proletarians.

What is being suggested, then, is that the 'deep structure' of this story of Chinese economic reform does not begin with the third plenum of the Eleventh Central Committee of the Communist Party in December 1978, but in England, some time between the fifteenth and nineteenth century. In addition, what is also being suggested is that this process is not explicable by reference to Deng Xiao-ping's selected works, but rather by reference to Marx's *Capital*. It is in *Capital* that Marx explains the general effects of the tendencies unleashed as a result of the English laws around enclosure and vagrancy. It is with an understanding of these two legal changes that one can begin to see the significance of the collapse of the Chinese household registration laws and the tightening of laws against vagrancy in China. In other words, to understand the key dynamics producing human rights abuses in China today, it is necessary to take Queen Victoria's advice and 'close

11  Karl Marx, *Capital* [Trans. Ben Fowkes], 3 vols (Middlesex: Penguin, 1976), vol. 1.
12  Karl Marx, *Grundrisse* [Trans. Martin Nicholaus] (Middlesex: Penguin, 1973), p. 508.

your eyes and think of England!' By remembering England, some of the key tendencies unleashed by the English Industrial Revolution are also remembered and enable the Chinese economic revolution to be contextualised.

## Close Your Eyes

The English enclosure laws placed limits on the use of certain common lands which were previously available to all (including the peasants) as open grazing lands. Peasants relied heavily on the traditional right to graze, but more often than not, they lacked adequate property holdings to secure an economically viable herd. Without this right to the use of the commons, they could not survive. From the fifteenth century onward, this right was gradually withdrawn to allow larger pastoral enterprises to come into being. Gradually, the lands were enclosed (hence the name of the legislation). Farmers without land or capital to refinance their enterprise were forced into the city in search of work in the burgeoning industrial sector. For Marx:

> The prelude of the revolution that laid the foundation of the capitalist mode of production was played out in the last third of the fifteenth, and the first decades of the sixteenth century. A mass of 'free' and unattached proletarians was hurled onto the labour-market by the dissolution of the bands of feudal retainers.[13]

In China there were no enclosure laws, but the collapse of the tightly policed household register which kept people on the land, and the recognition of the need for a migrant labour force—recognised albeit in the margins by tell-tale signs such as the issuance of the (more mobile) resident identity card system—had much the same effect.

In both cases, these changes resulted in wholesale movements of rural populations to the cities. In China, literally millions of peasants were given the 'freedom of movement' despite restrictions still in place if one were to read the letter of the law. The degree of movement (something like forty to eighty million on any given day) is stunning, and the changes brought on because of it, considerable.

Throughout the 1950s, rural population migration into the cities only ever amounted to about 3 per cent of the cities' total residential population. In hard times, this increased. After 1957, the disastrous Great Leap Forward led to a dramatic increase in the number of transients, but even then it grew to only about 5 per cent of the total city population, reaching a high point of 8 per cent in the early 1960s when the famine was at its height. Improvements in the economy brought it back down to 5 per cent of the total permanent city population and this was the general level until the Cultural Revolution, when the policy of establishing 'great [revolutionary] ties' led to large numbers of people entering the cities. The number of people who actually entered the cities at this time, however, is impossible to know as the Ministry of Public Security came under attack and the entire system of household registration, like much else in that period, was severely disrupted. Nevertheless, on the basis of very incomplete statistics from a number

---

13 Marx, *Capital*, 878.

of cities, it can be estimated that the number of people who entered the cities as a percentage of the total permanent population of the cities was 10 per cent or higher. After the third plenum (1978), which brought on economic reform, things changed and the figure would outstrip all that went before.

The current transient population, on even the most conservative estimates, is put at a daily flow rate of over 40 million people, among whom 20 million-odd people would be heading for the cities.[14] This accounts for something like 15 per cent of the total cities' permanent population. Other estimates put the figure at double this. The system simply could not cope even on these conservative figures. For example, in Beijing there are over a million transients, but only 50,000 beds in hotels and specially designated places. Transients are therefore forced to accommodate themselves either on the streets or illegally. The point about all of these figures is not their veracity, but rather that they indicate an almost 'crisis-like' mentality within the Ministry of Public Security. The police neither know the number of transients nor how to deal with them. In other words, the population flow reached the point whereby the police could not cope and this, in turn, induced something of a social panic. Consequently, harsh and *ad hoc* policing measures were implemented (eg. the police measures included hotels within the list of those work units they describe as 'special professions'. See Part II, 2). This situation is, once again, not unlike the England of which Marx speaks.

Marx points out that the enclosure laws may well have freed peasants so that they could become 'free labour' in the cities, but, he adds, they were far too productive in this task. Marx notes that the process of enclosure led to too many potential proletarians coming into the cities and, out of this, came not only the means by which to keep wages down (that is, a reserve army of unemployed) but also conditions that could potentially produce social and political unrest. The State response to this was harsh. Marx:

> these men, suddenly dragged from their accustomed mode of life, could not immedi-ately adapt themselves to the discipline of their new condition. They were turned in massive quantities into beggars, robbers, and vagabonds, partly from inclination, in most cases under the force of circumstances. Hence, at the end of the fifteenth and during the whole of the sixteenth century, a bloody legislation against vagabondage was enforced throughout Western Europe. The fathers of the present working-class were chastised for their enforced transformation into vagabonds and paupers. Legislators treated them as 'voluntary' criminals, and assumed that it depended on their own good will to go on working under conditions that no longer existed'.[15]

Marx goes on to explain the brutality of the policing measures used against these people. We are told of how some are 'tied to the cart-tail and whipped until the blood streams from their bodies, then they are to swear on oath to go back to their birthplace' or to where they have lived the last three years and to 'put them-selves to labour'.[16] Contrast these measures to the ordinances detailing Chinese

---

14 Xu Hanmin, *Forty Years of People's Public Security* (Beijing: Police Officers Educational Publishing House, 1992), 136.

15 Marx, *Capital*, 896.

16 Marx, *Capital*, 896.

police responses to vagrants and beggars (see Part II, 3). A tight disciplinary regime is put into effect and the purpose of this is to teach the discipline of the proletarian. The beggar, the vagrant, like the criminal and the malcontent, is 'temporarily housed, re-educated and then sent back to work'. For those without homes or papers but who are still fit for work, banishment to outlying farms is also possible. Even local beggars could suffer incarceration and banishment, for the city is no place for the mendacious and lazy.

If the laws against vagrancy seem harsh, those against prostitution seem positively draconian. Prostitution has long been seen as such a shame on the woman that draconian penalties seemed unnecessary. This shame, when revealed, seemed punishment enough. In the current period, when shame itself is no longer enough, there are police calls for the prostitute to be punished and repeat offenders to be dealt with under the harsh anti-hoodlum laws. This sea change in police attitudes is due to the massive rise in the number of prostitutes which has emerged with economic reform and the free movement of vast numbers of country girls into the city in search of work.

The contrasting accounts of the prostitute and the *baomu* are, I think, quite revealing. Both are said to undergo what is described as a 'material and ideological transformation' as a result of living in the city, yet their transformations are in opposite moral and ethical directions. One learns little from the city other than vice; the other, we are told, becomes a more modern woman who goes back to the village as an emissary of the modern (see Beijing *Baomu*, Part II, 4). One knows her place, the other flaunts decency. Here, then, is the dual face of modernity: spiritual civilisation and pollution captured in the figure of woman.

Here, also, is a gendered account of the disciplining of labour presented in Marx under the sign of the vagabond. The contrast between the migrant prostitute and *baomu* could not be more stark: not only is the *baomu* a 'good woman', but she is also a good *working* woman. She is no longer a mere transient, but becomes a good temporary worker housed by her employer and, therefore, no longer 'floating'. The *baomu* story is simply the 'other side' of the migrant prostitute's tale. Both come to the city to sell their labour power. One 'sells' in the highly paid, but chancy, world of prostitution; the other in the very lowly paid and squalid work of cleaning someone else's laundry. In both cases, the work is on the margins, and even in the rather gilded account of the *baomu*'s life given in this collection, one should note the working conditions: low wages, a lack of permanent rights to reside, the lack of regulations governing treatment and so forth. Be it *baomu* or prostitute, one begins to realise that socialism with Chinese characteristics is a very strange creature indeed. It is a form of socialism where class *does* count, where a different accent, a low level of education or a lack of appropriate cultural capital all conspire to render the transient the Chinese voice of subalternity.

It is the subalterns who are punished most harshly, policed most closely and incarcerated in the most squalid of conditions. It is they who are the victims of human rights abuse which generally prove to be far worse and far more intrusive than anything suffered by student dissidents. Yet it is their claims, their stories and their lives that always seem to elude the telling in the great rush to identify the grand heroes and representatives of Western-style values within China. They become visible only when their tactics of deception fail, for their tactics always involve keeping a low profile. For the most part, they become visible only as names on a file or actions taken down in police records. It is in this way that they are made visible and speak—not with their own tongues or in one voice but in the heterogeneous trails they leave in the form of new legislation and police and legal commentaries about them. Their failed tactics are productive for they lead to stories being told of their lives and their actions. Such stories are vastly different to the grand statements of the dissident students who speak to uphold certain general principles. When the subaltern speaks, it is to outwit or outmanoeuvre poverty and authority. It is in taking my cue from the tactics of the subaltern that I begin *Streetlife China* with Chinese governmental concerns about human rights and their insistence on the centrality of the rights to subsistence (*wenbao*). Tactically, then, this way of examining rights offers the possibility of both taking Chinese rights discourse seriously, while simultaneously focusing on those areas of rights discourse most in need of attention. By focusing on the subaltern and their conditions of existence we are offered no heroes to eulogise, but only numerous accounts of victims. Victims in a social system that insists that they are the true rulers. This is the starting point of *Streetlife China* and the start of a journey that will ultimately lead back to the issue of commodification. But that story, for the moment at least, is further down the road.

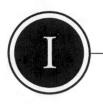

**Something happened on the Avenue of Eternal Peace at noon on Monday that is going to make a lot of people think about the meaning of courage.**

James Sterba[1]

# RIGHTS, TRADITIONS, DAILY LIFE AND DEVIANCE

There is only one streetscene in China worth remembering in Western eyes. That is the scene of the man and the tank, shot on Beijing's Avenue of Eternal Peace at the height of the 'troubles' in 1989. It is the streetscene that constitutes the mind's-flash image of the Western world: when it thinks of the name 'China' and weds it to the term 'repression'. The representation is so powerful that it demolishes all other understandings. This streetscene, this time and this event, have come to constitute the compass point for virtually all Western journeys into the interior of the contemporary political and cultural life of China. It is an event that announces the arrival of an anonymous heroic figure who broke from the crowds and jumped in front of a column of army tanks. He not only made history, but forced contemporary Chinese history into a single, solitary frame that featured his anonymous heroic body in contest with the powerful but equally anonymous forces of the State. In one second, and in a single click of a Western journalist's camera, this streetscene was transformed into iconography. China would henceforth be remembered as the land of the man and the tank; a land that epitomised human rights violations.

History stopped at this point, and so too did the analytical diversity of Western historians, sociologists and cultural critics. From this time onward, most accounts of things Chinese would be retold through the lens of the man versus the tank. Representations of contemporary Chinese history that had been chronicling the fast-forward motion of economic reform up to this time would grind to a standstill. The buzzwords of the eighties—economic reform and opening up to the Western world—would be replaced by new words such as repression and totalitarianism. China, the land of the instant image, where portraits of Chairman Mao, the Great Wall or a panda bear once stood in place of understanding, now had a new and even more powerful iconic representation. It was on this that Western eyes and minds would fixate, and utilise to essentialise and totalise the lives of 1.2 billion people. The man and the tank would live on beyond the few tense moments of the encounter to become a permanent and universal symbol of resistance to terror. Everything the West had ever abhorred about the Chinese Communist state was now summarised in this single image.

This power to frame, to 'stand in for', and to (re)define the Chinese nation tells us something of the sea-change in Western attitudes toward China after 1989, but more interestingly, the choice of this image to convey the story says something of the Western gaze generally. The real power of this image was not in what it

---

1   Quoted in Trevor Watson, *Tremble and Obey* (Sydney: ABC Books, 1990), 139.

depicted, but the formulaic nature of the depiction. Relying on a familiar semiotic code that was almost theological in intent, the man and the tank fulfilled Western yearnings for an individual ethics of heroism and an interpretation of the world through the prism of simplistic binary opposites.

Like a page from the 'primitive language' of Adam, the imagery of man and tank 'spoke to us without words'. Here was the perfect, transparent signifier. Here was the story of State power at a standstill, faced down by heroic resistance. Here was an image that offered a perfect photographic 'reproduction' in the modern age of the 'memory' of Jesus at Calvary. 'Truth' nailed to a cross by the Roman state that wished to silence his freedom song but which transformed it into an eternity instead. The cross becomes freedom's symbol in no less poignant a way than this image becomes the Chinese variant. Despite the death of God and the rise of mammon, Western morality prays that this ethic of the heroic individual, in which so much still remains invested, can remain alive and universal.

'No more arresting emblems of the modern culture of nationalism exist', says Benedict Anderson, 'than cenotaphs and tombs of the Unknown Soldiers'.[2] It is an arresting emblem, he goes on to note, because the anonymity of the soldier announces a void which is then 'saturated with ghostly national imaginings'. The image of the anonymous man before the tank awakens such ghostly imaginings but does so to honour a transcendental notion of humanity through individual heroism. Read, as it so easily is, through the Cartesian divide of good and evil, this imagery falls easily into place in the Western analytical trope of knowledge and life. From cinematic representations of the human versus the machine-monster through to Western human rights and political science discourse where such notions are 'translated' into the discursive space of the State versus 'civil society', such oppositions form the brick and mortar of Western methodological endeavours. Such a metaphysics of opposition, buoyed by an adversarial Roman legal tradition, has often enchanted Chinese, but lacks a place in traditional Chinese cosmology. There is no clear parallel in traditional Chinese discourse and so, the very grounds on which Western human rights discourse is built are, arguably, absent.

In traditional China, the moral and ethical focus of life centred on the promotion of mutual love and support rather than restraint or control, on individual obligation rather than rights, and, as a corollary, on the mediation rather than litigation of disputes. It was a cosmology built upon an hierarchical set of social relations that not only led to an obsession with stability but also established the basis and nature of social 'face'. 'Face', in turn, worked against clear lines of right and wrong being pushed to the extreme. Thus the self-evident moral logic of the man and the tank, so reliant for its semiotic meaning on a Western ethics of opposites to speak without words, begins to crumble when confronted with this other way of seeing.

The absence of a discursive category called 'human rights' in this other way of seeing does not mean that there is any less humanity, only that matters covered under the rubric of human rights in the West are dispersed and considered

---

2   Benedict Anderson, *Imagined Communities: Reflections on the Origin and Spread of Nationalism* (London: Verso, 1983), 17.

differently elsewhere and at other times. This, at least, is the argument proffered by Xia Yong. While Xia Yong's piece is written in a voice suggesting classical applicability, it provides a useful and necessary starting point through which to consider the possibility of dealing with human rights discourse—not to mention the ethics of life itself—in other ways. Through his unique reading of human rights and the Confucian notion of 'great harmony' Xia Yong helps signpost the importance of tradition. For him the centrality of the Confucian notion of harmony within traditional philosophy leaves no room for the articulation of clear, individually based rights that can be fought for.

A similar problem exists in relation to other Confucian notions such as that of benevolence. The Confucian notion of benevolence is about collective responsibilities, not individual rights. But how are we to know this 'hidden' additional meaning of the word? In the case of 'benevolence', Chinese scholars have long pointed out that this unstated meaning is visible in the character form of the word itself. The pictographic form of the Chinese character for benevolence, 仁 ren is made up of two parts: one being 人 ren meaning 'person'; the other, 二 er, meaning two.[3] Buried in the character form, then, are assumptions about the domain of applicability of this notion of 'benevolence' that a straight translation of the word would leave unpacked and unexpressed. Nevertheless, characters do not always carry the deeper semiotic coding of the word any more than they will tell of the historical terrain the word has travelled.

How words and philosophical traditions came to form and frame a contemporary ethics of the self in China is examined in the work of the Taiwanese scholar Li Yiyuan and the mainland scholar Xu Ping. These two pieces help us understand the way in which the 'high culture' values of traditional China became part of an ingrained and everyday set of assumptions about life, love and community. What their work helps uncover is the 'magical' process of mimesis[4] through which traditional values are transformed and transported into contemporary, popular, everyday Chinese life. It is in the process of mimetic transformation that these 'traditional' values are veiled and (re)appear as purely Marxist inventions. At the same time, and at an unconscious level, the magic of mimesis does its work to blur this purity. Through the unconscious kinship connection it forges between traditional concepts and the 'new' pure Marxian ones, the latter constructions are made to appear 'natural', legitimate and eternal. The way in which this 'kinship' connection has reinforced contemporary Marxist values becomes evident if we examine the current Chinese Communist Party's position on human rights. Their insistence on 'subsistence rights' as the most basic of rights, their demand that collective rights should prevail over individual forms, and their emphasis on obligation rather than rights are positions that can all be traced back as easily to traditional Chinese conceptions as they can to Marxist ones. Thus, while Chinese Marxism speaks, thinks and 'does' in the language of historical materialism, it also

---

3  For a detailed exposition see Ma Zhengfeng, *Benevolence and Humanity: The Philosophical Thought of Confucius* (Beijing: China's Social Science Publishing House, 1993). [ 马振锋, <<仁. 人道: 孔子的哲学思想>>. ] . See also Xu Ping's article in Part I, 1.
4  Michael Taussig, *Mimesis and Alterity* (New York: Routledge, 1993), 13.

operates—unconsciously and in part—in a sensual frame that is in harmony with many past traditional forms. This not only reinforces an unconscious and unarticulated sense of 'tradition', but reifies, in a modified contemporary form, a radically different way of configuring subjectivity and inter-subjectivity. Here are issues much more central to the Chinese lifeworld than the existence or otherwise of a human rights tradition or discourse. What is being discussed here are the ethical procedures and circumstances that frame both Marxism and a contemporary Chinese sense of self. Recognition of this helps move debate beyond the frozen 'disciplinary blockade' of the man and the tank and on to a more mundane and bio-technical framing of life. Such an approach takes us beyond human rights discourse and the question of totalitarianism and enables us to turn the spotlight onto the question of the government of self. The 'difference' of the Chinese debates over human rights, therefore, is interesting because it points to the way in which social subjects are brought into discourse and the way certain repertoires of conduct in everyday life in China are constructed. Central to this construction process in socialist China has been the work unit.

It is in the classic form of Chinese Marxist organisation in China—the work unit—that the paradoxical process of mimetic reaffirmation of past social forms is most dramatically and graphically 'on display'. The work units of China are organs built around a mathematical-based desire to calculate society and social wealth. Early Bolshevik dreams of an 'algebraic society' made operable and visible through a 'gigantic statistical bureau based on exact calculation for the purpose of distributing labour power and the instruments of labour'[5] find echo in the Chinese notion of a work unit. Theoretically, the work unit would function as the basic social unit of accounting, enabling central planners to calculate the totality of productive society as the sum total of all these (work) units. It is, therefore, not by chance that the term 'unit', as described in the *Modern Chinese Dictionary* quoted by He Xinhan, speaks of it as 'a standard of measurement'. Yet the transparency essential for such institutions to function as 'units' of measurement is radically undercut by a dynamic, 'obscene' underside that enables the 'work' of the 'unit' to be carried out. This work operates not on the planners' 'economy of measurement' but on an opaque, unstated economy of the gift. This 'economy of the gift' in China is, as Xu Ping's work illustrates, tied to a very traditional Confucian cosmology in which gifts forge the bond of love between a giver and a receiver. Generalised as an on-going social norm this emotive, incalculable relationship provides the social basis for the idea of 'great harmony' to take root. It is this 'economy of the gift', mimetically reconfigured as 关系 *guanxi*, 'connections' or 'relations' that, in the contemporary period, provides both the medicine that keeps work units productive and the poison that sends them to the wall.[6]

---

5  A. A. Bogdanov, *A Short Course of Economic Science* [Trans. J. Fineburg] (London: Labour Publishing Company, 1923), 466.

6  The incalculable 'economy of the gift' will be explored in much greater detail in my forthcoming book *AnOther China*. In many respects a companion piece to this work, *AnOther China* is in part a genealogy of the mimetic transformation of the Maussian gift-like relations in China into commodity forms.

Thus, while He Xinhan's article offers a very general account of the basic form of the Chinese work unit and an account of how an entire nation has been unconsciously influenced by work unit culture, it is in the articles by Lu Feng and Yi Zhongtian that the less visible and more traditional social dynamics of the work unit come into view. Lu Feng's work offers an understanding of the way the work unit harnesses the power of the traditional Chinese lineage group through mimetic appropriation of its dynamic regime of interpersonal relations. Read against the grain of the critique being mounted, Lu Feng supplies material that not only demonstrates the inherent problems of the work unit system, but, more significantly, its symbolic strength in mimetically appropriating the power of patriarchy and making that power its own.

Yi Zhongtian's work operates even more overtly to tie work unit culture to traditional value systems. Work units become a tangled web of 'face-based' relations. Work units are not simply a state-supplied 'iron rice bowl' that satisfies the desire for stability, but are also state-sponsored units for the production and reproduction of social 'face'. In comparing the work unit to the customary desire to display the coffin prior to death, Yi highlights the basis of the Chinese desire for stability, harmony and a home which, he notes, even transcends life itself. To be without a 'unit' is to be without a home and, to be without this, one is robbed of one's roots, and simultaneously, devoid of any sense of obligation. To 'float' without a work unit is to be an outsider, a stranger, a vagrant. In this code of life, to be an outsider in any sense is to be a potential danger. The traditional nature of this distinction, between stability and safety, and movement and fear, is again captured etymologically in the extract from Chen Baoliang's work, which highlights the character 流 *liu*, meaning to float, in the definition of the 流氓 *liumang* or hoodlum.

Austin once suggested contemporary words are often shadowed by etymological vapour trails and, from these, one can gain an appreciation of the deep structural understanding of the word that a 'straight' translation would be unable to convey. In this respect, words prove themselves no less opaque than images. The meaning they 'carry' is often unconscious and, without an archaeology of the word, these 'other' meanings will remain permanently in the shadows. Nevertheless, while such an archaeology of the word is important it should also be recognised that words are irreducible to their etymology. Words in use take on other, more contingent, meanings. Meaning is, therefore, quite often found in use. Hence, while Chen's piece on the etymology of the word *liumang* helps to locate the hidden meanings carried in the word, the definition of the term *liumang* would be incomplete without an examination of its contemporary use. How it is used is illustrated by example, and it is in the sensational tone of a work like Ge Fei's that 'typical' examples of *liumang* activity are recalled and rehearsed. Through this merging of language description (Chen) and action (Ge Fei) we begin to build up a range of images of what is meant, in Chinese, by the term *liumang*. Yet one must also be tentative at this point. The term *liumang* goes beyond criminal activity to incorporate all those people who, in Chen's words, are 'without a place': the most obvious forms of *liumang* are those outside the work unit.

There are, however, many ways to be 'placeless' in China. Whether one adopts Chen's etymological approach or Yi's sociology of the work unit and place, quite clearly the meaning of 'place' cannot be rendered purely in spatial terms. Place, in both accounts, means social place. To be without a place is to be excluded from a social place and this points to a definition that sweeps in far more people than the common criminal or those outside the work unit.

An equally important area of exclusion relates to sexuality. In China this is a domain with tight social boundaries surrounding acceptable behaviour. As the tone of Jin Ren's article on homosexuals in Beijing makes clear, the sexual behaviour one displays marks the boundary between the 'insider' and the 'outsider', and a very broad 'economy of the outsider' is operative in China today.

For the subaltern 'outsider'—be they sexually, socially, economically or politically outside—there are immediate and grave consequences. For this reason, all outsiders, all *liumang*, avoid the spotlight. Yet the very act of avoidance is an indication that to be discovered has severe consequences. Hence, all *liumang* have their tactics of avoidance and secret codes of communication. Jin Ren's discussion on 'pick-ups' and ways to avoid error in the gay community parallel the wily ways of the criminal eluding error and arrest. The floodlight shone on the man and the tank all too often blinds us to the forms of dissent taking place in the shadows. It is for this reason that it is now time to move away from the well-lit main streets of China and into the tiny alleyways, populated by figures who are collectively labelled 'outsiders' in their own land.

## HUMAN RIGHTS AND CHINESE TRADITION[1]

**XIA YONG**

In the 1990s, the issue of human rights has again come to the fore. This time, however, it is not simply dismissed as a slogan of the bourgeoisie. Within China, a whole range of scholars have already clearly shown that 'human rights are not patented by the bourgeoisie'. Even though the bourgeoisie first coined the term human rights, the proletariat have their own human rights slogans and their own rights needs. Moreover, Marxism itself offers its own form of advocacy for human rights. The question, then, must surely be whether the West has a patent over this concept. To deal with this issue involves examining three inter-related questions. Firstly, whether or not the West was alone in producing this type of concept. Secondly, whether or not there is congeniality between the East and the West on this point. Thirdly, whether or not the recognition and advocacy of human rights as basically emanating from the West will inevitably lead to a westernisation process taking place.

### Chinese Tradition and Human Rights Discourse

It is true that, traditionally, the concept of human rights did not exist in China. There are possibly two different explanations for this: the first would suggest that within traditional Chinese society, there was extreme political, spiritual and economic repression. Under such conditions, it was utterly impossible to initiate and practise human rights.[2] The second line of argument follows a different tack. It points out that whatever the political, spiritual or economic repression suffered during the classical period in China, it was far less draconian than the type of repression carried out in classical Western culture. In addition, Chinese culture laid great stress on humanity and pursued this through the concept of 'great harmony for humankind'. The pursuit of

---

1  Xia Yong, *The Origin of Human Rights Conceptions* (Beijing: Chinese Political Science and Law Publishing House, 1992), 177–86.[夏勇,《人权概念起源》.] Xia Yong is a researcher in the law school of the Chinese Academy of Social Sciences, Beijing.

2  Since the May Fourth Movement (1919) and, in particular, in the last decade, this viewpoint has tended to prevail in China. See my article in the collection *Comparative Law*, volume 1, 1991.

equality, freedom, social peace and wealth, which are ideas at the core of Western notions of human rights, therefore, could be pursued in China without the need for the rights principle or the rule of law.[3]

Both these positions, I should point out, are not unreasonable, but they are a bit simplistic and one-sided. It is probably better to understand them as products of two distinct cultural and intellectual trends evident in China since the time of the May Fourth Movement. The former position reflects the views of those who belittled and deserted Chinese tradition and who saw salvation in the West. Those who held the latter view had hoped for a rejuvenation of Chinese tradition which would then be the basis of a new beginning for the nation.

Both explanations still have inspirational significance. For my part, I think that the humanitarian and harmonious spirit that human rights embodies was not only present in traditional Chinese society, but that it was quite bountiful. If anything was lacking, it was the spirit of a rule of law. It is fair to say that humanism was a fundamental characteristic of traditional Chinese culture. Even though historically China had no ideology of human rights, within traditional Chinese ideology there were undoubtedly concepts such as the need for a moral law and the equality of persons which went beyond the existing laws of that time. Within Confucianism, Taoism and Buddhism there is abundant evidence of the concept of freedom. The problem is that these ideas are related to introspection, self-fulfilment and detachment, and only very rarely lend themselves to commentary upon social selfishness, self-aggrandisement, self-protection or social antagonisms. Hence the idea of rights could not be developed or deduced from this source. Nevertheless, the absence of discussion of human rights in traditional China and the lack of stress upon the concept do not make Chinese tradition and ideas of human rights incompatible.

Not that the cultural traditions of China and the West are as different as some scholars who carry out comparative cultural studies would suggest—in fact, it could be said that there are more similarities than differences. If there is a key reason why, in Chinese history, there was not the production of a conception of human rights as there was in the West it must surely be because, in Chinese tradition, pushing forward humanism and seeking 'great harmony' turned on individual obligation rather than the promotion of individual rights, and it relied on the rule of morality rather than the rule of law. Here, my meaning of the term 'turned on or relied on' is not the same as 'drawing support from' or 'being aided by'. This is not to suggest that Chinese traditional society offered absolutely no evidence of discussions on human rights or the rule of law. The so-called 'petitioning to the law' to adjudicate disputes between commoners, the idea of a life for a life, and the mandatory requirement that debts be repaid were all undoubtedly built on the allocation of rights to litigants. In attempting to redress any injustice, the

---

3   For an example of this line of argument see J. C. Hsiung, *Human Rights in East Asia*, 1985, 10, 12, 90.

common people enjoyed the right to beat drums in court and lodge complaints against perceived injustices (that is, petition the higher authorities). These were all types of rights which were used to appeal for a redress of certain wrongs and they were, at the very least, recognised in Chinese customary law. The view that 'human behaviour must be in accordance with propriety' or the idea that 'defining rights and obligations is done to prevent disputation' as well as the thought that 'rights and obligations must accord with the laws of propriety all have a certain affinity with the idea of *fazhi* or 'rule by law'. Naturally, this idea of 'rule by law' is not the same as the 'rule of law'. The so-called reliance upon individual obligation and morality is a far cry from a reliance upon individual rights and the law. The bottom line here is that it means relying on the positivity of people's mutual love and approval rather than on negatively constructed mutual restraint and control, and it is this which is used to push forward humanism and realise 'great harmony'. The ancient sages never lectured on human rights, nor did they discuss the need to struggle for the rights of the common people. Instead, they offered discourses on human character, humanism, and benevolence, regarding benevolence as the way to a universal fraternity and a system of government in which the king is of little weight, and it is the people who are truly valuable. The significance of these discourses is the difference they signify between China and the West regarding procedure. Far more important is the fact that not only is the traditional Chinese view of harmony at one with notions of human rights, but the former can be absorbed by the latter, and will even go some way toward improving traditional Western notions of human rights.

## Why Has Traditional Chinese Society Never Paid Attention to Human Rights?

From the perspective of those proposing means by which to rule the country, traditional Chinese politics sought to use the rule of propriety rather than the rule of restriction. The spiritual meaning of the politics of the rule of propriety has three points which are worthy of attention. First, only when one has achieved virtue can one set out to rule. Secondly, only by abiding by propriety can one adhere to morality and justice. Thirdly, only with a correct moral standing can one become a sage. On what did they rely in order to explain the political order? What methods were used and to what end?

The Confucian school long advocated *renzhi* the 'rule of man'. But the premise of the 'rule of man' is the rule of the virtuous sage. That is to say, as Mencius noted, 'only the sage can occupy positions of rank'—in contrast to the argument that anyone can fulfil the role. This notion is remarkably similar to the Platonic idea of the 'philosopher king'. But unlike Plato's philosopher king, the personality of the Chinese sage is governed by the idea that 'only when one has achieved virtue can one set out to rule'. For the cultivation of virtuous and moral character, one needed to correct the management of the family, the administration of the country and control and manage all affairs under heaven. This was a unified and total process. If the emperor was not a sage, then he needed to promote and extend the spirit of benevolence using his own morality to fulfil the will of heaven and to bring about a benevolent polis. It was only in this way that a good socio-political order could be established and long-term order and a lasting peace be maintained. This is best illustrated by the proverbs 'with a moral and virtuous sage king, harmony will reign under heaven' and 'if the king is just and true, the state will be at peace with itself'. The logic behind all this is that it is the people who determine politics. This argument emphasises the duties and obligations toward civil society of those who rule. The right to rule is derived from duty and obligation and not from the law and this, in turn, comes from spontaneous self-cultivation.

A very special and crucial characteristic of Chinese traditional politics and legal culture was 'taking obligation and duty as the heart of matters'. If we take as our starting point the stress laid on the duty and obligation of the ruler as a means for administering the country, then we can say that everything rests on the spirit of 'taking duty and obligation as the heart of the matter'. If we look at this notion and compare it with Western politico-legal culture, we discover that its moral boundaries and level of logic are quite different to Western discourse. However, this type of duty and obligation that political men of worth advocate is entirely dependent on them holding political power. That is to say, it becomes possible to protect the country and love the people only if the small group of moral leaders who have realised power have not degenerated, they control themselves and continue to devote themselves to the public. Naturally, a good socio-political order is not simply contingent upon the outward morality of the worthy sage. Social regularities and laws also need to embody the laws of propriety. Propriety has not only become part of the natural customary law of the ordinary people, it is also the moral law which has been expounded and interpreted by the just and worthy sages. It is also a part of the sovereign's law but it is definitely not a product of one particular social class, nor is it a social pact. Propriety is not the basis upon which people scramble for profit and power or struggle with each other. Rather, people rely on harmony without struggle, without litigation. It is here that morality, religion, law, politics and society come together. The function of propriety is not simply to inform a definite socio-political order (that is, the so-called 'governed state') that guarantees social peace, maintains social stratification and offers benefits to the next generation. Much more important is the Confucian idea that 'benevolence rules all under heaven', that is, people abide by the laws of propriety.

In the final analysis, the Confucian scholars wanted to influence people unconsciously, through rites (propriety). Confucius advocated rule by rites and opposed the rule of punishment. The object was to make everyone into completely moral people; as they became good, they became sage-like. That was Confucius's deeper purpose. In accordance with the ideals of the Confucian school, one should abide by the laws of propriety and advocate righteousness simultaneously. In ancient China, righteousness and self-cultivation were closely related and were the antithesis of individual self-interest. On this basis, the personal relations between people were not relations of fear and profit, struggle and extortion. Rather, it was a type of moral relationship within which people should love and help one another, have heart-to-heart relations based upon mutually accepted moral claims without any desire to use one another and calculate the benefits of the relationship. This is the only consummate form of social life. Hence, the ideal socio-political principle of classical Chinese was benevolence and righteousness—the doctrine of the mean, and harmony. In this respect, China was different to the West where the concept of justice related to disputes over rights and obligations. Furthermore, Chinese conceptions of justice placed particular emphasis on duty and obligation and this was quite unlike the West where stress was placed on rights.

In the classical period in the West, Plato's ideal of a philosopher king was never realised and Plato was finally forced to give up this ideal. The aristocrats of classical Greece replaced the sovereign's autocracy. This move had all the hallmarks of a change in the character of political power. Aristocratic power was a type of socio-political contract that operated prior to the question of political power being decided. Under these conditions, a number of wealthy and powerful people vied and compromised with each other and, later, utilised the law to form a social compact to restrain one another. In every social class, the relative wealth of a person and their relative power was directly reflected in the legal status allocated to them. The socio-political compacts utilised the notion of rights as its basis. People's real interests and benefits were the political starting points. Participation in politics and grasping political power were all undertaken in order to protect and increase self-interest, through the implementation of one's own rights. No matter which class, faction or group one was in, every person openly put their own self-interests first. Recognition and protection of the rights of others and social rights was a type of compromise and concession. To establish and protect the socio-political order, there was little choice other than to implement the rule of law. At the same time, the notion of justice became the most important socio-political principle. Justice was used and regarded as significant in so far as it helped resolve disputes and protected rights. The degree to which justice was realised could be determined by the degree it was able to maximise self-interest.

In traditional China, no attention was ever paid to human rights. To understand why, one only needs to examine the subject of rights. Rights are a relational concept that express a type of societal relationship between people. This type of relation has, as a precondition, the relative separation and independence of subjects. Rights, duties and obligations not only express an individual's existence and mutual relations but, even more importantly, they express the social relations of giving and receiving between social members. Give and take is a conceptualisation of the unity of opposites. In the history of the West, developed systems of rights have, as their precondition, not only the significance of self-constraint, but also the antagonistic contradictions and division between individuals and classes. As the subject of rights, duties and obligations divide, antagonistic contradictions grow strong, demands for rights increase and the rule by law develops. It was really very different in traditional Chinese society.

In relation to the economy, one family as one household and the autocratic small-scale peasant economy were the basic form of the whole of the traditional Chinese economy. Individuals belonged to the family and were not independent producers or managers. Nor were they independent economic subjects. The patriarch enjoyed considerable power over family members and bore the obligations and duties for family members. Natural blood relations were the key basis for people to enter into labour-based co-operation and social ventures. This natural economy and these 'natural' relations were quite different to those which dominated Europe in ancient times. The mixing of ethnic groups, the slave wars, the assaults upon traditional society by the mercantile economy all led to the gradual development of centrifugal forces. These centrifugal forces, in turn, led individuals to become more autonomous 'players' within society, ethnic groups and the market. In contrast, in China, the lineage group or clan offered the individual warmth and protection. Within traditional Chinese society, the individual as the subject of benefits and interests who has divided interests and antagonistic independent initiatives in relation to the processes of production, exchange, distribution and commodities is very rare indeed. People's dependence upon mutual relations is clearly the most important thing in China. Chinese people live in that way and their philosophy and morality are also thus inclined. If this economy were to place great stress on individual rights, if the relations between people were to be more clearly demarcated, then, it would be virtually impossible for the society to operate. In fact, one could even go so far as to say that the very basis of the demands for existence and the need for social order could not be met. As we know, in the process of the disintegration of the Western feudal economic order, the demands for rights by outsiders, the urban dwellers and the bourgeois led to the gradual increase in rights to the point where they produced modern human rights discourse. However, these three new subjects of rights and, especially the latter, the bourgeoisie, simply did not exist in traditional Chinese society.

The individual in classical China did not achieve the independent socio-political status like that attributable to the 'citizen'. The status of every person is determined first and foremost by their ethical capacity, that is, status is determined by blood, as in the case of the father, son, younger or older brother, male, female, husband or wife. Because family and nation are as one, the individual's social status, such as one's position as Emperor, minister, official, commoner or as lowly servant or superior sage is derived from one's status within the family. Rights, obligations and duties are based upon, and produced as a result of, these different capacities of (social) agents. One can also say that, other than the mercantile economy and the destruction of blood relations as a result of ethnic wars, the history of the West also had the notion of citizenship and religion operating as a corrosive force upon family status. In addition, in the West, human rights, freedom and liberation were often attributed the same meaning. These stood in sharp contrast to the authority of God and the spiritual control exercised by the church. Traditional China did not have this conception of God nor this religious system. Nor did China have feudal domination by kings and lords. In China, the system of imperial domination was aided by the warmth of familial blood links and the extremely patriarchal nature of power. This, in turn, was further reinforced by the ethical programme of Confucius. Therefore, compared to the West, institutions within ancient China that opposed spiritual oppression and governmental control and promoted demands for a free and independent concept of the individual, were all rather weak.

Within the cultural arena, ancient China lacked Western notions of an atomised, antagonistic and absolute conception of the individual. The Confucian notion of heaven was a place where the Confucian concepts of righteousness and justice prevailed. Similarly, a human was a person committed to these Confucian concepts. Every person's character was defined by their social relations. Moreover, the individual belonged to, and served, the collective. A person's interrelations, social relations and natural relations could all be considered to have a unified ontological character.

China lacked the intense relationship between humans and God which was evident in the West. In Chinese tradition, the relationship between humans and the supernatural was never all that important. The tendency within traditional Chinese philosophy was to treat humankind as its essence and, in so doing, placed stress on practical and useful things. Rarely did it 'depart from reality to raise abstract forms of argument'. Within Western history, apart from the intense relationship between the individual and others in economic and political life, other intense relationships included those relationships between humanity and nature, God and mammon, experiences and paranormal experiences, social justice and natural justice. It is in this type of dualistic relationship that the individual is able to receive the help of the divine powers in order to obtain certain types of absolute and isolated abstract formulations. It is these absolute and divine conceptions of the individual that protect the abstract existential notions of the self and these two notions must enjoy in common an absolute divine and abstract notion of rights. These rights have long been defined as innate; they are the so-called natural rights—human rights. Natural rights are the basis of social opposition. The more individuals are isolated, the more they are in opposition to society, and the more they run into conflict with others. The more rights are made absolute, the more they are guaranteed and the more we can talk about human rights. The basis of duty and obligation is derived from rights themselves. Regulating duties and obligation is carried out in order to protect rights. The implementation of rights is not based upon any internally generated love or benevolence. Rather, it emanates from contrary demands which are founded on divine and legal power. In the view of the Chinese ancestors, such a position would be considered inconceivable. This isn't because traditional China had no conception of the individual nor because the dignity and worth of humans were undervalued. Rather, it is because Chinese culture had its own special form and category of the person. For example, 'to overcome all worldly thoughts and enter sainthood' or to reach nirvana is totally dependent upon the individual's moral commitment. Such commitment is embodied in the dignity and worth of the individual. Moreover, this way of conceptualising dignity and worth is superior to Western forms, which are derived from Christianity, for the Chinese forms are neither supernaturally based, innate nor hypothetical. Only through self-sublimation can this dignity and worth clearly emerge. From the above, it is obvious that the individual in Chinese culture is introspective, yielding, generous of spirit and in harmony with others. These are not traits brought on by external controls, forms of extortion or employed for self-benefit as part of a struggle over conflicting interest. This form of individuation can very easily become the subject of duty and obligation, but there is little possibility of such a form constituting the ordinary subject of rights. The fact that the Chinese notion of the individual is unlikely to be the subject of rights is not to suggest that this form is lacking in a social reformist spirit nor that it lacks a spirit of combating evil.

Max Weber offers an interesting insight on this. He believed Confucianism advocated self-restraint and compliance with the laws of propriety. In his words, '[In] not reaching beyond this world, the individual necessarily lacked an autonomous counterweight in confronting this world'. It is this mental attitude, he claims, that 'could not allow man an inward aspiration toward a "unified personality"… Hence, there was no leverage for influencing conduct through inner forces freed of tradition and convention.'[4]

Weber's views have gained great popularity among Western Sinologists, but I think Weber really only concentrated on the restraining aspects of the rules of propriety. He failed to notice the even more important Confucian concept of benevolence which has a very stimulating function. The notion of benevolence displays a type of moral character that promotes initiative. While benevolence and propriety have a very close affinity, it is the notion of benevolence which is the more important of the two. The philosophy of benevolence is deeper and more complete than that of propriety. It is the internal dynamic of the notion of benevolence that can stimulate things and, from beginning to end, ancient China had always had a tradition that involved a struggle against the realities of politics.[5] In classical times, many intellectuals lay down their lives for justice and died as martyrs without any compromises for the dark and corrupt political forces.

---

4   Max Weber, *Religions of China* (New York: Free Press, 1951), 235–6.
5   Zhang Duanhui, *Heaven and Earth*, Lianjing Publishing House, no date.

They did this to advocate the right to eliminate the despot. This power to oppose tyranny and save the people and society did not come from God. Rather, it was internal and came from a sense of benevolence. Because these values are internal, the Confucian school cannot become the basis of worldly rights and one cannot derive the notion of human rights from this tradition of benevolence.

## ★ THE TRADITIONAL CHINESE VIEW OF THE COSMOS AND THE PRACTICES OF DAILY LIFE[6]

### LI YIYUAN

It is important to have an overall view of how Confucianism passes into different parts of the social system and is expressed in action. It is especially important to highlight those moments wherein non-intellectual practices of everyday life are fused with Confucian theoretical and philosophic forms. In actuality, between the philosophy of the Confucian classics and the actions of ordinary people, there exists a common cultural logic which forms the basis for the fatalistic principles of popular Chinese cosmology. Because of these common cultural norms, the two levels of culture (that is, the 'great tradition' and the 'popular tradition'), lead to common actions. This essay uses this observation to enable a deeper discussion of the relationship between Confucian culture and action, and to examine how it takes advantage of the social structure and social processes.

### The Three Levels of Balance

I once proposed a model of Chinese traditional cosmology that suggested it operated as three balanced tiers. I argued that when it came to harmony and balance, Chinese cosmology and the basic laws of fate were much the same because the intentions expressed in the 'Classics' involved 致中和 'a search for harmony'. In order to reach the highest state of balance and harmony—a perfect state—one needed to reach harmony and balance at each of these three levels. To have harmony at only one level is to have a very unstable situation. These three levels of balance and harmony are expressed in Figure 1.

The goal of achieving perfection requires that each of these three levels systematically operates to preserve the balanced harmony. This is true irrespective of whether one is discussing cultural imaginings within the great tradition of the gentry or simply those within the minor traditions of the ordinary people. This is also true in relation to the health of an individual's body as much as it holds true for the fate of the whole cosmos.

---

6  Li Yiyuan, 'Traditional Cosmology and Economic Development', *21st Century*, 20 (1993), 146–58.〔李亦園, "传统宇宙观与经济发展"《二十一世纪》.〕

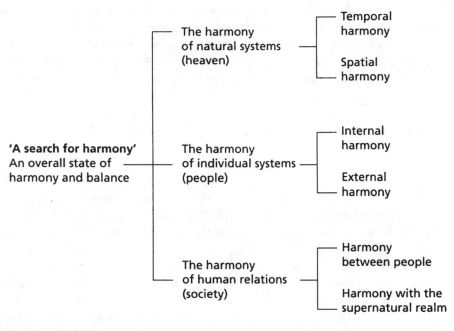

Three levels of balance

## Balances within the Natural System

In pursuing harmony in relation to nature or heaven, traditional culture can best be explained by reference to two facets of activity: one covering time, the other space. There was little difference here between the ordinary people and the gentry because harmony was expressed as the temporal alignment of an individual fate with the cosmos.

Every individual's year, month, day and time of birth is plotted and these four points plot the heavenly stems and earthly branches—a traditional system of temporal calculation prior to the westernisation of the calendar. This was popularly known as *bazi*, the eight characters, which were expressed in pairs, and indicated the year, month, day and time of birth. Each pair consisted of one heavenly stem and one earthly branch. This calculation was central to certain traditional divinational practices based on the correlation of these times. The 'eight characters' of birth in turn determined one's life course. This was one's 'fate', 命 *ming*. In popular religions, one's fate was sealed at birth and so 'fate was destined to be'. Nevertheless, every individual's life course and cosmos is in accord with contingencies that govern each phase and each of these is governed by different fortunes, some of which are auspicious, while others are inauspicious. This is called fortune, 运 *yun*. In traditional popular religious belief 'fate' is actually a form of predestination, 命定 *mingding*, and cannot be altered. Fortune, on the other hand, can be altered. Moreover, one can take advantage of one's different powers to bring about that change. Among the common folk, it is in the pursuit of temporal harmony that one notes the ability to change through fortune. Sometimes a temporal alignment of the individual and the cosmos may occur, leading to harmony. This period of alignment is auspicious and is therefore a very lucky period. A lack of harmony is inauspicious and can lead to calamities. Because of this basic concept of time, many Chinese will often want to find out each of the points of good and bad luck that face them through life's course and try to maximise their good luck and avoid the bad. This is the basic rationale behind the fortune-telling practice of divination. The age-old practice of fortune telling is an important part of the cycle in Chinese spiritual life. But in the rapidly changing conditions of modern society, the pursuit of the traditional concept of temporal harmony has taken on a more popular face. In Taiwan, an example I will use to illustrate my case, it is clear that not only are ordinary people informed by this value system, but intellectuals are too. At times, it proves a very popular belief system.

To preserve the harmonic balance with nature, to only look at temporality is inadequate. Only when guidance is also sought in relation to space can one preserve overall harmony. Without this, the system of harmony cannot lead to complete fulfilment. Within traditional culture, consideration of the concept of spatial harmony starts with the ideas of 阴 *yin* and 阳 *yang* and moves on to 五行 *wuxing*, the five elements, and divination based on the eight characters. It is these comprehensive range of factors that we find expressed in 风水 *fengshui* or geomancy.

Take popular religions in Taiwan as a guide: even though the ideas of geomancy are incomplete when compared with ancient times, they are still given a special place. In relation to land they can be said to lie at the heart of popular religious views on space. This is especially true when it comes to the search for an ancestral burial ground, but it plays a role in other things such as deciding upon the choice of dwelling and the layout of rooms.

## Balance and Harmony in Individual Bodies

To preserve balance and harmony throughout one's body one must, apart from working for harmony with nature, also ensure bodily harmony through care of the self. Within popular cultural systems, to preserve one's bodily harmony one can divide the care of the self into two parts: one to attend to an inner essential harmony, the other, to attend to external harmony. Within traditional Chinese culture, the individual body was viewed as a small cosmos. Hence the oppositional concepts of *yin* and *yang* can be used to explain the balanced harmony within this small cosmos. Nowhere is this oppositional conception of *yin* and *yang* better exemplified than in relation to conceptions of hot, 热 *re*, and cold, 冷 *leng*, as well as in the extension into popular life of the idea of *jinbu* 进补, meaning striving for attainment. This basic concept of harmony between hot and cold extends into all aspects of the culinary world, where things are attributed the properties of either hot, cold or are labelled neutral. This is done entirely to strive for food that preserves the internal harmonious balance of the small cosmos of the individual subject in order to bring about or preserve one's health. The *yin–yang*, hot–cold conceptualisation has a very long lineage and so it is very influential, not only in relation to food, but also medicine. Food customs and cooking habits, and at the same time traditional Chinese medicine, are in this way as one, and this constitutes one of the most significant characteristics of Chinese daily life.

While the preservation of hot and cold bodily balance is essential, it is still not enough. One also requires a balance in one's external manifestation and, only with this, can overall balance be assured. The external manifestation of balance is expressed in the naming of a person. In the traditional study of names, the name given to a person is attributed a transformational power. The transformational power of the first name and the surname, by and large, can be divided into two parts: the first is found in the influence of the five elements or *wuxing*, while the other is expressed in the written form of the name. Both are geared towards achieving external harmony for the subject. In contemporary Taiwan, it is fair to say that far more attention is paid to the external form of balance than to the internal. Moreover, in the method of writing and giving names, people are particularly fond of using the method which uses the five properties, and this is an important special characteristic of contemporary society as it undergoes rapid change. (See Li Yiyuan, Part III, 1.)

## Harmony in Interpersonal Relations

Harmony in interpersonal relations has been the loftiest goal of the Chinese cultural value system. It is here that one discovers the significance of 'this world' ethics. As professor Jin Yanji has noted in two famous essays he penned on 'networks': 'A question of concern to Confucian social ethics is the establishment of an harmonious secular order with people at its heart.' In addition, 'this reality can be thought of as the source of Confucian social ethics. Confucian social ethics are most concerned with the establishment of a social order based on harmonious social relations. Ethics are the pillar upon which this social order is built. The basic hypothesis of Confucian scholarship rests upon various types of relations and it is these relations that then form the various aspects of the ethics.'

There are two approaches to consider when examining the pursuit of these types of human relations and social order from the perspective of tradition. One takes a synchronic view of harmony in human relations, while the other takes a diachronic view. The former approach begins with 'family' and builds an ethics of relations between clan members. This is then extended to include other people. It was this that Fei Xiaotong meant when he discussed the 'layered nature' of human relations. Within these layers are extremely complex methods and processes for preserving the harmony of the different levels of human relations.

The diachronic approach to relational harmony leads to the preservation of human relations for living humans and, from there, is extended to cover relations with the non-living. This can be extended even further to include supernatural relations with deities. This is a point emphasised by scholars who research popular traditions, but is one almost completely ignored by other scholars. From this, however, one can see the way living and deceased family members can form one entity. It is the harmony and balance that one creates between the living and the dead that enables genuine balance to be achieved. This is a very important characteristic of interpersonal relations within Chinese culture. This basic concept is deeply ingrained and so the patriarchal clan system is given a definite process through which it can be preserved. Along with this, there exists the popular preservation of the patriarchal system of ancestor worship. Moreover, the extension of this ancestor worship leads to a whole range of other supernatural forms of worship becoming popular.

It is in these different diachronic spaces of harmonious interpersonal relations that the traditional culture draws together popular and high culture. High culture lays stress on the abstract, while popular culture tends to emphasise real practices. However, in the final analysis, both are concerned with these two spaces of engagement.

In summary, the three levels of balanced harmony are but three stages in the Chinese people's belief in overall harmony. But this vertical form crisscrosses parts of both popular and high culture. Within the traditions of popular culture balanced harmony is pursued most fully in actions at the level of daily practice. Hence one finds that the goal of achieving comprehensive harmony, for the most part, is restricted to the harmony of body and family and, in this area, it flourishes. Within the great tradition of the gentry, the pursuit of harmonious balance is expressed in fairly abstract cosmological conceptions and in the search for national and social happiness. Moreover, the idea of a 'search for harmony' becomes the highest standard by which to judge harmonious balance. This idea of pursuing harmonious balance still forms the basis upon which the actions of Chinese, be they in China or outside, takes place. At the same time, because these three levels are so ingeniously intertwined, it means that the popular culture of the everyday and the high culture of systemic thought have gradually become deeply and intricately interwoven.

## 报 *Bao*, Recompense/revenge, 缘 *Yuan*, Predestined Relationships: Expressive Actions of Chinese Interpersonal Relations

Interpersonal relational harmony relies on interpersonal association which, within the social sciences, is often designated as 'exchange'. In discussions of the processes of 'exchange' (交换) one can explain things from the position of economics, society or psychology. A cultural perspective, however, is possibly the most suitable way of seeing the essential expression of the way in which Chinese carry out exchange. Morever, looking at things in this way enables us to tie it into such things as personal emotion (人情), networks or relations (关系) and 'face' (面子).

I want to deal firstly with the familiar concept of 报 *bao*. Everybody knows that it was Yang Liansheng who first discussed the concept of *bao* in a systematic fashion in his paper '*Bao*—one basis of Chinese social relations' and then later in a paper 'The significance of 报 *bao*, 保 *bao* and 包 *bao* in Chinese culture', with a Hong Kong Chinese University scholar, Qian Shisi. He began by saying: 'In Chinese the word *bao* has a very wide meaning. It includes the words for 'report' (报告) 'repay' (报答), 'recompense' (报偿), 'revenge' (报仇), as well as [the Buddhist concept of] 'retribution' (报应). The key meaning for this term, however, is either 'retribution' (报应) or 'repay' (还报). This conception is of fundamental importance within Chinese social relations. Chinese people believe that an action's mutuality (交互性)—that is, love and hate, reward and punishment—from interpersonal relations right through to the relations between the person and the supernatural, ought to be predicated on a cause-and-effect relation. Hence, in any form of action by a Chinese person, it can ordinarily be said that they will calculate that action on the basis of a prediction of the likely 'retribution' or 'repayment' it will bring about. To offer others an advantage was therefore regarded as a form of 'social investment' which would, in due course, bring forth an appropriate form of repayment.

In his analysis, Yang used the term 'mutuality', which was a neutral word to explain these actions but, in actuality, the term 'exchange' is much more appropriate. In Yang and Qian's joint paper, they elected to use two English terms to fully describe 报 *bao*. These were reciprocation and retribution, and it should be said that these two terms are also very appropriate. Ordinarily, when people use the term 报 *bao* the idea of repayment, 回报 *huibao*, comes to mind. The problem with this, however, is that its scope is limited to those people outside the family relation. Yang emphasises the point that the term 报 *bao* really must include relations with relatives and family. Hence, he says we are really quite clear about the fact that the principles underlying the terms 'repay' (还报) and 'reciprocate'/'retaliate' (回报) are based upon practices within the family system. Reward and punishment, to bless and curse, these things can all be transformed in the family … The principle of mutual reward is both transformed and strengthened within the family system. 'For example, to be a filial son or daughter is the most appropriate demonstration of the principle of 'repayment' (还报). On the basis of this analysis we can go beyond the earlier argument where balance is the pillar upon which harmonious relations are built and are extended beyond the family to other people. Yang also suggests that the concepts of 报 *bao* and 祭 *ji*, which means to make a ceremonial sacrifice, are tied together. He considers the concept of *ji* as a kind of 报 *bao*, for not only does it relate to the question of repaying (回报) of parents and ancestors, but at the same time, it also relates to sacrificial repayments to the gods. From this point, we reach an understanding of the significance of Yang's thesis, which really is like the point we noted earlier. That is, harmonious human relations are pushed into complete synchronicity with relations between humans and supernatural deities.

Quite apart from this point, however, Yang also believes that the extension of 报 *bao*, along with the natural world, corresponds to harmony throughout the seasons. He says:

> The attitude of continuously utilising mutuality as a principle is not only in accordance with reality, but even if one were to turn to the animal and insect kingdoms, one would discover that this expression of 报 *bao* is even in accordance with the natural laws. Dong Zhongshu also holds a very similar view to this one. This Han dynasty theorist developed a theory of the unity of heaven and earth, within which the social system of the nation needs to be in correspondence with that of the cosmos. This demonstrates that nature and humankind are in a relation of repayment ( 还报 ) with one another. Dong Zhongshu's theory is that the performance of the political system must imitate the operation of heaven. This so-called 'four parts of government' must be in accord with the four seasons of the natural world.

This shows the need to protect the balances within interpersonal relations as one gives consideration to the harmonious balance humans must have with the natural world. Hence, in this way, one can see that when Yang says that the character 报 *bao* is a basis upon which Chinese social relations are built, he is really pointing to something very important.

Following on from Yang Lianshan's work, Professor Wen Chongyi has written on the question of 报 *bao*. In this work *The Debt of Gratitude and Revenge—An Analysis of the Act of Exchange*, he presents the following argument:

> The two basic principles governing the operation of the terms *bao'en* ( 报恩 )—to pay a debt of gratitude—and *baochou* ( 报仇 )—revenge, is that 'one receives' ( 来而不往非礼也 ); 'to not avenge is unsage-like' ( 此仇不报，非君子 ). To have a favour bestowed on one must lead to a response that is in excess of the original favour bestowed. Revenge must also be sought when required, but this need not be in excess, and can be equal to, or even less than, the original wrong committed. This type of mutual relation is one readily acknowledged by China's own history and cannot be denied.

After laying out a range of different historical case materials Wen concludes that revenge tends to be far more numerous, and identifies revenge as a key element in the mutual relations produced under 报 *bao*. If one accepts the double-faceted nature of these relations of mutuality, then it becomes rather easy to understand the point of this article: in interpersonal relations of mutuality, the basic principle is to establish balanced relations, and the maintenance of that balance is of utmost concern. This even reaches the point whereby, whatever measures one adopts and whatever measures one needs will all be formulated with regard to the different circumstances one faces.

Whether it be the positive face of *bao'en* —to repay a debt of gratitude—or the negative face of *baochou*—revenge—both come about because the individual does not wish to be burdened by owing any favours. The aim is to maintain balance. If one uses this system of mutual exchange to inform an understanding of the principles governing traditional Chinese cosmology, and actions that flow from it, then things become more intelligible.

One other Chinese character that is worthy of discussion is 缘 *yuan*, which means reason or predestined relationships. There are two predominant readings of the character *yuan* within the social sciences. One is suggested by Professor Li Peiliang in 'Social Science and Concepts From Here: Using Medicine and Predestined Relationships as an Example'. The other view comes from Professor Yang Guoshu in 'Concept and Function of the Chinese People's 缘 *yuan*.' In Li's thesis, the concept of *yuan* is a special kind of predestined relation that brings people together, 缘份 *yuanfen*. So, for example, one could say the relationship between a patient and a doctor was a medical *yuan*. Yang's research is very comprehensive and deep, but the two readings end up supporting one another through the cases they examine. Li Peiliang begins his work by arguing:

> 缘份 *Yuanfen* or predestined relations that bring people together, is an important concept in Chinese society. It has been quite a number of years now since its usage was enlarged and it became part of popular expression wherein it influenced popular perception and action about the world around it.
>
> But, quite apart from any material meaning it may have, the concept of *yuanfen* can also mean predetermination and can have significance in relation to external controls upon people … It has to be admitted that the concept of *yuanfen* has a negative side, leading people simply to accept their fate, but it must also be said that it has a positive side, making people try their best and, only after that, accepting the judgement of fate. For example, an individual can do good deeds and, through begging alms, enable themselves or their family to establish relations with all creation.

Yang, in the course of his exposition, suggests that:

> The importance of *yuan* in Chinese social life, leads to the protection of human relations and harmony. If we examine this from the perspective of social psychology, then predestination ( 缘份 *yuanfen* ) or chance ( 机缘 *jiyuan* ) can be thought of as a kind of process of attribution, for it is through them that the existence, nature and duration of human relations are conceived. Hence, human relations are determined not by individual free choice but by processes of attribution that are also thought to be predetermined. This, then, determines the existence (or otherwise) and relative worth of human relations; whether they are easily accepted or just endured. Moreover, this will then satisfy others and allow relations to be ordered and set and this, in turn, gives a stability to the relations that exist between lineage groups and people.

It can be seen that the significance of the character 缘 *yuan* is still designed to guarantee the harmony and stability of interpersonal relations. Moreover, in accordance with the analysis of Yang Guoshu, the notion of yuan has a different expression shifting between 良缘 *liangyuan*, meaning 'a good match', or 孽缘 *nieyuan*, meaning a bad fate. Therefore, the meaning and significance of *yuan* can be either negative or positive and, in this respect, it is quite similar to the idea of 报 *bao*. Its importance in the protection of relations is very clear.

## Transformation in the Model of Harmonious Balance

From the above discussion, we can begin to see and understand that the ties between the 'great tradition' and popular cultural traditions are based on principles of movement and operation and are expressed in the three-tiered concern for harmonious balance. It really is because of this commonality in deeper cultural conceptions that it is possible to have movement between 'great' and popular culture. At the same time, this shared 'ground' between 'great' and popular traditions acts as an extremely ingenious mechanism to facilitate change.

One of the pillars of this deep and shared culture is cemented to the fact that in traditional times, it provided senior officials or Confucian scholars with a philosophical basis on which to ground their work, but it also acted as a means by which the common people could come to an understanding of the world around them. It helped in arranging how people got along with one another. Nevertheless, in times of change and especially in the changes wrought by industrialisation, it tended to make the transformational tendency appear as the natural tendency and made people's lives adapt accordingly. This is especially true in relation to the common people, wherein it made it relatively easy to transform their attitudes and get them to adopt an attitude of functional utility. I, as well as a range of others from my country, have previously discussed the utilitarian tendencies of religion in relation to contemporary Taiwanese society. It is obvious, however, that a similar kind of utilitarian pragmatic social tendency is also at work in mainland China. In Hong Kong, especially in relation to the birth of commerce there, the situation is possibly best expressed in the words of Jin Yanji. He says that economic development in Hong Kong is 'a traditionalism of instrumental rationality'.

## THE GIFT OF SELF

The only gift worth giving, Emerson once wrote, 'is a portion of thyself'. Hence, poets give poems, shepherds lamb, farmers corn and sailors coral and shells. A gift of this kind, he continued, 'is right and pleasing, for it restores society ... to its primary basis, when man's biography is conveyed in a gift'.[7] Compare this sentiment to that expressed in the classical Chinese text, the *Liji*:

> Whenever people meet for the first time, the emperor will bring wine, the princes will bring an elongated pointed tablet of Jade [used in ceremonies which were held by the ancient rulers on ceremonial occasions], high government officials give lambs, scholars bring geese, ordinary people bring ducks, children put gifts on the floor and then quietly depart, field officers do not have gifts to offer so they must give ribbons, leather belts and arrows.[8]

---

7 Ralph Waldo Emerson, *Emerson's Essays* (Philadelphia: Spencer Press, 1936), 358.
8 Quotation drawn from the *Liji: zhengyi*, in *The Thirteen Classics*, 3 vols (Beijing: Zhonghua shuju reproduction, 1983), vol. 1, p. 1270. [《礼记．正义》卷 5《十三经注疏》.]

Gift-giving is, in both instances, not about the 'thing' given but about the 'secret' of self definition and social status. In Xu Ping's piece, the affinity between the Confucian notion of propriety, rites and ceremony, *li* (礼), and the *li* (礼) of the 'gift' is highlighted by reference to the identity of their pictographic form. This is not fortuitous but built upon the symbolic nature of any act of giving and receiving. While these two concepts emanate from different sources, the etymological identity suggests a certain 'spiritual' kinship.

The 'gift' functioned in traditional China as the symbolic capital enabling both self-definition and the ideas one holds about others to be translated into a material act. All human exchanges begin with this type of gift expressed perfectly in the old Chinese expression that: 'Without polite welcoming words, there can be no connection, without *li* [gifts] there can be no audience.'

Xu Ping's argument that the Chinese tradition of gift giving became, in part, related to traditional Confucian ethical concerns offers us a path through which we begin to see the deeper ethical considerations attached to the idea of gift giving, which allow us to refocus attention away from its material form. Self-definition and one's views of others take a material form through this exchange and are in this way, brought into popular discourse. Thus, over and above material considerations, gift relations are the symbolic exchange of tokens of recognition. The *li* of the gift is thereby tied to the *li* of propriety but also, as an exchange of recognition, to the Confucian concept of benevolence. Reading the exchange of gifts as a sign of deeper and more symbolic processes of self and social recognition enables the move to contemporary Chinese social relations and the suggestion I would like to make that the contemporary notion of relational networks, or *guanxi*, is 'gift-like' in so far as one gives 'self'. It is for this reason that this piece offers a profound insight into the structuring of contemporary social relations.

## ⊛ THE 'GIFT' AND THE CONFUCIAN NOTION OF PROPRIETY, *LI*[9]
### XU PING

In China, the 礼 *li* of 'present' or 'gift', and the system of *li* 礼制, which is used in the Confucian ethical code, are the same character. Despite the fact that these two concepts came from different cultural 'channels', there is a profound symbolic meaning in the fact that they share the same character form.

The character 礼 *li* in the Chinese language can be attributed at least four distinct meanings. Firstly, it means 祭神, 'ceremony'. In the *Book of Explanations* it states: '*Li* 礼 falls into the following category; *li* is of value in ceremony to bring forth good fortune.' Secondly, *li* is the name given to that which is used to regulate all social action in laws, rules and ceremonies. In the *Analects, On Government* it is stated: 'If they be led by morals and uniformity sought to be given them

9   Xu Ping, *The Etiquette and Customs Attached to the Presentation of Gifts* (Beijing: Overseas Chinese Press, 1990), 8–9. 〔许平, 《馈赠礼俗》. 〕 Xu Ping has a PhD in Chinese folk art and is a scholar in Nanjing.

by 礼 *li* then they will have a sense of shame and will change so that they become good.' In Xunzi's theory of *li* it states: 'The former Kings hated chaos, therefore they instituted a system of propriety, *li*, and justice to maintain order.' This then, is the *li* of propriety.

Thirdly, there is the use of *li* as a means by which to receive people. Here it is used to show one's respect. In the *Liji yueling* it states: 'In the spring, a famous scholar will be appointed to pay tribute to the scholar sage.' This, then, is the *li* of etiquette, protocol and courtesy. Fourthly, *li* as gift. This is expressed in the *Liji biaoji*: 'Without polite welcoming words, there can be no connection, without *li* [gifts] there can be no audience.' This, then, is the *li* of the gift.

From this, we can conclude that the character *li* offers criteria for activities which include those relating to spiritual matters, for greeting people and for worldly things. The *li* of the Confucian ethical code and the *li* of the gift intersect at this point.

For long periods in the feudal culture of traditional times, *li* was used to rule the State, while benevolence or 仁 *ren* was at the heart of human matters. Moreover, *li* was the only way to reach *ren*, and hence, 'to cultivate self and return to the [true] *li* meant *ren*.' Benevolence offers a means with which to handle interpersonal relations. The *Book of Explanations* states: 'The character *ren* is closeness and is made by combining [the characters for] people and two (仁，亲也，从人从二)'. This really is, then, a semiotics of interpersonal relations. The Song Dynasty Premier, Xu Xuan, said: 'Benevolence is tender love, so it involves two people (仁者，兼爱，故从二).' Equality of friendship and the gift of mutual aid were demonstrations of intimacy and universal love, and were a type of civilised procedure through which one developed interpersonal relations. 'Without polite welcoming words, there can be no connection, without *li* [gifts] there can be no audience' shows that the *li* of gift must reach the *li* of ceremony, propriety or etiquette. Moreover, the formation of the Confucian notion of propriety, which includes the *li* of the gift, is a type of guarantee of a sense of propriety.

Understood in this way, the *li* of the gift, like the *li* of propriety or the *li* of protocol, all fall within the loftiest principle of the Confucian notion of *li* and come to form a type of model social order and an effective control system for interpersonal relations. Apart from the internal civilising connotation of this ideal model, there is the ethical connotation imposing limits and it is important not to underestimate the ingenious nature of this structure.

## DAILY LIFE
## IN THE WORK UNIT

**2**

'Feudalism in a period of industrialisation' is how Fox Butterfield, the former *New York Times* reporter to China, is said to have described the Chinese work unit structure. The pieces gathered together in this part of the work would concur with that assessment. It is, perhaps, perverse that this should be argued. After all, as both He Xinghan and Lu Feng point out, the socialist work unit of China was supposed to be 'a socialist new thing'. It was supposed to herald the beginning of a new centralised and rational distribution of human and material resources. It was supposed to herald the beginning of a new way of life and promised to fulfil those dreams that socialism had claimed would bring forth human liberation. Perhaps those claims were too bold, too radical, too frightening, and people unconsciously returned to older ways of doing things. The result: a mimetic process slowly transformed the socialist dream of the new into a history lesson. Never underestimate the power of the past to haunt the present, nor the power of memory to recall ways of doing that decree alone could not abolish. This is not to say that the work unit has become a lineage group. Rather, what is being suggested in all three pieces gathered here, is that cultural memory has the ability to transform the new into something malleable enough to enable old ways of doing to still operate. These old ways of doing, in turn, end up reinforcing commitments to far more traditional ways of seeing, and it is these that fuel the daily routines of life.

## PEOPLE OF THE WORK UNIT[1]

### HE XINGHAN

By my side was the book, *Alive in the Bitter Sea*, by the *New York Times* journalist, Fox Butterfield. In the book he describes his experiences in China shortly after he arrived in Beijing in 1979. It has made a lasting impression on me.

Indeed, I guess it is possible to say that the experiences he talks about are ones familiar to all ordinary Chinese. Butterfield recounts going to the Beijing Hotel and requesting a room at the reception desk. The only problem was that the receptionist repeatedly asked, 'So what is the name of your work unit?' and that, of course, had Butterfield stumped.

---

1  He Xinghan, 'People in the work unit', in Shao Yanxiang, Lin Xianzhi (eds), *People and Prose* (Guangzhou: Huachen Publishing House, 1993), 157–66. [贺星寒, '人在单位中', 邵燕祥, 林贤治 (编),《散文与人》.]

The receptionist then pointed out: 'We only book rooms for work units, we don't book rooms for individuals.' After saying this, the receptionist went on to explain: 'Look, everyone in the whole of China has a work unit, you had better get onto yours, otherwise there is no way we can give you a room.'

Hence the first thing any journalist who wants to open an office in Beijing must do is find themselves a work unit. The news bureau, China Travel Service and the Chinese Foreign Services Corporation all slammed the door in Butterfield's face. Finally, Butterfield asked the US embassy for help. The ambassador wrote a letter to the Chinese Ministry of Foreign Affairs, asking for their help, and they agreed to look after Butterfield and allowed him to use them as his work unit. Only after that could he get a hotel room.

So, while I read Butterfield, I sighed with regret because of the bureaucratism and formalism of the Chinese style of work. There was one foreign fellow who had some interesting insights on this topic. He had spent time at Harvard University studying Chinese history and, from there, went on to become a journalist in Taiwan and Hong Kong. For him, he said, the work unit was kind of like a Chinese 'identity card', and second only to nationality in terms of its importance for most Chinese. Everyone exists in China in terms of a work unit. When meeting for the first time, they will usually ask each other what work unit they are from. When ringing someone, the first question likely to be asked is 'what is your work unit?', which usually precedes the question of one's own name. When registering in a hotel, the registrar will list the guest in terms of 'guest from such and such a work unit'.

This question is so common in contemporary China that it is treated as a normal state of affairs. Once Butterfield made his point, of course, it made me reflect on the issue. Speaking metaphorically, it can be said that it proves that it is impossible for the Chinese to identify the shape of Lu Mountain because we are so much a part of the mountain's landscape. According to my foreign friend, the contemporary Chinese mind-set is so much attached to, and a part of, the work unit that we Chinese have lost ourselves within the landscape of the work unit.

The *Modern Chinese Dictionary* gives two definitions for the term (work) unit. One identifies it as a standard of measurement, a metre, a gram, a second, and so forth. Let us leave unit at that for the time being. The second talks of the unit as an organisation, a department, a sub-division or a sub-section. Obviously, given the aforementioned discussion, the current usage of the term (work) unit has broken through the limitations imposed by the standard dictionary definitions. Little wonder that Butterfield would discuss the Chinese (work) unit as the brick and mortar of Chinese society. In Chinese tradition, he adds, there is no such thing as a work unit.

The contemporary Chinese work unit, then, is really quite extraordinary. Apart from functioning as a department or organisation, the work unit is also in charge of the management of the household register, the staple and non-staple food supply, all medical services, and all housing. It is also in charge of ideological remoulding, political study, policing and security matters, marriages and divorce, entry into the Chinese Communist Youth League and into the Party, awarding merit and carrying out disciplinary action. If one wants to run for election as a deputy for either the National People's Congress or the Chinese People's Consultative Congress, one must firstly get the permission of one's work unit. When administrative sanctions are deployed to detain somebody, or they are to be sent for labour reform, then the authorities must consult with the work unit. 'I am a person working in a work unit' is worn as a badge of pride in China; conversely, the expression 'I don't have a work unit' basically identifies the speaker as little short of a swindler. In actuality, the true swindler requires an awful lot of letters of introduction from various work units in order to survive. These are the 'capital' requirements of a swindler.

The thing about the work unit, however, is that it is a generic term that covers all sorts of institutions. There are big units and there are small ones, there are enterprises and businesses, there are publicly owned units as well as collectively owned utilities, there are even Party, government and military units. Even Buddhist temples can be divided into rank order in this way, with prefectural level and county level units and so on. In a good and powerful unit, all the problems one encounters from the time of birth to the time one passes away can be resolved. Even in the worst of units, one can still be given an 'iron rice bowl' (that is, lifetime-tenured employment). It is the work unit which can help out in hard times with subsidies and can help sort out problems when one of its members is criticised for committing some sort of error. Can the old People's Commune, the production brigades or the production teams be thought of as work units? Not according to the dictionary, although former commune members are all too ready to acknowledge the relationship. This is because the commune functioned to allocate human resources and jobs, to register one's work points, to grant members their grain ration and offer relief grain. They also offered the space on which domestic dwellings could be built and were responsible for approving the birth rate targets. Moreover, in times when an area was struck by famine, people felt secure and self-assured if they had some documentation from their production team which gave them permission to move.

Prior to economic reform, it was the dream of all Chinese to move on to a better work unit. People had a sense of self-importance if they could say that they were moving on to a work unit run by the Party Central Committee or provincial-level government. To belong to a work unit that offered excellent welfare services was to be the envy of all. Who could not recognise the talents of a person from a scientific or research unit, or the talents of a member of a literature or artistic unit? Work units related to security matters are known to consist of members whose family backgrounds are exemplary and political status extremely high. On the other hand, if you came from an ordinary production unit or a collectively owned store, it is probably best to keep that information to yourself when looking for a partner or trying to borrow money.

The work unit doesn't just constitute a kind of identity certificate. It also relates to subsistence and to other issues from birth through to death and also to the value attributed to the individual. If one is in a good work unit, one is set for life and one's status can even be inherited by one's children.

There is also a huge difference in the political atmosphere between one unit and another. In one unit, a few words attacking 'a certain leading cadre from the centre' may lead to a few years at a reform through labour unit, while the same 'crime' in a more relaxed unit may simply lead to you being called in and offered some advice.

What if people have particularly brilliant talents in a certain field? If they want to go to an appropriately specialised unit, there is little scope for them. The best they can do is struggle on in their original work unit and moonlight in their area of interest. But if they do this, there is every likelihood that, if discovered, they will end up being criticised for ignoring their professional occupation. Once they get into a position like this in a certain work unit, they will experience conflict all their lives up until the day they end up like 'rusty old screws'. The alternative is to try to arrange a move out of the unit. The problem is that 'moving out' is almost a dirty word in China and is regarded as a sign that someone does not know their place in life.

For Fox Butterfield, the heart of the work unit system lies in the way it ties the individual to the work unit, which, he suggests, is a sort of 'feudalism in a period of industrialisation'. There are also many pejorative labels one can use here. In feudalism, the basic social unit was, of course, the lineage group. Isn't it suprising, then, to discover that the work unit is described as a variant on the lineage group? Of course it is quite wrong to think of the work unit as a lineage group. Even though both are dominated by big gateways, are surrounded by enclosing walls and all members live in the common compound, once inside the walls, the situation is quite different. Within the work unit, one lives with comrades and relations are dominated by politics, whereas inside the lineage group compound there are family members and the dominant relation is based on blood. Shortly after the revolution in 1949, there still existed a variety of forms of address for colleagues. After an ongoing series of political campaigns, great stress was put on one's ideological outlook and on class position. This was reflected in the term 'comrade' that was universally adopted as a uniform form of address. It was like the kiss of death and a sure sign that one was about to be expelled if one was not referred to as comrade. It is, of course, impossible to break the blood ties of a lineage group. It is, however, still not impossible for a lineage group to break off contact and expel those who are regarded as unfilial. Whether a comrade or a relative, a work unit or a lineage group, all forms reinforced stability, with neither the place of residence nor the group members ever changing. Hence, while Confucius said that while the father lived, one should not venture too far from the family home, the work unit demanded that all should stay at their work posts.

There is no contractual obligation attached to either the political relations of the work unit nor the blood relations of the lineage group. Hence, these institutions prove difficult sites in which to implement the rule of law. Since the 1949 revolution, the goal of the political relation has dissolved while the capital basis of the lineage relation has come under attack. As a result, both face a crisis of disintegration. Ideology now constitutes the basis of stability. The unity of ideology is itself contingent upon the distribution of benefits. In the lineage group, it was always the patriarch who controlled the wealth. Those who disobeyed would have part of their wealth deducted or, in very severe cases, would be completely disinherited. Within the work unit, there are even more plentiful means available by which to penalise those with unorthodox or heretical views. The unit can withdraw opportunities to advanced skills training programmes, to promotion, to a higher waged position, to be elected as an advanced worker and so forth. If such relations were put on a contractual basis, then this would all be another matter. As one Chinese who works in the United States pointed out with much feeling: 'In America, the boss couldn't give a toss if you abuse the president; loaf on the job though, and you're out on your ear.' In contrast, it is no big deal to work slowly or stay away from work without any good reason in China, but it is absolutely out of the question to speak ill of those in charge.

The position of a lineage member is determined at birth. The status is decided by their age, seniority, and whether the member was by the wife or concubine. To rise in rank the lineage member must await the death of others and, only after many years as the loyal wife of a son, can one rise to become an elder grandmother. One's position in a work unit is contingent upon when one joined the revolution. This is the basis from which one begins and it is from here that one advances. To get ahead, one must not only be prepared to wait but must also be prepared to be on one's best behaviour. As long as a work unit member makes no really serious mistakes, then there is little chance of them dropping in rank. At least in this one regard, both the lineage group and the work unit have one thing in common: they both offer life-long tenure.

Chinese have a love–hate relationship with the work unit. On the one hand, they cannot stand it, but on the other, they are unable to live without it. The work unit is like their family: they must love their commune as they love their family, love their factory as they love their home, and love their shop as they would their kin. In work units with a very rigid system, one's rank within the unit is a symbol of one's status; the individual's worth is realised in the rank attributed to them. Whether one's name is first or last, the order of arrival at the unit, their address, their living conditions, what transport is available to them, their access to documents of varying levels of classification are all things of great concern and are fought over at great length.

'We are of the same work unit' at once captures the warmth and feeling between sisters and brothers, but also potentially signifies the enmity between those in the grip of an on-going struggle. Because the traditional conception of self is so dim, it is only within a life built around human inter-relationships that Chinese people feel comfortable. From the traditional Chinese perspective, individuality is invariably a pejorative term, and this is best captured in the traditional saying: 'persisting in one's ways, no matter what others say' or in the accusation that one is 'clinging obstinately to one's own course'. Individuality also evokes feelings of pity because such people are thought to have little other alternative. The case of 'a widowed mother living with only her young son or daughter' is a good example of this. Other traditional phrases such as 'to be lonely, wretched and helpless' and 'lonely souls have only shadows to stand by their side' are examples of this. So, even though the work unit isn't perfect, it is preferable to being lonely and roaming around in society without one. It is the deep structure of Chinese culture which forms the bedrock upon which the work unit is built.

In the 1970s in China, the perfect state of human feeling was expressed in the saying 'utter devotion to others and without a single thought for self'. There is a joke from that time about a foreigner coming to China and watching twenty-odd people all seated at a round table having a meal. What were the table manners of these Chinese and how would they be able to eat their food? The foreigner soon discovered their technique. Each person had a very long set of chopsticks which was used to pick up portions of food and then stretch across the table and put the portion in the mouth of the person opposite. The admiring foreigner was greatly impressed by such self-sacrificing devotion.

For Chinese, the work unit is their very own big round table. People care for and love their fellow workers; they are no longer friendless and wretched since they are always surrounded by those they know. The best method by which to bring people together is to call on them to 'show great consideration for the masses'. If you expend 'human feeling' (人情) then you will ultimately earn a debt and be compensated. However, when others are showing concern for you, you may begin to feel your personal space encroached upon. There is always something for everyone to be concerned about, be it the type of residency in which you live, your love life, your family, the way you talk, your ideology or your clothes—you will always feel the need to bend to others' expectations.

There is also another side to this weakness in the notion of self: careerists within the ranks of a work unit will often use slogans such as 'serve the collective' or 'serve the masses' to mask their own intrigues against colleagues whom they are in competition with. It was in the work units that the so-called 'strife within the nest' really started, for it was the work unit which formed the best of all such nestings. The work unit is one part of a hierarchical tree (at the top is the ministry, below is the bureau, then the departments, then the sections and so on). All these parts form the tree's branches along with other work units which constitute the foliage. So those who engage in struggles in one work unit can, if successful, 'fly off' and nest in higher parts of the tree and carry out even greater struggles. Those less successful may move out to other branches, but they too, will find somewhere to nest. There are thousands of years of tradition at play here, and while it may be easy to talk of overcoming it, in practice, it is really quite difficult.

Other than China, few countries could claim to have such a dense type of work unit system. Prior to economic reform, the areas of work unit control seemed limitless. Indeed, without the work unit there could be no basis for subsistence. One billion people, and all of them in work units. A fitting question would no doubt be, how did the work unit come into this world? At this point, there is no harm in reviewing a little history.

After the revolutionary victory and the founding of the People's Republic, the old government was replaced by the new. This constituted the first phase of the development of the work unit. In order to extend the revolution and control the direction of the country, the government had to go beyond its ordinary State structures and control ideology. This, in turn, led to the schooling system being taken over by the State. Cultural workers were brought together to form a 'literary front'. This was made up of newspapers, bookstores (publishers), broadcasters and so forth, all of which were remodelled as work units. Advisory groups under the State Council, the democratic committees under the State Council and various religious organisations and so forth were all thought to be of value in the promotion of the united front, and so they, too, became work units.

This led to the second phase of socialist transformation (1953–56), a kind of high revolutionary tide which led to the formation of joint state and private enterprises and co-operatives, all of which sprouted in this climate like bamboo shoots after a spring rain. During the third phase, the education of the peasants was now thought to be essential if the revolution was to be pushed forward. The people's communes (of the Great Leap Forward period) became the channel through which this would all be accomplished. The free canteen system, whereby one could eat one's fill, came into being. In fact, it reached the point whereby people looked to the work unit as the only means of achieving their dreams which were, at that time, all about living in multi-storeyed houses with electric lights and telephones. Unfortunately, all this was not to be and the dream vanished into thin air. So the people's communes degenerated into nondescript work units that failed to provide the much sought-after 'iron rice bowl' (*tie fan wan*) and offered instead an 'iron walled enclosure' (*tie weiqiang*).

But the work unit would once again have its day. During the Great Proletarian Cultural Revolution, the whole country rose to Mao Zedong's revolutionary call. Campaigns were launched against class enemies in the name of the revolution, and the old structures were smashed and replaced by new work unit structures. As a result, work units were reproduced at an ever-increasing rate. At the same time another type of revolution came in the form of the 'transformation of ownership'. What this meant was that, in the name of the revolution, all forms of ownership throughout the country would be incrementally upgraded so that both higher and lower forms would go one step higher. On this basis, production groups became co-operatives, small collectively owned enterprises merged to form large collectively owned enterprises, and State ownership replaced collective local ownership. In turn, State ownership would be taken over by the central authorities and the 'bourgeois right' would be gradually eliminated, leading, ultimately, to a communist utopia.

If the history of the People's Republic tells us anything, it is that every time there is 'revolutionary action', there is also a huge growth in the number of work units. It is quite tempting to suggest that the revolution is pregnant with the expectation of the work unit!

It is best, however, not to be quite so impetuous. Let us look back on the past and recognise that not all revolutions gave rise to the notion of the work unit. Neither the American revolutionary War of Independence nor the revolutionary change which led to the Magna Carta produced this by-product. Why?

These revolutions were simply not the same as the Chinese one. In general terms and in terms of their form, it could be said that the American and English revolutions were confined to the political arena. Other matters, for instance those dealing with the economy or culture, would be settled in those areas themselves. There was no need to rush things, they just did one thing at a time and gradually things were reformed. The Constitutional Revolution (*lixian geming*) limited political power through constitutional controls so that it could never again interfere with the non-political arena. This transformed the old form of government into a new one, but left the original size of the structure intact.

Prior to the founding of the People's Republic of China, the Communist Party of China roused the peasant masses to carry out revolutionary activity and divide up the land under the land reform policy. The Party was, therefore, greatly loved. After the founding of the People's Republic, the Party mobilised urban residents through the work unit which operated like an emotional magnet to the people. Within the work unit, the prevailing ethos of caring, protecting and helping one another satisfied the traditional human needs of the Chinese. The benefit of the job allocation system for the Party was that it functioned as a useful mechanism by which to unify ideology. To make a thorough-going revolution which upset the political apple cart was indeed a joyful thing to do. But the revolution also had a heavy load to carry, hence the need for the work unit.

We can illustrate this with an example from the cultural arena. In the early part of the 1950s, actors, artists, raconteurs and acrobats were organised into groups to promulgate propaganda in favour of land reform and to support the war to resist US aggression and aid Korea. These artists needed to be fed and clothed, so the 'literary front' was born. After these campaigns passed, these artists basically lost the capacity to organise themselves. At the same time, they had participated in the revolution and therefore had a right to expect a share in the fruits of revolutionary successes. Moreover, the ever-broadening definition of politics informing the revolution meant that people should not simply participate but should deepen their commitment. In the process of all this, some were criticised and some did the criticising. Nevertheless, all remained in the work unit and, depending upon their position (as critic or as the person being criticised), were entitled to the benefits.

As political control developed so, too, did the reach of government. And as government became bigger so, too, did the work unit. This continued day after day until, eventually, a wise old man came forward and pointed out that the entire edifice was shaky at the foundations and the nation was beginning to subside. He quickly and loudly called out: economic construction in command!

The work unit has always faced obstacles. From birth it was suffused with politics. The daily time-table of the revolution was to prepare the way for the use of traditional notions of love and benevolence so that a new generation of publicly spirited people would develop. Unfortunately for the revolution, what motivates humans to carry out activities is largely the pursuit of their own personal interests. China was a closed society then, and those who tried early on to change things, or to leave their work unit or become self-employed ended up in terrible straits. Everyone gave tacit consent to the power and authority of the work unit. Within the unit itself, they attempted to get hold of, or get more out of, the 'big pot' which everyone shared. As its contents did not increase, the competition and struggle over control of it did. Someone who ended up being a 'loser' and unable to extract more would simply do less work to compensate. It was in this way that intelligence was squandered. To struggle over housing, to fight so that you could pass on your position to your children, to take state-allocated medicine for your own use and pass it on to the whole family, to collect up travel tickets and then apply for reimbursement, to refuse to give permission for someone to do something unless they have greased your palm, the list is, in fact, endless. The work unit was like a person with a huge cancerous tumour.

Then came the open door policy and the promotion of economic reform. The system of fixing output quotas on a household basis (*baochan daohu*) basically ruptured the dream of the work unit. For commune members, no longer would the big pot be available for all, irrespective of their laziness or diligence. The reformation of district (*qu*) and township (*xiang*) governments meant that the unbridled political spread of the past was railed in to manageable administrative levels. The rich 10,000–*yuan* (US$1205) household and specialist households now offered a challenge to the work unit for they were, in fact, non-work units and not terribly orthodox. Following on from this, the tide moved on and into the cities. Those who had, in the past, fallen foul of the work unit system— people without fixed duties, various types of miscellaneous personnel, and those regarded as trouble makers—now had the opportunity to open their own private businesses right at the gate of the old work units. It wasn't all that long before they started making quite a lot of money. While other work unit members may have been jealous, they were less than diffident. All it would take was one more revolution and they would be left empty-handed because the hen that lays the golden egg would fly from its coop and all the eggs would be broken. Meanwhile, the work unit would be left unaffected.

But this revolution would never come. Individual traders and private entrepreneurs amassed fortunes so quickly that they came to constitute the most serious of challenges to the work unit. Events outside the work unit were drawing people away, and the magnet force of ambiguous human sensibilities was replaced by the more open distribution of benefits and profits. The spirit of wealth generation drove out the political preaching; there would be a desperate struggle to oppose the cosy, friendly relationships of cooperation and the free market tended to upset the unified plan. In this more pluralistic social environment, the work unit began to feel its own weaknesses.

People within the work unit were also on the horns of a dilemma. The iron rice bowl became a chicken's rib—offering little flavour, but better than nothing. The safest thing to do in such circumstances was to stay behind the work unit fence and complain: after all, it is better to try to cut with derisive quips than be sliced by a surgeon's scalpel. These people were happy to entrust their fate to the work unit but sadly, and for a whole range of reasons, the work unit was unable to live up to their expectations. The work unit recognised that the ground on which it was built was moving. This movement was shaking the work unit, hitting small points at first, but gradually enveloping larger areas. It was a movement that grew stronger and could not be stopped.

The Party no longer takes class struggle as the key link, and, in abandoning this, it has, for all intents and purposes, withdrawn the right to life of any future work units. In separating itself from the government, the Party has, in effect, said that ideological control is no longer the central task of the work unit. As more rights devolve to local levels, as work units have output and profit quotas set and as more people sign work contracts or take work assignments, the link between the government and the work unit is weakened considerably.

Work units themselves have taken opportunities to break away from the government when such opportunities arise. There are indications to suggest that the work unit is attempting to overcome central control. The emergence of 'small gold storage centres' (*xiaojinku*) where departments can salt away their centrally allocated funds so that they do not have to send them back, is one example. Another is the emergence of 'invisible wages' (*yinxing gongzi*), which makes a mockery of the stated wage because so much is added in the form of bonuses and over-award payments. In addition, there is also the emphasis on short-term activity which may rapidly increase production but does irreparable damage to plant and machinery. Because managers are working on production-based contracts, however, and plant and machinery are the State's responsibility, it is the short-term production and profit which are all important.

The work unit has also broken away from the hierarchical relationship, with the centre often doing what it thinks is best for it. It is now trying to pull away from the formally mentioned hierarchical tree of which it is a part, listening less and less to the Ministry above. At the same time, it is asserting its absolute independence from, rather than cooperation with, other Ministry branches which are its equal. It is as though they are saying, 'If you want to control me where is your investment because I want to milk you; if you loosen control over me, I'll simply eat off my fat and waste myself away. After all, it is not like the control over the work unit property is in the hands of an individual.'

History is merciless. Who could possibly have predicted the growth of this type of work unit, and who could possibly be expected to stomach such a bitter fruit?

Those who have been working for a long time in work units have become accustomed to following orders and have already lost their capacity to think on their feet. But even these people must change. The contract system is now with us, and this means that within the work unit, the contractual relationship is now established and the political atmosphere has faded. Only in newspapers, on broadcasts, or at official functions does one hear the word 'comrade' used as a term of address. In social intercourse, the most frequently used term of address is either 'mister' or 'miss'. While work units demand to be untied, individuals demand their own rights. In the past, people would be ashamed to raise issues like duties and obligations, rights and power, and profits and interests. Today, these have become the crucial points of demarcation in interrelations. Have the Chinese started to degenerate? Not at all. On the contrary, after the utopianism of the past, the Chinese have finally begun to return to earth and now have their feet planted firmly on the ground.

The ruling Party has made the decision that reform must continue. The housing reform, along with attempts to 'smash the three irons' (*posantie*),[2] are in the vanguard of the struggle. For the work unit, this means reform is something of a relief fund to them while, simultaneously, bringing on a cardiac arrest. The reform process will always be a double-edged sword. The housing reform produces a break in the dependent relationship between employee and work unit, while the smashing of the three irons shakes up the current system of the work units. The government tests the level of tolerance the masses have for reform, while the masses in turn see how much reform the government is willing to tolerate.

There is a new turn in the reform with enterprise work units becoming the focal point of attention. The government has decided to devolve all rights to the work unit, but the problem is that these units still have no rights. This is proving a real headache. Restless with anxiety, most employees are playing very careful attention to see what will happen next. It is, after all, the employees who increase the value of a work unit, so all of them should be recompensed for work done.

The restructuring underway in the work units is not only formidable, but also extremely profound. As the old Chinese saying goes: once the ice is broken, dawn will rise. At this point one needs to add one further sentence: the development of the productive forces will bring about the thorough-going liberation of humankind and it is in this that its value lies. In order to get there, however, means surmounting much and the work unit stands at the threshold.

I believe that in the future, it will be possible to return the (work) unit to its original dictionary meaning, perhaps with the dictionary itself undergoing revision. It is important that governmental and non-governmental matters be kept

---

2 The 'three irons' were the security of job tenure, guaranteed wage and (for cadres) guaranteed status.

separate. Perhaps the only ones who will talk of them in the same breath are the very old who have seen much and the very young who have seen nothing. That is apart, of course, from the great humorists who will find much to joke about.

## THE WORK UNIT: A UNIQUE FORM OF SOCIAL ORGANISATION[3]
### LU FENG

In China, everyone calls the social organisation in which they are employed—whether it be a factory, shop, school, hospital, research institute, cultural troupe or Party organ etc.—by the generic term work unit. This phenomenon clearly shows that, over and above their individual characteristics resulting from the social distribution of labour, all types of social organisations in China have a common characteristic: the characteristic of being a work unit.

The work unit is a unique form of social organisation universally used by all types of social organisation in China. It is the basis of China's political, economic and social system. Without understanding its unique organisational characteristics and its behavioural tendencies, one cannot understand the nature of China's current system and its operational mechanisms.

### The Origins of the Work Unit

In the long revolutionary struggle to seize political power the Communist Party adopted the peasantry as its main revolutionary force. The most important method used to seize power was the establishment of base areas in the countryside from where military struggle was waged. In order to motivate the masses, the Party penetrated the grass roots level of society and established many types of mass organisations in the base areas. Through these organisations they led the masses to carry out class struggle, land reform and support for the war effort. As the base areas expanded and the number of people increased, all sorts of publicly owned economic, social service, educational and cultural organisations were set up. These organisations were subordinate to Party organs and the army, their sole objective being to serve the needs of the revolutionary war. Their staff members belonged to the revolutionary ranks. Due to material shortages, all members of the revolutionary ranks had to carry out a military-style communist supply system. All the organisations within the base areas often had to engage in production to support themselves and to supplement the war-time shortages. These organisations created in the revolutionary base areas were in fact the earliest embryonic form of the work unit. The experience of the base areas had a deep influence on the leadership and on the organisational style later used by the Party

---

3  Lu Feng, 'The Work Unit: A Special Form of Social Organisation', *Chinese Social Sciences*, 1 (1989), 71–88.
[ 路风，《单位：一种特殊的社会组织形式》。]

throughout the whole country. In the early period after the founding of the People's Republic, following the process of military takeover, all levels of political organisation were, in fact, directly derived from the Party's organisational system and this Party structure became the glue that held society together.

In a very definite sense, the socialist revolution led by the Communist Party was China's political reaction to the challenge of modernisation. But the only model of socialism which people knew about was the Soviet model. The Party, having grasped the machinery of State, adopted methods of top-down administrative power, militarised organisational forms and incited the fervour of the masses. In the process of this reorganisation of society, the work unit became the basic form of all social organisation.

In terms of social organisation, the structure whereby society may only function through dependence upon the work unit organisational form can be termed the 'work unit system'. The basic constituents of this system are: all micro-level social organisations are work units; and the centralised system for controlling and regulating the functioning of society as a whole is formed by an administrative organisation which is closely linked to the Party structure. In order to move from an extremely low economic level to rapid industrialisation the State had no option but to practise coercive accumulation. This aim necessitated a policy of State monopoly over the purchase and sale of important agricultural products, which, in turn, cut off the market relations between the countryside and the cities. Through the institution of a residency permit system, the urban and rural populations were completely cut off from one another. Thus, under conditions whereby individuals were not free to select their own jobs, the differences between peasants and urban residents, between workers in publicly owned enterprises and workers in collective enterprises, between cadres and workers, and other such categories determined by residence permits or planned management, became innate differences in status. The rights and benefits accorded to status meant that individual lives came under control of the state administration through the medium of the work unit organisation.

Under the work unit system, individual inventiveness, the autonomy of social organisations and market mechanisms all disappeared. Top-down state administrative power controlled every work unit, and through the work unit, controlled every individual. This type of social organisational structure has played an important historical role in China: a highly centralised and unified political system has been established; hundreds of millions of people have been organised to remodel society; vast resources have been mobilised towards industrialisation; an unprecedented level of social equality has been achieved through administrative control over distribution and so on.

## The Clan-like Nature of the Work Unit and its Code of Conduct

History, however, has brought forth a contradiction: while private individuals cannot make use of capital to oppress others, the realisation of the new principle of social fairness in the policy of distribution according to work was actually predicated upon the sacrifice of individual freedom and property ownership rights. The leading role played by the State administration in carrying out these new social principles meant that all social organisations were transformed into either administrative or work unit-type structures.

As a labour or work organisation relying upon direct state management, the work unit's rational norms of action became completely determined by the regulatory system established by the State and its administrative organs. This style of management had one innate defect: it lacked the independent spirit of initiative of individuals and grass roots organisations. Even more serious was the fact that even the few rules and regulations which did exist disintegrated during the political movements which began in the latter half of the 1950s. Indeed, during the chaos of the Cultural Revolution, there seemed to be nothing left of them at all. The results of this process were: firstly, there still existed a limitless authority of State over work unit and work unit over individual; and secondly, within this chain of relationships there was still no rational standard for day-to-day management. Thus, traditional cultural elements which had been hiding quietly behind 'left' despotism gradually filled up the vacuum left within the work unit's organisational order.

Although the work unit is the basic organisational form of State-run modern industry, its multiple functions, non-contractual relationships and immobility of resources has meant that it has gradually become a closed structure. This is in direct opposition to the nature of the socialisation of production. From the point of view of individual workers, the significance of the work unit as the site of social life for its members has gradually overtaken its significance as a site of organised labour or work, and the significance of the work unit as the provider of welfare benefits to its members has gradually overtaken its significance as a provider of products and services to society. From the government's point of view, the significance of the work unit in maintaining political order and in bearing social responsibilities[4] has gradually taken over its significance as part of the specialised social division of labour.

Within the unique set of social conditions present in China, the work unit has gradually evolved into a lineage or clan-like organisation. As the basic form of social organisation, lineage groups in traditional China performed many social functions. In modern China, the family, especially in urban areas, for the most part does not perform these functions. However, the clan functions which have disappeared have not been replaced by the general process of socialisation, rather they have been taken up by another form of social organisation, the work unit. In form, the work unit and the traditional-style lineage group or clan have a lot in common: they both exert a patriarchal authority over their members; the responsibility of individuals to the group is emphasised more than individual rights,

---

4 A typical example of this was the policy practised between 1982 and 1986 in which children could directly take over the jobs of their retiring parents.

while the group takes total responsibility for the care of its members. This process of transformation occurred within the formal State structure, where control and dependence became the source of power for the clan style governing practices of the work unit.

### The Importance of Interpersonal Relationships

The work unit is a community in which members know each other very well due to long periods of working together. This alone determines the importance of interpersonal relationships between work unit members. The organisational links between work unit members are founded upon relationships of status which are based on the state's administrative power. There are three levels to these relationships:

1.  Between work unit leaders (the representatives of State capital) and ordinary workers there exists an authoritarian relationship in which orders must be obeyed.
2.  Work unit leaders have limited authority as they lack the right to dismiss workers (unless they have committed a crime).
3.  Unreasonable behaviour of work unit members such as laziness has no effect on their benefits, since there is no direct connection between efficiency and individual benefit.

This has produced a kind of exchange based on connections: the motivation for cooperation between leaders and staff and between colleagues must obey the principle of mutual benefit or 'saving face'. Otherwise there could be slow-downs in work, sabotage or even physical attacks on persons. Under these circumstances, where exchange based on connections dominates, perception rather than reason becomes the standard by which individuals are judged. The abilities and achievements of an individual are not important, rather it is their connections—above, below, left and right—which count. Without connections one would have a very difficult time within the work unit.

### Egalitarianism

Because work units are held together by status rather than contractual relationships, internal competition based on individual ability and achievement would prove very harmful to group affinity. This is because it would erode feelings of harmony among group members, thereby destroying the principle of exchanges based on connections which allows for the smooth functioning of the work unit. Harmony among group members is founded upon the egalitarian distribution of material benefits. Only in this way can destructive behaviour such as jealousy, rumours and work slow-downs be avoided.

### Authority

There have always been two types of authority within work units—formal and informal. The essence of the formal relationships of authority is the direct administration carried out by the Party and the State. This type of authority reaches down into the organisational structure of the Party and State administration within the work unit and past experience of political movements shows that it exerts a decisive influence over the fate of the individual.

The major aspect of informal authority within the work unit is an ethical order based on an internal code of conduct. This order uses public opinion and moral condemnation to force individuals to adhere to the accepted norms of conduct. As the autonomy of the work unit expands, the informal relationships of authority within the work unit will become more and more important. However, whether these relationships will take a rational or irrational form will be decided by a whole range of factors.

There is a very strong collectivist tendency within Chinese cultural tradition which is certainly not a bad thing. Experience proves that the collectivist spirit of team cooperation can make a highly rational and valuable contribution to modern economic development—Japan is an example. However, because of the work unit's internal code of conduct, rationalisation of work unit behaviour and labour is impossible. This is due to the fundamental flaws in the work unit form of organisation. Irrational organisational behaviour leads to low rates of productivity, which would result in the elimination of the organisation in market or other forms of competition. The reason why an unproductive work unit can continue to exist is not only because there is no competition in the work unit system, it is also because the cost of low productivity is borne by the state. This is the inevitable outcome resulting from the relationship of control and dependence between the two sides.

State control over the work unit and the work unit's reliance upon the State determine the most important aspect of the work unit's external code of conduct: the need to strive for State patronage. There are two aspects to the motivation which necessitates this conduct: the active and the passive. On the active side, the work unit does its best to win more State resources in order to expand in scale and to improve production and welfare conditions. On the passive side, the work unit, either consciously or unconsciously, seeks to shift the burden of low productivity created by inherent inadequacies on to the State. This shift mainly occurs through such shortcuts as State subsidies, reduction in taxes and increases in the price of products. The macro-level result of this tendency is 'supply' not meeting expanding 'demand', thereby leading to shortages.

Reforms in the 1980s led to changes in the external environment in which the work unit functioned and in the internal organisational form of the work unit itself. In the external environment, rural communes were disbanded, an array of economic activity developed outside of the work unit system, market mechanisms expanded, avenues of employment increased and the work unit became more reliant on the market as the scope of central planning shrank. With regard to internal organisation, the State has instituted a system whereby the units may keep a certain percentage of profits to invest as it sees fit, the bonus system for workers has been revived, the autonomy of the work unit has expanded, and its political role has weakened as the focus of Party work has shifted and as the legal system developed.

However, the situation whereby the work unit is the basic form of social organisation in China has not fundamentally changed. The work unit organisational form is an historical creation, and organisational fluctuations within the reforms are also part of an historical process. Since the work unit is the organisational basis of the traditional political and economic system, any changes to the fundamental organisational style of the work unit will bring on changes in the structure of the whole of society.

## THE WORK UNIT: 'FACE' AND PLACE[5]
### YI ZHONGTIAN

Human relations and emotions are forms of psychological activity that are often intrinsic, spontaneous processes that emanate from innately human properties. Nothing else can compare with such relations and emotions when discussing the formation and survival of the collective. At the same time, we must recognise that they are a form of human psychology: they will always be intangible, immeasurable, and uncertain in nature. Therefore, if an ethnic group or nation relies solely upon such 'human emotion' to bind them, there might be trouble and chances are, the emotions will not be sustainable. So, in order to consolidate the stability of the group and the social order, a more socially useful and 'reliable' mode of expression is needed—a structure strong enough to restrict emotions, yet also one that could harness them. It needs to be a structure, that is both powerful and readily implementable. It has to be a form that regulates and restricts as well as guarantees that the collective will not descend into a 'loose sheet of sand'.

This type of structure is known as the work unit.

For Chinese, the work unit is crucially important. It is second to none in securing the conditions for the supply of food, clothing, 'face' and human relations. When two Chinese 'face' each other they will, if they are 'close', greet each other with 'Have you eaten yet?' If they are 'strangers' or if they haven't been formally introduced, most often they will simply ask something like 'Which work unit are you from?' The work unit can more or less be said to be the basis of Chinese existence.

The work unit is one's rice bowl but it is also one's 'face'. So if a person doesn't have a work unit then they will have no face. Not only does the lack of a work unit exclude the possibility of a person having face, but even worse, without a work unit they are often pigeon-holed as being 'suspicious characters' or 'dangerous

---

5   Yi Zhongtian, *Casually Talking Chinese* (Beijing: Hualing Publishing House, 1996), 187–236. 〔易中天，《闲话中国人》。〕

persons'. One can even go so far as to say that, without a work unit, such people come to be regarded as 'unemployed idlers'.

The work unit represents a person's status and, when two people first come into contact, they will ask and come to know of each other's status within the work unit. They will use this information to judge their own sense of propriety toward the other person. Work units are also about human relations. If two people's work unit has 关系 *guanxi*, 'relations', then, irrespective of whether or not these two people have personal relations, they will be able to relate to one another. If these work units have a hierarchical relation wherein one is a subsidiary of the other, or they are regarded as having 'brotherly' or 'neighbourly' relations, or one unit is the customer of the other, then their *guanxi* or 'relations' will blossom. For example, if one unit needed something, then the other would aid them no matter what. Moreover, they would not consider such a task a chore, nor would they think of it as trouble. This is because 'if they wouldn't do it for this other unit, who would they do it for'? In this way, both work units gain 'face' and also strengthen their interpersonal relations. Alternatively, this also works in individual cases where the work units have no formal relation but where someone in one unit has a close friend in another. These personal relations will be employed to 'make connections' and enable their friend to get in through 'the backdoor' (that is, cut through the red tape). Because the personal blends into the work unit, when units want to establish relations with one another, they go through the people in their unit who have 'relations' or close friends in the other unit. It will then be their responsibility to make the linkages and they will do this by 'cottoning up to them'.

Of more significance than all these relations is the fact that the work unit is like one's parents and one's family; it is the cradle in which one sits and the swaddling clothes one wears. Ordinarily in China we talk of the 'work unit' in terms of responsibilities and rights or explain that it fulfils a range of responsibilities such as arranging work, food, accommodation, entertainment, political study, pensions as well as being the place that looks after each employee's 'personnel dossier'. Hence, if Chinese are able to find a 'good work unit', they look upon it as a series of lifelong benefits. Little wonder that parents are often concerned about their daughter's boyfriend's work unit because it is the work unit that will take care of their future. Work unit participation is double-sided. On the one hand, when outside the unit, workers will protect its name. On the other hand, when they get back to their work unit, they display their family face and say things without reserve and do things without fear.

Logically, all this might appear strange and irrational but these things are generally acknowledged to be 'quite natural' because, irrespective of whether one is a leader or simply one of the masses, all work unit members recognise that the work unit and the individual have fused into one 'unit'. It is not difficult to see how this feeds into a 'mass consciousness' central to Chinese culture. It is in the work unit' that this type of mass consciousness is most fully embodied and develops into a perfected form. The work unit becomes more than a mere place where an individual works. Rather, it can be said to be a way of structuring a strong mass consciousness and holding together group relations.

What the work unit produces is a mass consciousness. What is this mass or group consciousness? This begins by considering people to be first and foremost 'social beings'. If people leave the group, then they are not people and cannot survive. So the individual cannot leave the group even for a moment; the group is the 'home' for each Chinese to get on with life and live in peace. The so-called place where one lives one's life in peace is a place that can be relied upon both materially and spiritually. Without this place to rely upon, this site upon which one can depend, one becomes rootless; like a fish out of water, the 'body' is suspended in mid-air and one's mind has no place to go. It is as if one's heart were 'like a well from which seven buckets had been drawn and then eight dropped back in', leaving one in a constant state of anxiety.

Chinese are dependent on this need to have a place not only while they are alive. Even in death a place to settle is crucial. Hence one discovers the expression 'to enter the ground is to enter peace' (*rutu wei'an*). Those with money such as an emperor, will secure their burial place by building a tomb. Poorer people will have coffins made. All this is done while they are still alive. In traditional China, people would all put a little money aside before their death so they could get the coffin of their choice. This would then be placed in the home in a grand manner offering these aging people comfort and decoration. A filial son would have a coffin made for his parents prior to their death. This would make them very happy. Sick people who were nearing the end of their life would have the coffin brought before them so that they could see it and this would give them great satisfaction. It was as though all the hard work of life was purely directed toward their return home in the after-life. One might as well think of these coffins as very small work units! Chinese who wanted good luck and feared death would, contrary to expectations, treat the coffin as though it were 'a special attachment'.

Superficially, this is unimaginably strange but, on closer inspection, there are some important reasons for this. While it is admittedly true that the fear of death is great, Chinese people are even more scared of 'dying and being without a place of burial'. Should this happen, they would be nothing more than 'orphan ghosts and strange ghosts'. Therefore, to place the coffin in the house is a glorious and auspicious thing to do. In fact, one does not call the coffin a 'coffin' (*guancai*) but refers to it as the 'wood of good fortune and long life' (*shoumu*). Every year, these 'woods' were repainted. The more times the 'wood of good fortune' was repainted, the more glorious it was; the more glorious, the more auspicious it was. The significance of the coffin and its placement in the house prior to death lay not only in the belief that it brought forth longevity, but also that it demon-strated the wisdom of the aged who had prepared well for their after-life. To examine the opposite case, if one died and preparations hadn't been made such that the corpse didn't even have a coffin, then many people would think that 'this corpse had nothing to rely upon' (*shenwu suoping*).

In summary then, no matter whether it is in life or in death, everybody wants a place that they can rely on. They want a place to settle down, and if they don't get this it could very easily lead to a strong sense of loss and a feeling that they are like homeless dogs.

From the perspective of traditional Chinese society, the day when every single person has a place that will secure their fate and enable them to have a roof over their head is the day when there will truly be great order under heaven. The opposite of this, of course, is a state of great confusion. This state has one obvious manifestation and that is when the people are 流离失所 *liuli shisuo*, or forced to 'wander about without a home'. In this traditional Chinese expression, the character 流 *liu*, which means 'to flow', actually means 流失 *liushi*, 'to drop out or drain away'. That is to say, the individual breaks away from the group. The character 离 *li*, meaning 'to leave', actually means 离散 *lisan*, which is when relatives are scattered or dispersed. Thus this expression is designed to convey a sense that there is a tendency toward the disintegration of the group. The characters 失所 *shisuo* obviously mean that the people do not have a 'roof over their heads'. For most people, the idea of wandering about destitute or 流落 *liuluo*, means leaving their native place. The term 流浪 *liulang*, meaning 'to roam about', ends up becoming 流民 *liumin*, wanderers or refugees or even 流寇 *liukou* a roving band of rebels. Under these circumstances, how could great disorder under heaven be avoided? A 'state of great disorder under heaven' has, as its natural corollary, a state in which the mind of the people is greatly unsettled. To put this more accurately, because the minds of the people are in an unsettled state, then there is 'great disorder under heaven'. 'Floating' or drifting, 浮 *fu*, is a form of 'movement', 动 *dong* and movement leads to chaos, 乱 *luan*. Chaos or *luan* are the cause of 'floating' or drifting (浮 *fu*) and this means that there can be no 'assured place' (着落). Without an assured place, one is left 'hanging', 悬 *xuan*, and this is called 悬浮 *xuanfu* or being in a state of 'suspension'. Therefore, peace and stability under heaven can be taken to mean helping people overcome their misery or literally, 'helping people who have been left suspended upside-down'. This means helping people find a certain place to settle down (厝 *çuo*), where they will have food to eat, clothes to wear and a place to shelter. This means that everyone has their own 'place' or 所 *suo*. The classical meaning for this term 'place' (所 *suo*), when translated into a contemporary colloquialism, would be 'work unit'.

# 3

# DEFINING 'OUTSIDERS', LABELLING *LIUMANG*

Etymology and contingency haunt the structure of this chapter on the naming of groups outside 'acceptable' social structures. Chen Baoliang's piece details how the term 流氓 *liumang*, hooligan or hoodlum, came to take its current linguistic form. In Chinese, *liumang* or hooligan, is a compound made up of two characters. The first is 流 *liu*, meaning 'to flow', the second 氓 *mang*, which currently means 'common people'. In traditional times, however, this latter character was pronounced *meng* and meant 'to leave, or be forced to leave one's land'. In other words, etymologically, *liumang* is tied back to the idea of the outsider, the unsettled, and, by implication, the unreliable. Not for them the tight, complex and intimate relations of the clan, the group, or, in more recent times, the work unit. They are always outsiders.

Yet to be outside is not always a physical or spatial phenomenon. The meaning of the word is not only shadowed by literal past understandings encoded in the characters but is also constantly reworked by more contingent, contemporary concerns. Ge Fei's article gathers together some contemporary examples of *liumang* activity and these sit alongside Jin Ren's exploration of the 'forbidden world' of the homosexual in China. Through the citing of examples, the contemporary meaning of *liumang* is filled out. The very definition of *liumang* 'floats' into a contemporary register with their work.

From the etymologically based understanding to a range of activities, the *liumang* begins to enter contemporary discourse and it is from this that one begins to understand that the term *liumang* goes beyond criminal activity to incorporate all those people who, in Chen's words, are 'without a place'. To be without a place means more than being without a work unit for here is an understanding of place that goes beyond the spatial. To be without a place means exclusion from the norm and exclusion from an acceptable social position. In China, there is a strict policing of the boundaries of acceptable social behaviour and, while the metaphor of exclusion from the walled compound of the work unit helps one picture the degree of expulsion, it is inadequate in conveying the wider meaning of *liumang*.

Jin Ren's article on homosexuals in Beijing helps explore those who may be inside the walled compound but whose sexuality takes them outside its strictures. This wider 'economy of the outsider' points to a heterogeneous collection of bodies defined more by what they are not than anything else. What they are not is 'normal' and it is their 'abnormalities' that moves them beyond the controls on normal life and into the dimly lit world of the *liumang*. How they enter discourse—as etymological effects, as examples of criminality or as specimens examined in the new field of sex studies—point to the way they are unable to define themselves. Their voices are muffled in this 'scientific' assessment, but it is this process that gives them voice, no matter how faint the murmur.

## TO BE DEFINED A *LIUMANG*[1]
### CHEN BAOLIANG

How would one define 流氓 *liumang*, the hooligan, and how has the definition changed?

The origin of the word described a person without a place, but this is quite distant from the current usage of the term. The term more fully means transient (流者 *liuzhe*), nothing (亡也 *wangye*), flee (逸也 *yiye*), vagrant (游也 *youye*). The current term *liumang* 'hooligan' consists of two parts. The second character 氓 is now pronounced as '*mang*' but in classical times it was pronounced '*meng*'. The meaning at that time was also quite different. In classical times this character 氓 *meng* actually meant 'to leave, or be forced to leave one's land' (流亡之民). So, discussed in relation to its origins *liumang* can be said to mean 'to leave or be forced to leave one's land', a meaning in those times that was closer to drifter (流民 *liumin*) or vagrant (游民 *youmin*).

The contemporary pejorative meaning of *liumang* came into being near the end of the Qing dynasty in Shanghai, when the term 流氓, pronounced *liumang* and meaning hooligan, and a type of biting insect (流虻, which was also pronounced *liumang*), became synonymous. Ge Yuanxu's *Notes About a Shanghai Sojourn* states: 'In Shanghai business and shopping districts there were many types of vagrants who caused trouble and, as a result, they became known as *liumang* (流氓). Because the term *mang* could also mean a type of insect which was one which "would bite people" … so people started to use it metaphorically with regard to those vagrants who would "bite".' The character *mang*—also pronounced *meng* 虻, meaning horsefly—was also used but it was eventually replaced by *mang* 氓, because, in the end, even hooligans are people and not insects. From this came the contemporary term for hooligan.

The terms 流 *liu* and 游 *you* are sometimes attributed the same meaning; the so-called *liumang* really means 游民 *youmin* or vagrant. So what is a *youmin*? Looking at the changes to the term over a long period of history it can be said that a *youmin* is anyone other than a scholar, peasant, artisan, or merchant. This meaning of the term existed all the way through to the Ming Dynasty (1368–1644), and only began to change at that time. In the time of Ming Taizu the emperor said, 'Concerning those who do not cultivate the land, that is those who specialise in small scale, low status, itinerant type services, these people can be described as *youmin* and they can be taken into custody.'[2] By the time of the

---

1  Chen Baoliang, *A History of Chinese Hooligans* (Beijing: Chinese Social Science Publishing House, 1993), 2–7; 21–2; 386–88. 〔陈宝良, 《中国流氓史》. 〕
2  Quoted from *The Records of Ming Taizu*, juan 208. 〔《明太祖实录》. 〕

Qing Dynasty (1644–1911), an even more exact definition of *youmin* was developed. *Youmin* became a specialised term for all those who did not engage in farming, artisan work or mercantile activity, and also included all those who did not offer their labour power on the market.

Generally speaking, the term 流 *liu*, to flow, in *liumang* can be contrasted with the term 土 *tu*, earth or 地 *di*, land.[3]

## Differences and Similarities between *Liumang* and *Youmin*

Rapid socio-economic development led many people in the society to drift out of the traditional social structure. The massive changes and divisions within the society caused by such changes led to the dispossessed becoming an itinerant body (游民群体 *youmin qunti*). Moreover, this group were quite separate from the respectable category of the four subjects (四民 *simin*), for they did not work on the land, were not artisans, were not involved in mercantile activities and were not scholars.

The difference between the term *liumin* (流民) and *youmin* (游民) is absolutely clear. Yang Jingren, from the Qing Dynasty, said: '*liumin* (流民) are *jimin* (饥民)—refugees from a famine'.[4] From this it is clear, the term *liumin* applies to those who suffer as a result of sudden calamities and who have nowhere to live and nothing to eat and so, for these reasons, go off in search of food and shelter and become *jimin*. Once the calamity passes, these people then return to their homes and pick up their lives. So, the term *liumin* applies to those people who are suddenly placed in this predicament and are there temporarily. Moreover, their situation is not an isolated one; it is suffered by an entire group. The difference between *liumin* and *youmin* is that the latter is constantly present. Moreover, the *youmin*, whether working in one area or travelling around to different places, are always idle drifters. It is this idle drifting which is their chief characteristic.

Many *liumin* become *liumang*, but even more *liumang* come from the ranks of the *youmin*. They are a special group who loiter, 游荡 *youdang*, disturb social order, and do all sorts of evil business. Despite the fact that the *liumin* are the 'reserve army' of the *liumang*, they can generally be thought of as *jimin* or refugees from a famine who abide by the law and know their place. Their pressing concern is to find the basic conditions of life, that is, land and grain. Once this becomes possible, they return to their homes and rely on their land for a living.

Broadly, *youmin* can be thought of as *liumang*. But there are also differences between these two groups. While *liumang* have become an independent social class they are, nevertheless, part of the broader category of *youmin*. They are the 'professional group' within the *youmin* who wander from village to town without

---

3  Earth (*tu*) or land (*di*) are stable and indicate security and safety, while the former are without roots. See Yi Zhongtian (Part II, 1).
4  Yang Jingren, *Qingchao jingshe wenbiao*, huzheng 16, kuangzheng 1 [杨景仁，《清朝经世文编》。]

any work or reason for wandering. The Chinese *liumang* is a *youmin*, a person without household registration (无籍之徒). *Liumang* are a group of people without visible means of support who idle away their time and do not engage in labour and avoid work, they are not only the surplus labour in the countryside but also the surplus labour in the cities.

## SECOND-CLASS CITIZEN[5]
### GE FEI

One summer's afternoon on a country road that lazily weaved its way through the green curtain of tall crops like a stiff dozing snake in winter, there came a pair of newly weds. The pretty and charming young woman opened her florally designed umbrella and, as the sunlight shone down on the nylon surface of the parasol, it projected a bright red-coloured shadow which further heightened the alcohol-induced redness of this beautiful woman's face. This new bride was returning to her bridal home on a bicycle pushed by her new husband. Eager to show off his

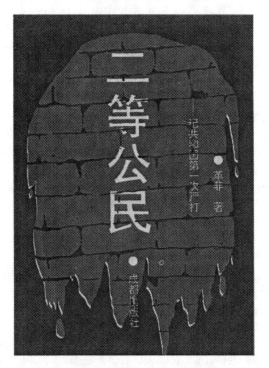

The cover of Ge Fei's *Second-class Citizen*.

---

5  Ge Fei, *Second-class Citizen: A Record of China's First 'Severe Strike' Campaign* (Chengdu Publishing House, 1992), 1–6. [革非, 《二等公民: 共和国 '严打' 纪实》.]

strength, he was determined to push the bike even up the steep inclines. The bride, however, saw how much effort it took her new husband and decided instead to walk with him.

Little did they realise that, even as they walked, disaster was about to befall them.

Suddenly, from behind the tall green curtain of grass sprang four evil bandits. Rushing out, they swamped the happy couple before they had a chance to turn around. Both were quickly bundled off into the maize field by the side of the road. The husband was beaten until he was unconscious, the couple's watches were stolen and all their money taken. After that, the four bandits gang raped the bride. They then stripped them both of their clothes and finally swaggered off. The bride, having suffered such a severe attack, never regained consciousness. The bridegroom, ashamed at their nakedness, dared not call for help. With the temperature reaching forty-odd degrees, it is unlikely that they would have ever been found had it not been for a peasant discovering them.

Analogous cases appear time and again in the city and suburbs. Such brazen criminal acts carried out in broad daylight are a challenge to society. But while such monsters climb one foot, righteousness is able to scale ten, and the long arm of the law always stretches out to catch such villains. In the end, the crime fighters were able to bring the seven thieves and rapists who organised and perpetrated this crime to justice. Four of them would pay the ultimate price. Nevertheless, it is worth noting that, of these seven criminals, six of them already had records, and five had already spent time in either reform-through-labour institutes or labour education centres for larceny and robbery.

In another city many miles from this, in a different and far off province, there was an even more cold-blooded case that would make one bristle with anger. This crime was also carried out blatantly in daylight and in full public view. A long-distance bus was stopped by scoundrels who stood in the middle of the road. After they got on the coach, two of their accomplices pulled out daggers and blocked the exits. While they did this, the other two criminals brazenly started to 'clean up'. Of the entire forty-odd passengers, not one was lucky enough to escape. In total, the thieves got away with over one thousand *yuan*. Only one young seventeen-year-old girl resisted this terrifying outrage. For her trouble, this brave girl was dragged off the bus, and had her clothes ripped from her body and there, by the side of the road, right before the eyes of the other passengers, was gang raped. The sun just hung in the sky.

Again it proved difficult for these four scoundrels to evade the wide net of the law. After being caught, two of them were sentenced to death while the other two received death sentences with a two-year reprieve. In the People's Court notice it was stressed: of the four, two already had records for larceny. In fact, in 1983, these two had spent three and four years respectively in prison. From the time of their release until their most recent crime only two years had elapsed.

On a train, nine men and one woman formed a 'north east tiger' group and cleaned out four carriages, robbing over four hundred victims. One young woman who opposed them was sexually assaulted by having her breasts molested. One other young peasant was stabbed and badly injured. After their cases were heard, these ten 'north east tigers' were executed. The remainder of their group received prison sentences that varied between life imprisonment and set term imprisonment. In the public notice of the People's Court accompanying this decision, it was written that, of the ten, three 'tigers' already had records for train robbery. These sorts of evils are not restricted to the countryside, you even get them being perpetrated in large and medium-sized cities.

Desperados who busied themselves in one particular area were surrounded by police and tried to fight their way out. The police were worried about casualties and, because of a lack of experience in dealing with such situations, suffered four casualties. There were also two fatalities, one a police officer, the other an innocent bystander. With the loss of one of their number, the police's power to resist was affected. When they were brought to justice these criminals were given the death penalty. The court notice promulgating the sentence also revealed that two of the convicted criminals already had criminal records.

In the dead of night three murderers rushed into a bank, stabbing and seriously wounding two of the night security guards and stealing all the ready cash. After the case was brought to trial, three of the criminals were given the death sentence. The court notice in this case also noted that the principal criminal already had a record.

There is one case of a couple of infamous bandits who carried out robberies in more than ten provinces and, when they were finally brought to justice, were given a suspended death sentence with a two-year reprieve. Both of them had previous histories.

There was also a case of one couple using their place as a brothel for a number of prostitutes to practise their trade. After the case was cracked, they were both given the same sentence. It was discovered that the husband had once been imprisoned on robbery charges.

These sorts of serious criminal cases, which significantly and adversely affect social order would, if discovered even ten years ago, have been thought of as shocking. Today, however, they don't even raise a murmur let alone create a stir. These crimes are often undertaken in full view of the public. We have even reached the stage whereby people say they are 'accustomed' to such things.

There has also been a tendency for criminality to increase in scope and take on new forms. Within criminal ranks, one discovers that secret societies and criminal armed gangs are once again being formed. These organisations are not only involved in traditional criminal forms, such as armed robbery, rape and theft, but are also reviving prostitution, transnational drug trafficking and smuggling. On the soil of mainland China, we now discover organised criminal gangs vying with each other for power, carrying out killings and openly enacting gang fights. They even surround and encircle the forces of law and order, carrying out violent armed struggle against them.

On the basis of statistics from a number of the larger southern provinces, in the ten-year period from 1978 through to 1988, the number of criminal cases of all types has increased six-fold. This includes property crimes (robbery, theft, embezzlement as well as other crimes carried out in the course of these crimes such as rape and murder), which now constitute something like 70 per cent of all crimes. In the space of ten years, this type of crime has grown by 4.2 times.

The national campaign issued forth a 'severe strike against criminal elements who seriously jeopardise social peace'—known simply as the 'severe strike' or 严 打 *yanda*. Over the last three years, it failed to effectively keep within limits the black tide of wild crimes, leading the Chinese People's Republic, six years on, to relaunch the 'severe strike'.

Kind-hearted folk have expressed serious concerns regarding the severe public security situation, and their hearts are heavy with the dark cloud of crime that envelopes society.

In a number of northern provinces, a large-scale survey undertaken found that 95 per cent of the people surveyed were unsatisfied with the contemporary security situation. Some large cities that conducted this type of research found 94.5 per cent unsatisfied with the security situation.[6]

The deteriorating security situation in contemporary China has important lessons and offers some previously unknown challenges to the law in the People's Republic. The economic reform process has inadvertently led to a crime wave casting a dark and evil shadow over the normally peaceful life of the citizens of the People's Republic. These crimes have shocked the People's Republic.

Social order has become the most talked about problem among the public and one of the 'hot stories' of the media, not to mention the key concern of leaders in the social arena. Despite the severe strikes mounted by the public security and justice authorities against those criminal elements who seriously disrupt social order, and despite the fact that they often attach the big red tick to their notices of conviction,[7] we still read that the court officials are quite anxious about the situation. The problem of re-offence among those who are released from reform-through-labour or reform-through-education is a source of great concern. There are many serious cases whereby those released reoffend but who, upon discovery, not only don't give up but resist arrest, becoming desperados and sometimes murderers.

To be fair, the number of people released from these two forms of penal labour centres as a percentage of the overall population is very small. From the summer of 1983, when the 'severe strike' campaign was launched through to the end of 1984, less than two million people were incarcerated, constituting a little over 0.1

---

6    Ge Fei is referring to an internal study undertaken by the research unit of the Public Security Ministry, from the first report which came out in 1991. For details of the results see *Do You Feel Safe?*, Ministry of Public Security Research Unit, Masses Press (1991).

7    Indicating that the subject of the poster has been sentenced to death.

per cent of the population and, in recent years, the overall number of criminals of all types vis-à-vis the population as a whole doesn't even amount to 1 per cent of the population.

Nevertheless, given the overall size of the population, even less than 1 per cent of the population still means an awful lot of people. Quite apart from this though, it is important to note that it is the youth and the relatively youthful members of the population who are most represented among this group and that, within this group, the predominant gender is male. Moreover, this trend is continuing at an increasing rate.

There has been a ten-fold increase in the number of people released from incarceration in the two types of labour centres and the number of people released stands at about 10 per cent of all cases. Not only this, but the majority of those who re-offend do so within three years of having been released. The number of those who re-offend within that time frame as a percentage of overall releases has grown every year at a quite significant rate. Nevertheless, while it has not reached 30 per cent of cases in terms of overall population, there is more than a ten-fold chance of these people committing crimes rather than others.

Why are those who have already received some form of penalty more likely to re-offend than ordinary people? Within the household registration management system, there is a term known as the 'special population' (*zhongdian renkou*).[8] 'Special population' refers to those people released either from reform through labour or education. Police records of the 'special population' indicate what crimes they have committed, when they did it and what types of penalty they received.

Through the special population files those who are released from reform through labour or education are supervised and controlled by the police.

The masses really hate this criminal evil and detest these people released from the reform through labour and education centres, and pay a lot of attention to them—'the level of freedom' for criminals is much less than for ordinary people. People from the reform through labour and reform through education centres call themselves 'second-class citizens' and this definition clearly shows their mixed emotions. While part of it is attributable to an inferiority complex, it also reflects that they have nothing to lose.

Nevertheless, it should be asked why they are under special controls, have special attention paid to them by the rest of the population, and why they have less freedom than other citizens. These factors contribute to the development of a feeling of inferiority as expressed in the term 'second-class citizen' and easily lead these people back into crime.

---

8   Ge Fei refers to a category that is supposed to remain internal to the public security forces (see Yu Lei, 'Special Population', Part II, 3) and its appearance here in what is 'pulp literature' is indicative of the power of the market.

## HOMOSEXUALS IN BEIJING[9]
### JIN REN

For the vast majority of citizens of mainland China, homosexuality is quite alien. Nevertheless, one has to recognise that the endlessly increasing reports of homosexuality within the mainland probably means that people that are close to us, or even living within our midst, are that way inclined.

The first semi-public gay 'salon' dance party was held on 14 February 1993 during the 'sweetheart festival'. This dance, organised in one of the many dance halls in Beijing's Xidan district, was called 'men's world'. In the soft glow of the dim light, the music lingered and the couples swayed, yet all of these lovers were male.

On the afternoon of the same day in the Dongdan Park in Beijing, there were even more homosexuals out celebrating the 'sweetheart festival'. Some people, recalling that day, said that it was like going to a fairground.

How many homosexuals are there in Beijing? No one is able to accurately calculate, but one gay guy who is pretty familiar with the scene and a frequent visitor to Dongdan Park, says he can recognise about 1000 regulars. The American scholar Alfred Kinsey, who conducted a survey on homosexuality in the United States, discovered something like 4 per cent of the American population were homosexual. This figure seems to vary little between cultures.

Those 'in the know' suggest that there are about 55 regular homosexual meeting places in Beijing and, of these, the vast majority are public toilet blocks. Most of the regular toilet block haunts are around public parks or greens. Another popular spot for gays in Beijing are the public baths. Hotels, bars and dance halls also appear to be regular meeting places. In these latter establishments, the gay community is not the principal source of revenue. But by far the most famous site in Beijing is the aforementioned Dongdan Park—one does not need to buy a ticket to enter and so it is easy to come and go and this allows the visitor a certain anonymity. This fact, coupled with its relative proximity to the city centre, makes Dongdan Park a popular gay haunt 24 hours a day.

On the basis of one researcher's work on the gay scene, it is clear that homosexuality has always existed in Beijing. Nevertheless, there have been a number of recent reports about homosexuality, and this has brought it to the public's attention. In earlier times, the public lavatories on either side of Tiananmen Square were pretty popular sites, and they were jokingly named the 'East and West Palaces' by the gay community.

There is no way of telling the difference between a gay and straight person just in terms of appearance. Nevertheless, just about every gay man you talk to says

---

9    Jin Ren, 'Homosexuals in Beijing', *Economic Evening News*, 23 April 1993. [ 津人，'同性恋在北京'，《经济晚报》。]

that if you go into a public place, recognising another gay guy isn't difficult, although the secret to their success may be difficult for 'straights' to fully understand. Gays will tell you it is easy to tell if you 'look into their eyes and spot their desire' or if 'you pay attention to someone and watch what they do'. One gay guy told me that 'when you meet another gay, actions speak louder than words and their eyes will do all the talking. This is true nine-tenths of the time. When one's eyes meet, it is such a charge and both men know what is going on.' In public baths, for example, the first contact is often made by touching the other person with your foot. If they find you desirable, they will respond.

Within the gay community, activities in public places are quite often divided into what they describe as 'social' (public) and non-social (private) activity. Their social activities consist of drinking together and chatting whereas their non-social activity often involves long-term, stable and relatively intimate relations with their gay partner. This can even go so far as to mean that they secretly live together. But it is very rare that they will only live this gay lifestyle. The homosexual, in choosing a partner, will pay particular attention to their lover's age, occupation, and education. Gay men from different backgrounds will find those differences reflected in their choice of partner.

Scholars in the fields of psychology, physiology and sociology have all undertaken investigations into the causes of homosexuality. Some experts disagree that physiological explanations can tell us much about homosexuality. They emphasise, instead, its culturally acquired nature. Currently, the weight of academic opinion tends to suggest that cultural explanations are the most useful. This argument will identify childhood experiences and the confusion in gender identity that some suffer at an early age as one reason. Another explanation points to puberty and the way in which, at this time, sexual differentiation can lead to inhibitions developing. Still another points to the way in which homosexuals can lead the young into this type of activity. Generally speaking, most homosexuals do not subscribe to cultural explanations, believing instead that they were simply born that way.

One gay guy told me that even from a very early age he had a yearning for those of the same sex and was completely uninterested in the opposite sex. His first homosexual encounter was during a *pingju* performance—*pingju* is the local opera form of north and north-eastern China—where he met a gay guy of the same age. After this initial experience, he longed to meet this person again. Later, when he was to leave Beijing for business, he met another homosexual man in a park who told him of the places where most gay men congregated. After he returned to Beijing, he really began to get into the scene and went to these places. These days though, he will only venture out a couple of times a month. The reason for this, he explains, is because he is in a fairly stable relationship.

In Beijing, gay men do not, to use a Western expression, 'come out'. There are some very famous figures within the homosexual community but even they do not 'come out' but try, instead, to hide their sexual preference from relatives, family and society. As far as gay men are concerned, to be exposed as homosexual in China would have dire consequences. The moral order of China is built upon the traditional values of Confucianism and the idea that 'there are three forms of unfilial activity but the greatest of them all is not bearing a son'. Hence, every healthy adult male has to marry and give birth to a child. The pressure to marry is such that the vast majority of homosexuals end up getting married. They will find women who are willing to join in their activities but, all too often, such unions end in divorce. There are those who are bisexual, who love the same sex as well as the opposite sex. Pure homosexuality is a rarity.

Dr Li Yinhe, a famous Chinese sociologist, has undertaken a survey on the question of marriage and has been able to categorise the responses into three different models of behaviour. In the first, the man will have a guilty conscience and will do his best to fulfil his duty as husband. In the second case, the gay man will try to turn his wife around so she accepts his sexuality. The third case includes those who fail to change their ways and also to change their wife's views.

For the homosexual, getting married is equivalent to losing one's position. It will not only mean they will lose face among their homosexual friends, but it also means that certain restrictions will be placed on their life from that time forth. Naturally, there are many homosexuals who, after marriage, still frequent the old haunts and renew their homosexual acquaintances. Of the 51 homosexuals interviewed for Dr Li's report, some 31 men had been, or were, married. Fourteen of the men had higher education, fifteen were workers, fourteen were government cadres, five worked in technical or artistic affairs and seventeen were either peasants or had some other occupation. The oldest of the 51 men surveyed was 70, while the youngest was 22 years of age.

Perhaps the average person is unacquainted with homosexuality and we could even go so far as to say that, when they think about it, they feel sick. One survey undertaken into this found that 71 per cent of respondents thought homosexuality an abnormality, or even a type of sickness, while 34 per cent believed it to be illegal. Only 12 per cent of those surveyed believed that it was a matter of free choice. After the 'sweetheart festival' dance party, the manager of the Beijing dance hall, where it was held, lost his job. There was an obvious link between these two events.

The vast majority of homosexual men believe themselves to be little different from straight men in everything bar sexual preference. Moreover, they do not regard homosexual behaviour as seriously anti-social. Professor Qiu Renzong of the Chinese Academy of Social Sciences points out that there is little reason for the public to view homosexuality as abnormal or illegal. From the point of view of the consequences of their actions, homosexual men may very well do some quite immoral and illegal things, but then, so do straight men. Immoral or illegal activities are the province of individuals rather than homosexuals generally. In terms of the morality and justice of their actions, there are many people who think, or could argue at least, that homosexuality is abnormal because it fails to promote procreation, hence it is abnormal and anti-life. But this is to pre-suppose that everyone wants children.

In mainland China at present, there are no clear regulations regarding homo-sexual activity. It, therefore, proves to be a rather tricky matter for the police. Under normal circumstances, the police do not interfere unless the homosexuals carry out their activity in public places or force someone to engage in homosexual sex. In October 1992, ten men were publicly engaged in homosexual acts in a number of bath houses in Beijing. These men were detained and fined by the police under provisions given in the 'Regulations governing penalties for the security management of public spaces'. At that time the police, in dealing with these matters, did not inform the work units of these people. Even today, only in cases where the people refuse to mend their ways will the work unit be informed.

There is no question that homosexuals are a high-risk group when it comes to the spreading of AIDS. It is not uncommon for one gay man to have quite a few partners, which makes them increasingly susceptible to the AIDS virus. A survey of 96 homosexual men discovered that, on average, every man had about seven part-ners. Some people say that AIDS is God's punishment on those who carry out abnormal sexual practices. The Chinese mainland had its first case of an HIV posi-tive person in 1989, and while there has not been another such discovery, this has not stopped the general public from worrying about it.

From the homosexual perspective, AIDS is a very sensitive topic, and there is little agreement within the community about it. Some gay men are aware of the protective measures needed to combat the disease and are therefore not afraid of it. When they engage in homosexual activity, they take precautions.

Some research institutes on the mainland have been engaged in work among the homosexual community. The Chinese Health Education Research Institute began an 'AIDS help hotline' in April last year and that has gained some head-way.[10] By the end of last year, the hotline had received a total of 1126 calls asking for help and 15.2 per cent of these calls were from self-proclaimed homosexual men. The hotline is operated by academically trained professionals in the area. The hotline also operates as a means by which to disseminate information on HIV/AIDS to the wider community. In places where homosexual activity is more numerous, information and advice services are also set up to try to alter the sexual practices of gay men so that they adopt safe sex practices. It was the hotline group that organised the 'men's world' cultural salon last year. Since October 1992, when the salon was held, they have held six other meetings to try to get a stable means of communication going about the virus. There is an unofficial group operating within the homosexual community which aims at disseminating infor-mation about the virus and about ways of preventing its spread. In March 1993,

---

10 This AIDS hotline was closed in 1993 because organisers began to agitate for gay rights. See Seth Faison, 'Tolerance Grows for Homosexuals in China', *The New York Times*, 2 September 1997.

one homosexual expert set up a social network in Beijing to help spread the word on AIDS and AIDS prevention. The Chinese Health Education Research Institute is about to open an advice line for gay males very soon.[11]

Getting homosexuals together is a step toward preventing the spread of this disease, and it is principally from this perspective that such programmes are being set up. As the director of the Chinese Health Education Research Institute, Chen Bingzhong, pointed out: 'All human groups have health problems. Moreover, the health problems of one group can quickly become the health problems of all. The relationship between AIDS, homosexuals and the masses is precisely this sort of relationship.'

Professor Qiu thinks that, today, consciousness of homosexuality will increase along with concern for society and public health. Without some sort of clarification of homosexuality in China there can be no way forward.

---

11 The gay hotline was said to have been proposed by a bisexual, Wan Yanhai, who is now in exile. He formally worked in the Health Ministry. In the end, the proposal was not accepted. Later on, an underground hotline did begin but, with no publicity and few telephone link-ups, it only received two calls per day. Personal correspondance with hotline activist, 10 April 1998.

# PART Ⅱ

# THE 'STRATEGIES' OF GOVERNMENT AND 'TACTICS' OF THE SUBALTERN

'A thick feudal cloud', says Gong Xikui, 'covers the post-revolutionary Chinese landscape.' It is a cloud raining down on the majority of the population despite the fine weather forecasts of equality given by the Communist Party leadership. The reason: the technologies of these social meteorologists are defective. A central mechanism devoted to securing the fine weather conditions of life (and thereby establishing the material basis for human rights), ended up reinforcing the hailstorms of traditional fatalist value systems and social and economic inequality. That mechanism was the household registration system of socialist China.

In some respects, Gong Xikui's argument is not unlike that of Li Yiyuan's and Xu Ping's in Part I. Li Yiyuan and Xu Ping discussed the way in which certain 'high culture' values permeated popular cultural practices by a slow process of osmosis. Gong Xikui's essay likewise argues that the socialist household registration system of contemporary China has slowly changed to become a shackle tying the peasants to the land and thereby sealing their fate. This form of social osmosis ensured that traditional value systems prevailed over revolutionary technologies, subverting the latter's egalitarian intentions and leading to a system that materially reinforced social difference. The result was the production of a pyramid of rights whereby the majority of the population, forced to remain forever in their place of birth, got the fewest material benefits the revolution had to offer. After the revolution, China may no longer have had a class system but, as Gong Xikui suggests, it very quickly developed a traditional caste structure based upon socialist technologies that reinforced traditional sedentary and 'feudal' forms.

Economic reform was the revolution that changed all this. This process, which began in 1979, required a 'free' and large labour force to aid the process of unbridled economic development. It forced a reconsideration of those mechanisms that kept the peasant caste on the land. This, in turn, resulted in government administrative reforms of the family-based household register Gong Xikui discusses. By the mid-1980s this system was being 'augmented' by the individually based identity card system briefly outlined in this section by Zhang Qingwu. More radical experiments were also on the way. By the mid-1990s, Beijing was experimenting with a trial 'user pays' system that reflected the 'class nature' of social relations in China today. Pay, and you can enter the cities, this legislation seemed to suggest.

Combining Gong Xikui's account of the caste-like nature of the household register with Zhou Daping's account of new (trial) legislation authorising the Beijing government to charge huge amounts for residency rights, allows us to plot the direction of the current social and economic reforms. Where once the system more or less foreclosed the possibility of movement into the cities and, as a consequence, produced a peasant caste, today money buys mobility and flags the existence of new 'class' considerations. The registration regime has not only come to plot the movement from the countryside into the city, but also the move from caste to class. No matter what the eventual fate of this local Beijing legislation, its trial does signal the tendency toward social commodification in China, whereby even the age-old problem of controlling the massive flow of rural migrants into the cities now gains a monetary representation. Economic reform unleashed the peasant caste from the bonds of land and labour, but only to reintroduce certain restrictions that would ensure they became wage slaves in the booming cities along the east coast. But it also produced conditions under which peasant desire to earn in the city outweighed the fear of regulatory transgression. The result was a massive growth in transients and itinerants known today in China as the 'float-ing population' (liudong renkou). This population is itself divided between the worthy and unworthy 'floater', with the former being short-term workers whose papers are in order, while the latter are suspicious characters, without homes or status. Indeed, this latter group are always in danger of being defined 流氓 liumang or 'hoodlums', as the expression used to described them, 盲流 mangliu seems to suggest. Mangliu is a compound word that is formed through a reversal of the character order that makes up the term 'hoodlum' and the replacement of the character 氓 mang meaning 'common people', with the 盲 mang of blindness. The result is mangliu—to flow blindly and without reason.

It is interesting how this idea of 'flowing' or 'floating', as opposed to being sedentary or stable, has once again registered as a crucial marker of social division in China, confirming many of the points made by Yi Zhongtian in his piece on the work unit. Clearly, this pejorative use of the term 流 liu—to flow—when applied to people, is flagging the fact that there is more invested in the household regis-ter than the utilitarian benefits derived from the planned socialist system would lead us to believe.

Read at this symbolic level, the 'market orientation' of the Beijing registration legislation controlling residency and population flow is, likewise, a 'tell-tale sign' of deeper psychological changes under way rather than a 'mere technique' to control population flow. It tells us of the changing face of Chinese society and the emergence of a form of 'socialism' in which life for the poor, uneducated and unattached migrant is subject to harsh regimes of control and exclusion. It is at these crucial points—those moments Michel Foucault describes as the most 'intense points' in people's lives[1]— that they enter, momentarily and in shadowy forms, into discourse. That such an entry allows but a murmur of the complexity of these outsiders' lives is exemplified by the material gathered together in Part 4 of this chapter.

The difficulties 'outsiders' encounter and the prejudices they face while in the cities are captured graphically in the personal stories of two migrants (Lu Naihong and Li Ninlong) and also in the account of Zhejiang village in Beijing. Here, on the outskirts of Beijing, the migrant 'foreigners' coped with their lowly group status

---

1    Michel Foucault, 'The Life of Infamous Men' [Trans. Paul Foss and Meaghan Morris], in Meaghan Morris and Paul Patton (eds), *Michel Foucault: Power, Truth, Strategy* (Sydney: Feral Publications, 1979), 80.

by gathering together and offering mutual support and help to one other. The rate of growth of the 'village' was staggering. In the early 1990s, people moved into the 'village' at a phenomenal rate and the result was a squalid shanty town. High crime rates and a sense of lawlessness, whereby ordinary Beijing folk avoided the area and police treated residents with suspicion eventually led to a police crackdown—the internal police report on this is included in this chapter. Despite the crackdown, the more general problem of migrancy remains, and the suspicion of Zhejiang village by Beijing residents is but a microcosm of this general fear. This fear is palpable in the excerpt from the highly controversial book, *A Third Eye On China*, written by 'Leuninger'. Banned shortly after its release, *A Third Eye* is strongly critical of the social effects of economic reform and represents a clear statement from those who long for a return to a more stable and socialist past. Many Chinese city residents would concur with the assessment of the peasant migrant offered in *A Third Eye*, yet that has not stopped them happily utilising the services these migrants provide.

Sun Xiaomei's article on Beijing's 保姆 *baomu*, nannies, highlights the value of such 'outside' labour to Beijing residents and tells us something of the middle-class aspirations of many Beijing residents. From the *baomu*'s perspective, the story is naturally different. Their story emerges, in part, out of the interview with Li Ninlong, a young *baomu* from the countryside who currently works in Beijing. Reading between the lines of her story, one is able to paint a picture of life as a migrant woman worker. Traditional patriarchal attitudes and a stable social culture seem to conspire, not only to make city residents suspicious of the foreigner, but also to make rural villagers doubtful of the virtue of the departed woman. Should she return to her village, she would be treated with suspicion. Should she stay in the city, she will be doubly exploited as migrant and as woman. Her work in the household domain is invariably 'service', not 'productive' work; her life in the city is always that of the foreigner. Little wonder transient women find this type of work unappealing and turn instead to prostitution, where the risks are high, but the wages higher.

Just how high the risks faced by the prostitute are in China is evidenced, to some extent, by the classified documents used to deal with the 'problem' of prostitution and vagrancy. These documents and the regulations they outline are not available to the general public. They operate silently, invisibly and constantly. One is never quite sure whether one is 'caught within the net' of police attention. To fall within the strategic gaze of the police seems all too easy. It could be as a result of a visit to the doctor or because one spent a night in a hotel. Hospitals, as these internal documents show, are ordered to check on all cases of sexually transmitted diseases and report them to the police for further investigation. Hotels fall within what are described by the police as 'special professions', and these are to be closely monitored (see Yu Lei). To be caught within this policing gaze could lead to a special file being opened. It is a file that the police will mark 'special population'. Once again, here is an internal category where restraints are placed on personal rights and the freedom of movement, all but denied. Human rights, at this level, take on a very basic and onerous form. It is through legislation such as this that, as I mentioned in Part I, something of a Marxian 'pincer movement' is at work in

China today. Greater freedom of movement is legislated into existence but it is always accompanied by tighter regulations against 'blind movement' and socially suspicious elements. The peasant migrant enters the city but is 'hemmed in' by local city regulations that increasingly charge huge amounts to grant them the right to reside (see Zhou Daping), by a police force who perceive them as a potential cause of serious social disorder and crime (see Yang Wenzhong and Wang Gongfan's article and the internal report on the crackdown at Zhejiang village), and by popular city attitudes that regard them as second-class citizens with dangerous inclinations (see A Third Eye). Yet, as all these documents make clear, the number of peasants on the move is such that even the most draconian regulations cannot halt the flow. A Third Eye is correct to point to police weakness, but it is wrong to think that this has resulted in impotence. Instead, it has resulted in an ad hoc regime of arbitrary, harsh and seemingly inconsistent regulation.

Perceived in this way, these 'subalterns' are left with little choice but to live by their wits. Their principal tactic is to avoid the spotlight and live in the shadows. Strangely, it is the spotlight of the police and the government, as they turn their attention and their (often internal) rules and regulations to this issue, that enables us to glimpse at the subaltern presence and form. The government documents, in their attempts to block subaltern tactics, tell us much about their way of life, even if they do so only because we read between the lines. So we turn to these documents in order to read between the lines and, from this, learn to read the 'life stories' of the Chinese subalterns.

ANALYSIS

# HOUSEHOLD REGISTRATION AND THE CASTE-LIKE QUALITY OF PEASANT LIFE[1]

**GONG XIKUI**

For the vast majority of people in China, the household register is of the utmost importance. One cannot avoid a close relationship with the register, it is there at births and at deaths, it helps in the arrangement of food, clothing and housing, it is there for the registration of marriages or funerals, it is there in the selection of work and in work transfers, and it is referred to when attempting to establish the status and identity of people. Hence, there is much to be gained from a deeper analysis of the household registration system in China.

## Special Characteristics and Function of the Household Registration System

The so-called household register is a volume within which each resident registers on the basis of their household. In traditional China it was known as the 'male register' (*dingji*), the 'yellow register' (*huangji*) or the 'record of accounts' (*jizhang*). Over time, it has had various types of investigative functions, such as checking on the population, levying taxes and arranging corvée. After 1932 and during the rule of Guomindang or Nationalist Party, the household register constituted part of the *baojia* system and was of use as a procedure by which to levy able-bodied men for military service, control the population and oppress the people. After the communist victory in 1949 the household record constituted the statistical basis upon which the population became known for it contained names, ages, nationality, work skills and so forth.

The contemporary system of household registration in China came into being after liberation in 1949. It was established along with each level of government organisation and the general tendency was that, as each area became secure, this system would be established. In the beginning, the functions of the household register were quite simple. It provided the Public Security Ministry or the local level governmental agencies (such as the village governments) with a means by

---

1 Gong Xikui, 'One perspective on the current household registration system in China', *Social Science*, Feb. (1989), 32–6. [宫希魁，'中国现行户籍制度透视'，《社会科学》。]

which to administer, through the administrative region or the local work unit, those who were to be in charge of the registration books. They would provide documentation to these localities and the record would thereby prove useful in supplying population statistics, in helping with providing security for the region, in providing evidence on the citizenry and so forth. At this time, the register was closely related to residency and provided evidence of who lived in what administrative district, which local level government was responsible for them, when they could buy their grain, and other issues relating to the supply of goods. Shortly after liberation, it wasn't the transfer of the household register that determined population movement but population movement which directed migration and reregistration of households. So, wherever one worked was also where one lived, and this was where one was registered.

Over time, however, the function of the register began to change. The nature of that change can be seen in the shifting function of the register from the time of its establishment through to its emergence as a structure by which to classify social stratum. In the immediate aftermath of the 1949 revolution, there was no idea that benefits could be derived from this structure. There was no conception of peasant household registers being somehow lower down on the pecking order than city-based registers. People at that stage didn't care where one lived or what one did for a living for everyone was a resident in the new People's Republic.

Later on, however, due to the fact that different places of residency produced different benefits, new social stratum and groups emerged and the allocating function of a household register brought with it certain 'inflationary effects'. Hence, as the registration structure was gradually established, it took on the form of a pagoda (*baotashi*) in that it cemented social status. Within this pagoda structure it was the household registers of the peasants which were at the base of the social structure and, as one progressed up the pagoda, one moved on to the non-peasant households, the township households, the city households, the big city households and the centrally administered city households.[2] The lower one went down this pyramid of rights, the more widespread and numerous were the number and type of households.

Within this structural form, movement between areas of equal value proves to be relatively easy. For example, movement from one rural region to another, from one town to another, from one middle-sized city to another, are all acceptable forms of movement. Yet, comparatively speaking, even with this form of movement there are quite a few problems. The other type of migration, which we can call vertical migration, is of two types: there are those who wish to migrate from the bottom up, but this is a little like the old saying, the road from Shanxi to Sichuan is even tougher to travel than the pathway to heaven (*shudao zhi nan, nanyu shang qingtian*). It is nigh on impossible for a peasant to transfer the household register to a non-rural or urban area without abundant reasons and some

---

2   The centrally administered cities are Beijing, Tianjin and Shanghai.

very special contacts. It is very hard indeed to jump up the ladder between each stratum. A much easier form of transfer to arrange is for those higher up on the ladder to migrate to places lower down on the social scale, but how many would be willing to leave the big cities to go and live in small towns or in border regions?

The ideological, cultural, political and economic sources of this form of stratification, made effective through the register, run deep. From an economic perspective, the concentration and level of development of the big cities is invariably higher than that of the medium-sized cities, which, in turn, are in a better position than the smaller cities, which are better off than villages. Villages bordering cities are themselves usually more developed than those distant villages which exist out in the provinces. This ladder of economic development is also reflected in the level of economic benefits available. From a political point of view, each level of government authority is divided in order of importance into those of the city, the town and the central villages (village government centres). This political structure leads to a protection of local interests and, taking into consideration political factors, means that these authorities cannot but give benefits to their own areas. From a social perspective, the bigger a city is, the higher the concentration of population. This, in turn, means that it will have higher levels of organisation and the residents will be more politically informed and their benefits more ably defended. In relation to ideological and cultural factors, it can be said that the biggest concentration of intellectuals is to be found in the central cities. The general cultural level of the residents in these areas is invariably higher than elsewhere and the intellectual superiority of the area is quite apparent. It is these factors that guide the differential benefits given and impel cities of different levels to act as mechanisms to protect and guard what they have. With different levels set up to block change and protect self-interests, and to strengthen and tighten the household registration system, the natural consequence is the development of a logic that will interpret transfers from lower levels to higher levels to be against their own interests.

Now that this type of pagoda structure has become stabilised, it forms a protective screen to consolidate social difference. After a person is born, the type of household register they will end up with is completely determined by that which has been given to their parents. The only hope of any change rests with rare opportunities or favourable circumstances. The reproduction of the household register is the reproduction of difference.

At the time of the completion of the household registration system, its purpose was to register the natural appearance of the people and families, but this changed so that it became a means by which people's social standing could be differentiated and standardised. The household register was originally the outcome of people's social activity, but it quickly changed to become a precondition for social activity. Originally, one was classified as a peasant household because one lived in a rural region and worked in agricultural activities. Today, this situation has been turned on its head. That is to say, it is because they have a peasant household registration that they can now only live in rural areas and therefore have no choice but to work in the agricultural sector. The household registration system has produced a contrary result to what was expected. It has become a means by which the people's freedoms are limited and, as a result, the problem of alienation has already reached amazing levels. At the present time, the household registration system carries within it many selfish, biased and discriminatory elements. This human-made system is simply an opportunity to increase unfairness and social inequality for the benefit, and in the service, of a few.

As the cities are already extremely crowded, isn't it appropriate to tighten the household registration regulations so as to limit the vertical migration of people? But to address the question in this way is to avoid confronting what is, in reality, the truly crucial problem. To strengthen the household registration system so as to control the deployment of human resources is not only irrational, but it will prove ineffective and won't get to the root of the problem. Behind the household registration system lies the large differences that exist in the distribution of benefits so that whoever attains registration in one area enjoys the benefits of registration in that area. If the government were to strengthen the household registration management system, then the other side of that decision would be a strengthening of the disparity in wealth between city and country. It is the solidification of this very inequitable structure which will be the nett result of this type of household registration system. Naturally, once the people realise this, they will try to destroy this system which acts as a fetter upon them. As the desire for equality rises among them, so they will be strengthened and their actions become more resolute. Hence, the only thing to do is to rectify the household registration system. Without any rectification of this system, which reinforces disparities in benefits, all the labour exerted on reforming the system will be wasted. This is because every time the system is strengthened, it gives birth to a new round of attempts to circumvent it.

Naturally, there are complex social and historical causes for the form that social inequality takes. To assume that these can be overcome by relying upon subjective will is quite unrealistic. Nevertheless, to recognise that these inequalities take on this form because of historical factors certainly is not the same as saying that it is reasonable for people to protect and extend such inequalities. Hence, one should not use the historical causes of the various forms of social inequalities as an excuse by which to paper over contemporary causes which really can be put down to policy error. If no action is undertaken to adjust the errors of this policy, but instead it is allowed to continue to grow at its own pace, then this will not only prove to be a major headache for the household registration system, but also possibly produce new reverberations in the economic, political and other arenas.

A number of points in conclusion:

1.  The contemporary household registration system in China is covered by a thick feudal cloud. The policy leads directly to tying people to the land. The

fact that differences in land lead to differences in benefits quickly forms the reality of differentiation of status in the household registration system. More than this, this differentiation of status has been turned around so that it is the household registration system which offers different benefits. Hence, it is because the household registration system's population registration books function as a means by which benefits are distributed that there is alienation with the system.

2. A key component of personal liberation is the freedom of choice in work and place of abode. The rhythm of social life has continuously accelerated. Consequently, the need for movement by people of different work stations and different places has also arisen. Moreover, the attempt by the household registration system to have a situation whereby places of residence and work are stable, runs counter to the main tendencies in contemporary society.

3. It is imperative that, year by year, the original features and function of the household registration system be restored so that the household register is no longer linked to questions of benefit and so that the register can face a situation whereby all people are equal. The household registration system cannot be allowed to decide who gets big and who gets small benefits, for this must be based upon skill and success in enterprise. In a similar way, household migration registration should not determine the flow of the population. On the contrary, it is the flow of population which should determine the registration of migration.

4. Gradually, the household registration management system must be turned around so that in place of rigidity, there is a certain amount of elasticity. With the creation of a competitive environment and limitations placed upon the register's role in the allocation of benefits, all the various limitations imposed upon those migrating within the existing household registration system can be gradually made more flexible. The system of checks imposed upon those migrating can be simplified so that the greatest of all restrictions brought into effect by this system can be turned into a new respect for the rights of people to choose where they want to live. This, of course, is a long-term aim. Before such a long-term aim can be realised, however, a series of provisional measures should be instituted, such as making the temporary registration of households function in a way that is decided by science and so forth.

---

★ FROM CASTE TO CLASS: A BRIEF INTRODUCTION TO *A THIRD EYE*
---

The following excerpt is drawn from the highly controversial book, *A Third Eye on China*. This book became infamous in intellectual circles in 1994 both because of the leftist argument it proffered (which led to it being banned shortly after its release), and because the author of the work claimed only to be its 'translator'.

Wang Shan, who was eventually 'outed', claimed that he was merely the translator of a work by a famous German scholar who was, he claimed, 'the most influential Sinologist in contemporary Europe'. The controversy around authorship, however, only fuelled interest in the text and ensured that, despite the ban, it became a 'best-seller'. As Liu Bingyan wryly remarked: 'This "device" [claiming to be the work of a foreign author] enabled the book to become quite a hit within China itself and that was one reason for the use of the *nom-de-plume*. If a foreigner wrote it, even if it was a Chinese person mimicking foreign habits, it would mean that, firstly, they could speak a little more freely and, secondly, most Chinese would think it more objective, *because it was a foreigner speaking*. For this reason, the *Third Eye* is blue eyed and that proves to be a lot more popular than brown eyes.'[3]

The controversy around authorship aside, the work does express a strong line on the floating population and it is this that is excerpted. The chapter on peasant movement begins by briefly sketching the history of the peasant in China. It focuses particularly on the Maoist period and the Party's relationship with the peasantry. It then moves on to the Deng era and suggests that the problems of policing the peasantry are even more acute in this era than they were in the past. It lists the reasons for this turn for the worse in the following manner …

The cover of Leuninger's *A Third Eye on China*.

3    Liu Binyan, 'A comment on *A Third Eye on China*', *Beijing Spring*, 17 (1994), 23–32. (Excerpt from p. 25)

## A THIRD EYE ON CHINA'S LIVING VOLCANO[4]
**LEUNINGER**

### A Peasant Flood

While the flow of peasants into the cities is necessary to help the economy grow, there are three factors that need to be watched.

The vast numbers of peasants flooding into the cities are not in proportion to the rate of economic development. So, apart from some cities, in most cases, the movement is not the result of the economic needs of these cities drawing in peasant labour power, but peasant labour needing to get into the cities. This, in turn, is reflected in the law needed and used to maintain the cities' economic order. Hence, the clash between the peasants and the law will become more heated and more regular. The speed of improvement of China's city residents' living standard and the general speed of economic development has been remarkably stable, but when it is compared with that of the income levels of the peasants, there is a marked contrast. Hence, when peasants first enter the city, all they can do is feel envious, inferior and impatient. This even reaches the point where they develop a hate complex. This complex not only prevents them from gradually entering into city life, but can even lead them into crime.

Up until the present time, the Chinese government has failed to come up with an adequate policy with which to deal with this floating population. The policy is characterised by government attempts to block their movement, but they are doing it without really knowing how to dredge them out, without really having any means to do the job. Moreover, when it comes to the overall management and education of these itinerant workers from the countryside, the government has simply let things drift. The few remaining measures that are still effective are there only for incidents (such as violent social movements) where the police and army can be used to suppress things. But when the time is right, these trouble-makers will almost certainly begin yelling a series of political or purely economic slogans and this will be used to focus their political aims and change them into a force to get trouble started (because there are still hundreds of thousands of young intellectuals). The government will again suppress such a movement, but will it be fearless in the face of interference and opposition from the international community?

### The Crime Wave

A new and global crime wave besets our times. Crime is a social problem even though it varies in form, reflecting different social tensions. Some types of crime

---

4   Leuninger [German], *A Third Eye on China* [Trans. Wang Shan] (Shanxi People's Publishing House, 1994), 62–8.

are an inevitable consequence of rapid economic development, others symbolise temporary effects brought on by changes in the socio-economic landscape, still others clearly express sharp or unresolved contradictions which are internal to the society.

Because the Chinese authorities have not publicly released any statistics, at the moment it is really difficult to get a sense of the ratio of peasants charged with criminal offences as a proportion of overall criminal cases. Nevertheless, from ten newspapers on law that were openly on sale on the streets of Beijing in one month, one was able to get a full range of statistics. From these it became clear that the peasants, as an occupation group, accounted for over 70 per cent of all crime. On the basis of this, it is clear that peasant crime has already become a serious social problem in China.

## The Tendency for Basic Level Political Authority in Rural Areas to Disintegrate

The basic level of political power in rural China is made up of the Communist Party branch and the elected rural residents' village committee (the village head). These two pillars of the established order prop each other up. Because there is no longer any real ideological work being undertaken in the countryside and also because the mass-judgement activities (mass trials) that were once used to enable the expression of political opinions and ideologically educate the people about crime are no more, the authority of the Party at the basic level has been weakened. In many places, the Party branch exists in name only, and various attempts to revamp it so that it once again carries out its duties regarding the peasantry have all failed.

The village committees (village heads) have two tasks: one is to take responsibility for collecting the grain quota and all sorts of taxes, the other is to carry out governmental duties. These latter duties include providing material and financial support for rural areas in times of crisis or shortage. As a result of these duties, some people think that these positions can become a type of power base in the countryside. This leads to quite a few people vying for them. The consequence is that such posts are now often rotated or even given to those who are thought to be the kindliest. So, as a result of the freedom given to peasants to buy goods and materials, and market-based reforms that produced commodity pricing, there has been a significant lessening in government influence in rural areas.

By far the greatest danger facing China in this respect is that the peasants will use this new found freedom, and simply decide to leave the land, leave the place where they are registered and head blindly into the cities. Once there, they will find social relations operate differently to the countryside because everything is based on personal responsibility and freedom. For the peasants of China, there is still no establised social welfare system. Hence, leaving the place of household registration means leaving their welfare base. The dangers for peasants in doing this, quite apart from the possibility of being chased or apprehended by criminals, is that they lose all connection with their government-based support system and governmental agencies. This, then, is one of the causes of peasants and their businesses slipping into crime and, in times of turbulence, becoming latent factors leading to large-scale turbulence. In the move to the city, the peasants not only lose their social connections, but also lose any restraints upon their actions. In this process, they also have little else to lose and are therefore without fear.

## ★ PEASANT MOVEMENT: A POLICE PERSPECTIVE[5]
### YANG WENZHONG AND WANG GONGFAN

The 1989 statistics indicate that the floating population in Beijing now stands at 1.3 million as against 0.3 million in 1982, an annual increase of 0.2 million people. This trend is regarded as irreversible, for the ever-increasing immigrant population from rural into urban areas is but an effect of the open-door policy and the invigoration of the economy. Some government departments predict that the immigrants in Beijing will increase at an annual rate of 5 per cent and reach 2 million by the year 2000.

There are two things to be said about this floating population. On the one hand, such immigration helps invigorate the urban market economy and make the life of urban residents more convenient. Statistics show that 73.1 per cent of immigrants are employed in the trades or in business, and have already come to form an economically oriented temporary residential population of the city. They provide daily necessities to the city people to the tune of 450 million *yuan* ($US54 million) per year. In 1987 alone, the vegetable trade turnover reached 730 million *jin* (365 million kilograms). The Beijing commercial departments make about 1.5 million *yuan* ($US180,000) from these immigrants in economic profits. So, it is easy to see that the immigrants have made a sizeable contribution to the economic development of the Chinese capital. On the other hand, however, such a large number of immigrants have become a heavy burden on the city as well as a new problem for the public security forces.

One discovers that with each passing year the number of criminals tracked down in Beijing from within the ranks of the immigrants increases. From 18.5 per cent of criminals in 1986, it increased to 18.6 per cent in 1987 and then jumped to 24.6 per cent in 1988. Transient criminals in Beijing numbered 1362 in 1986, 1336 in 1987 and 2137 in 1988.

---

5  Yang Wenzhong and Wang Gongfan, 'The Influence of the Floating Population Upon Social Order', *Police Research*, 2 (1989), 52–3. [杨文忠, 王功藩, '流动人口对社会治安的影响', 《公安研究》.] The authors are from the Research Office of the Beijing Public Security Bureau.

Beijing currently has 4048 buses and trolley buses and 174 bus routes. In 1988, 1175 transient criminals were caught picking pockets on Beijing's buses and trolley buses. This constituted 60.8 per cent of the total number of transients arrested in that year and represented a 2.3 per cent increase over 1987.

Additionally, the number of detained and convicted transients and transients sent by Beijing public security units to other areas for reform through education has also shown a notable increase. There was a rise of 39 per cent in the number of such people between 1985 and 1986, while the 1987 figures indicate a further rise of 32.5 per cent.[6]

The transient criminals are easily recognised by the following characteristics:

1.  Their crimes are mainly in the economic and financial field. Since 1987, when Beijing launched campaigns against law-breaking activities harmful to the on-going reforms, 50 per cent of all those convicted were transients. Some of them were very serious cases indeed. Two cigarette merchants from Qingdao in Shandong province came to Beijing and, with just one trip, illegally sold more than 80 crates of famous-brand cigarettes worth more than 60,000 *yuan* ($US7300). Several felons from Qian'an in Hebei province bought from the Beijing free markets grain ration coupons with a face value of over 400,000 *jin*. They then used these to purchase 420,000 *jin* of rice and wheat flour which they illegally resold in Hebei markets for a profit of 12,000 *yuan* ($US1400). One criminal gang was found to be specialising in forging train tickets. In just one year, they turned out more than 2100 false tickets and sold them, netting a profit of 31,000 *yuan* ($US3700). All these law-breaking activities have seriously affected the economic construction in Beijing.

2.  Criminal gangs stand out. Investigations into transient criminals at the Beijing railway station in 1987 led to the discovery of eighteen criminal gangs involving some 27 persons. One gang from Panshi county in Jilin province came to Beijing and specialised in illegal cigarette trading. They had 'connections' which enabled them to buy, store, transport and sell cigarettes. Every deal they made yielded, on average, a 1000 *yuan* ($US120) profit. When the gang was finally tracked down, more than 7000 packets of famous-brand cigarettes worth 6700 *yuan* ($US800) were discovered.

3.  In the process of reform, new social contradictions continuously emerge and those with particular resentments or ill will head to the capital in order to wreak revenge on society. They often make quite deliberate trips to the capital and, once there, involve themselves in violent crimes which they hope will have significant political repercussions. In 1987, for example, a Hubei man by the name of Deng Qilin made two abortive, and one successful,

---

6   What Yang and Wang are pointing to here is the treatment of this group by means of administrative detention rather than criminal detention.

attempt to set off bombs in Tiananmen Square in the centre of Beijing. In August 1988, a coastal guard from the naval air force base in Liaoning province came to Beijing with a stolen 54-calibre pistol and attempted to commit violent criminal acts. Nothing came of this though, because he was detected and caught by police patrols.

Apart from this, it is also important to note the increase in the number of cases of visitors or non-residents being attacked, which has now reached the point of becoming a serious problem. Business people who carry with them huge sums of money, traders and young women who blindly enter the cities in search of employment and have no relatives in these cities to turn to, all prove easy targets for criminal gangs. In 1987, there were 586 robberies and thefts of this type reported. In the first nine months of 1988, this had risen to 684 cases.

Sociologists believe that it is a normal occurrence and tendency for people to immigrate into urban areas during a process of industrialisation. They also recognise that it is one factor leading to disturbances and social disorder in the urban areas. As a result, when Western scholars examine the problems of crime, floating populations are invariably noted as one important factor. They argue that in the process of industrialisation, large numbers of peasants who are poorly prepared for urban life head to the cities in search of work. Once there, they discover that there are few jobs available and few places to reside. The conditions for criminal activities are thus created. One contemporary American criminologist, Louis Shelly states, in his book *Crime and Modernization*, that 'criminal offences can be tied back to the transition from "small collectives" to "big societies". When people leave the traditional and stable family life behind and join the impersonal, capricious and unpredictable lifestyles of the urban dweller a transition takes place.' He adds that, 'In any capitalist countries where no control is exercised over urban immigration, the most urbanized areas record the highest rate of crime.'

In China, the migration of rural labour into urban areas is an inevitable outcome of the open-door policy, and a natural tendency brought on by the deepening of the reform process and the invigoration of the economy. While, in essence, this is quite different from the way the process took place in the capitalist countries, it should, nevertheless, be noted that the large numbers of immigrants entering Beijing have raised security problems in that city and that these problems are both serious and complicated. From the situation we have outlined, and the statistics quoted, it is not difficult to understand that there are increasing numbers of problems relating to public security, that there are very significant increases in the urban crime rate, and that all of these things correspond to the rise in the number of rural immigrants. In the period when society was not open, the crimes committed by the floating population were not as obvious as they are today. This is simply a fact of life. At present, China is in an historic period of transition, from an old to a new development phase. Before new administrative mechanisms can be established, it is hard to imagine that the public security problems which have arisen as a result of the floating population will be solved.

Strengthening management over the floating population will lead to increased efficiency in the control of crime, reduce the number of security problems, and defend and promote the smooth progress of reform. This is a new item on the agenda of organs concerned with public security. In view of the situation in Beijing, it has been initially decided that the management of the floating population should be strengthened and improved in the following ways:

1. Stricter law enforcement.
2. Continue to strengthen the management of key areas. The non-Beijing construction teams, rental accommodation and labour markets are three areas where the floating population tends to congregate. Because of the high mobility of people in these three areas, they prove very difficult places to administer. Beijing has devoted special efforts to the management of these areas.
3. Gradually socialising the administration of this sector. Strengthening the management of the floating population is not only the preserve of public security departments. It should employ a multi-tiered system which offers different management styles and different forms of administration all operating under the principle of 'the chief officer takes the lead' (*shei zhuguan, shei fuze*) and under the guidance of the municipal government.
4. Strengthen control over downtown areas. Police patrols should be introduced in downtown areas in line with the principle of 'police having beats'.
5. Establish a management structure for the floating population over the entire municipal area.

# 2

# GOVERNMENT
# STRATEGIES (1)

As millions of peasants head into the cities of China, most have in their pockets and wallets small plastic cards with a barcode at the base and a name and a face on the surface. The first major reform of the household registration laws since 1949 gave birth to this item, the residency identity card. It must be carried by every citizen at all times. Here was a new approach to the policing of populations. No longer would the population be held in check in their place of birth. With this card, the ability to check was made mobile. Each card would be tied via a number at the bottom of the card to a registration file, and each file would tell a life story. Millions of peasants with millions of stories, summarised on a barcode and carried around in their pockets. An outline of this new technology of biography, that enables a life story to be reduced to a numerical code, begins this section.

Yet this pocket portable file, while proving to be an aid to police as they attempt to monitor, control and limit population movement, is itself in need of augmentation. Zhou Daping's article on trial city levies on immigrants illustrates the type of augmentation some local governments are investigating and implementing. In the past, population was controlled by coercive policing strategies. Today, a market mentality is, in part, replacing certain aspects of this coercive style of the past. In the reform period, movement and residency are secured by monetary expenditure. In today's China, profits can be made out of migration. The map of China is in danger of becoming an index of wealth. Only those with an income can move into the cities and those with an income invariably have work. The gypsy, the transient, the beggar, they are the ones refused. The 'pincer movement' continues and gets sharper as a new category of acceptable migrant emerges. The new acceptable immigrant carries two 'name cards', one being the obligatory identity card in their wallet, the other, the dollar bills that sit next to it.

Once in the city, they are policed by a regime which still bears the hallmarks of Maoism. Mass-line approaches to community policing are 'augmented' by local neighbourhood security groups that support police actions and maintain daily order. A vast network of police stations is supported by an even greater number of mass-line citizen groups. The story of one model police station (Beef Street) and one neighbourhood committee (Weikeng) allows us a glimpse of how the story line is supposed to continue. In the next section, we will have an opportunity to see how such strategies can also go awry.

## THE RESIDENT IDENTITY CARD AND THE HOUSEHOLD REGISTER[1]
### ZHANG QINGWU

### Regulations Governing the Resident Identity Card

On 6 September 1985, the 'Regulations governing the resident identity card of the People's Republic of China' (henceforth referred to as the Regulations) were approved by the Standing Committee of the Sixth National People's Congress and simultaneously promulgated by the State president. There were twenty articles in all. The formulation of these regulations enabled residents to legally establish their identity.

On the basis of these Regulations, any citizen who resides within the boundaries of the People's Republic, and is over the age of sixteen, should apply for a resident identity card. Identity cards for active service personnel and for the armed police will be arranged by the military and police departments respectively. Foreigners or stateless persons who reside within the boundaries of the People's Republic do not fall under this legislation.

The resident identity card registers a range of items including one's name, sex, nationality, date of birth and address. On the basis of age, the expiry date of cards will vary. There are three expiry dates: one which occurs after ten years, another after twenty, and a third which offers long-term use. These cards will be printed, distributed and managed in a unified fashion by the public security organs. In the course of carrying out their regular duties, security organs have the right to check and examine a resident's identity card.

When a citizen is carrying out certain activities which require them to identify themselves or prove their political, economic and social rights and responsibilities, then they can produce their resident identity card. However, a work unit may not seize a card or take a person's card as a form of insurance. Any such breaches of the regulations will be dealt with on the basis of the severity of the breach, and, on the basis of the law, administrative punishments will be enacted or the matter will be examined to ascertain the level of criminal culpability.

Why did China decide to introduce this resident identity card system? Article one of the Regulations clearly allows us to answer this: 'In order to guarantee a resident's status, make social intercourse easier for a citizen, protect social order and guarantee the appropriate legal rights and interests of the citizen'. The implementation of the resident identity card system is an act of enormous importance for China's one billion people. On the basis of past practices, it was possible to identify one's occupation, unit and place of work by using one's work card or a

---

1 Zhang Qingwu, *A Handbook on the Household Register* (Beijing: Masses Press, 1987), 116–19; 124. 〔张庆五，《户籍手册》.〕 Zhang Qingwu is the head of the population research centre in the Chinese Public Security University in Beijing.

letter of introduction. For city residents, it was even possible to use the household registration book. However, because the workbooks and letters of introduction came in all shapes and sizes, there was no unified system of identification. Such materials could only be used in special, limited ways for they did not offer a comprehensive form of identification, nor did they have any legal standing. Moreover, such documentation was easily altered, forged or modified to hide one's original identity and so they were of great benefit to criminal elements. In fact, in many ways, the system itself helped criminals to cover their tracks. The problem for work units receiving such documentation was that even when they were faced with documents which appeared suspicious, it was difficult to ascertain within a limited time period the truth of the matter. It was therefore much easier for them to simply give a person the benefit of the doubt. This reached the point whereby such forms of documentation led to large-scale paralysis, with many people and units being cheated or tricked and great harm being caused. The household register was little better. There was only one volume for every household and that volume only had a legal status in the area of issuance. The register also proved cumbersome for those who wished to carry it. From the above, then, it is fairly clear that any attempt to use the household register or a letter of introduction as a means by which to identify a citizen was really inappropriate. Nor does this method of identification help in the management of the population. Hence, in order to prove a citizen's identity, make social intercourse easier and guarantee a citizen's legal rights and interests, it has been both necessary and imperative for the State to introduce the resident identity card which has a unified legal status and effect. The implementation of the resident identity card system constitutes an important reform of the household registration management system. It allows for professional skills to be effectively developed in the task of managing the household register; it offers even more protection to the social order; it allows citizens the means by which to protect their rights and interests and it serves socialist construction.

With the promulgation of the resident identity card, some people have even questioned whether this will lead to the abolition of the household registration book. From the perspective of household registration work, however, it can be said that even though the resident identity card is a unified national document issued throughout the nation, it cannot fully replace the register. This is because, in dealing with the problems of contemporary life, the household register could be used to fulfil the role of the resident identity card but it would be quite difficult for the reverse to occur.

1. The household registration book can verify the registered address of family household members; it can be of use in distinguishing city and town registration from that of rural household registration, it can be used to differentiate agricultural from non-agricultural workers, and it can be used as a basis by which to confirm the relations of registered family members—pointing out their different occupations, educational level and so on.

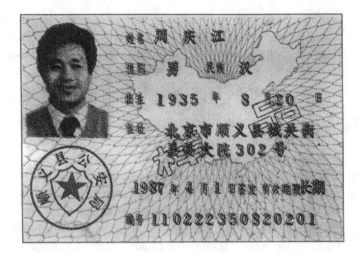

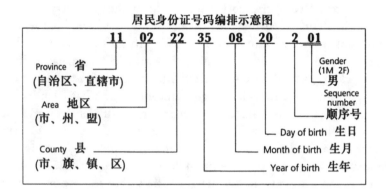

Codes used in resident identity cards.

2. The household register is still used as the basis for city administrative planning and supply calculations. For example, in the supply of basic rationed foodstuffs, in the allocation of housing stock and in the supply of coal for daily city life, it is the register which forms the basis of all calculations.

3. The State still has not promulgated a unified and legally binding form of birth certificate and therefore, the identity certificate of family members who are below the age of sixteen years is still based upon the household registration book. This is exemplified by the fact that for all children who wish to attend creche, kindergarten or school or who enjoy public welfare facilities, the necessary certification of a child's age and all such forms of certification, if they are legally binding, are based upon the birth date recorded on the register.

4. Population statistics which use the registered items given in the household registration book all come from the original material which was transcribed on to the register. Hence vital statistics, such as the number of households in the nation, the overall population, its sex and age, birth and death rates all come from this source.

5. From the material recorded in the household registration book about the household head and the relationship the head has with other household members, it is possible to analyse the scope of any household, to study the differences in form and structure which exist between households, and to note changes in the composition of the family. It is also possible to investigate single-person households and study why and how they departed from their original residence. It is possible to investigate how long they have been away and, in this respect, examine the relationship between the household register and people's life. All such data would emanate from the material recorded in the household registration book.

According to the above analysis, then, it is clear that the resident identity card cannot replace the household registration book. It is likely that, for a very long time to come, these two items will be operating alongside each other.

## REGISTRATION FILES, REGISTRATION CARDS
### YU LEI

### Household Registration Files[2]

Within the household registration system the household registration file constitutes an important professional item. It is necessary that every person have a household registration file and that it be divided into an original and duplicate copy. The original material may be provided to external bodies who may use it for a variety of ends, including drawing upon it as legal documentation in relation to a range of problems. Material on the original register may be valuable as a form of certifiable data relating to investigations or as evidential material about particular persons and confessions they may have made. Additionally, it may be of use as material to help with examinations undertaken which relate to particular persons or it may be of help in offering relevant data and material relating to a person's political and historical backgrounds which are under investigation and require verification. The duplicate material should be made available only to public security units. The material on the duplicate volume will include reference to assessments made about particular persons in any mass denunciation or any type of

---

2  Yu Lei (ed.), *The Study of Public Security Administrative Management* (Beijing: China's Public Security University Press, 1987), 91–2. 〔俞雷, （主编） 《治安行政管理学总论》。〕 Yu Lei is the former deputy minister of Public Security.

material which exposes them, as well as any other registration material or registration documents which have been written for internal use only. Indeed, systems need to be established with which to police the transmission, consultation and storage of records.

## Population Registration Cards

In the cities, the units in charge of city household registration establish a system based upon individuals which itemises the household register. This is called the population registration card. It is administered by a centralised management structure put in place by the city's Public Security Bureau Household Registration Management Department. It is handled on the basis of a scientific arrangement of materials, which allows for both management and easy access to materials needed in any investigation or search. Hence it is of great use as a means of enquiring into the general circumstances of the population. It can be utilised in the following manner:

1. In coordinating the struggle against the enemy, it can be used to check up and investigate, and locate the whereabouts of counter-revolutionary or criminal elements.
2. To help investigators from elsewhere track down the whereabouts and general situation of a person under investigation.
3. To help overseas Chinese, people from Hong Kong, Macao or Taiwan find their relatives.
4. To help other departments locate the address of residents. This could include aiding the postal department locate the addresses of people whose mail has been addressed inadequately or wrongly and other such things.
5. After the population card system has been properly instituted, it can be used to cross-check household registration details, locating strengths, weaknesses, errors and omissions and, in this way, improve the quality of the management system.

Along with scientific and technical developments and the reform of the household registration system, in 1985, China introduced the resident identity card system. This was a very significant reform in household registration management and also in public security administration, which could be tightened up as a result. The card system allowed for a person's status to be easily determined and proven; it enabled the monitoring of the floating population, the strengthening of the management over temporary residents; and limits could be placed on any possible criminal activity caused by transient criminals. As a result, the methods used in the work of investigating such things as the genuine names and addresses of criminal elements were greatly facilitated.

## BEIJING'S FEE FOR RESIDENCY SCHEME

On 8 September 1994, the twelfth meeting of the Beijing City People's Congress passed local legislation levying fees upon all those who applied for permanent residency in the Beijing city area. The levy was to go into effect in November of that year and be put on trial for a year. The fee scale was significant in so far as it signalled that restriction by cost was now at the forefront of thinking. For that reason, the scale is worth detailing in full:

|  | Fee per head (flat fee) |
|---|---|
| For ten or more people | $100,000 RMB ($US12,048) |
| Inner-city or inner-suburban residency | $50,000 RMB ($US6022) |
| Outer suburban, county, town area residency | $20,000 RMB ($US2409) |
| Residency in outer county or rural area | $10,000 RMB ($US1204) |

When asked why such local legislation was needed, Sun Jiaqi, the then head of the Beijing Finance Bureau replied that migration was proving a massive strain on city resources. By 1992, the city was growing by about 100,000 people per year and 75 per cent of these people were migrants. Controls were needed because infrastructural conditions and the supply of basic necessities could not keep pace with this growth rate. Sun insisted, however, that money alone would not buy entry. People who had specialised skills needed in the city, those who held a Masters or doctorate degree, or those who, for other reasons, were supported by the city government, would be granted an 80 per cent reduction in fees. Moreover, a range of other special exemptions were put into effect.[3]

Concerns and disquiet about this trial legislation remained and, behind the scenes, much debate ensued.[4] The police pointed out that it actually complicated the already-difficult task of getting people to register. The fee was so high, that even otherwise honest people would dodge registration and this would complicate their jobs enormously. Others complained it would cut off useful human resources. Still others saw it as anti-Constitutional.

Irrespective of the veracity of these criticisms, or the duration of the life of this legislation, it is significant in that it points to a kind of 'commodification' of residency. Later on, we will look at the new 'nationalities theme park' where, for the price of an entry ticket, one can partake in the national imagining. Here, we see an even more dramatic example of this commodification of society with the capital city itself becoming the desired theme park and the cost of entry being the price one has to pay to achieve residency rights. The reified and desired address, the place where commodities are fully on display—these are the places where the fees are highest and only those who purchase a ticket have the right to partake in the new imaginings.

---

3 Information drawn from *Legal Daily*, 25 September 1994, 1 and *Beijing Daily*, 1 November 1994, 3.
4 Interviews, 6 February 1995.

## USER PAYS BEIJING[5]

**ZHOU DAPING**

In recent years it can hardly be called news that cities have begun to levy fees for outsiders wishing to reside there; nevertheless the capital, Beijing, has been unique in that it has passed a local regulation restricting and limiting the entry of inter-provincial cadres and graduates into the capital. This new regulation-limiting residency makes Beijing the first city in China to officially levy a living allowance fee, and puts it right at the centre of a major debate.

On 22 November 1994, some 21 days after the government had passed the 'Regulations concerning the levying of fees for those who wish to reside in Beijing', they were faced with some very different opinions about its worth. Therefore, in the leadership spirit shown by the Central Committee Office, the local government decided to open up discussion on the issue by firstly inviting comment on their new rules from a number of representatives of the National People's Congress and some local Central Committee and Ministerial Committee members. What they were interested in was how to police this new regulation, but what they got was a heated argument and the meeting broke up in discord. In fact, even now, there is not one aspect of this legislation that can be agreed on.

### Beijing is Not Just a Capital City of Beijing People

Recently, the head of the finance bureau in Beijing, Sun Jiaqi, explained the ratio-nale behind the levying of fees on residents who were not from Beijing. In recent years, the city's population growth has risen dramatically and, in this process of large-scale change, there is an increasing contradiction between the city's overall needs and what can be supplied. There are very real limits on natural and social resources, which are strained, and therefore do not allow for an appropriate level of allocation. This is especially true in relation to basic resources like water, elec-tricity, gas, heating, roads, communications, education, health care and housing. An unsuitably rapid growth rate would lead to the Beijing economy and the live-lihood of its residents being put at risk. In order to control population increases brought on by immigration, there is a need for certain administrative procedures to be adopted that can be supplemented by economic ones. With this new measure in place, it has been calculated that in one year alone, the Beijing city government will gain between 200 and 300 million *yuan* ($US240,900–361,450), and this can then be allocated in a concentrated manner to help improve and provide basic city infrastructure.

This type of thinking, which advantages the residents and takes them into consideration, is very admirable, but is it logical? A number of scholars have very

5   Zhou Daping, 'Levying a Fee for Residing in Beijing: Reasons for the Surge in Beijing's Population', *Outlook*, 51 (1994): 8–9. 〔周大平，'征收城市容纳费－北京缘何起波澜'，《了望》。〕

quickly discovered some problems. Controlling the population increases and obtaining the living allowance fee are in actual fact two quite separate issues. If limitations are placed on the provincially registered population who wish to re-settle in Beijing, then one will not get the fee. If the fee is able to be collected, it then means that the population is still on the increase.

A specialist from the Ministry of Labour analysed it in this way: even if one could assume that this regulation could limit the number of immigrants, the question would then have to be asked, what kind of people are being denied settlement in Beijing? The 'fee annulment method' makes it quite clear that those people with a Beijing household register who are forced to leave the city to study, are conscripted into the army or who go overseas to study, are entitled to fee annulment. With this provision, it is clear that the only ones who will be affected by these regulations which are designed to limit the growth of the population are those who would otherwise be suitable candidates from other parts of the country to migrate to Beijing. Moreover, because the residency fee is set so high people who are not wealthy lose hope, shrinking at the mere sight of it.

China's People's University student section head, Su Zhangqing, thinks that Beijing is not only for Beijing people but is the political, economic and cultural centre for the whole country, and therefore in need of more specialist human resources. All aspects of employment development in Beijing are inextricably linked to the various skills and contributions available. Song Qiusheng, the deputy director of the labour allocation section of the Academy of Sciences, confirmed that of the scientists at the Academy, two-thirds come from outside Beijing. Every year they receive some 500 to 600 specialists and 90 per cent are from other parts of the country.

According to the Beijing City Higher Education Bureau, there are close to 20,000 postgraduates who come to Beijing from other places to settle in the capital. Based on the enforcement measures of this regulation, Beijing graduates will be offered greater employment opportunities, but a work unit's ability to choose the best talent will be infringed because they won't have the ability to choose outsiders.

In the current economic reform period, one of the key factors acting as a restriction upon economic development is a lack of talented people. In higher education institutions, salaries are very low indeed. Consequently, every year there are less and less people willing to do the work. In this climate, utilising measures to try to control the entry of outstanding talent into the cities is not really a very sensible measure.

## The Problem of Tighter Measures

Any reform measures, if they neglect to take note of the various positive and negative aspects, will fail. When the Beijing People's Congress passed the 'Regula-tions severely restricting the rearing of dogs' on 30 November 1994, they did so after wide-ranging consultation with many Beijing residents. In direct contrast to this, and despite the fact that it took two years to draft and discuss, the 'Regulations concerning the levying of fees for those who wish to reside in Beijing' clearly lacked satisfactory or adequate discussion with the appropriate people or work units that would be affected. This lack of planning has resulted in lost opportunities to discuss the levy and introduce limits and moderate the amounts of money demanded. Such carelessness has not only led to this embarrassing regulation being passed, but it has also led to it being virtually unenforceable. Moreover, the regulation is in conflict with a range of other policies.

On the basis of reports, the first places to actually start levying charges on immigrants who wanted city residency were Tianjin and Shanghai. From 1986 and 1987 respectively, these two places began to levy a fee on all incoming migrants who wanted long-term residency. The fee levied in Tianjin was 20,000 *yuan* ($US2409), while Shanghai levied 50,000 *yuan* ($US6024). This money was used in city infrastructural development. After that, cities like Changsha and Shenzhen also adopted these sorts of administrative measures. But all of these cities adopted measures that shared one common characteristic: they all issued exemptions for any out-of-town university graduates who chose to migrate to their city.

Within legal circles, it is said that Beijing is the first city to utilise local legal forms to put such fees into effect. In using legally devised measures to implement this, Beijing is actually leading the way. Moreover, as the capital, it will naturally be something of a model for all other centres. Indeed, it is known that, at present, six other cities have already followed Beijing's lead. The key point of the arguments that have been raised in discussions against these measures so far is the possibility that, along with limiting the population of the city, the measures will also operate to restrict the inward flow of talent. But one expert from the Ministry of Labour took another position. He argued that one of the effects would be that a lot of people who were unable to pay this fee would simply avoid household registration altogether and this would have a serious deleterious effect upon the management of the household register. At the same time, it also ran counter to the attempts to use the household-register-based identity card system as a basis to institute a system of monitoring the mobile population. The outcome is unlikely to be of use in limiting the population that was originally denied settlement in Beijing and will probably limit a work unit's ability to pick up talent.

If this legislation goes ahead from the State's finance section to attach what is a 'head-hunting fee' (*rentoufei*), then Party Committees, government ministries and enterprises will all be placed in a rather invidious situation. Both the organisational departments responsible for the annual transfer of tens of thousands of cadres from around the country into Beijing and the Personnel Ministry have made the same point: the central authorities and the various ministerial committees have no financial means to pay the fees being levied. But if the State centre's finances do not increase allocations by hundreds of millions of dollars to cover the costs incurred, then this measure will influence the development of central organs of State political power. Qinghua University, in a submission requesting the Beijing government to waive the fee, wrote that, on the basis of their calculations, something like 20,000 *yuan* $US2409) per person would be required to cover the fees for the relocation of people in Beijing. This cost, when added to the cost of teacher training and teacher replacement, would amount to an overall cost of 6 million *yuan* ($US722,891) annually, and Qinghua University was in no position to carry such a heavy financial burden.

Essentially, what the drafters of this legislation have not taken into account is the way it would attack Beijing's ability to train and attract the highly talented. It appears no one seemed to know that the State Council had already passed legislation ensuring that doctorate graduates should not be limited in their choice of employment, place of employment or household registration. How do these Beijing measures tally with this? In the meantime, the number of students going overseas or heading off to Shenzhen or Shanghai is increasing dramatically. Zhang Guaying, who is the deputy director of student management of the Beijing University Graduate Studies Institute, expressed regret at the fact that many of the most outstanding graduates were enquiring into, or applying for, study overseas because they could not meet the costs of this levy. A number of professors in basic research areas are concerned about the limited possibilities for graduate employment in Beijing as a result of this fee, and wonder what effect this will have on student entry next year.

## THE 'BILL' OF BEEF STREET[6]

To the south of Beijing city sits a mosque which is one thousand years old. This mosque is located in the Beef Street area, which is an area made up predominantly of the Islamic Hui nationality Chinese with Han and Man nationalities. Mongolian people make up the remainder of the population. For a long time now, these various nationalities have lived together peacefully, creating an auspicious and harmonious place and a healthy atmosphere. The officers at the local police station are charged with the responsibility of looking after the household registration and of the public security management of this area. They have utilised honest administration and a love of the people as a means by which to carefully administer things for the people. In eighteen years there have been no breaches of discipline, and the reputation of the Beef Street station is known far and wide.

Beef Street station has 51 officers. Since 1985, the station officers have been collectively cited, once for 'meritorious conduct second class', and five times for

6   'A Report From the Beijing City Public Security Bureau Beef Street Station', *People's Public Security Newspaper*, 9 December 1993, p. 1. [《人民公安报》. ]

Scene from Beef Street

'meritorious conduct, third class'. For the past four years, the station has been named by city and district governments as a 'unit with an advanced sense of spiritual civilisation', and it has twice been named a 'collective vanguard in the unity of nationalities' by the city and district. Moreover, it is an 'advanced unit for honest administration and love of the people'.

If you want to think about bringing forth a team with mastery over any situation, you must firstly think about the strength of the leadership group. Over the past eighteen years, leadership at this station has changed hands, but no matter who has been the leader, they have always grasped the ideological issues, and stressed unity and cooperation. They have stressed being clear, upright, maintaining and protecting the tradition of taking the lead, and acting as a good example. They take the lead and act as good examples, by vigorously doing all the work before them and working exhaustively on all the duties they face. They have strictly abided by the 'six points' which are:

1. Get to work early.
2. Leave late.
3. When eating, go to the rear (of any queue).
4. Decline any offers which may lead to a compromising situation.
5. Help each other out in work.
6. Fairly mete out justice.

No matter whether it was blisteringly hot or freezing cold, the leaders of this station, for many years, turned up half an hour early for work each day and, if they discovered that a task hadn't been completed by the time work was due to end, they would work that little bit extra. In the last three years, the station leaders have collectively worked more than 500 days per year. The leaders all help one another within the station and, when tasks are decided upon, they are strictly implemented; no-one pulls the rug from under anybody else or 'white-ants' someone behind their back.

Because the station's financial situation is precarious it received offers of bits and pieces from units outside the precinct and from the masses who are keen to help resolve some of their needs. But station leaders have always refused such 'good intentions'. Hence, there are two or three officers to one room and, while on duty, they must rest in the reception room of the household registration office, which has absolutely no creature comforts.

'Love the police, love the profession and love Beef Street' is the shared understanding of police officers at the Beef Street Station. Because the predominant residential population of Beef Street are of the Hui nationality, the people's police officers in this precinct all study the Party's policy on national minorities and all take classes so that they can cultivate an understanding of the customs and habits of the Hui. Most of the officers on the staff of the station are Han Chinese, but they all believe that 'when in Rome, one must do as the Romans do' (*ruxiang suisu*) and the station persists with opening only a Hui nationality kitchen and respecting Hui customs.

The mosque is the holy site at the centre of the hearts of Hui people, and the police station has put in enormous effort, working its fingers to the bone for the mosque. It regularly helps to wash out the mosque, provide it with firewood, sweep out the courtyard and clean the toilets. The Hui nationality are a much respected and ancient people. After the old people go to the mosque and find that it is clean and tidy, they are extremely happy and, consequently they are really effusive in their praise of the police whom they say are polite and understanding of their customs.

At Beef Street Station, the household registration office is the station's 'civilised window' (*wenming chuangkou*), and on the wall hangs the opinion box, the comments book, a road and rail map, a map of the streets of the area, as well as household registration rules and a place for public notices. Above the entrance still hangs the slogan 'serve the people' and, in 1990 alone, they actively registered an extra 870 people as new residents of the area. The nineteen officers who patrol beats in the precinct have also set aside a special time to aid the 56 people in the area who are old and lonely. They help them wash their clothes and clean the floors. They get coal for their stoves and, at festive times, they come to greet them. They take them to the hospital to seek sick friends, and they ensure that the old are taken out to have a good time and, at the same time, make sure they are warm. For the rest of the masses, the station also helps to resolve disputes. Thus far it has helped resolve 3000 cases, received over twenty silk banners and 200 letters of praise.

To be a police officer all one's life means being honest and upright for one's entire life. There are in excess of 100 officers working at this station, yet for the past eighteen years, there have been no reports of ill discipline. There have been over 900 invitations to dinner and offers of presents, but all such offers have been turned down. Among the offers made was one worth 40,000 *yuan* ($US4819) and some 130 gifts. In 1992, the entire station handled some 100 cases and all of these were dealt with according to due legal process.

In the eyes of the masses, you cannot separate the station from the smashing of criminal cases and the arrest of bad elements. So for the people at the Beef Street Station, they believe they can best express their love for the people by ensuring that the management of the precinct guarantees good social order. In recent years, the station has mastered their basic duties, developed comprehensive security management, promoted and strengthened mass defence and mass security (groups), and actively attacked criminal activity, resulting in the social order of this precinct being very good indeed and the masses feeling safe and satisfied.

## Strict Management and Caring and Protection

In the work of management, the station's leaders persevere with diligence in patrolling, in keeping watch, being circumspect in speech and careful in management. In one instance, two officers at the station worked day and night for five days to crack one particularly serious case of car theft. When finally caught, the criminal was very abusive, and these two officers, being quite indignant at this, pushed the prisoner around a little. When the leaders heard about this, even though the infringement was minor, they did not cover for the officers. So at the same time as they were being congratulated for cracking the case, they were severely reprimanded for their erroneous actions and made to write a report and take responsibility for their actions.

At the same time as advocating strict management, the station leaders also actively encourage officers to help mediate disputes and to help resolve concrete problems faced by the people in daily life and, in this way, the officers of the station become more 'human' and are almost accepted as part of the 'family'. Because station officers cannot leave their posts and be with their families and relatives on New Year's Day and other festive occasions, the station leaders invite the families and relatives to visit the station on such occasions so that these people are given an account of life at the station. This has been successful, with the families all sharing a meal together. The officers all say that life for them is the collective life.

## MASS-LINE POLICING: WEIKENG PUBLIC SECURITY COMMITTEE, BEIJING[7]

### FENG RUI

Since 1978, the Weikeng public security committee of Xicheng district in Beijing has mobilised and organised the masses so that public security work is more effectively executed. From that time onwards, there have been no reports of criminal cases or public security incidents in that area.

Additionally, there was a drop in the number of juveniles[8] committing crimes, from 60 in 1978 to the 1988 figure of five. The number of civil disputes also dropped by 35 per cent between 1981 and 1982. Currently there have been only fifteen cases and all of these have been promptly and satisfactorily resolved through mediation. Hence the masses say: 'To live in Weikeng means one can safely go to work and feel free to walk the streets, one does not have to worry about locking doors in this place'. The success of Weikeng rests upon the following important factors.

## Mobilising the Masses

The public security committee is an important link between the public security units and the masses. Therefore, they must never separate themselves from the masses while working on public security matters. In the last few years, members of the public security committee have worked hard and surmounted many difficulties to help the masses resolve various problems. They have, among other things, made arrangements to supply lunches to the children of parents who go out to work, and they have helped parents find and employ nannies for their infants and youngsters. They have contacted the department in charge of housing when repairs are needed to the houses of residents in their area, and they have helped sick people get to the hospital. The old, single, widowed residents of

---

7 'The Weikeng Public Security Committee of Beijing mobilises the masses in security surveillance and prevention work', *Reports on the Experiences of the Work of the Social Order Committees* (Beijing: Masses Press, 1984), 5–8. [ '北京市苇坑治保会发动群众搞好安全防范工作' ，《治安保卫委员会工作经验汇编》。]

8 The term juvenile (*qing shaonian*) in Chinese is quite ambiguous but generally means those persons between the ages of 14 to 25. For further elaboration of the difficulty of definition see Feng Rui, 'One must pay attention to a number of limits in handling under-age crime', in *Yearbook of Chinese Juvenile Delinquency Studies–1987* (Beijing: Spring and Autumn Press, 1988), 777. [ 冯锐，'处理未成年犯应注意的几个界限'，《中国青少年犯罪研究年鉴》。]

the area have been of special concern to them. For this group, public security committee personnel do many things such as installing fan heaters in their homes during winter and going out to the local store and buying them their Chinese cabbage.

There was one case of an old woman of about seventy years of age who lived together with her two grandsons on East Xinjiekou street and whose son had gone out to Shunyi county to work. This old woman had a recurring and fairly serious health problem which required periodic hospitalisation. Every time she needed to go to the hospital it was the comrades from the public security committee who came around with a small vehicle to ferry her there. She died last year and the public security committee then had a hand in helping her family to make the funeral arrangements. Touched by their support, her son said: 'It really is the case that you have been more caring of her than I.' Over a very long period of time, this committee has persistently done good deeds for the community and, as a result, they won the praise and support of the masses. Some of the masses said, 'We live and work safely because of these old ladies[9] and we would certainly lose out if they weren't around to keep an eye on things. We must give a lot of assistance to you if you need.' Numbers within the public security committee have also increased. In 1978, there were only 40 activists in this committee, whereas today there are some 225 people. Hence the 'ears' of the public security committee are clearer and its 'eyes' sharper.

## Organising Activists to Form Public Security Brigades

Conditions for the Weikeng public security committee are made difficult by the number of narrow streets, lanes and byways which crisscross this area. Yet their work is built upon a solid foundation. Prior to the Cultural Revolution, this particular public security committee was a 'red banner' winner. As such, it was widely regarded as an advanced unit in the public security field throughout Beijing. During the Cultural Revolution though, many of its members were persecuted, and not until the smashing of the 'Gang of Four' was the work of security and crime prevention once again put on a regular footing so that it became a powerful fighting force in the struggle against crime. The reasons for this being the case seem clear: firstly, the cadres of the leading group are united as one. There are five in responsible positions in the public security committee who take charge, the others act as deputies. Nevertheless, when it comes to work, it is all mutually coordinated and supported. Secondly, members of the public security committee have called upon the residents by going from door to door. They have thus merged themselves with the masses to become one force. In making

---

9  The neighbourhood committees are, more often than not, dominated by older female residents so much so that they were, in the past, often referred to as the 'old women's committee' (*lao taitai weiyuanhui* or *lao ma weiyuanhui*). Because many of these older women had bound feet they were, in some places, also referred to as 'the little feet brigade to track down and arrest people' (*xiaojiao zhenji dui*).

frequent calls upon various residents in the neighbourhood committee, activists are able to quickly discover, remedy and correct any loopholes or defects. Thirdly, the cadres and activists have a high sense of responsibility for the work of security and crime prevention. Among the members of the public security committee some are responsible for caring for handicapped family members while still others are responsible for the old and infirm. These people willingly put to one side their own personal concerns and work on this security committee for neither fame nor profit, despite the possibility of revenge attacks upon them by criminals.

A good example of this was when one activist, seventy-two-year-old Zhang Shuiying, while out on patrol, found some youngsters suspiciously standing in the doorway of a large courtyard. Just nearby, she discovered a further 20 to 30 of them, but this time she discovered they were armed with wooden clubs, daggers and firearms. She quickly realised that she had stumbled upon a gang fight and so she very resourcefully extricated herself and rushed back to the neighbourhood security committee and the local police station to put in a report. As a result of Zhang's report, the People's police were quickly dispatched to the scene of the incident and they arrived in time to stop a dangerous fight between hooligans.

## Strict Measures for Public Security and Crime Prevention

The Weikeng public security committee is organised into three detachments. The first detachment is made up of over 40 people who are allocated patrol duties. They, in turn, are sub-divided into seven teams and each of these is led by a head or one of the deputy heads of the neighbourhood committee when they go out on patrol. Over the last few years, these teams have continuously patrolled the area in all sorts of weather.

The second detachment organised by the Weikeng public security committee is made up of 123 residents who watch over household entrances and guard compounds. The basis of this work rests upon organising responsible persons to take charge of security within every compound household. Their job would be to keep an eye on things within the compound and promptly report any problems they discover.

The third detachment offers support and help to the committee when it carries out the work of crime prevention and maintenance of social order. This support group is made up of local retirees, those living in the area convalescing after illness, women at home looking after children, and other persons who take exercise or walk in the morning or in the evening. The Weikeng public security committee, by organising and using these three types of detachments, was able to build up a strict network of security and crime prevention personnel. It was also able to establish a system by which absenteeism could be checked up on. Moreover, it established the basis of a relation upon which comparisons and appraisals could be made and advanced persons and exemplary deeds cited and praised.

Another thing the public security committee did was to regularise and promote the four measures of prevention or *sifang* as they are known in

Chinese.[10] This has been made possible because of the education and propaganda spread through various meetings, both large and small, which are combined with hygiene checks. Additionally, educating and propagandising the masses have also been achieved by other means such as utilising street blackboard newspapers, slogans, posters and slide shows. Through these means, the level of vigilance of the masses is raised, their respect for the socialist legal system grows, and they more fully comply with existing social ethics and morals.

In order to more fully develop the public security work, cadres select a number of typical cases which are useful in the education of the masses and heighten their sense of struggle as well as their skills. In bringing the masses into play in the implementation of the four measures of prevention work, particularly close attention is paid by the security committee to seizing hold of the focal point and carrying them over into all areas of work. They very often get together with the People's police to analyse the local situation with regard to public order and determine any distinguishing features displayed by the criminal. Through this type of investigation, it was discovered that most burglary cases occurred in compounds which were empty, or where the houses faced the road or the lane, or where the house was unoccupied during the day. Hence, upon analysis they discovered that 36 compound households in the area fitted this description. Consequently, these compound households became the focal point of their work. Special personnel were dispatched to keep guard over these houses and security patrols were required to include them on their tours of duty. The result was that these loopholes were plugged up very effectively.

Before 1978, people used to park their bicycles in any old way and didn't worry too much about locking them. This was especially true of bicycles parked in front of Jishuitan Hospital, or in front of the local grocery shops, restaurants or food shops. Consequently, many of these bicycles were stolen. Weikeng public security committee focused on key areas and immediately organised propaganda on this issue, regulated the parking arrangements and demanded that all riders lock their bicycles. As a result, the past five years have been free of bicycle thefts.

## Expending Effort to Educate and Help Transform Juveniles who Have Gone Astray

The first thing to note is that these juveniles should not be shunned or discriminated against. Rather, the public security committee cares for them as if they were their parents, providing help and education so that the juveniles realise the error of their ways and correct their own mistakes.

Secondly, the public security committee must try every available means to find employment for them. Comrades from the neighbourhood committee and the

---

10  The four measures of prevention or *sifang* are as follows: 1. prevent spying; 2. prevent theft; 3. prevent fires; 4. prevent incidents which disrupt social order. Zhang Wenqing (ed.), *A Dictionary of Chinese Policing* (Shenyang Publishing House: 1990), 334. [张文清(编), 《中国警察辞典》.]

public security committee have surmounted many kinds of obstacles and arranged employment for 21 wayward juveniles. Indeed, at the current time, there are only two wayward youths awaiting a job allocation in this district—all the rest have already found work.

Thirdly, the Weikeng public security committee has implemented a programme of moral education and the raising of lofty ideals for these wayward youths so as to foster a collective spirit within them and encourage them to take an active part in various social activities such as tree planting and protecting the environment so that they, too, can enthusiastically engage in practices which serve the community. These wayward youths have quite often corrected their mistakes and been reformed because of the correct guidance, patient education and very practical help given to them. From among the ranks of these juveniles, some have gone on to be chosen as advanced workers, others have joined the army, while still others have been admitted into the Communist Youth League.

# 3

# GOVERNMENT STRATEGIES (2)

The Chinese character 报 *bao* can, depending on its context, mean either reciprocity or revenge. As Li Yiyuan pointed out earlier (Part I, 1), this character and the ethical stance it represents have become a 'lived norm' in everyday China. But only part of the story of this norm can be told 'sunny side up'. Illustrations of this side of *bao*—the side that faces the sun—could be read between the lines of the accounts of life in the Beef Street police station and the Weikeng neighbourhood committee. In these two stories of local 'mass-line' policing the reciprocal, positive side of this unconsciously accepted ethical norm is in full view. Yet such reciprocity and community mutuality is never free of its ugly twin. Reciprocity is possible, but only within limits and, once the line is crossed, a very different regime comes into effect. Reciprocity is backed up by a range of coercive measures that ensure that the other negative meaning of *bao* always shadows such happy stories. Aspects of that shadowy, other figure who lurks behind the public face of *bao* emerge in a range of 'internal' literature, a sample of which is gathered here. With these documents, one moves from the sunny stories of Beef Street to more coercive aspects of the mass line in policing. Those who step out of (the mass) line too often, or for too long, end up being marked 'special' in a highly undesirable way. Key businesses are monitored, key elements of the population covertly kept in check. This is the darker side of policing.

It is the shameful face of *bao* that clouds the sunny stories and, for that reason, it is kept from view. If locals are checked in this manner, imagine what fate befalls the stranger or the moral polluter. Their fates are determined by a range of local 'internal' documents. These internal rules cover virtually all aspects of life, but the sample gathered here is restricted to those dealing with the treatment of and penalties for prostitutes, beggars and vagrants. As these all too clearly illustrate, for the morally questionable, the stranger, or the socially irresponsible, *bao* will always be in danger of turning its face to darkness.

## THE SPECIAL PROFESSIONS[1]
### YU LEI

## Management Work in Hotels, Engraving Works and Second-hand Stores

Within the lexicon of policing, the security management practices operating in hotels, engraving works and second-hand stores used to refer to this type of work as security operations within the 'special professions' (*tezhong hangye*). Taking advantage of the particular nature of these special professions, many criminals have used these services in a variety of ways. These special professions are of potential use to the criminal in that, through them, they could hide or conceal their profits; they could forge or alter seals, documents or certificates; or they could use their services as a means of disposing stolen goods. Therefore, policing these trades becomes a very vital and basic task in the struggle against crime.

### The 'Special Professions'

#### The Hotel Service Industry

The hotel industry is characterised by the transient nature of its clientele. Guests come from different places and are all very mobile. As a consequence, it is very difficult to correctly ascertain their status. Criminals take advantage of this fact and can be found frequently mingling with other travellers. They do this for a variety of reasons. Sometimes they do it to avoid detection, at other times, they do it to commit various crimes such as stealing, swindling or engaging in hooliganism.

#### Engraving Services

Generally speaking, the engraving industry includes engraving factories, engraving shops and stores, as well as street-peddlers who engrave characters onto seals and pictures. These are included because criminals frequently forge official seals or various types of certificates.

#### Second-hand and Junk Dealers

Second-hand shops and stores,[2] scrap yards and disposal points. Essentially, these dealers are persons engaged in purchasing, consigning or selling on a commissioned basis unwanted items. Some criminals utilise this trade to conceal and dispose of a variety of stolen goods.

---

1   Yu Lei *et al.*, *The Study of Public Security Administrative Management* (Beijing: China's Public Security University Press, 1987), 80–2. [俞雷，'特种行业治安管理'，《治安行政管理学》.]

2   These stores are more like commissioned agents than true second-hand dealers. A person will approach the shop and ask the storeholder to sell a particular item for them. Upon the sale of that item, the seller will receive the money but the shop owner will deduct a commission.

In addition to the trades mentioned, others can also be included in the category of the 'special professions' if, on the basis of any particular condition, the government deems it an appropriate course of action. If so deemed, then any such business will be administered in a special way by the public security units.

## The Basis on which the Special Professions are Policed

Those who wish to start up businesses in these particular 'special professions' must have their proposals examined and approved by the responsible departments and by the commercial administrative department. After receiving their business licence, those who wish to engage in these trades must apply for approval to commence business from the county or city (or city branch) public security bureau, and these organs must then administer them and carry out security checks and supervision. Public security organs, in conjunction with other relevant departments, must work out a clear set of security conditions which can be applied to each new business. On the basis of these guidelines, the relevant departments can then examine and approve any business venture.

In these particular trades, the responsibility for security work rests with the businesses themselves. On the basis of the special circumstances of these particular industries, an overall security contract responsibility system, offering a comprehensive set of security measures, needs to be put in place. The role of the public security organs will be to offer leadership and carry out security checks.

In order to discover and control illegal or criminal activities and keep abreast of circumstances surrounding the transient population, all businesses engaging in these special trades are to implement a strict system of registration. This will mean, for example, that those who stay in hotels will all have to register; that all contracted work within the engraving industry be registered; and for the second-hand trade, all goods put up for sale or sold as scrap will be put on a register.

On the basis of the relevant regulations, any person within these industries who knows of any criminal or illegal activity, or of any suspicious persons or items, is duty bound to report such people, activities or items. The duty of the public security organs is to improve the various measures of investigating and controlling crime while, simultaneously, recognising the special character of these industries. With these things in mind, the public security organs set up information networks within these industries through which cases can be reported and criminals investigated and arrested.

## Management

It is critical that, in the policy formulation and professional work of these businesses, stress be placed upon the tight and continuous supervision and examination duties of management. Therefore, the public security units need to set up management structures which are appropriate to these industries and also deploy specialised personnel to carry out security management. These specialised personnel must be conversant with the profession, have an understanding of relevant policies covering these industries, and understand the way they should be managed. With this knowledge, they will be in a position to implement the security responsibility system.

The public security agencies need to establish, within these industries, various types of internal security organisations. If the security personnel are able to maintain close contact with a wide body of workers in these particular industries, then it will be possible to put in place the 'four measures of prevention' (*sifang*).[3] Meanwhile, public security organs should strengthen their leadership over these security organisations. They should organise and supervise study sessions for security members on a regular basis so that they are conversant with relevant policies and professional matters. In this way, their professional skills will be enhanced and the security bureau's leadership in the struggle strengthened. This, then, aids the development of security and preventative work. In addition, in order to more effectively control and prevent crime, the security organs should also seek out staff in these trades who are in a good position to identify suspicious activities or characters who are able to get close to criminals. These people should be recruited as informers.

Public security organs, in conjunction with other departments, should organise security programmes for workers in these industries whose job it is to receive, verify, register and evaluate goods and items.

The public security bureau and local police stations in the cities and counties must regularly carry out checks and supervision so that they are in a position to discover and solve any policing problems. Through this method, the police will be able to promptly solve any problems and institute any measures necessary to plug loopholes in the system.

---

## THE SPECIAL POPULATION[4]
### YU LEI

The 'special population' (*zhongdian renkou*) is a specialised term used by the public security organs. The administration of the 'special population' is not only an important internal and basic vocational task performed by the public security organisation, but it is also a focal point in the administration of the household register and an important task of local police stations and other basic security units.

### How the 'Special Population' is Administered

On the basis of the 'Regulations concerning the management of the special population', issued by the Ministry of Public Security, the following types of people should be listed as being part of the 'special population':

---

3 For an explanation of *sifang* see Feng Rui, Part II, 2. See the same chapter for examples of how these measures have also been implemented in neighbourhood committee work.
4 Yu Lei, *Administrative Management*, 89–91.

1. Those suspected of having committed counter-revolutionary crimes. Into this category would fall all those who are suspected of having hijacked aircraft, ships, naval vessels, trams or motor vehicles or are suspected of having sabotaged trains. It would also include those suspected of being engaged in spying or espionage activities, those suspected of writing counter-revolutionary slogans, leaflets, anonymous letters and those suspected of being engaged in counter-revolutionary crimes of a religious nature. Lastly, it would also include those suspected of committing counter-revolutionary crimes of any other type which are not mentioned above.

2. Those suspected of common criminal activities. Such crimes as murder, arson, setting off explosives, spreading poison, robbing, raping, stealing, swindling, smuggling and selling and transporting narcotics and other illegal drugs would fall into this category, as would those with membership of a criminal gang or a transient with criminal intent. Those suspected of illegally manufacturing, trading, stealing, snatching or concealing weapons that will be used for criminal purposes would also be included, as would any other common criminal activity not listed above.

3. Those suspected of endangering public order, including those who engage in hooligan activities or continue to engage in any other activity which disturbs the peace. Those suspected of regularly taking part in gambling activities or of organising gambling for a percentage of the purse. Whoever roams from place to place, without work, without being enrolled in an academic institution, and without a home to return to, would also fall into this category, as would all other people suspected of being a threat to public order.

4. Those who have been engaged in civil disputes which could potentially lead to criminal activity and even murder.

5. Whoever has been sentenced to control through public surveillance, has been deprived of their political rights, has been given a suspended sentence, is on parole, or is out on bail pending trial. All such people should be subject to residential surveillance.

6. Those who have been released from reform through labour units, reform through education institutes, and criminal rehabilitation detention centres (*shourong jiaoyang*).

## Administrative Methods Used by Public Security Units

The principle to be applied in policing the 'special population' must combine the specialist management skills of the public security units with a reliance upon the masses. In the administration of these people, a whole range of tactics—everything from secret forms of control, help and education, right through to legally based reform through surveillance—should be utilised.

## 确定重点人口呈批表

| 姓 名 Name | | 性别 Sex | | 出 生<br>日 期 Date of<br>birth | | 文 化<br>程 度 Education<br>level | |
|---|---|---|---|---|---|---|---|
| 别 名 Any other<br>names | | 籍贯 Native place or<br>place of origin | | | 身 体<br>特 征 Any defining<br>bodily parts | | |
| 工作单位<br>及 职 务 Work unit and job | | | 现住址 Current place of abode | | | | |
| 家庭主要<br>成员情况 Main family characteristics | | | | | | | |
| 简 历 Summary history | | | | | | | |
| 主<br>要<br>问<br>题<br>和<br>表<br>现 The main problems with the person and how<br>they were expressed in actions | | | | | | | |
| 基层单位<br>意 见 The Basic Unit's recommendation | | | | | | | |
| 批准单位<br>意 见 The opinion of the approving work unit | | | | | | | |
| 备 考 Points for reference | | | | | | | |

填表单位: Applying unit     填表人: Applicant     填表日期: Application date

The decision form to place someone in the special population.

## The Administrative System Used in Policing the 'Special Population'

In relation to who is to be listed and who is to be taken off the list of those in the 'special population' category, a very strict system exists. This system includes a process of examination and approval, regular investigations and prompt handling, and it is one in which a wide range of related departments are consulted and their opinions canvassed. Particularly in relation to those suspects who cross various administrative districts, who move between urban and rural centres, or who are actively involved in the organisation of criminal gangs, it is imperative that the police force institute both a strict division of labour and also a tight system of cooperation. This division of labour and close coordination should be between the local police stations concerned, the police officers who have been especially appointed to rural areas and the security units at a departmental (*chu*), sectional (*ke*) or subsectional level (*gu*).

---

## BEGGARS, PROSTITUTES AND UNDESIRABLES: THE INTERNAL RULES OF THE STATE

---

In this section, a number of regulations on how to deal with certain 'subaltern elements' have been summarised, transcribed or, in part, translated. These documents all come from a volume entitled *A Collection of Rules, Regulations and Policies on the Comprehensive Handling of Social Order*, Masses Press, Beijing, 1992. I have retained the original format of these documents, which are nothing more than lists of rules. These lists of rules, however, are not publicly promulgated and, therefore, are known only to the field officers in the area of policing to which they are to be applied. China has a detailed hierarchy of classification and these documents would be on what could be described as the second tier. That is, they are not just 'classified' but have an added rider attached which is 'classified and available only for workers in security related work units'. Nevertheless, this level of classification is not very high given that most public security workers need to have access to such documents to do their jobs. Hence, one finds certain statistics, regarded as too sensitive to be generally distributed among the public security forces, deleted from some of these documents. In place of the statistics or names you will find 'XX,XXX'. The 'X' has numerical significance. For example XX,XXX indicates figures of ten thousand or more.

The sorts of rules outlined are issued by a range of authorities (from the Central Committee through to provincial ministries) and are not designed to be—nor by their very localised nature could they ever claim to be—comprehensive. Part of the point is just that. They are an illustration of a regulatory practice designed either to augment the very general and publicly promulgated laws which do cover aspects of the area in question, or to 'plug holes' in areas of policing where laws have not yet been formulated or promulgated but action is regarded as being needed.

Three sets of rules are given:

1. Relates to the treatment of beggars. This includes two sets of regulations.
2. Relates to the treatment of prostitutes and the sexually promiscuous and includes two sets of regulations.

    2.1 Relates to the incarceration of suspected prostitutes.

## TRANSIENT BEGGARS IN THE CITY

SUMMARY TRANSLATION OF DOCUMENT ONE[5]

**Section one**: In order to help educate and redeploy city beggars and maintain social order in the cities these special measures have been formulated.

**Section two**: Listed below are the type of people who can be detained and expelled:

1. Families that enter the city from the countryside and practise begging.
2. City residents who have become vagrants and hang around city streets begging.
3. Other types of people who spend their nights on the street and have no visible means of support.

**Section three**: The detention work relating to these people is the responsibility of civil authorities and the Public Security Ministry. Concrete methods are to be determined locally on the basis of conditions that exist in that particular place.

**Section four**: Big and medium-sized cities, open cities and other important transportation route points where the vagrant beggar population is large need to establish detention repatriation stations (*shourong qiansong zhan*).

**Section five**: The detention repatriation stations must promptly get acquainted with the beggars' names, identity, family address etc. They must arrange a reasonable life for them, and strengthen their ideological and political education. They should also dispatch them promptly to their original place of household registration.

**Section six**: Those detained must abide by the following rules:

1. They must obey the detention and repatriation order.
2. They must clearly give their name, their identity and family situation.
3. They must obey State laws.
4. They must respect the regulation system of detention and repatriation.

**Section seven**: Repatriation must be swift and people should not be held for long periods.

---

5  State Council notice concerning 'Trial method of detaining and repatriating the vagrant beggars in the cities' ['城市流浪乞讨人员收容遣送办法实施细则 (试行)', (国务院通知: 12 May 1982)] in *A Collection of Rules, Regulations and Policies on the Comprehensive Handling of Social Order* (Beijing: Masses Press, 1992), pp. 306–8 (12 sections). [《社会治安综合治理政策法规汇编》.]

**Section eight:** The process of repatriation and transfer is to be unified and co-ordinated and carried out in a co-operative manner between province, city, and autonomous region.

**Section nine:** Finding employment and housing for those detained is the responsibility of the local People's government in the place from whence the beggar departed. This latter government should contact the commune, team or street committee where the people in question were once resident and they should then take over responsibility and resolutely resolve their work and life problems. For those without a family, the civil authorities must take responsibility. Those whose household registration has been cancelled since their departure should be reinstated on the record.

**Section ten:** Workers at the detention repatriation stations must abide by the law.

**Section eleven:** The concrete implementation of the methods for implementing these rules is to be worked out by the Public Security Ministry and the civil authorities.

**Section twelve:** This regulation comes into effect as of today.

## SUMMARY TRANSLATION OF DOCUMENT TWO[6]

**Section one:** This document has been written on the basis of [Document 1, 'Method ...'] section 11 above.

**Section two:** Detention repatriation stations (*shourong qiansong zhan*) are a non-profit governmental unit designed to carry out relief, education, detention and repatriation.

**Section three:** Detention repatriation stations are established on the basis of section four [Document 1, above].

**Section four:** Detention repatriation stations are, other than in a few cities, under the responsibility of the civil authorities.

**Section five:** The object of the detention repatriation stations is to strictly implement section two of 'Methods' [Document one, above] and to prevent arbitrary or erroneous detention. If the detention repatriation stations' personnel discover criminal or suspicious characters among the occupants of the detention repatriation stations, they must inform the Public Security Ministry department who will carry out an investigation.

**Section six:** On the basis of (the above) 'Methods', section 3, formulate concrete actions on the basis of the requirements of the province, city, autonomous region or centrally administered city people's governments. People's government and Public Security

---

6 Civil Administration, Public Security Ministry notice concerning the printing and distribution of 'The implementation of detailed (trial) rules and regulations covering the methods of detention and repatriation of the vagrant beggars of the city' ['城市流浪乞讨人员收容遣送办法实施细则 (试行)', (国务院通知: 12 May 1982)] in *A Collection of Rules, Regulations and Policies on the Comprehensive Handling of Social Order* (Beijing: Masses Press, 1992), 309–14. (26 sections).

Ministry departments divide up the responsibilities, coordinate closely and work together very well.

**Section seven:** The detention repatriation workers' clothing, documentation, badges etc. are made and issued by the department in charge and on the basis of the concrete regulations of the province, city, autonomous region and centrally administered cities People's governments.

**Section eight:** In relation to those vagrant beggars who are detained, there is a need to promptly investigate and establish the names, identity, and family addresses, the causes of the vagrancy and times of vagrancy. This will require the establishment of a file and, on this basis, political education will be undertaken.

**Section nine:** Detention repatriation stations need to care for the relief of the detained, guaranteeing food, and ensuring that it is hygienic. Concerning the old, the young, the invalid, and the handicapped, we have to offer them appropriate support.

**Section ten:** Detention repatriation stations need to pay close attention to improving hygiene. For those detained who are seriously ill, prompt medical services need to be offered and for those with contagious diseases, isolation measures should be implemented.

One must ensure that unusual deaths are prevented and, for those who die while in custody, checks should be made to ascertain the causes of death and a legal death certificate made out. A report on this should be given to the department in charge.

**Section eleven:** In detention, there is to be a strict segregation of the sexes and women detainees are to be dealt with by female personnel.

**Section twelve:** Apart from strictly abiding by section 6 in the (above) 'Methods', those detained in detention repatriation stations need to obey the following disciplinary requirements:

1. Conscientiously answer questions put to them during interview.
2. Comply with work personnel management.
3. They are not allowed to damage public property.
4. They are not allowed to fight, nor are they allowed to carry dangerous weapons which could cause bodily harm.
5. While in detention, detainees are not allowed to be 'scalpers'.
6. Detainees are not allowed to carry out any other illegal activity.

If it is discovered that any of the detainees have been engaged in illegal activities while in detention, this information is to be passed on to the Public Security Ministry authorities who will handle it on the basis of the law.

**Section thirteen:** Detention repatriation stations need to promptly organise repatriation. Those detained should be held at the station for no longer than fifteen days if they are detained within their own province or one month if detained outside it.

Under the following conditions, it is possible to extend the time limit of detention:

1. With a doctor's certificate indicating a contagious, dangerous disease which requires further medical treatment or continued diagnosis and observation.
2. Where the household register of the detainee is in a border region or where climatic conditions are severe.
3. Where the detainee is mentally retarded and time is needed to check the address given.

**Section fourteen:** Each province, autonomous region and centrally administered city needs to take appropriate steps to repatriate detainees.

**Section fifteen:** Units in charge should get help from the railway and transportation ministries to buy tickets for these people and the train and boat guards should also be notified of their presence.

**Section sixteen:** Detention repatriation stations need to put into effect a repatriation work responsibility system. Repatriation work within a particular province, autonomous region or centrally administered city involves sending the detainee to the place of their household register. Once there, the county (city) People's government needs to organise departments to take care of them and receive them. Upon reception, the unit involved needs to sign a receipt indicating the vagrant's return.

**Section seventeen:** In transit, if the transient vagrant needs to change trains, then arrangements have to be made to provide for them en-route.

**Section eighteen:** The employment of the detainee is the responsibility of the local authority which issued them with the household registration in the first place. If their registration has been cancelled in their absence, then it has to be restored and the civil authorities must make arrangements with the vagrant's (former) commune, team and street committee to employ these people.

**Section nineteen:** For those who have been detained but are without a home to return to from places where their place of household registration has labour power problems or really has other serious difficulties, the civil authorities' department can ask provincial, autonomous region or centrally administered city departments or bureaus to approve their dispatch to a farm.

**Section twenty:** For city detainees with no home to return to and no labour potential, approval of the household registration people at the civil authorities department at a county (or city) level or above, can lead to them being sent to city social welfare units for care.

Those from the countryside with no home to return to and no labour power to offer can, after going through the household registration units of the People's government department at a county (or city) level or above, be sent to an old people's home in their village or distributed to other places and given the five guarantees.[7]

**Section twenty-one**: The civil authorities must guarantee to pay the following costs and ensure the following conditions:

1. Food etc. and transportation costs of sending people back.
2. Costs associated with detainees.
3. The wages of detention repatriation station workers.
4. Cost of maintenance and repair of the detention repatriation stations.
5. Other associated costs.
6. Women are not to be abused.

**Section twenty-two**: When the detention repatriation stations get the detainees to work, the wages should go toward the cost of maintaining and transporting them.

**Section twenty-three**: On the basis of the regulations, units can also arrange to give workers at the station a subsidy.

**Section twenty-four**: The rules for the workers at the detention repatriation stations are as follows:

1. They cannot abuse, fine or mistreat detainees.
2. They cannot cheat detainees out of their belongings.
3. They cannot embezzle the food and finances of the station.
4. They are not allowed to check letters.
5. They are not allowed to make a personal profit out of the work of detainees.

**Section twenty-five**: A reward system should be introduced to encourage work.

**Section twenty-six**: These regulations come into effect from today.

---

7   The five guarantees are that childless people without financial resources are to be guaranteed food, clothing, medical care, housing and burial expenses.

## PROSTITUTION

> ### SUMMARY OF SOME POINTS IN DOCUMENT ONE[8]
>
> In the last two years, nationally, there were already more than X ten thousand prostitutes but early estimates of those investigated and detained indicates that the number was, in reality, three to four times that figure. In addition, the national figures for those with STDs (sexually transmitted diseases) in recent years has reached XX,XXX people and the figure is increasing by X.X times annually. In the first half of 1989, police units handled XX,XXX prostitution cases which was a XXX per cent increase over 1988.
>
> Hence the Public Security Ministry Notice (1989) to the State Council advised that concrete steps needed to be taken to deal with this and research needed to be done before the establishment of detention education (*shourong jiaoyusuo*). The document focuses on a meeting chaired by Wang Fang on 9 January 1989 which outlined some possible ways of dealing with this growing problem.
>
> Repeating the points made previously about the growth in prostitute numbers the meeting also highlighted the increasing difficulty in identifying prostitutes as a group because it suggested cadres, Party members, and army people accounting for quite a few within their ranks. The prostitutes are also leading the surge in STDs, with figures from recent years indicating XX,XXX people and an annual increase of X.X annually. So it is already a major threat to social order and needs to be controlled.
>
> What measures can be used to combat the threat? One is to legally establish the work of detention education centres for prostitutes. This is an administrative measure to force education and treatment upon them. It is a measure to halt the spread of prostitution and suppress it and because it has had pretty good results in the past, it should continue to be utilised. Nevertheless, along with the rise in mass understanding of the law, a number of aspects and a range of people have raised potential questions about these places because, while the detention education places impose limits on the degree of personal freedom, they do so without any clear legal basis. That is, they are without regulations or rules governing their activities or formation. It is really in a minority of cases that the arrested prostitutes deserve to be arrested (on criminal charges)

---

8 'A summary of the minutes of the meeting concerning researching the attack and suppression on prostitution activities' (State Council Document [1989], Number 18) [《关于研究打击取缔卖淫嫖娼活动的会议纪要》.] in *A Collection of Rules, Regulations and Policies on the Comprehensive Handling of Social Order*, pp. 141–44.

and sent to youth reeducation centres (*shaonian guanjiao suo*)[9] or reform through education centres. In the vast majority of cases, they can be handled through public security detention, fines, warnings and education, after which they can be released. These punishments would be difficult to fit the goals of reform through education as pre-punishment, post-cautionary, methods. Hence, there is an urgent need to introduce a clause on punishment. In order for these practices to be established on the basis of the law we need to get such practices legalised.

## A SUMMARY TRANSLATION OF THE DECISION[10]

The document starts by explaining that, in order to prohibit prostitution and protect society, there need to be the following additions and amendments to the criminal law:

**One**—In relation to appropriate penalties to impose for those who organise prostitution. Penalties of ten years' imprisonment to life are regarded as acceptable. This can be accompanied by fines of up to 10,000 *yuan* ($US1204) and confiscation of property. Serious cases can be given the death sentence with property confiscation.
—Helping to organise prostitution rackets should lead to a penalty of no less than three years' imprisonment and a maximum of ten. Added to this should be a fine of up to 10,000 *yuan* ($US1204) and, in serious cases, up to ten years' imprisonment, a 10,000 *yuan* ($US1204) fine as well as property confiscation.

**Two**—Those discovered to be forcing people into prostitution should be given sentences ranging from five years' imprisonment through to a maximum of ten years imprisonment with a fine of up to 10,000 *yuan* ($US1204). Under certain extreme circumstances, which are listed below, the sentence considered should be harsher—from ten years to life with a 10,000 *yuan* fine and property confiscations. For very serious cases within this latter category, a death sentence should also be considered and this can be accompanied by confiscations. Such very serious cases are as follows:

1. Where the victim being forced is under fourteen years of age at the time they became a prostitute.
2. Forcing many women or forcing one woman many times into prostitution.
3. Rape followed by forced prostitution.

---

9 For further details on these see Shao Mingzheng, Wang Mingdi and Niu Qingshan (eds), *The Encyclopedia on Chinese Reform Through Labour Laws* (Beijing: Chinese People's Public Security University Press, 1993), 630. [邵名正，王明迪，牛青山（主编），《中国劳改法学百科辞书》。]

10 'The National People's Congress Standing Committee decision concerning the strict prohibition on prostitution', 4 September 1991 ['全国人大常委会关于严禁卖淫嫖娼的决定'] in *A Collection of Rules, Regulations and Policies on the Comprehensive Handling of Social Order* (Beijing: Masses Press, 1992), 163–5.

4. Injuring or even killing the prostitute or acting in a way which leads to any other serious consequences of equal seriousness.

**Three**—Luring or taking somebody into, or introducing them to, prostitution should lead to a penalty of up to five years' imprisonment with a fine of up to 5000 *yuan* ($US602). In serious cases, more than five years' imprisonment and up to a 10,000 *yuan* ($US1204) fine can be considered. In lighter cases, the Public Security Management Regulations can be used instead of this notice.

**Four**—Ordinarily, prostitutes and their customers can be handled on the basis of the Public Security Management Regulations.

—On the basis of decisions of the public security and other related units, prostitutes can be legally sent for moral and labour transformation for between six months and two years. But those found prostituting themselves a second time are to be sent for reform through education and fined up to 5000 *yuan* ($US602).

—For prostitutes, there is one rule: All must have medical checkups. For those with STDs, treatment is to be given and this can be forced on them.

**Five**—Those who knowingly continue to carry out prostitution activities while infected with an STD are liable for up to five years criminal penalty, or detention or supervision and a fine of up to 5000 *yuan* ($US602).

—Those who hire an under-age prostitute (that is, one under fourteen years of age) are to be charged with rape.

**Six**—Work unit personnel at hotels, bars, nightclubs and taxi stations etc. who, in some way, aid prostitution, are to be dealt with under sections 1, 2 and 3 of the regulations. If the leaders of any of these units know of, or are involved in, the sex industry, they are to be dealt with harshly.

**Seven**—Work units like hotels, bars, nightclubs and taxi stations etc. who know of such things but do nothing, or who block investigations, can be fined between 10,000 *yuan* ($US1204) to 100,000 *yuan* ($US12,048).

**Eight**—Work unit-responsible personnel and staff at hotels, bars, nightclubs and taxi stations etc. who know of such things but do nothing, or who block investigations, are to be dealt with under section 162 of the criminal code.

## FEMALE EDUCATION AND FOSTERING CENTRE[11]

### SUMMARY OF SOME POINTS IN DOCUMENT ONE

'Female education and fostering centres' (funü jiaoyangsuo) are designed specifically to educate and raise females who are prostitutes or who have engaged in hoodlum activity. These centres have had good results and should be introduced in cities after the Public Security Ministry, civil government, health department, Women's Federation and other relevant departments have examined the concrete condition in their locales.

Once a woman is brought into detention, she is checked for diseases by doctors. If she has an STD, she is registered and a report written to higher level units. She is then put under the supervision of her work unit, neighbourhood committee or village or town leaders as well as the supervision of the doctors and health prevention workers. She is to be forced to have treatment and even made to undertake more radical curative measures if deemed necessary.

All hoodlums brought into custody are to be checked for transmittable diseases and, if a disease is discovered, they are to be registered, and a report written to higher authorities. For those with infectious sexual diseases, isolation and forced treatment are called for.

If hospital workers discover sexual diseases when checking a patient, they must register that person and write a report and clarify how the person was infected. That is to say, they must determine whether the person is a prostitute or customer etc. The hospital must quickly determine all details and pass them on to the Public Security authorities.

Payment for checks and treatment: In relation to detainees, this is to be borne by the local authorities, or the reform through labour unit or the family of the person themselves. If they are in no position to pay, then it is the responsibility of the local civil authorities.

### SUMMARY OF POINTS IN DOCUMENT[12]

—Those who have not reformed, or who have a sexually transmittable disease and keep working as a prostitute, thereby threaten-

---

11 From 'The Supreme Court and seven other departments on the attack on prostitution activity and the prevention of sexually transmitted diseases', 16 September 1985 ['最高人民法院等七个部门关于坚决打击取缔卖淫活动和防止性病蔓延的报告 (节录)'], 117–19.

12 The Office of the Central Committee of the Communist Party of China and the State Council on 'Notice concerning the severe attack and persevering with the suppression of prostitution and preventing the spread of STDs', 21 September 1987 ['关于严厉打击坚决取缔卖淫活动和制止性病蔓延的报告 (节录)'], in *A Collection of Rules, Regulations and Policies on the Comprehensive Handling of Social Order*, 132–34.

ing the health of others, can now be called hoodlums and they can be treated under the clauses in the criminal code relating to hoodlum activities.

For those whose crimes are insufficient to warrant criminal charges, work needs to be undertaken to determine the best methods of detention. If the person concerned has already been detained by the public security units in the past or has undergone education but has been caught again, then there is one rule: send them to re-education through labour. If their misdemeanour is insufficient to warrant this, send them to the specialised places of education (教育场所). All who are detained on prostitution charges (and this includes foreigners) are to be checked for STDs. Chinese nationals are to be forcibly treated and they have to pay for treatment themselves. Foreigners are to be expelled.

Put up places of education and STD monitoring structures. Currently, a number of cities have Public Security authorities and civil government authorities working in unison and, as a result, they have established eighteen centres as places of education where prostitutes are educated and forcibly treated for their sexually transmitted diseases. The health department has established sixteen STD monitoring stations (*xingbing jianudian*) but such centres have to get the approval of the civil authorities, Public Security, health, Women's Federation, and finance departments etc. before they are established. These units will look into the possibility of such centres, look at the cases involved and then send a recommendation on to the government.

# 4 SUBALTERN TACTICS, GOVERNMENT RESPONSE

The literature gathered in this part of the work cannot, by definition, replicate the 'comprehensive appearance' of government documents. Gathered here are reports from the edge. They are stories of the everyday and, other than the one survey of Beijing *baomu*s (nannies, char-ladies and housekeepers) undertaken by Sun Xiaomei, the material makes no pretence of being anything other than individual tales, observations or opinions. The first such commentary comes pictographically with two images of nursing, one from the Cultural Revolution, the second from a recent Chinese calendar. The juxtaposition of revolutionary and calendar girls flags the commodification of women's bodies in China today.

Female bodies are also bought for things other than sex, however, and the examination of the *baomu* in Beijing which follows this highlights other roles for the rural woman. This takes on a personal dimension with the interview conducted with a young rural woman working in Beijing as a nanny. This is followed by a second interview, this time, with a male peasant fruit seller. In both cases, their life stories, in part, reveal the 'tactics' they employ to avoid government regulation, employer wrath or their home village disdain.

Finally, there is the story of 'Zhejiang village'. Here, on the outskirts of Beijing, and much to the chagrin of the local police force, a village of tens of thousands of residents has grown up. The vast majority of these people are strangers to the city and come from the province of Zhejiang (hence the name). This village tale is unremarkable but for the fact that this small enclave exists on the margins of a society that Westerners think is totally controlled. Its existence is testimony to the power of economic reform and the limits of governmental 'pincer movements' to halt its emergence. Yet the internal document which closes this chapter highlights a governmental response that is little short of panic. Containment in Zhejiang village meant expulsion, demolition and disenfranchisement. Yet to read the police accounts of this 'campaign' one could easily believe we had returned to Beef Street on a sunny day. From these stories, one begins to realise that the 'sunny side up' face of China is changing. This change is bringing forth a new phenomenon, which, in other circumstances, we might mistake for the birth of the working class. Socialist China finally has the class it has desired for so long, yet the reforms ensure that this emerging class is treated in a manner whereby we really can, as I suggested in the introduction, close our eyes and think of (Victorian) England.

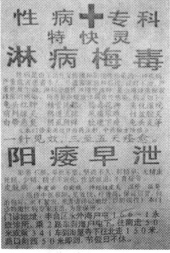

Above: Cultural Revolution nurse.

Top right: 'Chinese' calendar girl, 1995.

Bottom right: The now ubiquitous street poster advertising specialised medical help for those suffering from STDs and premature ejaculation.

## NURSING CHANGE

Through the changing portrayal of 'nursing', comes the changing face of China. It points to the obvious conclusion that in China today, 'white woman sells'.[1] What she sells, as the calendar girl so readily depicts, is the very idea of being for sale. Consumption takes on the appearance of a beautiful face, a beautiful body and a beautiful home—all of which can be bought, for all of these are offered for sale. 'Could it be', Schein continues, 'that the white woman ... is now guiding Chinese consumers-to-be into the privatised world of fetishized things?'[2]

---

1  Louisa Schein, 'The consumption of color and the politics of white skin in post-Mao China', *Social Text*, Winter (1994), 146.

2  Schein 147.

From this juxtaposition of the two portraits of women, the shifting sands of an unconscious portrayal of females—from the patronising innocence and pastoralism of the Cultural Revolution, to the seductive playboy/playgirl image of today—is revealed. Gone from the streets of consumer China is the egalitarianism of the Cultural Revolution period that repressed talk of sex and, in so doing, buried it. This burial only led to an aberrant form of the patriarchal code reappearing wherein women were gendered male and took their place as workers, soldiers or revolutionary comrades. Once this gender repression lifted, the code of difference returned in a virulent, reifying form. The male gaze fixed on the once taboo subject of the female body and allied it with another unobtainable form, the white, foreign, female. The 'revolutionary' depiction of a 'pure' woman/girl who stands before us 'selling' and instilling revolutionary virtue disappears. The comfort and care she offered the workers in the background is radically contested in the second frame where care is redeployed as a lustful moment and the background is the dream-envy of a bourgeois life.

The revolution that China has undergone in the process of economic reform has begun to lift the embargo on sex and its representation. Female bodies take their place alongside Mao watches as objects of desire and purchase. Economic reform sells sex as taboo and herein lies part of its value. But taboos, when breached, involve costs and the advertising hoarding selling cures for sexual ailments is the other side of sexual allure. Yet even on this 'other side' the market prevails, transforming cures into commodities.

The failure of Maoism lay not simply in its inability to 'transform people to their very souls', but to stop them desiring the impermissible. While the Cultural Revolution had tried to 'cure' desire by reducing life to a narrow puritanical revolutionary ethos, the consumer revolution sold heterogeneity. It was heterogeneous, however, only so long as everything from sex, to cure, to revolutionary virtue itself, could be rendered and reduced to the commodity form.

---

★ BEIJING *BAOMU*: TAKING BEIJING PEOPLE'S MONEY AND DOING BEIJINGERS' WORK[3]

**SUN XIAOMEI**

---

In 1993, we carried out a survey of 329 service persons, 91 of whom were sales people, 66 worked in the hotel industry and 172 were working in people's homes. We discovered that these women, who had been swept to the fore by the economy, were having an incalculable impact upon large city production.

## The Inspiration for 'Service Personnel'

The vast majority of the women entering Beijing are engaged in work in the tertiary sector and they bring with them a whole range of services to city families,

---

3  Sun Xiaomei, 'A group of outsider women inside Beijing', *Women's Studies*, 3 (1993), 22–7. 〔孙晓梅, '一群外来妹在北京', 《女性研究》.〕

promoting the growth of individual cafés and restaurants and the establishment of strings of individual markets. These conform with social demands and, at the same time, also have a tremendous influence on the society.

There are three ways of dealing with household work in China. The first is to do it yourself, the second is to share the burden with the social service sector, that is to say, socialise family work, and the third is to bring in people who specialise in this work, for example, bringing in family service personnel to undertake the tasks. Family chores become professionalised.

The first of these methods is one that is clearly in need of change because, in the modern Chinese family, both partners work, which leaves little time for anything else.

The second method, which is the realisation of the socialisation of family tasks, is certainly the most distinguished of routes but, under current conditions, it is not feasible. The productive forces are still quite under-developed and the conditions which make feasible the socialisation of family labour have definitely not developed at the same rate as female employment. Gadgetry, mail-order purchasing, laundry services and the fast food industry etc. have not reached a point whereby they have penetrated ordinary family affairs. Take the self-service supermarket, for example. Overseas, these places offer prices which under-cut department stores and these are appropriate places for professional women to get all their shopping done in one go. In China, however, these conditions do not exist. Hence, household work cannot be shared by the social service sector.

The third way—employing specialised personnel to undertake the household tasks—is the simplest in that it does not require a huge investment but only a very modest expenditure on wages. This has its advantages. In the first place, this person can carry out all the household duties such as washing, buying the groceries, making the meals, cleaning the house, looking after the old and the young in the house and so on. Compared to the duties involved in dividing up these tasks between different agencies, that is, taking the clothes to the laundry, buying vegetables at the market and taking the child to the kindergarten, help in the home is enormously more convenient. Secondly, this person can satisfy a range of different family requirements. For example, core families, older people living by themselves and so on. Different families have vastly different standards of living and great differences in customs and habits, and it is very difficult for society to satisfy each and every variant that exists, hence hiring a 保姆 *baomu* is clearly the most suitable of options.

The burdens of the city household are becoming great, the age of the population is increasing and the size of families is decreasing. These sorts of things have determined the current large numbers of household service personnel. The growth and development of this social grouping is a product of the development of city, social and economic life.

Along with the development of tertiary industry, there has been the continuous development of the individual private service sector. This is especially the case with regard to the food and catering sector and other types of service industries, all of which offer conveniences to city residents. In the last few years, a new trend has emerged—of people coming in and offering the family help with cooking, cleaning and the purchasing of daily necessities. Most of these young country women are employed in the catering trade and, after that, on private traders' stalls. The key factor determining which way they go is the wage they are offered.

For the majority of *baomu*, wages run between 50 and 100 *yuan* ($US6–12) per month, while the wage for waitresses and related catering positions is 100 to 200 *yuan* ($US12–24) and, for those employed in retail outlets, it is 150 to 250 *yuan* ($US18–30) per month. In private catering businesses, many employers also offer bonuses, provide food and accommodation. A great many private entrepreneurs are happy to employ these young women because they will do as they are told, they are willing to work, they accept being bossed about, and employers can offer them lower wages. The shift toward self-employed *baomu* workers contributes to the large-scale development of Beijing commercial life being of convenience to the residents and establishing the conditions for the socialising of family services.

The demand for labour in the city is the basic precondition for the flow of rural women into urban areas. The flow of large numbers of women into the city creates a kind of market there. Looking for work in this type of market, firstly, offers no protection and, secondly, should either the employee or employer discover problems or contradictions in the arrangements, the benefits of such arrangements cannot be guaranteed.

Under the leadership and organisation of the Women's Federation, from 1983 onwards, a number of district Women's Federation branches established '3.8' household service companies[4] to help resolve a range of problems emerging in this sector. From then on, and through liaison with Women's Federations in many provinces and cities, an arrangement for the placement of advertisements for family helpers began.

After these helpers join one of the huge number of families employing them in the city, the department concerned will, then, in a particular period, carry out a trace and go around and make some enquiries. The '3.8' service companies also utilise holiday periods to offer a range of training courses in sewing and hairdressing etc. By offering these home helpers this sort of training, they also increase their service skills.

## Supplying the Guarantee of Agricultural Economic Development

Beijing's outside labour force comes from two places. One is where there is little available cultivable land and a huge population, and the other is the poor and remote rural regions. After the establishment of the rural responsibility system

---

4    '3.8' stands for 8 March, which is International Women's Day.

The sign reads '3.8 Family Services Company'. 3.8
stands for 8 March. In these reformist days,
'Family Services' means itinerant women servants.

and the system of fixed output quotas for each household, the basic productive
unit became the family. The problem of excess labour power emerged, bringing
about a shift in the deployment of labour power from agricultural to non-agricultural production. Women occupied the dominant position in service personnel
work. After 1978, Beijing began to experience a female population flow into the
city from southern rural areas with little agricultural land and large populations
to feed. After 1984, females from poorer rural regions in the north-west began to
move into the city. Among the 329 service persons spoken to, 30.4 per cent came
from the southern province of Anhui and, even though we have no county breakdown of this figure, we do know that 71 of these women now in Beijing all came
from one village. Moreover, these women invariably send money back to their

hometowns to help their families and promote rural production. Quite a few have already returned to their rural homes, becoming advisers to others on money making.

## City Life Influences the Self-sufficiency of the Service Personnel

After a few years of city life, these women undergo a great change both materially and ideologically. Generally, the educational level of these women is pretty low, but they are very quickly able to adapt and develop themselves. From an analysis of the educational levels of the 329 women surveyed, it was discovered that 34.7 per cent of them had an elementary school education, 48.6 per cent had graduated from lower secondary and 5.2 per cent had an upper-level secondary certificate.

As a service person's cultural level rises, their own self-assessment undergoes a profound change. After the survey, it was quite clear that these people no longer fit the stereotype of the old *baomu* who were servile in all respects, and humble. The young household help, especially the ones who have received higher levels of education, feel the need for respect from their employer and society intensely. After a year in the city, these people speak fluent Mandarin Chinese, and their habits are becoming much more hygienic. When asked about this, 46.8 per cent of respondents considered the biggest change they felt after being in the city was learning about things they had previously never heard of.

## City Life Brings about an All-round Change in the Women

Young rural girls who are accustomed to village life come to the city with different expectations. Some really want to see the world, others feel the need for a change and for new opportunities, still others come because of the need to make a living. After arriving, all of them feel really out of place but, within two or three months, they begin to see things very differently.

They arrange their free time very sensibly, especially those who regard reading as the most important pastime. For example, of the 114 respondents who have only an elementary school education, 55.3 per cent of them buy books to read. This demonstrates that they are accumulating knowledge all the time, and their knowledge of a variety of different things is increasing such that they are becoming closer and closer to the city folk and start to talk the same language.

The higher level of material and cultural wealth of the city also has an imperceptible influence upon those female *baomu* with a higher level of middle-school education for they are directly motivated to take full advantage of the higher educational and cultural level of the city, and this forms a kind of supplementary course for them, creating the conditions for further learning. They are often hired by the families of the intelligentsia and, quite often, their remuneration is not something they are fussed about because they receive help and benefit from their employer with study matters.

In the 1950s and 1960s, such a situation was extremely rare. In one case, a country girl worked in the household of a lawyer, studied law herself, and then returned to the countryside to open a business offering legal advice. There is another case of a girl who worked in the household of a photographer, studied photographic techniques herself, and then returned to the countryside to open up her own studio. There are many other cases of such people returning to their hometowns with their new-found skills and employing them to contribute to an improvement of life in rural areas.

These service personnel have really independent characters. They have their own incomes and, while in the city, they work if they feel the need to, and leave if they want. Some even go off to new places and look for work there. The result is that very few of them put up with humiliating working conditions. Most employers in Beijing respect the personal traits of their employees. They have thrown out the traditional attitude of treating them as servants and, instead, establish a new type of relationship based upon equality and mutual respect. In this way, the *baomu* overcomes any inferiority complex or self-deprecating attitude she may hold. Moreover, these employers also take great care to ensure that the *baomu*'s living conditions are satisfactory. In the survey undertaken, we discovered that 105 of the 329 respondents, or 31.9 per cent of them, said that when they were not well, their employers took care of their medical expenses. When the *baomu* was careless about her work, we discovered that in 68 per cent of cases, or those involving 224 of the respondents, the employer called upon the employees to take greater care but did not abuse them. Two hundred and thirty-one respondents, or 70.2 per cent, said they regularly ate their meals with their employers, and 54.1 per cent, or 178 respondents, said they regularly received help from their employers.

Of the 329 women questioned, 82.7 per cent of them were young women who had never married. The vast majority of these women were between the ages of seventeen and twenty-five years. This is the period when their personality and ideological outlook is really being formed. Hence their ideology, their interests and their likes and dislikes are inevitably influenced and changed by the families with whom they live. In this way, they are influenced by the good marriage customs of the city dwellers. Of those who answered the questionnaire on the issue of choosing marriage partners, 139 respondents, or 42.2 per cent, stated that a person's character was the most important factor in determining the suitability of a partner and this was far more important than anything else. Hence, it is clear to see that these young women develop a healthy attitude toward the issue of love and marriage. This is especially progressive when compared to past attitudes, where the suitability of a partner was measured in terms of their economic circumstances.

China implements a system of household registration and, as these women do not have city household registration, it is very difficult for them to find suitable partners in the city. Basically, after a number of years, these women return to the countryside and generally get married there. Because few of the employers ask the *baomu* about their marital status, the survey found that 59.6 per cent of respondents thought that their employers did not care about their marital situation. Yet when asked about what makes them happy only two of the 329 respondents said that it was talking about love and marriage. For these *baomu* there are few opportunities in their work to talk about such matters.

Currently, *baomu* are faced with the following types of matrimonial situations. First, there are the cases of women who are betrothed before leaving the countryside. Upon their return to the countryside, they have gained new experiences and knowledge and consequently, are less than satisfied with their fiances and try to get out of the arrangement or agree reluctantly to go ahead with it. Second, there are those cases where, upon returning from the city, they are introduced to a partner or know someone and then become engaged. In these circumstances, dissatisfaction also arises because once they start a family, they quickly discover that there is no way of reaching the living standards they had grown used to in the city. Third, there are those who return to the countryside and recognise that, despite the suitability of any given candidate, there is no possibility of satisfying their desire for a life like that offered in the city. Four, they get together with peasant males who are also working in the city and return to the countryside with them. Fifth, in order to stay in the city, they find city men who themselves have difficulty finding partners (the so-called 'difficult households' (*kunnanhu*).[5] Such marriages are often not harmonious and both sides suffer heartaches.

The greatest feature of *baomu* attitudes on love and marriage is that, because of their rather extraordinary experience, there is no way they can be satisfied by an ordinary-style peasant marriage. They may well wish to fulfil their dreams, but the reality is quite different. Many of these women have come to the conclusion that their own future marriage arrangements will be well removed from what they desire.

## An Analysis of Causes and Problems

Workers offering home help have a huge number of different duties. Work in this sector has no wage scale, no limits on the work levels nor is it overseen by any government ministry. It is determined absolutely by the laws of supply and demand, and arranged on the basis of the labour market. Because of the transient nature of these women and the fact that they do not have Beijing city household registration, a series of problems emerge for all transient women workers.

In the catering and retail industries one very acute problem is the length of the working day. There are a number of employers who, in order to maximise their

---

5   A 'difficult household' is someone who has reached an age whereby it is hard for them to find a partner. In the cities, this age is usually from around the late twenties, early thirties for city women and mid-thirties for men. In the countryside, the ages are much lower.

profits, refuse to employ an adequate number of staff and, in order to compensate for this, make their young female staff work extraordinarily long hours. Moreover, the bonuses that are supposed to be awarded to stimulate work are actually, in part, to compensate for work actually undertaken. So while the wage of people in this sector is often 100 to 200 *yuan* ($US12–24), more than that earned by home helpers, the work done in this sector is often really tiring and the working days can stretch over eleven and twelve hours. For example, 66 respondents in the catering industry, that is, 37.9 per cent of all respondents, stated they worked more than twelve hours per day. In order to make money, they are willing to endure long periods of work.

Work in the service sector is not covered by any established regulations. Beijing's '3.8' family workers' labour service company has established rules which involve establishing a wage for new, inexperienced home help of between 55 and 60 *yuan* ($US6.50–7) per month. Later, and depending upon conditions, this can be increased but wages arranged on the basis of this regulation are simply too low. In the vast majority of cases, it is the employer who sets the wage and the two sides negotiate and settle on a rate. For example, on the basis of a questionnaire covering 82 employers of workers in the catering and retail sector, 26.8 per cent stated that they set the wage rates, and 47.6 per cent said they negotiated and settled on the rate with their employer. This way of doing things means that employers are able to build in loopholes and they are also able to wring the best deal out of their employees. For the employees though, this way of doing business creates the conditions where their bargaining power is at its weakest.

Service personnel basically have no rest periods and this is especially true of those who work in the catering sector or in retail networks. For example, of the 91 persons interviewed from the retail sector, 55 per cent said they were not given a day off. From the catering industry, the situation was much the same: 66 respondents, or 56.1 per cent of those in the industry, said they had no rest days. Hence, although these people earn quite a lot of money, their working days are long and the harm this does to their health is great.

Those hired as home help all live with their employers and it is the employers' responsibility to provide food and accommodation. Generally, it can be said that most live in reasonable conditions. If one were to compare the conditions of these workers with those that labour in the catering sector, the conditions of the latter are far worse for they, too, in the majority of cases, live where they work. During the day they work in the restaurant, while at night they sleep on the floor. For example, of the 66 people questioned from the catering sector, 48.5 per cent said they lived where they worked and, of these, 84.9 per cent said they lived with the other employees. This, of course, is far from hygienic and really detrimental to the health of the worker. They also lack any living space of their own.

Quite a number of service sector workers, especially young rural girls who have been hired through the illegal labour markets, are without any administrative cover. Once they run into problems, they have no understanding of the law, which then leads to new problems. Another problem is that, of the 329 service personnel questioned, 34.1 per cent of them had never undergone a medical check-up. Moreover, people have even been known to employ minors. Of the 329 women surveyed, nine were under the age of sixteen.

The problems I have noted have arisen for a range of reasons and, of these, the most important are as follows. Firstly, the management system is far from adequate. After economic reform and the open-door policy, the speed with which private entrepreneurs began to develop was really great, yet the problem of management was still a pretty new issue. In relation to problems associated with production, the Chinese authorities lacked both experience and a creative ability to deal with many of the management issues. Secondly, education is really insufficient. For example, the education of people in terms of the law, ideological worth and health consciousness is inadequate. Thirdly, there are no funds available for training or specialised structures and personnel. Of the 311 persons questioned, 258, or 83 per cent of them, have received no training whatsoever. Yet, when we surveyed 168 employers, we found that 62 per cent of them demanded greater levels of skilled staff. Various levels of the Women's Federation have undertaken some of this work, but the financial problems associated with this means that appropriate training is simply not possible. These problems need to be seriously addressed by the relevant departments.

## 'BAOMU BLUES'
### An Interview with LI NINLONG

Li is eighteen years of age and female. Like many peasants, she came to Beijing with an introduction to work . She became a *baomu* or nanny. She remits most of her pay back to her family. Her case offers an interesting example of the problems facing young rural women who come to the cities to work. Life for such women is difficult for their values often change and end up running counter to the ones dominant in the rural areas. Thus, while her life is still very much determined by the 'rural calendar', her own values seem to be increasingly at odds with this. This is  captured in the discussion of marriage, where her demand for a 'modern' husband illustrates her own dissatisfaction with traditional rural males. By rural standards, she is now at marriage age and the thought of becoming *kunnanhu*, a 'problem household', that is, missing the marriage age and being left 'on the shelf', still looms large. The interview was conducted in January 1995.

*MD: Let me begin by asking you to tell me a little about yourself.*
**LN:** Sure. I came to Beijing in 1993. When I first thought of coming to Beijing I had no idea I would end up a nanny. I really was happy to find any kind of gainful employment. When I first came I was only sixteen years of age. I got a job as a babysitter and nanny through my sister who knew these people because she had been a classmate of the woman so we had a connection with their household. That is quite important. I come from the countryside and our family is pretty big. There are six of us in all: my parents, grandfather and my sisters and brothers. Our average income is about 300 *yuan* ($US36) per person per year.

My current employment is really good because I make 200 *yuan* ($US24) per month which is more than my whole family's monthly income combined!

*Do you repatriate much of that?*
Of course. Most of it goes back. I like to keep a little for myself, but the bulk of it goes back to my parents.

*Do you have much contact with the other* baomu *around this place?*
I wouldn't say I have 'contact' with them. Sure, when we all take the children down to the swings and slides I will chat with them. That is only natural, but we don't really get together. In fact, the only person I see regularly like that is my sister who comes around occasionally. I also sometimes see some of my classmates who are also here in Beijing working.

*Is your income the same as other* baomu?
Yes, my wage is pretty similar to most and, like most *baomu*, we are all pretty much here to help out the family back home.

*Was it easy to leave home and come to the city?*
For men it is really very easy. For women it is another matter. It really depends upon the family. Some families don't allow it, others do. My family did not prevent me from coming here but that was probably because I have relatives in Beijing who could help out if I ran into problems. If I didn't have close relatives here I cannot imagine my parents allowing me to come. It really would not be safe enough and they would worry too much. Crime in the city is pretty bad these days.

*Has your family raised the issue of marriage with you?*
Not in so many words. I haven't really been concerned with the issue up until now, but it is becoming a consideration. Most of the girls in my hometown are talking about it. Mostly, they are interested in getting a man with a lot of money who lives, or wants to live, in our town. I am less concerned with wealth than where the person lives. I really want to live on the east coast where things are developing rapidly.

*So do you find men from those developing areas different from those in your hometown?*
Mostly, I find them pretty similar. But I do think there is a cultural issue that can make them different. If a man has been reasonably well educated, then he is really quite different to those who are not. I also find that those that are only sons can be painful and selfish. What I am looking for in a boyfriend is someone who can bear hardships along with me.

*What do people in your hometown think of people who go to the cities in search of work?*
The most common view is that it is good that they are able to go to the city, make money and send it back home. Many people do have worries, though. Some worry that these people won't return home or that they will get themselves into trouble in the city. Families are really concerned that their boys come home for they hope that they will come back and provide for their aged parents. For women, the problems are different. Many people think that the women who leave and return take on city airs and come back different people. Also, they are sometimes suspicious of the types of jobs they have done to make so much money in the city. The result is that many who leave don't go back to their home-town to find a partner because these men are too conservative. Most of us in the city don't consider ourselves to have any kind of 'behaviour problem'.

*Do you think you have been influenced by city life?*
I think I have. I really much prefer life in the city to that of the countryside. I really want to find a man who is well educated and open minded but you won't find those types in the countryside.

*So how do most women find a boyfriend back in your hometown?*
Most of them meet through introduction. Where I come from, men and women rarely meet partners by themselves. There are really few opportunities to meet people in that way. The result is that you often don't know your partner very well before marriage. Arranged marriages are standard practice in the countryside. I have been introduced to boys in that way but I really don't like this system very much and my parents have been very good, they have not pressed me into marriage. The important thing for me is that I am given a say in this process and, if I don't like the man, I have the right to veto any arrangements. I think that this is one way in which a job in the city has had an influence on me. It has not only led me to be more independent in the way I think about these things, but it has also given me a degree of financial independence.

*But don't you feel that city people look down on you?*
No, not at all.

*How do you handle your income?*
I deposit it in the bank. I don't really need to spend very much money because the family takes care of most of my expenses and I live in their house and eat with them, which is included in my wage. You can make a lot of money in the city. For example, I know some people from my hometown who have made a stack of

money while here. I mean, they have made something like 20,000 to 30,000 *yuan* ($US2409–3614). This means that they can support their whole family and even build themselves a big house back in their hometown. Where I come from, it is the duty of every parent to build their son's houses when they are married. This often leads parents into real financial difficulty. So if you can earn a lot of money and help your parents to pay off the house, then that is a real honour.

*What is the average age of marriage in your hometown?*
I couldn't say exactly but it is usually pretty early by city standards. Probably around 17 or 18 years of age for most. I am 18 years old this year but have until now not really been all that worried about it. I am not really worried because I am in the city. If I were in the countryside though, that would be another matter and I would probably be engaged by now. I think this is really terrible and I am reluctant to be a part of it. I think 18 years of age is too young to get married. Also, once you are married, the pressure doesn't stop. After marriage they all wait for you to give birth and they all want you to give birth to a son. Even my parents are like that. All grandparents want a grandson.

*And what are your views on this now?*
I don't think there should be any difference between a girl and a boy. It should be thought of as an equally joyful occasion. I should say that I did not think this way before I came to the city. At that time, I thought the marriage would only be fulfilled once a son was born. Certainly, my parents continue to think in this way. Their view is, no son, no future generations of the family. Most young men who come to the city do so to get enough money so that they are thought of as 'good prospects' and can find a good partner for marriage.

*Does the same thing apply for women who work in the city?*
No. It is more difficult for them. Few of them come back unchanged by city life. They tend to have different attitudes and ideas to when they left. They have greater expectations of their partner and aren't really all that satisfied by what is on offer back in the hometown.

*Do women who stay in the village marry at about the same time as those who go to the city to work?*
No. Generally they marry earlier than those who go to the city.

*Do people who come to work in the city end up feeling superior to those who stay in the countryside?*
Well, I would not say they feel superior but some things do change. For example, some married men often make quite a lot of money in the city and, while there, they take the opportunity to have affairs. Women, too, are faced with a lot of ethical problems although they tend to be different. In the countryside, married women rarely leave the hometown—the husbands simply would not allow it. It is the husband who rules the house and he decides on such things and the woman must follow.

*Do you think you have learned much from coming to the city?*
Yes. My views on things have changed a lot. Everybody comments on this whenever I return home. I feel I have a much broader education now.

*Do you want to go back?*
No. I don't want to go back. It is too poor. I want to be independent and to be independent you have to be mobile.

*Do many women leave your hometown and come into the cities?*
No, not very many. Most who do, come here and rely on relatives or close friends. Very few would leave without a relative or close friend backing them. A few of my classmates have made it into the city. Most of these are younger and better educated. If you are twenty years old it is very hard—the issue of marriage looms too large to consider leaving, and most families would not allow it.

## 'LIFE ON THE OUTSIDE'
### An Interview with an Itinerant Worker, LU NAIHONG

Lu is male and was born in 1962. He is typical of many peasants who go into the city to find work. He is part of the transient population who have, in recent years, 'floated' into cities like Beijing in search of work and a better life. Life in his home county of Huaiyuan, Henan province, proved very hard. His hardships were accentuated because, like many peasants, he was obsessed with raising a boy which has caused him much financial hardship. This has meant that he has continued to have children in excess of the plan. Yet another reason for not going back to his home county is that Beijing offers the anonymity he needs to avoid paying the fines that are accruing for his breaches of the population control laws. The interview was conducted in January 1995.

**MD:** *Why did you leave Henan and come to Beijing? Was it because of the poverty there?*
**LN:** Yes. My hometown was plagued by a lack of land and a very high population density. If you combined the land allocation my wife and I were given with the low yield of the land, our financial ability did not really amount to all that much. I mean to say, we could only get a wheat yield of about 600 to 800 kilograms per *mu* (1 *mu* is 0.667 hectares) and we only got a few shillings for each kilo of wheat we sold. We only had a land allocation for the two of us yet we have three children. Effectively, we were unable to survive on the land we had been allocated. If we changed to vegetables, things would be better, but with wheat and rice it is hopeless. I simply couldn't feed my family and so I had to find other means to support them.

*And on top of all this you still had to give a portion of the grain as tax in kind?*
Yes, of course. In our area the rate was about 90 kilos per person per annum. The amount one gave also depended on the 'five guarantees'[6] which meant that the more family members one had, the more grain one had to give. In my household, this rule meant that I had to give about 600 kilos of wheat per year, which was untenable.

*So you came to Beijing to find work?*
Yes.

*How long have you lived in Beijing?*
I have lived in Beijing for about six years. Two years ago my wife and children joined me. I rent a small room from a local peasant on the outskirts of the city and I pay 150 *yuan* ($US18) per month for a 10-square-metre space. I used to pay 80 *yuan* ($US9.50) but it has slowly gone up.

*Do you have temporary household registration in Beijing?*
I did. Every year I had to register and it cost me about 100 *yuan* ($US12).

*How do you find life in Beijing compared to Henan?*
Oh, it's a lot better than in my hometown. In Beijing I can sell fruit in summer and earn up to 1000 *yuan* ($US120) per month. In winter, I sell vegetables and rice and earn around 500 *yuan* ($US60) per month. Winter is the off-season. We really have to watch what we eat and consume but we are still a lot better off now. In fact, we can actually put a little away each month.

*How many children do you have?*
Three. All girls. The oldest is five. Actually, I really wanted a boy and we will keep having children until I get one. People in the countryside all share this view. We must have a boy. Unfortunately, I have had no luck so far.

*But weren't you fined for being in breach of the one child policy?*
Of course I was. I was fined 1000 *yuan* ($US120) for the last one we had. Luckily I am no longer in my hometown so I don't have to pay right now. In fact, I am not going to pay a cent until I have a boy. The last child has proven to be a real burden. We only found out it was a girl in the seventh month of my wife's pregnancy and, by that time, it was too late for an abortion.

*Under the responsibility system in agriculture, your land allocation is dependent on the size of your family but, because you have breached the family planning laws, you do not get additional land for the additional children, is that right?*
Yes, that is right. I got no extra land for my two extra children and that makes things very difficult. Moreover, the allocation that was given is set for fifteen years, so I guess that is all I am going to get for quite a while.

---

6   For details of the 'five guarantees', see page 124, footnote 7.

*So how did you actually arrange to come to Beijing?*
Well, a relative knew I needed more money and arranged an introduction for me here. I left my hometown to come to Beijing to take up a job as an unskilled labourer on a building site. All that had been arranged for me before I left. After working on a building site for two years, I was able to save up enough money to apply for a licence to sell vegetables. It was only then that I started to make a bit of money and was financially able to have my family join me. Sometimes I sell vegetables with others from my area but most of the time I am in this by myself.

*What about the land allocation back in Henan—who is taking care of that?*
My parents look after that. The way we work it is as follows. I'll pay the land tax, which, as I have said is about 80 to 90 *yuan* ($US9.50–11) per person per annum, and they take care of the land. I will also give them money when I can. When I go there on holidays I give them money which, as you know, is our custom. While we are still very poor, we are much better off in Beijing doing this than working the land back in Henan. In fact, now my brother and his family want to come to Beijing and work!

*Actually, that brings up the whole issue of the floating population, have you any general views on that?*
It seems obvious to me that the increasing number of peasants in the city is pretty much inevitable. In the past, the government kept a very tight rein on the population. They stopped us from moving but could not provide enough for us to feed and clothe our families. Now, if there is no money around, we can at least move on to places where there is money. This is also good for our hometown for a lot of the money we make here in Beijing ends up being repatriated.

*Life still seems pretty hard though …*
Oh, yes, that is true. Everyday I have to get up really early—around 5 a.m. each morning—and I don't get home till after dark.

*And how much is the trader tax?*
About 10 *yuan* ($US1.20) per day. Of course, it depends on what I am selling. Fruit, for example, is a lot higher, but it averages out at about 10 *yuan* per day.

*And do you want to stay in Beijing?*
You bet. I really don't want to go back to my hometown because there is absolutely nothing there for me now and there is no work and nothing to do. At least in Beijing, I can feed my family.

*What do you think about the situation with regard to law and order in the capital?*
Well, it is getting worse. A lot of transients are involved in criminal activities and that is bad for everyone. There is certainly a lot more robbery and theft than when I first arrived. Also, they target people like me. I can buy a bike cart to carry my vegetables and it will cost me around 900 *yuan* ($US108). These types steal it and sell it for 20 or 30 *yuan* ($US2–3). They really are just lazy loafers and they should be heavily punished.

*Are you forced to pay the police bribes?*
No. That sort of thing really only happens at the wholesale market where there is a lot more money. It is the wholesale managers who pay the police off.

*If the police don't bother you, how about the mass organisations that carry out policing duties? I am thinking of organs like the joint defence teams—do they give you any trouble?*
No, not really. The only trouble we get are from some smart-arse Beijing types rather than from organisations. For example, a couple of weeks ago one smart-arse Beijinger came around to collect our tax. We paid him, only to find out a little later on that he was not the responsible officer at all and had done this to shake us down. Well, of course, we went after him and taught him a bit of a lesson. So what did the police then do? They dragged us in over the bashing. I was fined 50 *yuan* ($US6) for starting a fight. Can you believe that? It was worth it, though. We certainly won't be getting any more Beijingers pulling that sort of a stunt again.

*Do you find that Beijing people look down on you?*
Oh yeah, of course they do. Beijing people think that anyone from other parts of the country—especially peasants—are quite inferior. They really discriminate against you. But I have found that they are a bit better if you have your family with you.

## ZHEJIANG VILLAGE, BEIJING: A VISIT

From 8 November 1995 to 10 January 1996, a small army descended upon a southern suburb of Beijing with a 'final solution' to deal with problems of illegality there. The place in question was known in local parlance as Zhejiang village (浙江村) because of the high density of Zhejiang residents. The 'small army' was all Beijing and all government: 1500 police from fourteen different Beijing units, 1500 armed police from the Beijing number two regiment and 1700 local cadres from the area itself made up this 'strike force', and strike they did. Forcibly evicted were 18,621 people without appropriate residency papers, 9917 houses were demolished and 1645 unlicensed businesses closed.[7] Zhejiang village was demolished and in this act of destruction a warning went out to all illegal 'outsiders'. They were not welcome and would not be tolerated.

The scale of the police action, decided at the very highest level by Premier Li Peng himself, would act as a warning to all others who ventured into cities illegally. This is a story told on a more minute scale throughout China every day and, while the full extent of Zhejiang village's tale remains hidden beneath the rubble, something of the tensions and dilemmas that led to this police action can be glimpsed at in this tale of the village. Here, the 'outsiders' tell the 'other side' of

7    'A summary report concerning the complete success of the tasks of cleaning up, rectifying and making secure the Big Red Gate area', Internal Unpublished Report of the Beijing Public Security Bureau (1996).

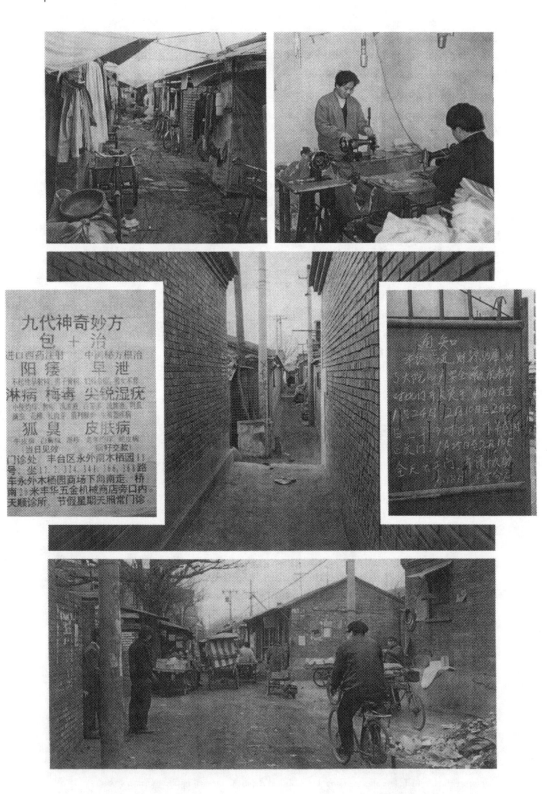

the police story. Theirs is an account of harassment, corruption and victimisation by a national police force that looks anything but national, guarding, as it does, the local and quite particular interests of the Beijing government in suppressing the 'floaters' or *mangliu* of Zhejiang village.

Zhejiang village was located in the south of Beijing in the Nanwan area, about 5 kilometres from the Qianmen commercial district. It was an area made up of about 26 previous villages and occupied about 26 square kilometres of land. It fell within the 大红门 Dahongmen or Big Red Gate, police station jurisdictional area. Like the rest of the southern part of Beijing, it was relatively poor and underdeveloped. Traditionally, the southern part of the city was for the poor, as summed up in the old Beijing adage, 'in the east are the wealthy, in the west live the aristocrats and bureaucrats, while in the south there is only poverty' (*dongfu xigui nanqiong*). It is to this area that the majority of the rural poor have gone, and it is the large numbers of migrants from Zhejiang province that have predominated. They began moving into this area around 1983, renting houses from local peasants and setting up businesses. Rental accommodation was initially cheap, with small houses being rented for 100 to 200 *yuan* per month ($US12–20). By 1994, this increased to 300 to 400 *yuan* ($US37–50), and just before the crackdown average rents were somewhere between 500 and 600 *yuan* per month ($US62–75). Despite the rent hikes, the 'village' grew rapidly over this period. In the ten-year period between 1983 to 1993, the village population reached 28,000 people with about a third being women. The total 'outsider' population peaked at about 30,000 residents which constituted somewhere in the vicinity of 60 per cent of all village residents.[8] A police crackdown and registration drive in July 1995 clarified the situation further. After this, it was discovered that the actual 'floating' population within the village stood at more than 37,000 people.[9] Clearly, with numbers escalating at such a rate more draconian action was thought necessary. The problem was that Zhejiang provincial authorities, who were much more sympathetic to the village population, opposed any harsh action. The central authorities were forced to adjudicate and the result was a huge registration crackdown beginning in November 1995. It resulted in many residents being forcibly repatriated to Zhejiang while others were forced to seek alternative accommodation elsewhere in the city.

The vast majority of village residents were from Zhejiang and, principally, the Leqing and Yongjia counties of Wenzhou city. Most residents were involved in the rag trade and businesses were usually very small and family based. They were typically sweatshops offering little protection for their workers. It was, however, not just at work that conditions were bad. The massive growth of the 'village' placed huge strains on city resources and amenities. There were few rubbish removal or hygiene services available, nor was there much support in terms of medical, educational or child-care facilities. Indeed, it had been rumoured that medical services were so bad that veterinary doctors had set themselves up as medical doctors in the area. Diseases were said to be a major concern and there was a widespread

---

8    Interview with senior police, 25 January 1995.
9    *Workers Daily*, 19 August 1995. 〔《工人日报》。〕

fear that a major epidemic could spread from the village into the city proper. Crime was also significant. For the government, tax avoidance was another major problem and led to considerable conflict with these 'migrant' residents. Another area of contention was the high proportion of contraband or fake products emanating from village factories. For the residents, other crimes were much more of a worry. Kidnapping, drug use, prostitution and gang activities were very serious problems in this area. Yet the Zhejiang migrant residents appeared to have little faith in the police force whom they regard as corrupt and 'alien', interested only in protecting Beijingers' rights and interests.

### A Visit to the Village, 21 January 1995

I visited the 'village' before the crackdowns and saw the conditions which had become infamous throughout Beijing. Every backstreet told of neglect. The village quite visibly lacked most amenities taken for granted in the rest of the city. The roads were dirt, there were no drainage facilities, no rubbish collection and the living conditions were squalid and easily the worst in Beijing. On virtually every corner of these dirt streets were posters advertising cures for various sexually transmitted diseases, physical evidence of the claim that the incidence of venereal disease in the village is high. Within the village itself, there was a huge compound entered via three gates that sealed it off from the rest of the area. Within this compound were houses and small sweatshops tightly clustered together. On the back of the entrance gates was a notice indicating that gates would only be opened in the morning at nine and closed at five in the afternoon. On festive occasions, the gates would remain locked. Some passers-by who lived in the compound explained that one gate that was guarded would remain open. It was as though, even within this village of the *mangliu*, the compound structure of Chinese life was again being unconsciously mimicked. Despite this security, crime was still a problem. When I asked residents whether there was much theft in this area, they laughed. 'There are too many thieves to count', said one. It was in one of these backstreets that I met some residents who told me of village life in more detail.

Three men were in a small house rented by one of them who lived there with his wife and child. He said the house (actually, it was one small room of about 8 square metres without heating or water) was owned by a Beijing landlord who rented it to them for 350 *yuan* ($US44) per month. All three men had been friends in Zhejiang. The first had moved to Beijing in 1987, the others followed in the early 1990s. They moved in search of work. Invited into their house we began to talk about the problems they encountered in Beijing, with Beijingers and with the police.

### On Movement

When asked why they came to Beijing, they said to make money.

Asked if they came directly from Zhejiang, one of them said he first went to Shanghai and only later came to Beijing. Asked why he did not stay in Shanghai, he said that there were too many Zhejiang people already in Shanghai and it was difficult to make a living.

*Income*

When asked what business was like, they said it was 'up and down'. The specific details of their financial situation were never made clear. Later on, I visited a small sweatshop filled with Zhejiang people making leather coats and goods—one of the main occupations of the villagers. The average income was estimated to be about 2000 *yuan* per month ($US250).

*Living Together*

Asked why they all live together in the village where conditions are deplorable, they said it was partly because of their Zhejiang friendship network and also because they could help each other with their work. They offered their own situation as an example to demonstrate what they meant. For example, those making leather jackets could do it in the village as the leather buttons, collars and even zips they needed are readily at hand and cheap in their friend's factory next door.

*Attitude Toward the Authorities*

When they were asked about Beijing people they had mixed feelings. They said they were not discriminated against but, when we got talking, they pointed out various ways in which, when they first arrived, Beijing people gave them trouble. At that time, Beijing residents, they said, would deliberately put their foot under their tricycles hauling goods and then demand compensation. The police, whom they described without hesitation as really terrible, would always support local Beijing people's claims. The official policy, they said, was one thing, but as this policy was adopted lower down the ladder, the system became more and more arbitrary. They complained, for example, that they would be at home playing mahjong with friends and the police would burst in and harass them. They claimed that, even when families were playing, they were accused of gambling and taken to the station to pay a fine which was never recorded and, therefore, clearly a form of extortion.

The *lianfang* (local work units and security groups) were even worse. At night they would grab any youths they discovered and rough them up, asking them if they had weapons and then frisk them for money. If any youth gave them 'lip', they would be given a beating. They said that the worst police in Beijing were those stationed at Big Red Gate (Dahongmen). All the police were local Beijing people and they had a very bad attitude to outsiders. They thought of Zhejiang village as 'their turf' and the Zhejiang people as 'outside invaders'. They treated Zhejiang people very much like second-class citizens.

*Gangs*

During our discussions, they also talked about the gang problem in the village. These 'black societies', as they are known in Chinese, were always on the lookout for opportunities to extort money. Hence, if it became known that any villager had a lot of money, they would be paid a visit and the money extorted. If they didn't have any at the time, they would be beaten and forced to sign an IOU in which they would indicate how much they owed the gang and when they would pay up.

Gangs were also involved in the kidnapping and ransoming of children in order to extort money. Last year, one villager's child was kidnapped and the parents told that if they wanted the child back, they had to give 5000 *yuan* ($US602). The village had an informal contact network, however, and ransoms could be negotiated through such friendship links. In this example, the parents' friends had some 'contacts' and were able to negotiate with the gang involved. Through these intermediaries, the money demanded was negotiated down. After giving over some money and ten bottles of alcohol and a couple of crates of apples, the child was released.

## ZHEJIANG VILLAGE: A GOVERNMENT TALE[10]

The task of cleaning up and rectifying the Big Red Gate area was completed successfully after two months' hard work. It began on 8 November 1995 and came to an end on 10 January 1996. The Central Committee leaders and citizens of Beijing were very concerned about this operation. It was important to do this task well because it was of such a large scale and involved complicated and wide-ranging matters. It required strong policies and strict implementation. Under the leadership of the Beijing City Committee, city government and city clean-up and rectify working group, and with the support of the Fengtai area and the people of Beijing, 3000 public security officers and armed police officers of the second division worked hard to guarantee that the clean-up and rectification work ran smoothly and successfully. There were no major problems and the achievements were remarkable. These were:

1.  A total of 18,621 people or 5320 households who did not meet the residential and working conditions were persuaded to move and the number of immigrants in the area dropped to 34,420 or 9834 households. In other words there was a 35.1 per cent drop in this immigrant population.

2.  A total of 9917 illegal buildings were demolished: 3627 of these belonged to local residents, while 6290 belonged to people who had moved to Beijing from Wenzhou, Zhejiang province. The differences before and after the clean-up were great with the pre-clean-up situation being dominated by crowded, illegally constructed dwellings and an area that was generally dirty, messy, shabby and quite chaotic.

3.  Improvements in social order. During November and December 1995, there were only eight cases of crime in the area, which was a 61.9 per cent drop in the crime rate from the same period in the preceding year.

4.  Road and traffic problems were solved when 190 illegal commercial stalls on Big Red Gate Northern Road were cleared away. This led to the previously 9-metre-wide road expanding to 18 metres. Moreover, the banning of over 600 illegal tricycles also helped to improve the traffic situation.

---

10 Beijing Public Security Bureau, 'Making secure the Big Red Gate area'.

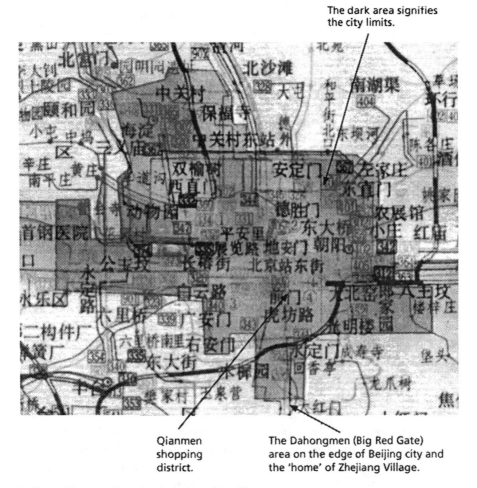

The dark area signifies the city limits.

Qianmen shopping district.

The Dahongmen (Big Red Gate) area on the edge of Beijing city and the 'home' of Zhejiang Village.

Zhejiang village, Beijing: On the edge of city life.

5. Also banned were 1645 unlicensed market stalls, as were 53 illegal medical clinics and 131 unlicensed medical practitioners. Two hundred and ten illegally operating restaurants and hairdressing salons were banned, as were 215 illegally run food-processing plants that were selling bogus and bad quality food. Two illegally operating large-scale markets were also banned.

6. During the clean-up and rectification operation, there were no incidents where officers or cadres were injured nor were there any industrial accidents during the period of persuasion of landlords and residents, demolition of dwellings and removal of illegal residents. There were no serious public security, traffic and fire problems, nor were there any cases of collective appeals to higher authorities due to the improper handling of matters. Moreover, there were no cases that caused political embarrassment or led to the news focusing upon the operation.

These achievements were praised by Central Committee leaders. On 29 November 1995, in *Current Information (Dangri shiqing)*, Premier Li Peng stated: 'Well done on this matter, comrades Jianxing and Qiyan. This indicates that the Beijing Party and government organisations at all levels have a strong work force and a great attitude. I hope you keep this up and set up regulations to deal with these matters in a manner that consolidates what you have already achieved.'

## Correct Central Committee Policies and the Determination of the City Committee and Government

In cleaning this area up, the police were faced with a particularly complicated social situation. Since 1983, an immigrant population, mainly from Zhejiang, had descended upon the Big Red Gate area. By the end of 1995, the number of outsiders who had taken up residency in this area had reached 53,000 people. In some parts of Big Red Gate, the ratio of immigrant residents to local residents was as high as three to one. This immigrant population lived mainly in houses rented from local farmers. There were some 14,600 houses rented from local farmers. Apart from these, there were another 6400 illegally built houses on rented land that made up 45 compounds. The high density of this immigrant population created many social problems: environmental conditions deteriorated, rubbish piled up, serious deficiencies emerged in water and electricity supplies, serious traffic congestion ensued, markets were in chaos, and a large number of houses were being rented at inflated rates. The public security situation in particular deteriorated rapidly. Serious crimes such as armed robberies and murder were frequent occurrences, while drug trafficking and abuse increased. Although there have been a few large-scale clean-up and rectification operations since 1985, the problems were so widespread that they remained basically unresolved. Whether these problems could be solved, and how to go about solving them, remained in question, even in the minds of the leaders in charge of these matters in the Beijing Public Security Bureau.

On 25 September 1995, Premier Li Peng, reflecting upon the serious situation in Big Red Gate, made an important point in the document *Internal Information (Neican qingkuang)*. He said 'the uncontrolled situation occurring in Beijing's "Zhejiang village" should not be allowed to develop further, otherwise it will bring forth serious problems for Beijing's security … [we must] show the determination necessary to resolve this problem.' Ren Jianxin and Luo Gan were sent as special envoys of the Party Central Committee and State Council to listen to the report from the city committee and government on the clean-up, rectification and security work in the Big Red Gate area. The city committee and government made it clear that they would firmly implement the Central Committee leadership's instructions.

The work at Big Red Gate was to prove very complicated. The area was over-populated with outsiders and large numbers of migrant labourers. Local farmers were leasing their houses to these people while a few very big investors who were VIPs in other provinces had investments there. Thus, while it was necessary to crack down on illegal building it was also important to take into consideration the handling of provincial relations and this made the clean-up and rectification work very sensitive. The Beijing Public Security Bureau Communist Party organisation suggested that initiatives be undertaken which anticipate various scenarios. After careful study, twelve possible scenarios were rehearsed. These studies focused on various possibilities such as massive resistance, and set about to work out ways to resolve them. During the operations, most of the forecast scenarios would have become realities but for the counter-strategies already rehearsed which stopped them turning into major problems.

The clean-up and rectification work in the Big Red Gate area should have been the responsibility of the Fengtai area forces but, given its special status and complicated nature, the Beijing Public Security Bureau regarded it as their next major task after the International Women's Congress. A general security head-quarters was set up and Zhang Liangji, the head of the Beijing Public Security Bureau, was made commander-in-chief. He was assisted by four Deputy Bureau chiefs, the head of the second division of the People's Armed Police, and the head of the Fengtai Public Security Bureau. The Beijing Public Security Bureau Communist Party organisation also held several enlarged meetings to listen to preparatory reports. Some fourteen security headquarters were established throughout the Big Red Gate area to guide the operation. Five branch headquar-ters were also established in places like Shi village where workloads were high due to the heavy concentration of immigrants. From top to bottom, the leadership was strong, and well organised. This not only ensured that the operation ran smoothly, but also enhanced the capacity of the police force to handle any large-scale or sudden incident. Some 1500 police officers from the second division of the armed police were also put into this taskforce.

The main tasks in this operation were to eradicate illegal constructions and to persuade the so-called people of the 'three withouts' *sanwu*—that is, those with-out identity cards, without permission to work and without permission to temporarily reside—to leave Beijing voluntarily. To complete these tasks the approach taken had to be multi-faceted. The Beijing Public Security Bureau Communist Party organisation required that security work be carefully organised and in complete control. Control would be achieved by surrounding key opera-tional sites. For this reason, the five villages requiring heavy security were desig-nated key points and all nine surrounding traffic routes into these areas including Young Road, Big Red Gate Northern Road, and the Third Ring Road became 'battle lines'. Focusing on these key points, the whole of the Big Red Gate area became a territory where complete control was necessary, and when the operation began, the task of forces in these surrounding areas was to assist and support the overall operation.

The huge population concentration in Big Red Gate made the area a fire hazard. One part of the police operation focused on identifying and eliminating potential fire hazards. In a number of difficult spots or important places, fire officers were sent in as a precautionary measure to ensure that the danger of fire was minimised. To resolve traffic problems in the area, the Public Security Bureau launched a crackdown resulting in some 1356 traffic violations being prosecuted and more than 30,000 *yuan* ($US3614) in fines collected. In addition, 24 new traffic signs were erected in the area, 8000 metres of traffic lines repainted. These measures had a great impact on traffic order in the area. The Public Security Bureau also sent 300 police officers on patrol duties on the nine surrounding roads from 8 a.m. until midnight. In the course of this, a total of 131 public security related cases were settled, 157 criminals arrested, 267 people detained and deported, and five cases involving six foreign correspondents wanting to write stories on the crackdown without permission being caught. To ensure the operation achieved the best results, the Beijing Public Security Bureau Party organisation required that area and county branches around Big Red Gate cooperate with authorities in this area to tighten control over immigrants moving towards the area. Through these measures a new round of immigration would not take place once the pressure of the clean-up and rectification operation lifted.

### Giving Full Play to the Public Security Establishment's Functions, Providing the Clean-up and Rectification Operation with a Reliable Safety Guard

During the two-month operation, the police from our bureau gave professional assistance and advice and acted as a back-up force during the operation.

According to instructions from the Beijing City Public Security Bureau Communist Party organisation, police actions were to 'begin with a crackdown to clear away obstacles'. Police began by focusing attention on gangs, armed robbers, drug traffickers and abusers and hoodlum activities in the Big Red Gate area. This crackdown lasted one month. In all, 27 criminal cases were 'cracked' (six of which were deemed very serious), 61 criminals were arrested (57, or 93 per cent, of whom were immigrants), five drug dens were closed down and twenty drug abusers arrested. This preparation period crackdown had a great impact, clearing away obstacles that might block the full-scale clean-up and rectification operation. During the operation, the police force was effectively organised to detect crime and, in particular, serious cases. On 28 November 1995, during the operational phase of getting people to volunteer to have their illegal buildings pulled down, a 27-year-old business woman named Li from Leqing city, Zhejiang province, was killed at house number 67, Ma village, Big Red Gate. The Beijing Public Security Bureau immediately organised a taskforce to investigate. These investigations led them to Changshan county, Zhejiang, where investigations continued and resulted in the apprehension of the killer within a week. To further strengthen their impact upon criminal activities, the public security organs, the procuratorate and judicial organs worked hand in hand to organise and hold two mass trial meetings of those publicly arrested in the Big Red Gate area during the clean-up and rectification operation. In these meetings, thirteen criminals were arrested and four were denounced and given death sentences. These measures purified the social order and helped ensure that the clean-up and rectification operation ran smoothly.

A key to the success of the clean-up and rectification operation was the persuasive use of propaganda as well as the minimisation of opponents. The Bureau sent 300 police officers to work alongside the 1700 cadres of the Fengtai area committee and area government. They went into villages and households carrying out propaganda that convinced the masses. At the same time, they indicated that if there were any disturbances or violence perpetrated against the clean-up and rectification workers, the police would come down and ensure an end to such criminal activity. Due to this, there was not a single case of a clean-up and rectification worker being hurt, nor any safety-related accidents during the building-demolition process. Nor did any group of migrants or local residents apply for an audience with the higher authorities to appeal for help.

While all the clean-up and rectification tasks were arduous, the toughest related to the demolition of the illegally built compounds. The first step in this demolition work was to convince the landlords to accept the demolition of their buildings. During the clean-up and rectification operation, some landlords tried passive resistance. Some tried to avoid talking to the operation workers; others spent their time trying to find well-placed 'contacts'. Some claimed they would write letters to the Party Central Committee and State Council to complain about their huge losses due to the demolition of their property. According to the general security headquarters, the cadres and police officers used their initiative to get to know these owners with the aim of explaining the situation to them. This method, known as 'making the first steps easy and leaving the hard ones until last', was applied at meetings with each of the owners. Some owners agreed to serve notices of eviction upon their tenants, but some did not. Mr Wang from Leqing city, Zhejiang, was the owner of the Jilei compound and proved to be very uncooperative. Police officers had five meetings with him. After education and persuasion, he finally gave in and cooperated, and he persuaded his 42 tenants to move out. After that the demolition work began. The owners of the Jinou, Jinwen and Jixiang compounds, however, had no intention of demolishing their compounds. After investigation, we realised Mr Lu of Jinou was one of the biggest investors in Big Red Gate and an influential figure among the immigrants. So it was decided that the leaders of the city general headquarters should come down and personally meet him and help him settle any outstanding problems. The Jinou compound demolition work was carried out more speedily because of this. By 17 December, 45 out of 47 compounds in Big Red Gate had been demolished. The remaining two compounds remained untouched for they were found to be built in accordance with the law.

About 5000 cadres participated in the police campaign. Internal management focused upon the demand of the Public Security Bureau for united leadership. The general security headquarters set up weekly meetings to exchange information, adjust police deployments and modify work. As the operation developed, more forces were deployed. During the period when the illegal compounds were being demolished, a large number of garbage scavengers came to Big Red Gate. The general security headquarters responded by arranging for a detention centre to be set up and devoted to them. Some 73 scavengers were detained and this acted as an effective restraint upon the rest. External management focused on information exchange and mutual support.

## A Precondition for Achieving Success in the Clean-up and Rectification Work was the Continuous Nature of the Operation and Dedication of Police Officers

After the operations began at Big Red Gate, the police officers overcame all difficulties such as cold weather and harsh working conditions. They carried forward the spirit of continuous hard work and dedicated themselves to the operation. The police were highly praised by the leadership at all levels and also by the local cadres.

The large-scale nature of this operation required clear understanding of policies and their correct implementation. Decisions about who should be persuaded to leave Beijing, and which buildings should be demolished, involved a wide range of people and interests. During the operation, the police officers were very clear about who and what should be protected. Towards those people staying in Beijing without permission and those buildings that were illegal, the police officers held very firmly to policy.

One retired worker, Mr Yan, who lived in Nanmuqiyuan, had renovated his work unit's dormitories into a nine-room house that he then rented without permission. During the operation, he refused to demolish the structure and threatened to appeal to higher authorities and create difficulties for the operation. The Public Security Bureau sent out police officers to assist with the demolition work and educate those people who still hoped they could avoid having their illegal houses torn down.

Mr Lie, a local peasant who had built an illegal house at 227 Big Red Gate Northern Road, was one such person. Despite education and persuasion, he was still unwilling to demolish his house until, finally, the authorities moved in and did the job for him. Mr Lie then went to the branch headquarters to try to disturb their work and created chaos. He was then detained and educated according to the law. He remained detained until he admitted to his errors. By doing this, both Mr Lie and the surrounding masses received a good lesson. The owner of the Southern Compound in Deng Village collected money from his tenants and used this as a 'slush fund' to try to 'make connections' (*la guanxi*) and 'use the back door' (*zou houmen*) by finding the right contacts who could protect his compound from demolition. Police officers discovered his plans and warned him not to embark on any project that would slow down the progress of the operation. This way of handling his case had a great impact on the other compound owners who were reluctant to demolish their compounds.

The 3000 or so police and armed police involved in this clean-up and rectification operation worked together for two months. There were many touching stories told about this operation. The propaganda police only ever had one day a week off. There were 300 patrol police officers from the Public Security Bureau who took on 24-hour shifts, and who never even took sick leave. Among the total number of police officers, there were 223 officers who remained on duty despite sickness and 160 officers who overcame other difficulties to remain in the taskforce. Seven of these actually had to postpone their weddings. A total of 4292 days overtime was undertaken by these police officers.

During the operation, the police strictly followed discipline. By being committed to serving the people, they created a very positive image of the police force. No one was involved in the buying or selling of goods, although such goods were easy for them to gain access to due to the power they had in the field. When the police went into the village and into households to do propaganda work, they saw an old lady's belongings falling off a bicycle and immediately offered help to resecure her goods. This old lady, upon returning to Zhejiang said: 'Beijing's police are really very kind.' During the propaganda and persuasion period, police officers were very patient and kind to the immigrants and therefore, many people shook their hands and said goodbye before moving out. During the demolition of the Jingwen compound, the police found a television set and other belongings in one room. They kept the goods in a safe place until they could be returned to the rightful owner. Some of the Leqing city people who witnessed this said: 'You police are really doing good things for us.'

PART III

# NAMING, FRAMING, MARKING

'Let the use of words teach you their meaning', says Ludwig Wittgenstein.[1] But what happens when meanings are encrypted and use repressed? What happens when 'buried meanings' remain to haunt new uses to which words are put, inflecting this art of use such that meaning is more elliptical than first thought? Here, the politics of the semiotic code, a politics that reveals a mystic presence that goes beyond utilitarian use, comes into focus. As it does, I am reminded of a simple tale from the work of the late C. P. Fitzgerald that both exemplifies the issue of use and does so in the context of Chinese history.[2] This is a tale set in Qianmen around the time of the 1911 revolution and centres on the act of changing a bronze nameplate. It is the story of a city gate that began its life named the Great Ming Gate, continues to exist throughout the next dynasty as the Great Qing Gate and finally comes to take on a more revolutionary designation after 1911. To effect this change of name, the new Republican authorities dispatched two workers to remove the old plaque and attach the new. These workers replaced the old plaque but, fearing a return of the Qing, took out insurance. Rather than destroy the old Qing plaque, they put it in a loft above the gate. To their surprise, they discovered that they had placed the Qing bronze name plate on top of the original Ming plaque! It was as though history lay in a loft for hundreds of years, discarded but ready to return. It was as though the physical language of the workers (in tactically taking out insurance) was in radical dissonance with the message of the Republic that the past was dead.

How many more historical relics lay discarded but ready to return after the Communists took power? How many revolutionary workers bowed to the new, but took out insurance in case of a return? Anticipating the possibility of backsliding, the Communists seemed determined to change so much, so quickly, that no one would be able to remember that which went before in any other way than the way the Party spoke of it. In Beijing alone, 27 streets were renamed 'Red Sun' Road and that was but one of the revolutionary new names adopted. Moreover, this was long before the wholesale 'revision of names' that was the Cultural Revolution. Here was a use of words that would teach politics the meaning of life. This was the sea-change that would be metonymically linked to the name change. This is the history of the word that Yang Dongping tells in this chapter.

At an official level, Yang Dongping tells of the Party's language reform wherein a standard system of romanisation was invented, a simplified script introduced

---

1   Ludwig Wittgenstein, *Philosophical Investigations* (Oxford: Blackwell, 1953), 220.
2   C. P. Fitzgerald, *The Birth of Communist China* (Middlesex: Penguin Books, 1964), 15.

and a standard pronunciation proclaimed. Beneath this, at an unconscious and popular level, he highlights the radical change of names of the 'ordinary people.' He explains how they began to employ the vernacular to revolutionary ends. This new language of revolution was full of peasant and military metaphors, indicating the well from which the revolution had drawn its strength. It spoke with a strong northern accent, reflecting geographically where the revolution had been, and it spoke with new, non-hierarchised expressions and titles indicating, ideologically, where the revolution was going. The social revolution was thus translated into the vernacular. Translating revolutionary themes into the expressions of daily life unconsciously framed the way people thought about things and this even included the naming of their own 'revolutionary successors'.

Traditionally, as Li Yiyuan points out, the naming of a child in China was determined on the basis of detailed and complex sets of calculations that took into account the time of birth, one's position in the family and the appropriateness of the name to bring forth harmony with the elements. While these techniques were never forgotten they were, at least in the most revolutionary periods, swept from view. All that could be seen, at this time, was the colour red.

Six hundred million Chinese seemed to chant in unison the words 'class struggle', Chairman Mao and revolution. Moreover, they all seemed obsessed with ensuring that these revolutionary lines were chanted into the 'first names' of their babies. Yet appearances are slightly deceptive. Personal names all too often became personal struggles as the buried and unconscious commitments to past ways of life resurfaced in these new revolutionary times. The glow of revolution, for example, was insufficient to dim the desires of patriarchy to put forth feminine names for female babies. The Cultural Revolution may have promoted revolutionary androgyne, but parents did not. They struggled over how to demonstrate their faith in the revolution while maintaining an intrinsic deep-rooted faith in patriarchy. The names of many female children during the Cultural Revolution were the result of an unhappy marriage between these two considerations. 'Fragrant Soldier' 'Graceful Army' and 'Public Fragrance' were the unlikely combinations formed and, far from reinforcing the revolution, they seemed to mock it.

In moving from naming to framing in this chapter, we also move toward other forms of mockery. Structured around the acupunctural chart of the traditional Chinese doctor are a series of other charts and tables that playfully rework the themes of medicine into dissent. The first of these comes from the Chinese artist Zhang Hongtu, now in New York, who mimics the acupunctural chart structure to identify revolutionary values as acupunctural pressure points on the body of Mao. Zhang's playful use of the chart brings forth a shock and a smile. In his depiction, Mao's body is riddled with the virus 'revolution' and herein lies the value of his art as a diagnostic chart of the cultural revolution that had been, for him, psychically 'dammed up'.[3] His rebellion in art is loud, it is shocking and it is designed for pleasure, revelation and display. Other worlds of dissent encode their bodily pressure

---

3    Sigmund Freud, *Jokes and Their Relation to the Unconscious* [Trans. James Strachey] (Middlesex: Penguin Books, 1981), 166.

points less visibly and whisper rather than shout. It is in trying to frame these other worlds, the world of the thief, the hoodlum, the pickpocket, that I have borrowed Zhang's 'technique' and plotted their 'tactics' on a series of bodily forms. While the original acupuncturist's chart highlights the points of cure, and Zhang's the points of political infection, the hoodlum's chart highlights points of vulnerability. While both the acupuncturist's and Zhang's charts read the surface of the body as 'signs' of its internal workings, the hoodlum is interested only in surface phenomenon. The location of the wallet, the watch, the necklace—these are the quarry. Their location, however, is not enough. The thief must work simultaneously in a range of different vectors—some spatial, some temporal, some positional—and it is in the language they use to designate these different sites of activity at any given time that we begin to hear what de Certeau would no doubt describe as a 'murmur' of another kind of society:[4] the voice of opposition to the practices of everyday life. The 'tactics' of opposition become audible in the colloquial expressions of the hoodlum or *liumang*. Their slang works to 'disfigure' the meaning of words and phrases. Through double entendre and sly subversion the certainty of the word is eroded, becoming a joke for those 'in the know' and a riddle for those not. At its playful, subversive best, language is turned on itself. Secondary playful meanings become codes for the initiated. The depictions of bodily forms, stances and sexuality form the contours of this landscape that is always momentary, tactical and as creative as life itself. Yet there are permanent markers even in this nether world. When that world takes on a written form it is not one found in books or journals but on the graffiti on the sides of buildings or in toilet blocks or, more likely in China, on the arms, legs and torsos of the people themselves. The written language of the *liumang* is found on their body as tattoo. Here again, we see how 'undesirable elements' have tactically subverted dominant meanings and usurped what was once a sign of their disgrace as a flag of their rebellion.

Tattooing in traditional China was, from a very early period, known as the 'ink punishment' and was used by the State to stigmatise offenders, criminals and the socially deviant. The 'recovery' of the tattoo by criminal gangs as a kind of 'membership badge' constituted something of an example of the way in which the tactics of resistance often play with negative social signifiers and try to invert them. Yet this is not the only reason for the tattoo being cut into the body of the *liumang*. Jiang Fuyuan's survey of criminal tattoos is both a rare compilation of the various types of tattoo in China and a stunning example of the way the 'language of the tattoo' is being brought into discourse by social scientists. The need 'to know' creates a space 'to talk' which, in turn, produces what Foucault would describe as an 'incitement to discourse'. All this, taking place on a social canvas that, through the high valuation offered to the previously hidden, secret and taboo, produces an 'incitement to reveal'. Commodification has produced within popular culture this 'incitement to revelation', for to reveal is to be marketable and to be marketable is profitable. From rebellious rock songs through to

---

4   Michel de Certeau, 'On the Oppositional Practices of Everyday Life', *Social Text*, 3 (1980).

'pulp' literature, things that once went unseen, were buried, taboo or secret are now objects of open desire. As the avenues of profit broaden, so, too, do the problems of the State. In contemporary China, it has even reached the point where the Communist Party finds it hard to keep a secret for its secrets have a market value!

## REVOLUTIONARY CULTURE[1]

**YANG DONGPING**

### Revolutionary Culture and Language

Language, as a cultural instrument and the direct reflection of ideology in reality, is the lively surface of social culture. It is an important measure of temporal, social and cultural change. It incorporates changes to script, pronunciation, vocabulary and grammar. At its broadest level of significance, it also reflects changes in literary form and style.

From the early 1920s, the 'Prolekult'[2] faction within the Soviet Union asserted that the 'Bolshevik revolution had created its own language and literary form'. As a basic principle this is untenable. Language is a common social tool that advantages no one and has no class character. At the same time, one needs to recognise that it is relatively changeable. Indeed, in a short time span, language—and more especially vocabulary—can change in literary style and form, reflecting a new style quite different from 'the old'. In the social revolution in China, this type of transformation has been profound. From the time when vernacular language and script replaced classical styles there has been a big transformation in language—the debates over colloquial language, the spread of Esperanto, the Latinisation of script and so forth—which has been crucial in the cultural revolution which has run throughout twentieth-century history.

In 1951, at a time when new China had just been created, the nation began script reform. Three types of tasks were undertaken to simplify characters, promote standard Chinese and formulate and advance the *pinyin* method of Romanisation. Up until 1977, the State Council promulgated four programmes of language simplification. The simplification of characters meant that the number of characters employed, the writing of those characters (from left to right

---

1  Yang Dongping, *City Monsoon; The Spiritual Culture of Beijing and Shanghai*, (Beijing: Eastern Publishing House, 1994), 262–76[ 杨东平,《城市季风: 北京和上海文化精神》.] Yang Dongping is an educationalist, environmentalist and a pioneer of comparative regional cultural studies.

2  Prolekult was a revolutionary cultural organisation operative in the early years of the Russian revolution. It stood for proletarian culture which, as the name suggests, it tried to import into both the form and content of early Soviet artistic works.

and top to bottom) and the printing styles used to depict them were all modified. This led to mainland Chinese characters taking on a somewhat different appearance to those that were used formally and to those used by overseas Chinese, and yet they could still be readily recognised. In December 1977, the fourth simplification programme was announced, and this clearly had all the problems of the period of Cultural Revolution. Thus, with the fall of the Gang of Four, this fourth phase was speedily abandoned.

As revolutionary culture spread so too did the Cultural Revolution and it transformed both places and culture. At that time, there also developed another type of change in Beijing. The revolutionary culture used Beijing as its centre, and the materials and instruments reflecting ideology and culture absorbed Beijing culture. Moreover, Beijing became both the source and model for this new cultural system. These two types of cultural influences—one from Beijing and the other from the Revolution—drew close together and infiltrated each other and one can detect this in the changes implemented within standard Chinese.

This is because Chinese political domination has long been centred in the north and the structure of the northern dialect has been the standard language of social intercourse.

By the 1950s, there was a clear tendency wherein Beijing dialect and standard Chinese appeared to draw very close together. The large number of people from outside Beijing entering the city at this time joining institutions, work units and visiting the capital led to the development of a new language of exchange. This type of shift, in turn, meant that a new type of Beijing dialect emerged that had a more general and national use.

Apart from this, many people paid attention to what they regarded as the 'voice of the Central Committee'—central radio and television announcers all had a definite pronunciation style when broadcasting. This, then, became for revolutionary culture, 'the form of the voice of the Party'.

Vocabulary is one of the most sensitive and lively markers of political change. Revolutionary culture uses a new political vocabulary as its scriptural form and, from this, it clearly displays cultural composition. This includes using things like Marxist theoretical phraseology, drawing on terms from the Soviet Union such as 'Soviet', red army, Bolshevik and Politburo. A notable characteristic in all this is the large number of new vocabulary items that came from military terms. Some examples: 'repulse the savage offensive of the right faction', 'toward the anti Party and socialist black line vigorously open fire!', 'charge the enemy lines to promote the revolutionary line', 'the party branch needs to be brought into full play as a fighting bastion', 'the secretary of the Party committee needs to be a good squad leader'.

A large number of military terms that have been borrowed and are in official use are in fact relics of the wartime period. The degree to which this military experience and military culture is stressed or has influence varies and, in this way, we can see that language really is a 'semantic trap'. For example, if one were to use a very strict measure to check the frequency of, and intensity in, the use of military terminology, one would find that it roughly approximated the different degrees of intensity of the class struggle in various periods. Hence, the catch-cry 'use peaceful methods and persuasion' always emerges in times of political liberalisation.

Apart from this, there is also the penetration of language from the rural sector. After liberation, many terms from the rural sector took on a new meaning within the political sphere and became key elements in the construction of a revolutionary culture. For example, to praise an upright young revolutionary from an appropriate class background, one might say: 'a straight-rooted red seedling' (*gengzheng miaohong*). When discovering a bright young thing one would talk about 'discovering a seedling' (*faxian miaozi*), or when passing on revolutionary knowledge to the young one might be said 'to be an irrigation channel, heart and soul' (*jingxin jiaoguan*). In this way, the dialect of the leadership became the official and standard dialect and this language was adopted as soon as one left the cradle.

The replacement of the old vocabulary with the new directly reflected cultural changes at the social level. The basic characteristic of these changes is to take an original, clearly defined term and blur the edges, thereby widening and extending its meaning. For example, once it was only within the Communist Party that the term 'comrade' (*tongzhi*) would be used, whereas now it has spread to the whole of society and is a general term used to address people irrespective of their social standing, work status, age, sex or relation. The term *shifu*, which meant 'master worker' and was also a polite honorific form of address, has also changed. After the Cultural Revolution it was stripped of its reactionary political content. This type of change embodied the new superstructural ideology whereby differences in rank and profession gave way to equality and respect.

It is worth noting, at this point, the way this new language neglected gender difference. In the immediate days after 1949, there was a lot of activity leading to the eradication of talk about female beauty. In place of this, a social asceticism came to predominate. Analogous to this was the replacement of gender-specific language such as 'husband' and 'wife' with the gender neutral term 'partner', *airen*. The term 'friend' replaced 'darling' or 'beloved' and, in so doing, changed the degree of intimacy expressed. But the most interesting of all these changes was the one whereby marriage was redefined as 'a personal question', *geren wenti*. So, when people met they would say things like: 'have you solved your personal problem yet?' Invariably, what they meant by this was 'are you married and with a family?' Within this new discursive formation, love and marriage were perceived as 'personal matters', but really they were framed by a structure that organised and systematised them. It is very possible that the production and materiality of this term 'personal problem' is homologous to the term used in relation to Party entry and participation. This is described as being an 'organisational question' (*zuzhi wenti*).

There was also a transformation of familial terms. Males and females of the older generation were addressed by younger people as 'auntie', 'uncle' or 'older

sister'. This, or similar terms, were transformed remnants from traditional peasant discourse.

People's names were a particularly interesting area of transformation for they
were influenced greatly by the changing social environment. Within the current
period, they, too, have been touched by social changes and have themselves
adopted the characteristics of revolutionary culture.

These types of name changes and the locus of the changes were also reflected
in the naming of the cities. In the early part of the 1950s, Beijing's new suburbs
such as Hepingli, 'Place of Peace', Xingfucun, 'Village of Happiness', Qing-
nianhu, 'Lake of Youth', Tuanjiehu, 'Unity Lake', Bayihu, 'August 1st Lake',[3] all
transmitted the feeling of youth, newness and vigour. In the 'Cultural Revolution' there was a craze to rename places with names like Posijiu, 'Smash the Four
Olds',[4] Dongfanghong, 'The East is Red' and Hongnongbing, 'Red Peasant Militia'. In Beijing, 'east' was an all too common prefix for any alleyway, and some
475 roads included the term 'revolution'. There were only three 'The East is Red'
streets in Beijing, but 27 'Red Sun' roads. In addition to all this, there began a
very vulgar and crude renaming of alleys and lanes. Suddenly, there appeared
names like 'Young Red Militia Lane', 'Red Guard Alleyway', 'Study Chairman
Mao Alley' and 'Oppose Revisionism Lane' etc. By the end of the 1970s, the heat
had gone out of this process of renaming residential sites, for no matter who was
asked, whether cultured or illiterate, new or old residents, all were heartily sick of
the process. By the beginning of the 1980s, this process had stopped, and it was
at this time that old names began to be restored [yet] this revision still demon-
strated an embarrassing lack of culture.

## Cultural Revolution and Revolutionary Culture

The relationship between the revolutionary and traditional culture is really
complex. New Chinese culture has been defined as 'a national scientific mass-
based culture'. It finds itself flagged as a kind of 'national culture' that is both
non-government and non-Party but which, nevertheless, utilises the nationalism
that it promotes to mobilise for political ends. It is a Marxist–Leninist culture
born with the imprint of Chinese characteristics derived from the village, the
mountain and the gorge. It is a form that ties the construction of revolutionary
culture to tradition by employing, showing respect for and building on the
national historic cultural tradition. At the same time, the relation between the
revolutionary and the traditional is always flexible for the revolutionary goal
always stresses the profitable use-value of the traditional in the service of the
political and economic struggle.

---

3  1 August 1927 was the date of the Nanchang Rising which was later attributed to be the founding date of
   the Communist Red Army. The Red Army is the precursor to the People's Liberation Army of China.
4  These being 'old ideas, old culture, old customs and old habits'.

The conflict of values between traditional and contemporary culture was once rather abstractly labelled as the struggle between the indigenous and the foreign. Later, it was rather arbitrarily relabelled as being between either the 'proletarian' or the 'capitalist'. In the social life of the 1950s, the idea of 'culture' and 'cultural form' was really all over the place, being riddled with self-contradictory and quite mad ideas. For example, in the medical world, it was said to be 'capitalist idealism' that inspired opposition to the use of traditional Chinese medicine, while in architecture, the 'back to the ancients' advocacy of cultural forms was described as being a form of 'capitalist idealism'. The status of Chinese painting was particularly embarrassing: chock prints and prints for the spring festival were forbidden because everything had to revolve around the revolutionary, mass-based tradition. Ordinary oil paintings quickly gave way to the painting of the Soviet schools where political correctness was the key to their appropriateness. This continued right up until May 1957 when the establishment of the Chinese Academy of Art gradually led to respect being shown for paintings with 'national independent character and colour'. This really was the time when China strove to free itself of foreign (most notably, Soviet) influence and thus moved increasingly toward being a closed society.

## ★ WHAT'S IN A NAME: REVOLUTIONARY CHINA AND THE NEW COSMOLOGY OF THE NAME[5]

### YANG DONGPING

People's names in China were a particularly interesting area of transformation during the Cultural Revolution for they were influenced greatly by the changing social environment. Yet even at the time of the revolution in 1949 people's names were touched by the social changes and began to incorporate the characteristics of revolutionary culture. Indeed, one discovers that names were contingent upon socio-political ideology in China even in the earlier part of the twentieth century. At that time, names such as 'Equality' Li (Li Pingdeng) and 'Freedom' Shen (Shen Ziyou) were very popular. Nevertheless, the adoption of names then rested upon lofty ideals and the vast majority of them were aliases, pseudonyms or *noms de plume.*

In the 1950s, the giving of names could be said to fall into a number of different categories. In the first instance, there were those that directly adopted the new political vocabulary, with names like 'New China' Wang (Wang Xinhua), 'Construct the Nation' Gao (Gao Jianguo) and 'Victory' Chang (Chang Shengli). Abbreviations for terms like 'oppose imperialism' (*fandi*) and 'oppose revisionism' (*fanxiu*) were also popular, as were terms such as 'unite' (*tuanjie*), 'do battle'

5  Yang Dongping, *City Monsoon*, 267–68.

(*zhandou*), 'science' (*kexue*), 'culture' (*wenhua*), 'love the nation' (*aiguo*), 'youth' (*qingnian*) and 'east' (*dongfang*), which were adopted as names. The other tendency was to use particular times, political incidents and commemorative dates as the basis upon which to coin names. Examples of this are 'Resist America' Zhang (*Zhang Kangmei*) during the Korean War, 'Great Leap' Wang (*Wang Tiejin*) during the late 1950s, or 'Three Antis' Li (*Li Sanfan*) around 1951, which refers to the three antis campaign that focused on corruption, waste and bureaucracy. As well as this, significant dates such as 4 May (*Wusi*) and 1 August (*Bayi*) became the basis of names. The third type of name was one which captured a certain mood, and took the form of names like 'Tempest' Fang (Fang Fenglei) or 'Stormy' Wang (Wang Fengyun), and included other names like 'Towering Mountain' (*Gaoshan*), 'Great Ocean' (*Dahai*) and 'Great Yangtze River' (*Dajiang*). The fourth type of name tended to be one chosen by high-ranking cadres when naming their children. Such names were derived from the places where their fathers fought during the war against Japan and the civil war. These names indicate where the children were born. These places then became part of the children's names. Hence names like 'Born in Shanghai' Wang (*Wang Husheng*) or 'Born in Yan'an' Liu (*Liu Yansheng*) came into being. This sentiment often led to names like 'Little Beijing' or 'Born in Battle'. In the 1950s, it was not at all uncommon to find entire nursery schools filled with children called things like 'Construct the Nation', 'New China' or 'Resist America' and 'Aid Korea'.

In the Cultural Revolution, these customs underwent further change. First of all, the tendency to give children revolutionary names became hegemonic and names used along with the surname became slogan-like. Surnames like Gan which, in another context could also mean 'to do', were attached to a first name like Geming, which meant 'revolution', thus producing the compound slogan 'to make revolution'. Surnames like Zhao 赵 were joined to first names like Fan 反 and the resulting compound, if pronounced slightly differently as zaofan 造反 instead of zhaofan 赵反, meant to 'rise in rebellion'. Names like 'Eternally Red' or 'Protecting the East' were also popular. This high level of revolutionary consciousness during the Cultural Revolution even led people to change their original names and adopt more revolutionary ones. There was also the heavy use of military analogies in the choice of names. Words like army, soldier, hero and protect were extremely popular. Another popular feature of naming was to give single-character names. Hence, shorter names—like Zhang Dong, 'Eastern' Zhang, or Li Jun 'Army' Li—also became more popular than in the past. This use of shorter, single-character, names reflected the new and positive feeling toward the simple, clean, clear and speedy.

There was also an avoidance of individual, social or literary names, people opted instead to exemplify the depth and beauty of things of the revolution. This tendency quickly became a flood and by the 1970s, this replication of the extremely simple had reached a new height. This culminated in the draining away of social culture and the vulgarisation and impoverishment of spiritual civilisation.

In the vast majority of the examples cited, no distinction was made between male and female names. Traditionally popular names for girls such as Lan (orchid) or Fang (fragrant), lost their appeal or, more importantly, became so politically incorrect that the vast majority with names like this had them changed. At the same time, though, it is possible to identify a kind of mixed form whereby femininity and revolution are joined. This, very possibly, is one strategy for protecting a kind of femininity in naming, or maybe it is simply a vestige and secularised form of the heavy gender differentiation of the past. Either way, it led to a kind of 'heroic spirit' where rouge and lipstick combined with military uniformity producing compound names such as 'Fragrant Soldier' Lin, 'Graceful Army' Ma or 'Public Fragrance' Guo.

## ★ WHAT'S IN A NAME: TRADITIONAL CHINESE COSMOLOGY AND NAMING[6]
### LI YIYUAN

The relation between the name and the five elements or *wuxing* (gold, wood, water, fire and earth) is well known. Striving for balance between the five elements is unlike the balance one wants between hot and cold in relation to food, and, therefore, the methods used are quite different. Moreover, the symbolism of the external appearance necessitates selecting those factors in the person's name that would add to, or detract from, them. The method of achieving external harmony is pursued through the auspicious and inauspicious factors influential in the writing and giving of a name and, even though this basic idea is rather simple, it crosses over into superstition and involves a type of sorcery. There is a pattern to the lucky and unlucky aspects in the writing and naming of a child and, in the streets, many consult the calendar almanac.

6   Li Yiyuan, 'Traditional Cosmology and Economic Development', *21st Century*, 20 (1993), 149. [ 李亦园, '传统宇宙观与经济发展', 《二十一世纪》.]

# 2    FRAMING

Any idea that 'etymological vapour trails' point to origin and clarity is an illusion. Words take on different meanings in different contexts and the only way to understand a word is through use. There is, however, a politics of use. This politics of use is underlined in the charts of the human body that follow. This part begins with a standard acupunctural chart, but a turn of the page reveals the way in which this can be subverted.

Through metaphor and mimicry the acupunctural chart is playfully reconfigured into a series of political statements. Diverse forces chisel away at the certainty of its meaning. The subversive word games of the hoodlum or *liumang* demonstrate that etymological linkages alone are not enough to hold a single meaning together. Word associations replace object associations to force cracks in meaning and open words to other understandings and uses. These word games employ the same subversive tactics as certain 'joke-techniques', condensing, substituting, diverting and destabilising linguistic meaning or revealing hidden meanings that give rise to other understandings.[1] This subversion of the acupunctural chart plots the language game of the 'outsider' who employs them as tactical codes, leading to the jokes and the joys of all those 'in the know'.

Such meta-languages, however, are not confined to words. From the 'language of the look' in the gay pick-up that Jin Ren examined in Part I, 3, through to the tattooing of the criminal gang member to be examined in Part 4, bodily contact and marking become the tactical languages through which common interests are expressed and connections made. A coded language of bodily comportment and signs, a slang vocabulary of double meanings, a physical marking of the body to identify difference, these are all part of the language games of the weak. To play with language in this way is to subvert meaning in a manner that signals rebellion without the formal declaration of war. War, for these people, would only bring forth repression and extermination. Subversion like this offers the opportunity to manoeuvre.

The various uses of the acupunctural chart offer us a means by which to begin to calibrate this playful subversion of the familiar. To meddle with the chart in this way is to 'alienate it' from its popular and official usage. The result, as Zhang's chart all too clearly demonstrates, is art. Yet the art of the *liumang* is one that must always be concealed. Not for them the canvas or the page. After all, once their work appears on canvas or on the page, it enters the public domain and, once there, it becomes traceable and translatable. For the *liumang* caught out in this way, the game is well and truly up.

---

1   Sigmund Freud, *Jokes and Their Relation to the Unconscious* [Trans. James Strachey] (Middlesex: Penguin Books, 1981).

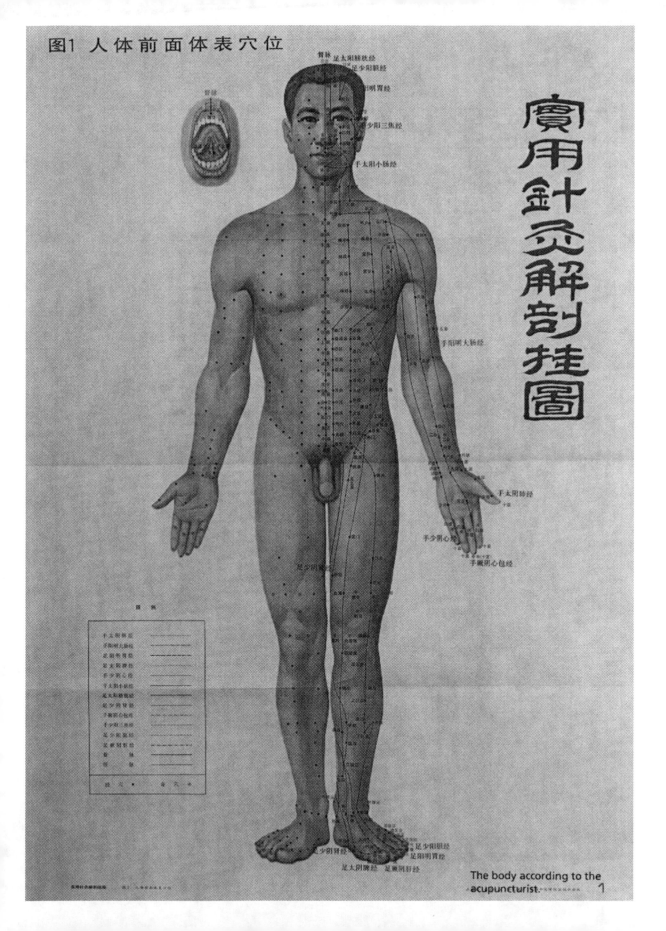

图1 人体前面体表穴位

实用针灸解剖挂图

The body according to the
acupuncturist.

1

# MAO'S BODY AS ACUPUNCTURAL ART
## ZHANG HONGTU

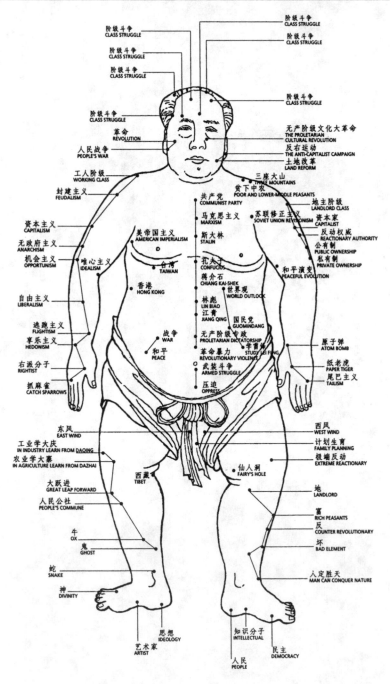

顶天 **ding tian** propping up heaven. Slang for hat.

靶 **ba** target: the place gang members would aim for when attacking. Heilongjiang slang for head.

拔叉子 **ba chazi** North-east slang for stealing from the top pocket.

拔管子 **ba guanzi** pulling on the pipe (because a pen is like a pipe). North-east slang for stealing a pen from the top pocket.

门帘 **menlian** literally, curtain over door (probably because there is a flap on the top pocket). Hebei slang for top pocket.

老天 **laotian** meaning 'heaven'. Heilongjiang slang for stealing from the top pocket.

明仓 **mingcang** open warehouse: because the top pocket will be open. Heilongjiang slang for stealing from the top pocket.

上仓 **shangcang** top warehouse. North-east slang for the top pocket.

天窗 **tianchuang** window of heaven: a pocket which opens at the top, offering a good opportunity. Slang for the top pocket.

上甘岭 **shanggan liang** in the Korean war, taking Shanggan Mount was probably the most costly of battles and huge numbers of soldiers died. This saying depicts a mark which offers real difficulty.

吃里怀 **chi lihuai** *chi*: to eat; *lihuai*: originally breast. To 'breastfeed' is *chi lihuai* but in the parlance of the thief it came to mean to steal from the breast pocket. 'Breastfeeding' for the thief became their 'milk of life'. Slang for stealing from the breast pocket.

里怀运动 **lihuai yundong** *yundong*: in contemporary China, 'campaigns' are a way of bringing about changes. The Cultural Revolution and anti-crime movements are all campaigns. Here the thieves mimic the communists. They organise their own campaigns: the campaign to steal from breast pockets. Slang for thieves in groups stealing from people's breast pocket.

天解 **tianjie** Something sent under guard from heaven. The thief takes what is sent to him/her under guard, i.e. the victim, by God. The thief indicates the justness of the act of liberating what is his or hers. Nationwide slang for stealing from the outside jacket pocket.

拔塞子 **ba caizi** *ba*: to pull out; *caizi*: cork or stopper. To pull out a cork. Slang for stealing a fountain pen from the top pocket.

下仓 **xiacang** lower warehouse, Heilongjiang slang for bottom front pockets.

地道战 **didaozhan** tunnel warfare. In the early 1960s there was a very famous Chinese movie called *Tunnel Warfare*, which was anti-Japanese. The soldiers would wait in the tunnel for the Japanese troops and then surprise them. This is analogous with a difficult theft from the lower pocket. North-east slang for stealing from a lower pocket with great difficulty.

敌后武工队 **dihou wu gongdui** armed guerillas behind enemy lines. The name of a famous movie where the guerillas surprised the enemy and succeeded. Heilongjiang slang for stealing from a lower pocket with great difficulty.

大圣 **dasheng** great sage. Slang for penis.

甩 **shuai** It is the shape of the character which determines its role and not the meaning invested in it. Slang for penis.

有眼无珠 **youyan wuzhu** have eyes but no pupil, i.e. only one hole. The head of the penis looks like an eye without a pupil. Slang for penis.

踢土 **titu** kicking the earth. Northern Chinese slang for shoes.

The male body according to the thief.

北京牌手表 **Beijing pai shoubiao** Beijing brand watch: Beijing is the seat of power and authority. Slang for handcuffs.

到三楼 **daosanlou** at the third floor. North-east slang for stealing from the vicinity of the upper part of the body.

地道 **didao** tunnel. Slang for stealing from the back pocket.
后门 **houmen** using the back door: a play on the political term which means to gain advantage by using somewhat nefarious means. Slang for stealing from the back pocket.
后仓 **houcang** back door warehouse. Slang for stealing from the back pocket.
屁门 **pimen** backside entrance. Slang for stealing from the back pocket.
白蛤 **baigei** 'A free gift', meaning an easy mark. Heilongjiang slang for wallet in the back pocket.
底仓 **dicang**; 底包 **dibao** lower warehouse. Heilongjiang slang for back pocket.
底帘 **dilian** lower the curtain. Heilongjiang slang for back pocket, probably with a flap over it.
底洞 **didong**; 地狱 **diyu** meaning hell. Heilongjiang slang for back pocket, probably hard to get at.

到二楼 **daoerlou** at the second floor. North-east slang for stealing from the vicinity of the middle part of the body.

到一楼 **daoyilou** at the first floor. North-east slang for stealing from the vicinity of the middle-lower part of the body.

一圆 **yiyuan** one dollar coin. Slang for arsehole, used in homosexual subculture.

下手 **xia shou** grabbing the legs. Slang for fetters on the feet.

The male body according to the thief.

吃天窗 **chi tianchuang** *chi*: to eat; *tianchuang*: window of heaven. The top shirt pocket opens at the top (i.e. heaven). Slang for stealing from the shirt pocket.

(吃) 天仓 **chi tiancang** (eating) from heaven's warehouse. Same as 'heavenly window', i.e. indicative of a good opportunity. Nationwide slang for stealing from the outside jacket pocket (but indicating an easy mark).

上扇 **shang shan** top leaf: to take from those top pockets which have lapels over them (hence the idea of a leaf). Nationwide slang for stealing from the top outside pocket which has lapels.

里叶子 **liyezi** inside leaf: probably so named because there is a flap over the shirt pocket. Heilongjiang slang for shirt pocket.

虎穴 **huxue** drawn from a longer saying 不入虎穴, 焉得虎子 *buru huxue, yande huzi*—how can you catch tiger cubs without entering the tiger's lair, meaning nothing ventured nothing gained. Saying *huxue* means 'difficult pocket but a reward in the risk'.

内仓 **neicang** inner warehouse. Heilongjiang slang for shirt pocket.

小窑 **xiaoyao** literally, small pit. The pocket is a small space for storage. Heilongjiang slang for inside breast pocket.

小仓 **xiaocang**; 小插 **xiaocha** small storage space. Heilongjiang slang for inside breast pocket.

旁门 **pangmen** side window. Slang for stealing from a side pocket.

吃平台 **chi pingtai** literally, eat from the platform. Slang for stealing from the outside pocket of someone of about the same height and therefore 'on the same platform'.

明插 **mingcha** publicly putting one's hand in someone's pocket; to publicly steal. Heilongjiang slang.

吃坐窗 **chi zuochuang** Stealing from a window seat. Beijing slang for stealing from a passenger seated on a bus or train.

The male body according to the thief.

牌儿 **pai'er**; 盘子 **panzi**; 盘儿 **pan'er** *pan'er/panzi*: plate. A round face on a woman is regarded as desirable. Indeed, if a woman is regarded as desirable she is called *pan'er liang* (beautiful plate). Slang for face.

傻兜 **shadou** stupid pocket: easy to get at and probably where the woman keeps her purse. Slang for the pocket on a woman's blouse.

梨 **li** pears, meaning breast. 啃梨 **ken li** to nibble on pears, meaning fondle a woman's breasts. Q thus named because breasts look like the letter Q.

门外一片松树林 **menwai yipian song shulin** outside the door there is a forest of pine trees (from the 1960s). Slang for pubic hair. 半天空中一座门 **bantian kongzhong yizuo men** the door in the middle of half the empty sky. Slang for clitoris.

排子枪 **pai ziqiang** machine gun; slang for multiple rape (gang bang). 爬山 **pa shan** climb the mountain; slang for making love. 拍婆子 **pai pozi** pat females; slang for chase women. 扑蜜 **pumi** *pu*: pounce on; *mi*: honey. Slang for chase women. 采蜜 **caimi** *cai*: gather; *mi*: honey. Slang for chase women.

The female body according to the thief.

## SLANG RELATING TO POLICE

棍警 **gunjing** baton-carrying police officer, because all police carry guns or a baton. Slang for police officer.

老交 **laojiao** *lao*: term of address; *jiao*: traffic. Slang for traffic cop.

看街狗 **kan jiegou** the dog that watches the street. Slang for traffic cop.

胶泥 **jiao ni** 'clay' (because the traffic cop just stays in the middle of the road). Slang for traffic cop.

板儿绿 **ban'er lu**; 板儿蓝 **ban'er lan** stiff green/blue, because the clothes of the police are very stiff and as green/blue as a board. (The *er* is Beijing dialect meaning very. Blue was the official police uniform colour prior to 1985.) Slang for army police.

包力士 **baolishi** porter: probably emanates from the fact that in the 1960s many visiting overseas Chinese mistook police for porters because they would help them carry luggage at stations etc. Slang for community police.

穿孝的 **chuan xiaode** wearing death clothes. In the 1960s in summertime the police uniform was white which, in China, is the colour of mourning. This of course is an insulting play on words for it suggests a death in the police officer's family. Slang for community police.

刺 **ci** thorn (in somebody's side). Slang for uniformed and plain-clothes police.

灯泡 **deng pao** lamp to shed light on a scene. Hunan slang for criminal investigation police.

澳洲黑 **aozhou hei** a black Australian. Sichuan slang for plain-clothes cop.

黑腿 **hei tui** black leg. Slang for plain-clothes cop.

看门狗 **kan men gou** dog watching the entrance. North China slang for armed police (because their main task is guarding buildings).

老二 **lao'er**; 二哥 **er'ge** elder second brother (also means cock). Slang for male police officer.

二舅 **er'jiu**; 舅舅 **jiujiu** mother's second (younger or older) brother. Also means cock. Slang for male police officer.

二姨 **eryi** father's second sister. Also means cunt. Slang for female police officer.

钩子 **gouzi** hook, but the pronunciation in Nanjing dialect is similar to dog. Nanjing slang for police officer.

狗 **gou** dog. Shenyang slang for police.

老抓 **laozhua** *lao*: a term of address literally meaning old but here means frequent. *Zhua*: meaning to grab somebody or detain somebody. The expression therefore means a person who frequently detains. Slang for police.

# 3 MARKING

Language, as this section makes clear, isn't always verbal. The tattoo is a form of language that is both expressive and non-verbal. It operates to both mark one 'out' but equally mark one 'in'. In traditional society, tattooing was used to mark out the criminal and the deviant with the so-called 'ink punishment'. The significance of this punishment was two-fold: it marked the deviant out, forewarning people of danger and, more importantly, shaming the offender. Yet, more importantly, in marking the body, the State also marked the family. In traditional China, one's body was not one's own, but a 'gift' from one's ancestor. It should, therefore, be neither marked nor disfigured in any way. This familial bond may have been eroded over time, but it has left its own mark on Chinese society. Even today, no 'respectable' person in China would ever consider tattooing his or her body.

Certainly, there have been attempts to subvert this taboo. Some secret societies attempted to turn it on its head when they began using tattoos to mark out their members. For them, no tattoo meant no favours. Yet such attempts to rehabilitate the tattoo met with little success and stayed confined to such marginal figures as the triad and gang members who were always outsiders and outlaws. In contemporary China, the traditional use of the tattoo as punishment has gone, and while the tattoo is once again being used by gangs as a 'membership badge', it is currently more commonly a sign of a more private and individual form of rebellion. Prisoners tattoo themselves to silently comment upon their conditions, commemorate their incarceration or remember their loves and lives outside the prison walls. On the arm of any tattooed person is a story in summary form, waiting to be told. There are millions of these stories, but the perversity of their collective expression, in a country that traditionally honours the unmarked body, makes the mark of a tattoo a particularly interesting phenomenon in China. In China, irrespective of what the tattoo itself means, it stands as a more general mark of the excluded and it is this which signals its interest.

## THE WORLD OF THE TATTOO[1]
### XU YIQING AND ZHANG HEXIAN

Tattoos mark a heightened sense of self prestige and are a means by which to intimidate others. Because tattoos require a painful operation, those within the black societies (secret societies) who have them regard themselves as heroic and daring. In the Tang Dynasty (618–907), Duan Chengshi wrote that tattooed people were, for the most part, 'young turks' out on the streets. They were 'these 髡 *kun* who had 肤扎 *fuza* on their arms which featured all sorts of designs and messages written within them. They operated within groups that would fight and carry out armed robberies, they would coil around saloons like snakes, and would use the sheep's bones to attack and rob patrons.'

The meaning of the character 髡 *kun* here is bald-headed criminal while 肤扎 *fuza* means tattoo. In some rare cases, officials had tattoos too, but if they did, it was because they either were or had been members of a secret society. For example, Duan Chengshi pointed out that one general from Sichuan, named Wei Shaoqing, was 'not fond of books but very fond of tattoos'. There was an official sent to Guizhou by the name of Cui Chengchong who had one side of his body covered with the tattoo of a snake with the head reaching all the way down to the right hand and the mouth of the reptile was formed by the gap between the thumb and the index finger. When he was with guests and friends, his hands would be covered by the sleeves of his jacket. However, when he drank, he was in the habit of raising his sleeves and he would use his arms to grab the minstrels who performed and would say to them: 'The snake will bite you!' and the minstrels would recoil in fear. This was all done by him for his personal entertainment. This type of unscrupulous prank seems most likely related to the fact that he joined the army when he was very young and drew sadistic pleasure in carrying out judicial torture.

There was also another case of an emperor Guo Wei from the later Zhou Dynastic period who was called 'sculpted green heaven' (signifying he had tattoos). Prior to taking the throne, he had been to many places and even stooped so low as to dig up bodies in order to steal, and then sell, their clothing. Prior to liberation, there was a group of hooligans who had blue dragons on their arms to identify them as gang members. Lumpen society had many types of secret societies and the vast majority used the tattoo as a mark to identify group members.

---

1 Xu Yiqing and Zhang Hexian, *A History of Life Faiths: The World of the Tattoo* (Chengdu: Sichuan People's Publishing House, 1988), pp. 224–26. [ 徐一青，张鹤仙，《信念的活史：文身世界》。]

## ★ TATTOOS: A REVIVAL[2]
**GAO JIAN**

### Tending Toward an Ancient Degenerate Art

Tattoos are a very ancient artform found in the very earliest forms of society. People would use needles or knives to dig into their skin, inscribing designs or Chinese characters and, afterwards, they would add colours, leaving a permanent mark on their skin that would stay with them until they died. In ancient times, primitive peoples would worship such things as the sun, moon, landscape, flowing rivers as well as dogs and sheep. These would be marked on their bodies as a sign of worship.

With social progress, the art of tattooing has not only continued, but also developed and its meaning broadened. It was useful as a means of expressing will. For example, Yue Fei's[3] mother marked his back with a four-character phrase tattoo which read: energise, be loyal to and protect the nation. This reinforced his determination to repay the debt owed to society for the kindness it had shown him. Others have tattoos on their bodies as a form of ornamentation. For example, in the classical novel the *Water Margin*, the character Shi Jin had nine dragons drawn on his back. People have called this 'the nine lines of the dragon of Shi Jin'.

Other uses for the tattoo came during the Warring States Period (475–221 BC) when some people, fearing that in those chaotic times they might lose track of their children, had a design or characters tattooed on them so as to mark them out as their own. Another use came about because of superstitious beliefs and this led people to have tattooed images of Buddha or a cross marked on their bodies as they thought this would help ward off evil and harm. An even more common use was the marking of criminals as both a measure to prevent their escape and as a form of punishment. For these people, marks would be cut into the face. Wu Song,[4] for example, had his face marked twice in this manner and was then sent into exile. The art of tattooing developed down to the modern period not as an ethnic cultural practice, but as a feudal form that displayed a murderous intent. Those most strongly associated with tattoos are generally young hoodlums who are associated with triads, bandits with their 'kings' occupying mountains and those without steady employment who simply wander around. In the eyes of the average person a tattoo is a sign of one thing: a secret society. After liberation, this phenomenon was basically eliminated.

In contemporary times, due to a range of influences and factors which reflected modern society as well as influences from Hong Kong, Taiwan and the

---

2   Gao Jian, 'Tattoos—A Revival', *Social News*, 690 (1993), 2–3. [高健，'文身：死灰复燃'，《社会报》。]
3   Yue Fei is a legendary hero of the Han.
4   A character from the classical Chinese novel, the *Water Margin*.

(Tattoo art on pages 160 and 183 by Simon Moody.)

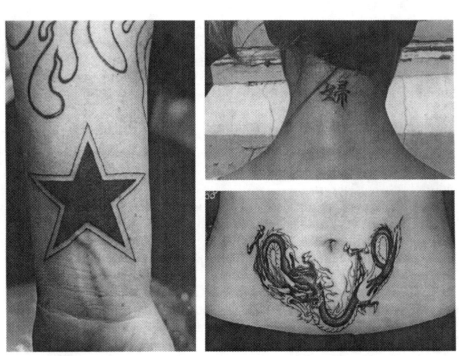

Tattooing the body.

West, this fashion of tattooing was to come back to life in China. This was especially true in the coastal city regions which attracted huge numbers of young people. On the basis of a sample survey carried out among young people at educational institutions, it was discovered that 7.6 per cent had tattoos. These figures also show that there is a higher percentage of youths with tattoos who have broken the law than there is among those youths without tattoos.

Why has there been a tattoo revival?

## The Charm of the Secret Society Tattoo

One day in Guangzhou, inside the bus for Dongwan, a pickpocket was staring at a passenger's bag behind him. He was looking for a good opportunity to steal it. Then, suddenly, he noticed on the man's forearm a tattoo of a 'death's head skull' and crossbones. The thief very quickly pulled his hands back from the bag and, while doing so said: 'I didn't see you clearly so I didn't realise I was on this journey with a friend. Let me offer you my most profound apologies.'

Within the criminal fraternity, the tattoo is regarded as something glorious. Some of them have designs of dragons, phoenixes, a pigeon holding a stalk of grass in its beak, a snake with an eagle's head or an arrow piercing a peach. These are often on their wrists, lower arms or upper arms. Others will have tigers' heads, panthers' heads, or skeletons tattooed on their heads, belly, back or ribs. Still others have their knees or lower legs tattooed with things like two dragons intertwined or a beautiful woman holding a peach in her hand. The tattoos on women who are hoodlums or prostitutes, for the most part, are to be found on their bellies and illustrate things like 'affectionate couples playing in water' or 'a host of arrows being shot into a peach'. Tattoos come in all shapes and sizes, from the ridiculous to the sculpted.

## The Hidden Meaning of this Ugliness

It is possible to split the tattoo into two main types: those which are character based and those which are pictorially based. However, they all very often carry within them an ugly message.

Those which are character based will often use characters meaning 'filial piety', 'loyalty', 'endurance', 'hate' or 'death'. In relation to filial piety, what they mean is 'filial piety toward the gang chief'. When they have written 'loyalty' it means loyalty toward their criminal brothers. Endurance signifies their determination to hang on when things are going against them. Hate signifies that when they hate, they really hate, while death testifies to their views that if death is upon them, then so be it. Apart from those, there are also some other forms like 'weapons cannot harm me', 'long live freedom' and 'the statue of liberty'.

One day, along with an old editor from the newspaper office, I boarded the Guangzhou city train at Zhangmutou railway station in Dongwan city. There was a young girl sitting opposite us on this train. She was of a good appearance, her skin was lovely and white and she looked quite beautiful wearing a short skirt and matching top. We more or less thought that if not a university student, then chances were that she was a dispatch officer for one of the larger companies. Then the old editor caught a glimpse of a tattoo on the young woman's arm which read 'statue of liberty'. He asked her to explain. She answered: 'When I look at you I see an old fart, don't you try to intimidate me with your words. I do what I want without any restraints on my romantic life.' When she had finished, she then cocked her head and pressed her mouth up against the old editor's ear and very quietly and secretly said, 'If you want it, I'm willing to give you ...' With all this going on, the old editor's face went as red as a beetroot and, I must say, I was also left pretty speechless.

I remember last summer, I was visiting a prison farm. While there, I went out into the fields where the prisoners were wearing very few clothes and, as I looked at them, I saw one of them had a tattoo on his leg of arrows going through a number of hearts. As I was accompanying the chief of the camp, I took the opportunity to inquire as to the meaning of the design. The chief told me that this person was a hoodlum and had slept with countless girls. The design stood for his 'conquests'. Some of the male hoodlums have tattoos on their bellies or thighs with designs of 'a beautiful woman picking pears'. Some of the female hoodlums have tattoos in the middle of their breasts of two dragons intertwined. All of these designs, of course, express dirty meanings. A tattoo of a snake coiled around an arrow designates a certain dissatisfaction with the current state of things and demonstrates a real hostility toward the Ministry of Justice. A tattoo of a pigeon holding a stalk of grass in its beak is a sign used by thieves telling those in the 'know' to take care otherwise their things will be taken. Those criminals who are repeat offenders also have their own tattoo which reads 'a hungry tiger down from the mountain'. Upon release, the criminals are like hungry tigers—long cooped up, and still want to get back into business. 'Linking circles' means that the group is all together, that they will suffer or succeed together, and nothing will come between gang members. These are but a few examples, for there are many kinds and they are all used to express harmful meanings.

## The Tattoo as a Record of the Heart

If we examine tattoos from a subjective position, we can see them as expressive of different heart-felt feelings. One is as a means of bringing a gang together and expressing solidarity. It constitutes a kind of 'membership badge' and also a kind of member's 'identity card'. These people are sworn brothers who will give their all for each other. They plan out their 'spheres of influence' within the arena of criminal activity such that some will commit armed robberies, while others will engage in fraud and hooliganism. Quite a number of people actually join these secret societies to avoid disaster, hurt or harm or are forced into being gang members. By being enmeshed in a web they themselves have spun, these people will later end up suffering the punishment of the law.

A second heart-felt feeling is expressed in the form of an inscription which sums up their spirit or character and this is something which will always be with that person. A number of people who have been sentenced by the judicial organs feel very resentful, either of the government or of particular production sites, and they express their feelings in their tattoos which read 'hate', 'revenge', 'death', or they have tattoos depicting 'a sword being unsheathed' and these are carved on their wrists. They carve out their hatred and their desire for revenge, still others will carve on their bodies their personal feelings of resentment or gratitude in relation to individuals. These will either be marked in characters or pictographi-cally and, when connected to revenge, it usually indicates that they are awaiting their opportunity.

The third type of heart-felt feeling is to express one's warmth of feeling or as a commemorative motif. This type of feeling is most evident in those who have morally degenerated or who are hoodlums to begin with. They use the tattoo to express their affections by writing 'darling' on their bodies as a commemorative mark, or they have a tattoo to commemorate some particularly important hood-lum activity they were involved in. Nevertheless, such solemn pledges of love are little other than hypocritical stances.

The fourth reason why people have them done is that they unthinkingly regard them as 'fun' and because they want to model themselves on somebody. The most important group in this regard is the adolescent teenager. Immaturity within this group often means they don't understand the significance of the tattoo and have no aesthetic sense by which to judge beauty. They see others getting them and they quite ignorantly think that they are 'cool' and blindly follow. There was once a case of a young middle-school student who, on his back, had written in a very shaky hand the character *ren*, meaning 'to endure' and he thought this looked very good indeed. After he had it done he told everybody and revealed it to the world. Later on, having failed to graduate from middle school, he decided to enlist in the army. He went to 'sign up' and when he stripped off for inspection during the physical, they discovered his tattoo. His chance of an army career was over.

## Too Late for Regrets

Tattoos, for the very young, can become a source of great harm. First of all, they can lead to dermatitis and, because they lead to a change in skin pigmentation which lasts forever, they can destroy the natural beauty of the body. Because one is pouring chemical pigmentation into the skin, this practice can lead to significant health problems and even cancer. According to newspaper reports, in a certain county in Jiangxi province, there was a couple who gave birth to extremely cute identical twins. Then one day the wife said to the husband: 'These two kids are identical, how are we going to know who is the eldest? It's going to be a bit tricky telling them apart. Maybe we should have them tattooed so that we can tell them apart?' The father agreed. So, they got together a sewing machine needle and some black ink, then they dipped the needle into the ink and got on with the job. They rested the arms of the children on the table and, as their skin was pricked, the children began to squeal, but this did not stop the parents. The result of all this pain were two characters on two different arms, one which read 'big one' the other which read 'little one'. Halfway into the night the two children began screaming, and both had high fevers. So, on the second day, they were taken to the hospital for observation and a check-up. When they were about to be given a needle, the tattoos were discovered. Checks followed and it was discovered that the ink had poisoned their skin, leaving them with dermatitis. And, while they were able to be treated for their ailment, the scars were permanent and the lessons from this grim indeed.

Tattoos can also damage a person psychologically. There was the case of one young fellow by the name of Little Wang who, when aged only eighteen, went along with a couple of his 'brothers' (best friends) and all of them had a dragon and a tiger tattooed on either shoulder blade. But this did not bring them good luck. Later on, they were involved in a gang fight and, as a result, Wang was given four years' imprisonment. After four years in prison, little Wang was determined to repent and turn over a new leaf. He opened a little store and managed the business with great diligence. Later on, he would meet a girl who was most interested in him. Unfortunately, when she caught sight of his back, she was thrown into a real spin. In social intercourse, to see a person with 'dragons' and 'tigers' can be quite disconcerting if not a real turn-off. They are thought of as being a little too strange. Little Wang was quite distraught about people's reactions and was hurt by them so he decided that the best thing to do was to use vinegar and try to get rid of them. All he managed to do, however, was to completely destroy large sections of his skin.

Another example relates to a young woman by the name of Ai Ying. Ai Ying, whose name conjures up someone who is really beautiful, in all respects matched her name with her beauty. But when she was just seventeen, she saw the Japanese movie *Life, Death and Love* and liked it so much that she had these three characters tattooed on her wrist. From then on, any plans she had to marry were doomed. When she was nineteen, she became romantically involved with a young man, but when he saw the three words, 'life, death, love' tattooed on her wrist, he wanted to know who she had been with whom she felt so strongly about. Poor Ai Ying was in an awful dilemma. She denied any previous intimacy, but who would believe her with those three characters tattooed on her wrist? The boy she was with found it impossible to believe her story and, in the end, left with the words, 'bye bye'. Afterwards, there were quite a few other boys interested in her, but all of them thought that with 'life, death, love' stamped on her arm, even a dip in the Yellow River would not be able to clean her sullied reputation, nor replace this eternal love she had felt so deeply about. She is now 27 and just stays in her room for she has not been able to make a life for herself. It is Ai Ying who has the final word when she said, 'I really do wish that I could just cut this hand off but, in reality, it is too late for regrets.'

## THE TATTOO OF THE CRIMINAL[5]
### JIANG FUYUAN

### The Physical Expression of Tattoos among the Contemporary Criminal Population

On the basis of a survey drawn from work done by the Hubei provincial reform through labour association and related departments, it was discovered that, of all those held in detention in the entire province, some 7200 inmates had tattoos. The breakdown was as follows:

> 6196 inmates with tattoos were in the reform through labour (prison) sector.
> 705 inmates with tattoos were in reform through education.[6]
> 299 inmates with tattoos were in lock-ups, watch houses or remand centres.

---

5 Jiang Fuyuan, 'A survey of criminal tattoos and how the situation should be rectified', *Special Teacher*, 5 (1989), 24–5. [姜福元，'对罪犯纹身的调查与矫正'《特殊园丁》.]

6 Reform through labour is a prison for those charged under the criminal code whereas reform through education is the detention centre used for those given an administrative sanction. While the latter is less serious than the former, inmates can still be sentenced to detention for up to 4 years.

Of these,

351 people had tattoos with both pictures and words and this accounted for 4.9 per cent of the total.

3604 had tattoos featuring animal figures (dragons, tigers, lions). This accounted for 50.1 per cent of the total.

Of those that were character (word) based, 1499 or 20.8 per cent had words like 'revenge', 'avenge', 'taken into custody', 'brought in for questioning', 'arrested', or their date of sentence, length of sentence or a woman's name tattooed).

The remaining tattoos featured the following designs:

| | |
|---|---|
| knife or sword figures | 1334 inmates or 18.5 per cent |
| female bodies | 541 tattoos or 7.5 per cent |
| group numbers | 7 tattoos or 0.1 per cent |
| floral designs | 481 tattoos or 6.7 per cent |
| other | 128 tattoos or 1.8 per cent |

Nearly half (48.8 per cent) or 3514 inmates had the tattoo done before they were locked up, while 3686 people (or 51.2 per cent) had them done after they were locked up.

In terms of age, the proportion of those who had tattoos were:

| | |
|---|---|
| 18–25-year-old | 4944 people or 71.4 per cent |
| 26–35-year-old | 1675 people or 24.2 per cent |
| over 36 years old | 581 persons or 8.1 per cent |

The proportion of those who had tattoos according to the types of crimes committed were:

| | |
|---|---|
| hooligan crimes | 2448 people or 34 per cent |
| rapists | 1224 persons or 17 per cent |
| armed robbers | 1224 persons or 17 per cent |
| thieves | 1369 persons or 19 per cent |
| grievous bodily harm | 421 people or 5.8 per cent |
| murderers | 360 people or 5 per cent |
| other | 124 people or 1.72 per cent |

The duration of the sentence of those with tattoos was as follows:

| | |
|---|---|
| those sentenced to 11 years or more | 1192 people or 19.5 per cent |
| those serving 6 to 10 years | 2325 people or 37.5 per cent |
| those serving 5 years or less | 2679 people or 43.24 per cent |

Those with lower level secondary qualifications or less (including the illiterate), 6120 people, or 85 per cent of the total number of people, were tattooed. Of those with tattoos 4309 people, or 59 per cent were from rural families.

## The Psychology of the Tattoo

### Ignorance

The survey revealed that a great many of the inmates who had tattoos had them because they were unenlightened, spiritually empty or seeking spiritual stimulation. There were 4092 people like this, constituting 56.8 per cent of all those who were tattooed. These included people who thought tattoos made them look really remarkable, gave them an air of freshness, were simply regarded as good fun or offered them an amazing mystical feeling. Under the influence of adverse social conditions, these people blindly moved from the standard social patterns of the masses.

### Revenge

After a prisoner has been sentenced, they 'came to a realisation about themselves'. They realised that they have suffered a setback, had a new status and an environment that now placed severe restrictions upon them. With no way of getting out of their situation, they increasingly developed a feeling of resentment, hopelessness, depression and defiance, resulting in them refusing even to recognise their criminal responsibility. Toward those who accused them, and those who took charge of the case against them, they developed a feeling of deep resentment. This spilt over into a desire for revenge, and they recorded this feeling with a tattoo. There were 257 such criminals and they constituted 3.6 per cent of those tattooed. Their tattoos are simply words like 'avenge' or 'revenge'. Some of them also include a knife or an assassin's sword piercing the object of their hatred. For example, the criminal Chen Xiangsheng (a rapist sentenced to thirteen years' imprisonment) had on his forearm a picture depicting a 'knife slicing off a beautiful woman's head' and, while he showed me this, he said: 'I hate the Public Security Bureau and those people that did this to me. I can tell you one thing, this is one revenge that will be sweet.'

### Flaunting one's superiority

There are 1283 people with tattoos that signal a sense of superiority. This constitutes 17.8 per cent of all prison tattoos. These people see others with tattoos of dragons, tigers, knives and swords and think they are really 'cool'. They think such things are really unique and a sign of a really virtuous hero. So they blindly believe they are like that. At the same time, they like the feeling of getting others to pay attention to them. The criminal Xie Feng (hooligan, sentenced to ten years' imprisonment) in an exchange with me said: 'I get into lots of fights, so I want people to be really scared of me and, for this reason, I had a coiled snake cut into me.'

### Sexual desire

The most vulgar of the tattoos are those featuring female bodies—410 prisoners have these sorts of tattoos, accounting for 5.7 per cent of the total. These types of people, for the most part, are hooligans, rapists and hardened criminals who express their motivation in the form of a tattoo. After they have been thrown into prison, there are strict systems of management and tight limits on their behaviour. This stops them doing what they like. Faced with this situation, they feel really frustrated because restrictions are placed on their sexual desires. Hence, they try to think of ways to strive to satisfy their desire, but their lopsided needs for sexual gratification are not satisfied by obscene publications, and, because of this, they use the tattoo to compensate for their sexual feelings. For example, the criminal Chen Jianxin (hoodlum sentenced to fourteen years' imprisonment) decided to carve a naked woman on his inner thigh, and on his arm, the half torso of a naked woman. When I asked him why he wanted the tattoos, he answered: 'I really like women, and don't like to be kept away from them.'

## Superstition

There are 308 people, who constitute 3 per cent of those tattooed, who fall into this category. These people have been influenced by the poison of feudal ideology. This takes the form of a decadent, old and decayed superstitious viewpoint being adhered to. An example of this comes in the form of the tattoo of the criminal Ma Xianbin (sentenced to three years' imprisonment for stealing). His tattoo combines a skull with a cross and demonstrates his belief in God and the hope that God will bless and protect him.

## Remorse

This category has 185 people within it, which constitutes 2.5 per cent of the tattooed prison population. The crimes committed by inmates who fall into this category usually aren't serious. They are often light or casual offenders, or they are guilty of unpremeditated crimes. Nevertheless, the problem is that once they have entered the prison, their remorse knows no bounds. They deeply believe that their crime has injured the people, themselves and their family. Most express the feeling that their 'one wrong step is in need of a thousand eternal regrets'. Under this type of psychological pressure, they opt for a tattoo to express their remorseful attitude. For example, the criminal Zhang Sheyuan (a rapist sentenced to ten years' imprisonment) had a tattoo of one word: 'repentant'. Another example relates to the criminal Yu Weihua (who was convicted of grievous bodily harm and given three years' imprisonment), who has a tattoo which reads 'the lessons of blood can never be forgotten'.

# P A R T

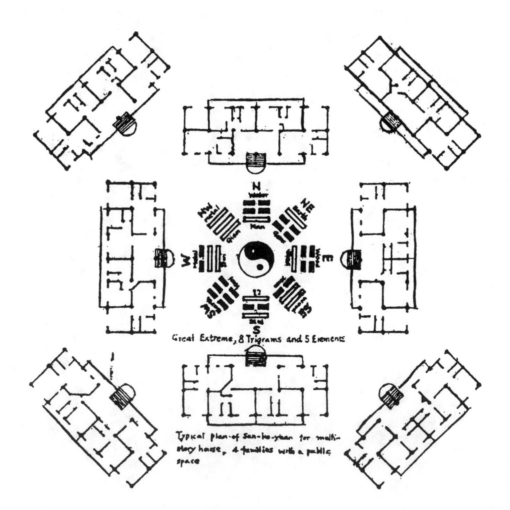

Great Extreme, 8 Trigrams and 5 Elements

Typical plan of San-ho-yuan for multi-story house, 4 families with a public space

# THE ARCHITECTURE OF LIFE

As tattoos mark the body, so buildings mark the landscape, and while the former can be a very private rebellion, the built environment offers no such privacy. The use of space is the grammar of any rhetoric of life, and the following translations decode the way in which spaces, places and lifestyles are negotiated and reconfigured in China. Architectural forms also exist as artefacts; relics of the way life was once lived. Such ways of life may no longer be operative, but they are 'remembered' in the structures, shapes and order of building forms. In this way, the building is like a 'note' to the historian. They are the skeletal forms (Rossi) of lived relations of former times. Just how fossilised and historical such skeletal forms can be is made clear by juxtaposing past and present structures. In the final chapter of this part, the juxtaposition of the old and the new allows the eye to wander and make the connection. Here, the picture replaces the word as the work unit living space, streetlife shopping space, national 'symbolic space' and even the space and place of revolution are all contrasted with earlier forms or former representations.

To understand the full import of such juxtapositions requires knowing something of the 'flesh and blood' of these skeletal forms. It is necessary to go beyond the diagram and picture. Hence, this part begins not with pictures or diagrams but with the words of Chinese architectural theorists who guide us through the symbolic order of Chinese architectural forms and offer a 'picture' of the past to sit alongside the present.

Traditionally, Chinese architecture was based on the compound household form (the *siheyuan*). This was a compound structure made up of 'connecting courtyards, each surrounded by dwelling forms' (the *shenzhai-dayuan* model).[1] Endlessly replicated and enlarged, this structure extended from household forms to urban design. Walls within walls and, behind those walls, more walls. Here is the story of both house and city in traditional China.

Zhao Dongri tells this story in relation to Beijing, but it is equally true of many other ancient Chinese cities, as Yang Dongping's contribution makes clear. Behind each wall there were discrete sites of activity. Walls then, were used not simply to keep people out, but to order those within. Beijing the city of walls was also Beijing the city of hierarchies. Different classes built different dwellings using different colours and living in different parts of the city. Thus despite the

---

1 Zhao Dongri, 'My understanding about and prospects for Chinese architecture', in Gu Mengchao and Zhang Zaiyuan (eds), *Criticism, Analysis and Prospects for Chinese Architecture* (Tianjin: Science and Technology Publishing House, 1989), 211. [赵冬日, '我对中国建筑的理解与展望', 顾孟潮, 张在元 (主编)《中国建筑评析与展望》.]

'transparent' utilitarian appearance of the traditional city layout a radically different cosmology was operative. Compare, as Zhao Dongri does, the traditional Chinese city with those of Europe. In this account, the absence of religious symbols—so central to traditional European city architecture—was a crucial marker of difference but not as one might imagine. Chinese did not lack spirituality but lacked display and, in place of this 'embedded' the spiritual in daily life practices. The hierarchised family order of Confucianism was both a spiritual and practical world and this was embedded in the spatial ordering of the compound house. Traditional China, then, was the land of a million churches, all of which were called home. How this cosmological ordering of space figures in any consideration of socialist building forms is explained as we return to the work unit and its architecture.

Earlier in this volume, Lu Feng and He Xinghan (Part I, 2) pointed to the way the work unit reinforced a lineage or clan-like mentality among its members. What they did not allude to, however, was how this mentality was captured, and indeed reinforced, by the architectonic resonances of work-unit building forms. Hence, this part of the book begins not with an examination of the work unit, but rather with a sociological reading of the idealised building form of clan household life and its relation to the work unit. Xu Ping's work highlights the use of space, reinforcing certain social relations between clan members. In other words, the clan-like bonds forged within the lineage group that Lu Feng and He Xinghan suggest are all too apparent in the contemporary Chinese work unit. These are in part 'propelled' by spatial arrangements. These spatial arrangements, I would argue, take on a more ubiquitous form under socialism and it is through Yang Dongping's work that this becomes apparent. Past architectural forms feed unconsciously into an architecture of life that is the work unit. Space is always calculated in terms of hierarchies. The compound wall makes these micro-orders of power discrete but intense as they cluster, first, around the family under the patriarchal order, and later under the work unit regime around the worker, cadre and Party. That this obsession with the walled form of life comes to unconsciously frame the organisation of that 'socialist new thing', the contemporary work unit, should come as no surprise. The work unit structure is, therefore, no ordinary factory form but a technology to produce a very definite kind of subjectivity and inter-subjectivity long after the original familial 'impulse' found in the household compound form had been forgotten. To understand the degree to which this architecture 'holds' the modern requires understanding something of its past ubiquitousness, its symbolic power and, through this, its ability to transcend conscious memory and 'inlay' a particular 'way of doing'.

As a note to the historian, this examination of architecture requires more than merely contemplating building design, it embodies a concrete frozen mentality of living. The ubiquitous nature of the compound wall reveals more about a mentality than a tradition of building. The study of the Chinese compound architectural structures adds detail to the arguments of Lu Feng, He Xinghan and Yi Zhongtian, graphically illustrating the point Yang Dongping makes when he refers to contemporary China as a 'walled culture'. Yang Dongping points to the way that in traditional times, the difference between rural and urban space (unlike the internal urban landscape) was never a sign of a social or hierarchical division. It mattered little whether one was from an urban or a rural background. Ironically, as Gong Xikui's earlier contribution (Part II, 1) makes clear, it is in contemporary socialist China, where the walls have come down, that these sorts of mental walls have gone up. Mental walls, spelling out in the architecture of the 'new' the word 'class', and also the expression, stolen from the final section of this book, that China has 'entered the market'.

# TRADITIONAL CHINESE ARCHITECTURE AND HIERARCHY[1]

**ZHAO DONGRI**

In traditional times, Europeans believed in the munificence of God and in the authority of religious rather than secular powers. The Chinese, on the other hand, placed humankind centre stage and esteemed and honoured both ancestors and heaven (the latter, in actuality, being to pay homage to nature). Indeed, the emperor who was the representative of heaven on earth was, after all, still considered a mortal. In European cities and towns, urban design centred on the church and the architectural form that structure took reflected its dignity and status. In China, it was quite different. The largest and most dignified architectural forms were the imperial palaces and imperial government mansions, while all forms of temple were treated as secondary. Buddhism and other religions were treated differently from the religions of the West for Chinese believed them to be the embodiment of human aspirations and they therefore should submit to imperial rule. The hierarchical nature of traditional Chinese architectural forms stems from ideas based on these formulations.

The hierarchical nature of traditional Chinese architecture is a reflection of the class structure of these former times. Regulations existed stipulating building forms appropriate to various classes, ranging from the imperial house through to those occupied by the common people. The Ming Dynasty (1311–1644), for example, operated under the feudal system and therefore stressed the Confucian-based patriarchal order. This led to the prevalence of large family dwellings—exemplified by the idealisation of the model family as being four generations under one roof—and this could even consist of housing a thousand family members. The standard residence of the ordinary citizen consisted of three bedrooms and five supporting frames. They were not permitted to use 斗拱 *dougong*[2] nor were they allowed to decorate with bright colours. The colour of any particular residence rested not upon taste, but social rank. In the Zhou

---

1 Zhao Dongri, 'Chinese Architecture', 208–9. Zhang Dongri is a leading architectural theorist in China.
2 *Dougong* is a system of brackets inserted between the top of a column and a crossbeam. Each bracket forms a double bow-shaped arm called a *gong*. Each is supported by a block of wood on each side and that is known as a *dou*. (From *A Chinese English Dictionary*, Beijing Foreign Languages Institute, 1978, 163. [《汉英词典》. ]

Dynasty (1100–211 BC), for example, red was the colour of nobility and, by the time of the Song Dynasty (960–1279), commoners were no longer permitted to decorate their houses in bright colours. In the Ming and Qing Dynasties, only the imperial household was permitted to use yellow glazing. For the nobility at that time, the colour green was deemed appropriate, while the common people were only allowed to use neutral colours. The guiding ideology of city construction was, therefore, to separate superior from inferior, and to identify the emperor as the paramount force. Religions such as Confucianism, Taoism, and Buddhism had little influence over the overall architectural structure. Thus, while religious icons were in evidence on the walls and inside the compound households, the architectural form was never really dominated by them.

## ON BEIJING[3]
### YANG DONGPING

Beijing is a model compound Chinese city. It is a famous and ancient capital with an illustrious heritage, but it was also a city surrounded by a city wall. This was typical of the traditional Chinese city structure. This compound character also exists in cities like Xi'an, Luoyang, Kaifeng, Nanjing, Handan, Zhenzhou, Hangzhou, Suzhou and Yangzhou. The sealed nature of the city is typical of a city form within an agricultural civilisation. It was the fusion of these two elements that formed the character of Beijing's 'ancient capital culture'.

In the Ming and Qing dynasties, the city had three tiers, each cordoned off and made discrete by a wall. At the centre was the City of the Palace (or Forbidden City), and this occupied the entire central city space. It took up an area of about three square kilometres, with the front area reserved for the imperial court buildings, and the rear given over to living quarters. The second tier was made up of the imperial city, and this occupied an area of some nine square kilometres. This area functioned as an administrative district and was full of government buildings. It also functioned as the residential quarter for court officials. The outermost part of the city took up an area of 23 square kilometres and was surrounded by a twelve metre-high wall with nine gateways. The city was divided into outer and inner city districts. In 1553, the outer city wall was built. Originally intended as a wall to replicate and completely surround the inner city wall, financial constraints imposed limits on this original idea, and only the southern section of the wall was built, thus producing the 凸 *tu* shape of the city. The original plan for the city had four strongly fortified walls, but when one adds to this the Great Wall, which lies outside the city in the mountains, one really can say that it became an 'impregnable site'. On the left-hand side of the Forbidden

---

3  Yang Dongping, *City Monsoon*, 29–33.

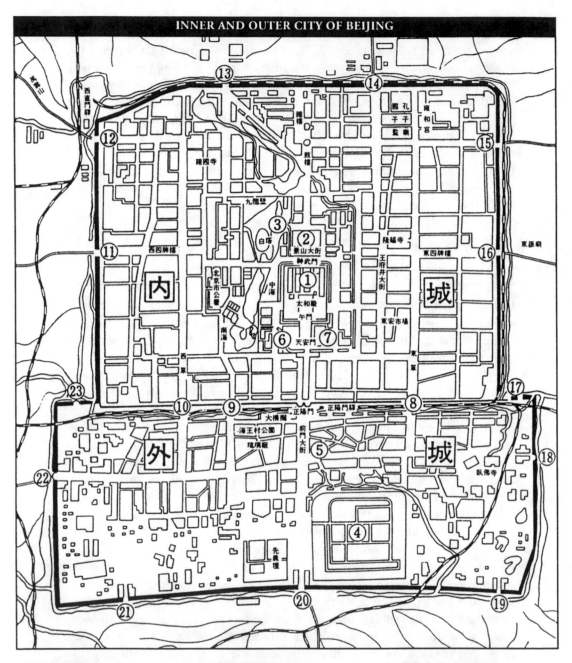

# INNER AND OUTER CITY OF BEIJING

1 紫禁城 Forbidden City
2 景山 Jingshan
3 北海公园 Beihai Park
4 天坛 Temple of Heaven
5 天桥 Tianqiao
6 中央公园 Central Park
7 太庙 Imperial Ancestral Temple
8 崇文门 Chongwenmen

9 和平门 Hepingmen
10 宣武门 Xuanwumen
11 阜城门 Fuchengmen
12 西直门 Xizhimen
13 德胜门 Deshengmen
14 安定门 Andingmen
15 东直门 Dongzhimen
16 朝阳门 Chaoyangmen

17 东便门 Dongbianmen
18 广渠门 Guangqumen
19 左安门 Zuoanmen
20 永定门 Yongdingmen
21 右安门 Youanmen
22 广安门 Guanganmen
23 西便门 Xibianmen

City was the ancestral temple of the ruling house, and on the right-hand side, a shrine to the gods of land and grain. At the very rear facing the city street was the drum tower.

The magnificence associated with the imperial spirit, together with the segmentation and stratification of the system and the arrangement of the city into a series of square compounds formed the basic characteristic and culture of ancient city construction in China. It was a construction that structurally reinforced the strict social separation of the nobility, officials and the commoner. Huge and innumerable contrasts existed in social and cultural life, and there were few channels for social intercourse between the upper and lower strata of society. Because of this lack of social intercourse, strong contrasts existed between the cultures of various groups. Hence, there were great differences between so-called palace culture, the culture of officials, intellectual culture, traditional systemic and ethnic cultures, and the culture of the secular society of common people. This really is one of the key factors to any understanding and knowledge of Beijing culture.

Both traditional Chinese and Western cities are products of agricultural civilisations. Research by urban sociologists clearly indicates that these 'pre-industrial society city forms' are principally centres of administration and religion. Their function as centres of commerce was very much secondary. Those parts of the city designated suitable for agriculture, defence and commerce were surrounded by city walls. An hereditary ruling élite held all political and religious power. Their position could be used to increase the size and influence of a lineage group, or increase or lessen the social position of their subjects within social groups. The central city space was given over to governmental or religious buildings. The heart of the city was reserved as the living space for those involved in religious or governmental affairs as well as those of means. Business people, artisans and workers were 'the market' in those times. The basic form of commercial activity took place at the regular and irregular 'trade fairs'. Close by the city wall, just outside it, were the lower-class people, the prostitutes, the foreigners and those regarded as untouchable.

Traditional Chinese cities shared many of the above-mentioned characteristics, but they also differed in some unique and distinctive ways. In the traditional Chinese cities, it was military and administrative functions which predominated, for rarely did they function as religious centres. Compared to the predominance of religious building forms and the central role of the church in the fortified cities of Europe, this was a highly significant difference. In China, the most famous temples are remote and mysterious, hidden in famous mountain ranges and by the side of famous rivers. Moreover, the role of the city in terms of commercial activity was also significantly less. However, by far the greatest difference of all lay in the relationship established between the country and the city. In the ancient cities of the West, the development of trade, commerce and commodity economy activity brought forth a new identity and status for the city resident. In Germany, there was an old saying suggesting that 'the city offered the air of freedom'. This slogan was derived from the legal regulations that entitled runaway slaves to be given residency rights and freedom should they survive in the city for more than one year. In contrast, as Professor Chen Zhengxian adroitly remarked, 'administration and culture largely symbolised the [Chinese] city. On the whole, there was little difference between the city and the country with few differences evident between the rights and penalties of city and non-city residents. It certainly was not a function of the wall to divide people in terms of the level of harm they were to endure.' Within the political and economic structure of Chinese feudalism, the city functioned as a dispatch point for officials posted to regions by the central government. They formed a vast control network over the agricultural society. Essentially, city and rural residents shared similar characteristics, and there was no separation from the peasants by the formation of a city resident identity. The city did not exist in opposition to the countryside, but derived from it; both had common characteristics.

## BEIJING: THE CITY AS COMPOUND[4]
### ZHAO DONGRI

The quintessential character of old Beijing with its traditional layout can best be seen by looking along its north–west axis routes which stretch eight kilometres in length across the city. This axis crosses four parts of the city, that is, those parts outside the former city wall (*wai cheng*), those parts within the walled part of the city, those parts within the royal part of the city and those within the Forbidden City (the Gugong). This imaginary axis also cuts through the nine city gates (that is, the 永定门 Yongdingmen, 正阴门 Zhengyingmen, 中华门 Zhonghuamen, 天安门 Tiananmen, 端门 Duanmen, 午门 Wumen, 太和门 Taihemen), reaching the great palaces of the Forbidden City. If one were to calculate from the 午门 Wumen or Meridian Gate and move in a northerly direction, this imaginary axis would cut through nine palace gateways—these being 太和门 Taihemen (the Gate of Great Harmony), 太和殿 Taihedian (Hall of Great Harmony), 中和殿 Zhonghedian (Hall of Middle Harmony), 保和殿 Baohedian (Hall of Preserving Harmony), 乾清门 Qianqingmen (Gate of Heavenly Purity), 乾清宫 Qianqinggong (Palace of Heavenly Purity), 交泰殿 Jiaotaidian (Hall of Unity), 坤宁宫 Kunninggong (Palace of Earthly Tranquillity), 坤宁门 Kunningmen (The Gate of

---

4   Zhao Dongri, in *Chinese Architecture*, 210.

*Opposite*: The Forbidden City. From top to bottom, the buildings are: the Palace of Earthly Tranquillity, the Hall of Unity, the Palace of Heavenly Purity, the Gate of Heavenly Purity. Next is the Hall of Preserving Harmony, the Hall of Middle Harmony and the Hall of Great Harmony. The Gate of Great Harmony and the Meridian Gate are at the foot of the illustration.

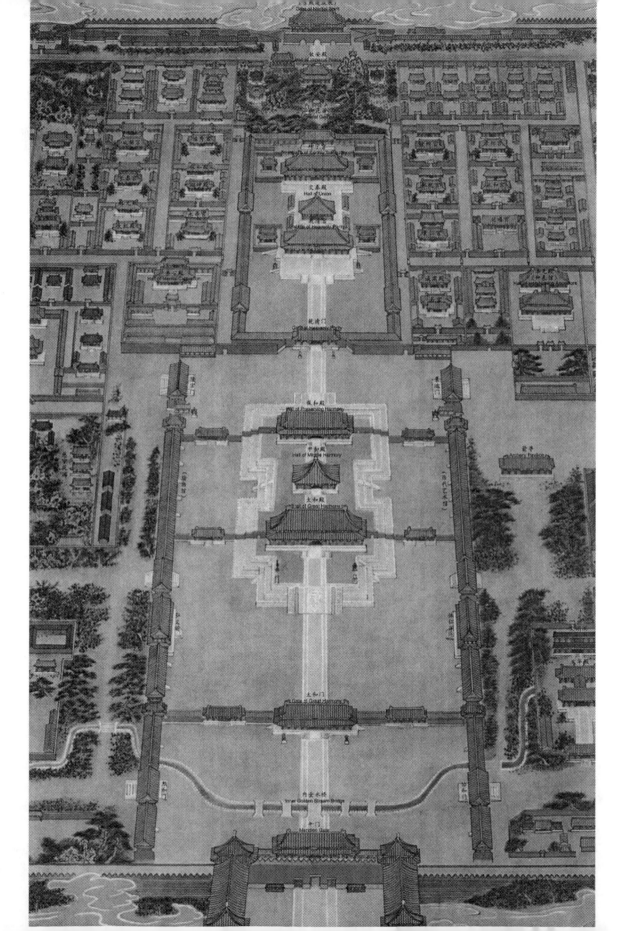

Earthly Tranquillity). Upon entry into the Forbidden City, the first three *dian* 殿 palaces are for State business, while those to the rear are for the court's personal use, housing the emperor and his concubines. This entire architectural form was built upon a compound model of connecting courtyards. Each of these is surrounded by dwellings (the *shenzhai-dayuan* model), which are built upon, and multiply, the compound household form surrounding a courtyard. That is to say, they are *siheyuan* or compound household structures.

# SOCIAL RELATIONS AND THE ARCHITECTURE OF LIFE

'Any edifice', writes Philippe Harmon, 'is by nature forgetful' and it is for this reason that decrepit building forms display 'explanatory plaques' to guide the viewer in reading their former meaning.[1] This introduction, although plaque-like in form, serves to engrave on the mind of the reader the suggestion that architectural structures don't just reflect social relations but play their part in structuring them. While the edifice may consciously forget, unconsciously, it remembers too well.

Earlier in this volume, the inward-looking and traditional nature of work unit social relations were alleged to be an unconscious inheritance (remembrance) of clan or lineage commitments mimetically reworked to suit the new social order of the work unit. Part of the reason for this, I would now suggest, is because of the compound architectural style of the work unit. This mimetically reworked traditional household and clan relations, and reinforced an unconscious analogy between past and present and led to traditional social forms reasserting themselves.

The work unit was, in its high socialist form, both a spatial as well as social phenomenon. Work units invariably used the traditional compound model of architecture to cluster their various buildings together and, in so doing, produced the work unit community. This meant that offices, residences, schools and even factories were—are—all within the same compound and cordoned off from the wider society by large walls and guarded public entrances with discrete open entrances for 'those in the know'. A person not only worked in a unit, they lived in it. They became, to use the words of He Xinghan (Part I, 2), 'people of the work unit'. This architecture lent itself to Lu Feng's critique (Part I, 2) that work units forged clan-like relations; it reinforced Yi Zhongtian's (Part I, 2) point about the formation of an internal work unit culture and even illustrated the point Yang Dongping makes when he calls the Chinese nation the land of the 'walled culture' (Part IV, 2).

Xu Ping's article dramatically illustrates the way traditional clan relations were forged in a similar spatial environment to the contemporary work unit. Indeed, he suggests that this form of architecture was crucial in directing the clans' gaze inward and producing a tight-knit relation between clan members. Yang Dongping's piece lends itself to an historical comparison of the technology of the wall in promoting discrete social spaces and communities. From the traditional compound household architecture of Northern China to the enclosed and hermet-

---

1   Philippe Harmon, *Expositions: Literature and Architecture in Nineteenth-century France* [Trans. Katia Sainson-Frank and Lisa Maguire] (Berkeley: University of California Press, 1992), 92–3.

ically sealed space of the work unit, the walled nature of life provides compelling evidence of some form of unconscious continuity. Both articles in fact point to the architectonic nature of compound design in structuring life and social relations.

The reason for the power of the wall to so dramatically frame the production of a particular type of subjectivity may, perhaps, be gleaned from Wang Shiren's contribution, which makes clear that this form, while dominating the household, formed the template for virtually all architectural structures in traditional China. The reason this compound architectural form spreads beyond the household is because it is tied into a cosmology of life reflected in the society at large. Hence, this architectural style spreads across the landscape not merely because of its utility, but also because it reflects, embodies and reinforces a traditional Chinese cosmological view of the world. Such form of argument reinforces the suggestions made earlier by Xia Yong and Li Yiyuan (Part I, 1) about social relations in traditional China. Their work demonstrates the way traditional belief systems saturated all aspects of life, but what we find here is that the compound building form, in creating a structure within which such beliefs could be lived, reinforced the sense that such relations were both natural and given.

Little wonder, then, that when work units replicated a similar architectural form, they encouraged similar sorts of social interaction. Socialist China became a nation of discrete work unit spaces and a distinctive Chinese mentality increasingly imposed its will on a more recently arrived view of socialist modernity.

## CLANS, GIFTS, ARCHITECTURE[2]
### XU PING

The circulation of gifts has changed. Gifts are still given within the clan and also between relations, but now one also finds the obligation includes the giving of gifts to subordinates, between student and teacher, between villagers and neighbours, and even between strangers. The many and various forms of gift giving no longer has as its only object the consolidation of interpersonal relations. Rather, gift giving has become significant in so far as it leads to a whole new way in which a space for new human relations can be opened up.

Within contemporary Chinese society one can note a clear decline in gifts related to those with whom one has close ties while gifts not designed for those with whom one has close ties have increased enormously, as demonstrated by the unprecedented increase and variety of gifts offered within enterprises. Behind this change is the implication that there has been an historical development in the location of interpersonal relations. With regard to traditional interpersonal relations, blood ties and those between relations were judged to be the loftiest kind. This high regard extended the importance of blood and kin relations which

---

2   Xu Ping, *The Etiquette and Customs Attached to the Presentation of Gifts* (Beijing: Overseas Chinese Press, 1990), 242–45. 〔许平，《馈赠礼俗》。〕

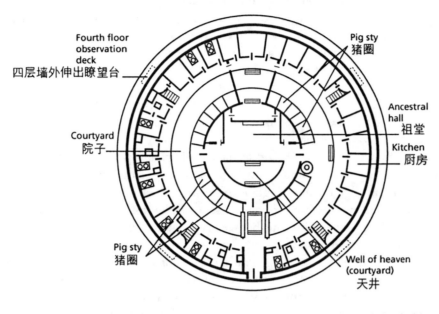

Fourth floor observation deck
四层墙外伸出瞭望台

Pig sty
猪圈

Courtyard
院子

Ancestral hall
祖堂

Kitchen
厨房

Pig sty
猪圈

Well of heaven (courtyard)
天井

Clan household.

together formed the basis of clan relations. These relations embodied the highest moral aims. Indeed, it can be said that in traditional China, human relationships were relations of close ties centring upon the clan. This reached the stage whereby a great many people not only lived their life restricted to just one place, but also restricted their human relations largely to the clan. In present-day Southern Jing (Nanjing) county, Fujian province, there exists a perfect example of this type of relation expressed in architectural form in the *huaiyuan* building. This is a building that is circular in shape and made of dirt and stone. From the outside it looks like a blockhouse. Indeed, at its base it even has a hole which looks just like an embrasure, ·clearly giving the feeling that outsiders wishing to enter would be blocked. In fact, in this entire structure, there is only one small entrance, which opens onto a central courtyard area of a circular shape. Half this central courtyard area is devoted to the 'well of heaven' (courtyard), while the other half is given over to an ancestral hall. No matter which way one looks, in all directions one can see the upper, middle and ground floors of this structure. The ground floor is devoted to animal pens and the like, while the first and second floors are for human habitation. These entire living arrangements operate on one rule: all doors open onto the central area. Within this big clan court, everything is arranged on the basis of clan seniority, with the aged living in the first-floor rooms. Ordinarily, men would leave the compound to work during the day, while women would remain within the compound carrying out all sorts of household chores. Because of the rather closed nature of the entire structure, and because life's daily necessities could all be found within the compound structure itself, there was, therefore, little need to leave the compound house. Hence, each clan member tended to live in the seclusion of their own compound. It can be said that this type of structure imposed a limit on one's living environment and one's social relations. It can also be pointed out that this type of circular building structure was far from small in scale since this structure covered a vast expanse and defined a place that the clan could guard for itself and cut itself off from the outside world. It thereby accurately reflected the closed nature of traditional Chinese forms of social interaction.

This is by way of a background to the gift obligation which is both an internally circulating relation and, most importantly, a relation tying one to one's parents, siblings, grandparents, grandchildren and older male and female relatives. Indeed, the widest circulation of presents within this economy of giving was restricted to the giving of presents between two clans connected by marriage. The goal of this operation was not to open up a space for new interpersonal relations, but rather to consolidate existing familial ones. Moreover, when this type of clan relational network was extended down to cover all the various elements, it already reached a scale that replicated a small society. Connections between relations established in this way also had a way of seeping into social relations. It was this form of giving that enveloped other types of gift-giving relations, such as those between neighbours or those that developed to reinforce scholarly or professional ties. It meant that such relations were themselves strongly coloured by the family relation. Indeed, this reached such a degree, that in the end they, too, acted like the relational gift-giving obligation for they became internally circulating.

Obviously, the internally circulating gift-giving obligation cannot be extended *ad infinitum*. This is because it loses the capacity to enhance cultural flow and hence it also loses external stimuli and promotional effect. As an internally circulating form, the culture of gifts itself gradually atrophies.

Modern human relations have changed—they have broken out of the birdcage of this traditional model. They have taken on a new pattern and style expressed clearly in their pro-active spirit, which is best reflected in two aspects: their elective nature and their changeable character. Their so-called elective nature can be seen if compared with what we can call the fixed nature of the traditional model. For example, blood relations can be described as non-elective, while marriage ties have changed from being passive compliance with parental orders and the matchmaker's words to a self-determining and self-deciding form of elective relation. Similarly, neighbourhood (area) ties, scholarly ties, and professional ties are all of this elective type.

The so-called changeable nature of contemporary relations is shown in comparison to the rigidity of the traditional model. Apart from blood relations, which are always non-elective, others, such as neighbourhood ties, scholarly ties, professional ties, and even marriage ties are all negotiable relations in contemporary society and can be altered. This is especially true with regard to living arrangements, going to study and engaging in a profession. All of these are now based on choice. In contemporary society, a person rarely makes a 'decision that will last a lifetime'; change, transfer, and movement are the norm. Hence, the new types of interpersonal relations, while centring on blood, marriage, neighbourhood, study and professional work are, for the most part, self-determining and open in structure. Gift giving within these types of interpersonal relations leads to a new and very strongly subjective form of social interactive structure and this, in the end, leads to a very different field of operation being put into play.

## TRADITIONAL CHINESE ARCHITECTURE AS SYMBOLIC HIERARCHY[3]

### WANG SHIREN

Besides expressing the functional nature of architecture through symbolic methods, which is itself an important and significant question, it should be added and stressed that in traditional China, architecture itself was of a symbolic form with symbolic implications. The basic architectural form of residency in China was the compound house, the *siheyuan*. It signified everything from lineage group relations through to societal forms. Indeed, the segmentation and hierarchisation of all such 'relations', be they between elders, betters or the lowly, blood relatives and non-blood relations and siblings, or even host and guest, constitute the very basis on which a relationship is built up between architecture and spatial representation. Hence, appropriate appellations are devised for those parts of the residence used by particular occupants. Rooms are described as 高堂 *gaotang*, which is the main room for parents or ancestors, 长房 *zhangfang*, that of the elder son, 内子 *neizi*, that of the wife, 外子 *waizi*, outer wife, 掌柜的 *zhanggui de*, the person responsible for the internal order of the household, 堂兄弟 *tangxiongdi* male cousins on the paternal side, 表姐妹 *biao jiemei*, female cousins on the maternal side, 塾师 *shushi*, family tutor, 门子 *menzi*, pupil/disciple, 廊下×房 *langxia × fang*, along the corridors (廊 *lang*) at the side of the compound house where various rooms occupied by family members are 'named' according to the occupant etc.

It is also suggested that the names used and the architectural forms chosen for the imperial palace are ordered so that they correspond with the heavenly equivalent. The Heavenly Temple in Beijing is therefore a circular building with a dominant blue colour throughout, and this stands as an architectonic metaphor for heaven itself. The Imperial Garden, with its lakes and three islands, is an earthly signification of *penglai* 'the home of the angels'. The first emperor of China, Qin Shihuang, built his palace in Xianyang to imitate the architectural forms of the six states he had vanquished. Chinese scenic and historic sites inspired the designs

---

3  Wang Shiren, 'The Wisdom of the Chinese Nation and the Vitality of Traditional Architecture' in Gu Mengchao and Zhang Zaiyuan (ed.), *Chinese Architecture*, pp. 140–41.

for the emperor Qian Long's palaces such as Yuanmingyuan and the Imperial summer villa in Chengde. This latter building, in turn, drew on the architecture of the whole nation and, in so doing, signified the Chinese state as a single, unified, domain.[4] Hence, whether we examine the buildings in terms of architectural style or decorative motif, it is obvious that these buildings have definite and significant implications. What is particularly significant to note here is the way such symbolism is deepened, reinforced and visibly demonstrated by the upright stone tablets, horizontal inscription boards, antithetical couplets, pillars and posts. This demonstrates not only the importance of symbolism in China, but also the architectural investment in symbolic forms through which the Chinese nation comes to an understanding of both society and the cosmos. This is an important dimension of the wisdom of the Chinese nation.

The unity of heaven and earth, which is the conceptual frame through which Chinese operate, leads to both a collective orientation as well as an active and pragmatic spirit being deployed in social practice. That is to say, it expresses well the humanist spirit. From an architectural perspective, this has led to the humanist spirit being coded into a way which emphasises social functionality, but which nevertheless allows for a full play of its spiritual role. It thus operates to bring reason and spirit together as one. Indeed, one could go so far as to say that it is an enrichment of architecture through investment in ethical concepts such as rites, music and harmony. Architecture connects reason and emotion, goodness and beauty, ethics and psychology, practical concepts and aesthetic appreciation so that they all emerge, fused as one, encapsulated in the physical form of the building.

---

## ⊛ CHANGING COMPOUNDS: FROM COMPOUND HOUSEHOLD TO WORK UNIT[5]

### YANG DONGPING

---

Typical of Beijing residential architecture is the *siheyuan*, or compound household, which fully embodies the 'taste of Beijing' and the spirit of Beijing culture.

Cultural anthropology would no doubt tell us that this residential architecture is the result of an adaptation to the natural environment which has become a kind of cultural symbol and environment within which human behaviour has been influenced in subtle but profound ways. The original model for this compound came from the residential house style of the northern Chinese farmer. It is the product of a traditional lifestyle and agricultural economy which always took the family as the basic unit. The single-storey house was built using a large amount of space. It embodied traditional Chinese cultural values and reinforced

---

4   See 'Buying Nation', Part IV, 4.
5   Yang Dongping, *City Monsoon*, 178–80.

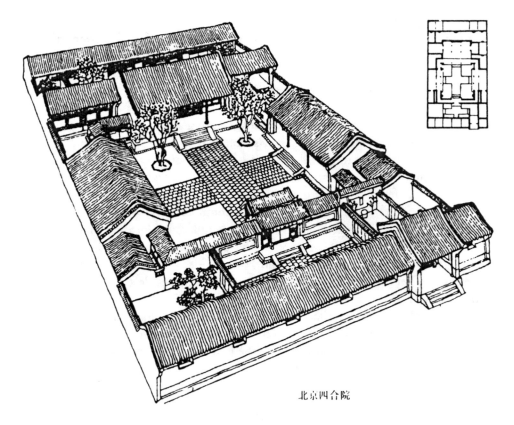

北京四合院

Compound household.

the social ideal of a patriarchal family system. Moreover, it underscored the survival skills of the northern Chinese farmer.

The typical compound house is set to the north and faces south. This ensures that the house has an ample amount of light. A bright and spacious courtyard is at the centre of the house, surrounded by rooms on all sides of the compound. The main room faces south and this is occupied by the most senior members of the family. The junior members of the household occupy rooms in the eastern and western wings. The southern room that faces north, usually serves as a lounge, a study or a servant's bedroom. The gate of the compound normally opens on the south-eastern corner of the house leading to the expression *kanzhai xunmen* 坎宅巽门 or the *kan* house and *xun* gate. Here, the *kan* is to the north, while the *xun* is to the south-east. They constitute the wind element in the five elements (*wuxing*) and it is believed that a gate that opens to the south-east will bring forth good luck. In the house of the wealthy, verandahs are used to connect two or more compounds and this creates a series of compounds and courtyards in the style of a prince's residence.

The compound household style embodies both the strictness and inflexibility of the traditional social order but also the sentimental comfort this connection affords. This emanates from its architectonic mimicry of the family order in which the old lead the young.

The compound household also embodies the idea of an harmonious relationship with nature. Deng Yunxiang believes that the strength of the compound household lies in its combination of closed and spacious elements. 'Closed' ensured the demarcation of one's own space, that is, the space of the family, 'spacious' made it easier to gain a good perspective on things ensuring few limitations on one's lines of vision within the compound.[6] This combination meant that one could feel the changing of the seasons and thereby remain sensitive to nature while still remaining closed within the compound.

However, as a residential structure, the compound house does lack practicality. Only the northern room is warm in winter and cool in summer. There is no sewerage system in the compound and few considerations seem to have been given to kitchens and toilets. Without a public toilet, people tended to simply urinate anywhere in the laneway.

Professor Xu Liangguang has compared residential housing styles in America and China. Typical American houses are surrounded and adorned by plants, but there are no walls or fences surrounding the household. Curtains and blinds are invariably used only as objects to separate the inside of the house from the outside. No one should 'invade' another's private space inside the house. Children are not allowed to rush into their parents' room. In fact, a right to privacy is even observed between husband and wife. In the Chinese compound, there are surrounding walls to make a 'natural surrounding'. The courtyard within the walls becomes the site of traditional patriarchal family life: sometimes there are no doors between rooms, parents have absolute rights to enter their children's private space and the children can use their parents' personal belongings as they wish. There is no privacy, and everyone learns to handle the complicated human relations that follow from this. The Chinese attitude towards life takes shape in this environment and it has the family at its core.

Surrounding walls demarcate the compound which, in turn, has the family as its basic unit. Courtyards and walls enclose the house, thus creating lanes. In the city, walls demarcate the prince's palaces, the emperor's palace, the inner city and outer city. The outer city is still surrounded by the great wall. Walls not only form the city's skeleton, they also form the parallel notion of the family-state. The walls not only block people's vision, they build up psychological barriers for city people. They re-shape and change personalities, creating the so-called 'walled culture'.

---

6   Deng Yunxiang, *The Compound House of Beijing* (People's Daily Press, 1990), 111. 〔邓云乡，《北京四合院》。〕

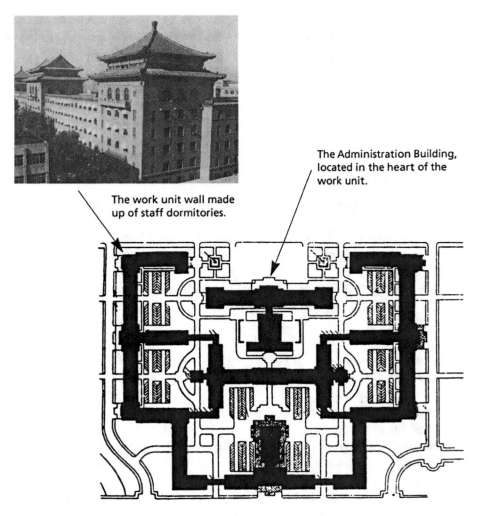

The Administration Building, located in the heart of the work unit.

The work unit wall made up of staff dormitories.

A work unit in Beijing.

## The Mimesis of the Compound Form[7]

In quite a number of the new large work unit compounds, one suddenly discovers the use of space in which the traditional courtyard form is accompanied by buildings with a traditional, national façade right down to the use of glazed tiles on the roof. In terms of their effect, however, they are absolutely different to past forms for they lack the atmosphere of warm friendship and closeness.

7   Zeng Zhaofen, *Design and Style in Contemporary Chinese Architecture* (Tianjin Science and Technology Press, 1989), 94–5. 〔曾昭奋，《创作与形式：当代中国建筑评论》。〕

The Sanlihe Central Committee unit's office block in Beijing was built at the beginning of the 1950s and has a ten-storey office block to the north and all the rest of the buildings are five storeys. These high-rise buildings form the wall of the enclosure. This, however, has a retrograde influence. There is little activity inside these walls and even within the 'heavenly well' courtyards there is little chance of growing flowers or trees. Thus, the traditional spatial form dies because the social atmosphere within dies. This type of death isn't bad because it is an effect of the technological progress that enabled us to build upward.

## From a City of Laneways to One Made Up of Work Units[8]

Go out from Tiananmen Square, pass by the Great Hall of the People or go past the Qianmen Watchtower and there, before one, is a sea of densely clustered houses, grey in colour and spreading across the horizon like waves. Until very recently, many thought of daily life in Beijing as the stories of compound houses and the inhabitants within. This is the Beijing of Lao She's *Teahouse* or *Four Generations under One Roof*. It is the city of Liu Xinwu's *Clock Tower*. It is a familiar picture: Beijing people living a warm yet desolate life under the light of a setting sun.

From the 1980s onward, another Beijing began to emerge from the pens of writers and the images of filmmakers. *The Girl from Huangshan* was one of the earliest depictions of this other Beijing. This was the story of a young *baomu* nanny from Anhui Province who moved into a big work unit compound where she lived and worked for a high-ranking official's family. Even the neighbours know nothing of these other lives behind the compound wall. Until the publication of three novels from Ke Yunlu, the lives of the officials behind the walls remained a mystery. In the novels *New Star*, *Day and Night* and *Decline and Prosper*, the lives behind the compound walls are revealed from a particular perspective: life in Beijing behind its big compound walls. Through these works people came to peek at the intelligentsia and the cultural élite coming into, and going out of, the walled compounds. They saw a little of the political rivalry that was taking place in the officials' lounge-rooms, they saw the manipulation that was going on, they spied on the private salons of the high-ranking cadre's family, and they glimpsed at the daily lives of writers, journalists, artists, researchers and other members of Beijing's 'high society'. The new political movements and cultural trends of Beijing no longer sprang from the tiny laneways. There was now a new type of Beijing person and a new type of community—the big walled compounds of the work unit became the epicentre of life in Beijing city.

No matter whether one goes out to the far end of west Chang'an Avenue, to the north of Muxudi, passing the Baishi Bridge or heads out to Zhongguancun, a

---

8    Yang Dongping, *City Monsoon*, 249–58.

different picture of Beijing begins to emerge. In these places, there are no laneways or compound houses covered with grey tiles. Nor are there any princely compounds or imperial court buildings. These areas were, in times gone by, the wastelands of the outer city. Today, it is a different story. As one moves down the road one discovers that walls connect to other walls and one work unit compound adjoins another. Ornate gateways, large enough to allow cars to enter and leave, identify the status of these various work unit compounds. In the vast majority of cases, these entrances do not have any sign to indicate what the unit is or which department it is attached to. In fact, all they have is a mysterious gate number displayed on the wall.

There are two types of compounds in Beijing: one is the leading establishments of the Party, the government, the army and the central departments, the other is the scientific, cultural and educational work unit or those of arts associations.

# 3

# OUT OF THE
# WORK UNIT

'What work unit are you from?' asks the DJ at the beginning of a Chinese radio show. 'Would it be okay if I just told you my identity card number', replies the young listener. So begins the article by Zhu Huaxin in this collection. It is a beginning that, in relation to this collection as a whole, quite overtly refers back to things already examined (identity cards and forms of identity) and forward to things about to be examined (the move out of the work unit system). At a deeper level, it also points to issues already covered. The article 'From work unit person to social person' illustrates the power of the name, the fear of identity, or, as Zhu reads it, the changing forms of subjectivity in China. Such changes do, of course, resonate throughout this volume.

What Zhu makes explicit is the changing nature of subjectivity in China brought on by the reform of the work unit system. These changes, he notes, are 'signalled' by 'little things' such as offering a number rather than a name, or considering oneself a social being rather than 'a work unit person'. These 'little changes' may not appear all that significant, but they are, in fact, of the greatest import as they are 'markers' of a changing sense of self among Chinese.

In this chapter, the move out of the once-ubiquitous work unit system is highlighted through an examination of the 'one family, two systems' model. To appreciate the significance of this 'little thing' requires an understanding of the importance of the work unit in the daily life of ordinary Chinese. Its importance goes well beyond material considerations and centres on the psychological and even spiritual support it brings to daily life. As previously noted, work unit life has been ordered by and built upon (radically modified) traditional forms of living. Herein lies both the original strength of the work unit and the dilemma that this form of social organisation now poses for reformers.

Economic reform demands of production units that they be assessed purely on economic grounds. The clan-like structure of the work unit militates against this. Work units operate by blurring the lines between economics, politics and social and moral issues. The work unit is, in this sense, more oeconomic than economic for it is tied to a moral and economic order. As economic reforms increasingly require the separation of these various domains, the once tight, organic, unified system of the work unit is broken down and the result is a shift in personal commitments away from the unit and toward broader society. It is a shift that Zhu celebrates but, such celebrations, I would argue, are premature.

While Zhu traces the shift away from the work unit tradition he studiously ignores the fact that 'vapour trails' of tradition—which Lu Feng (Part I, 2) earlier suggested transformed the work unit into a lineage-like organisation—are far more resilient than the work unit itself. Hence, the decline of the work unit is not coterminous with the 'end of history'. The lineage-based reciprocity inadvertently encouraged by the socialist work unit has, to my mind, not been extinguished by economic reform. Indeed, it has been one of the few aspects of work unit life temporarily woven into the social fabric of post-reform China. The collectivism and mutuality the work unit encouraged, and which acted as a 'tell-tale sign' of their lineage-like nature, is mimetically transformed rather than obliterated by the reform process and now takes a more petite and traditional form. This petite form of collectivist mutuality is familialism and it re-emerges as one member of the family leaves the unit to make money in private enterprise while the other remains in the unit to secure the on-going benefits. It is summed up in the new popular slogan 'one family, two systems' which is briefly examined by Zhu Huaxin, and dealt with in detail in the interview with Hu Lianpin. What is striking about the benefits Hu Lianpin describes as flowing from 'one family, two systems' is that they are not purely material but are strongly relational and dependent upon the 'social network' her husband can employ by staying in his current position. If one recalls Lu Feng's critique of the work unit structure (Part I, 2), it will be remembered that he suggests they reproduce the conditions under which 'relational networks' or *guanxi*, similar to those of the lineage group, are built up. What Hu's interview suggests is that 'relational networks' or *guanxi* may be substantially more enduring than the work unit structure.

Economic reform does not abolish the old, it dreams it anew and mimetically expresses it in different forms. Yet these different expressions of the familialist tradition do have consequences and may, in fact, be harbingers of a new and radically different way of life. After all, this new 'system' does enable family members to depart from the chrysalis of the work unit and engage in market activity while still feeling spiritually and materially secure. It is as though the 'head' of capitalism has emerged from the work unit cocoon and this 'head' is now supported by a family body that remains behind, and draws strength and resources from, the vestiges of the socialist work unit system. It is as though the work unit acts, in Marx's words, as its own grave digger.

## FROM A 'PERSON OF THE WORK UNIT' TO A 'SOCIAL PERSON': PSYCHOLOGICAL EVOLUTION UNDER THE IMPACT OF REFORM[1]

ZHU HUAXIN

In the music shows on the radio you often hear the disc jockey asking listeners who, with enormous difficulty, have phoned in: 'What work unit are you (from)?' The lucky listener, all too often some young kid, quite deliberately attempts, albeit in a very polite way, to twist the answer around a bit: 'Would it be okay if I just told you my identity card number?'

---

1 Zhu Huaxin, 'From 'a person of the work unit' to a 'social person': psychological evolution under the impact of reform', *People's Daily*, 14 December 1993, 11. [祝华新, 《人民日报》.]

This sort of thing may appear unintentional but it has, in reality, great sociological significance. It demonstrates that, for quite a few of the youngsters of the
current generation, the individual work unit consciousness has weakened and a
social consciousness has become stronger, indicating the gradual transition from
the person of the work unit to the social person.

Under the traditional system, the work unit was an 'iron rice bowl' and a 'big
pot', that is, the work unit guaranteed life-long tenure of employment and a wage
more or less similar to all other members. Once a person had achieved this status
there was nothing more to demand. While you were alive, you were a person of
the work unit, in death you were its ghost and the work unit would organise a
memorial meeting for you. In this way, the workers not only became loyal and
faithful to their work units, but also grew to depend upon them in a trusting and
nurturing relationship. A couple of years ago, the sociology research unit of the
Academy of Social Sciences in Beijing carried out a detailed sample survey of residents in 30 cities scattered across China. One of the questions asked was: which
of the items listed below do you regard as being the responsibility of your work
unit? Of those surveyed 97.5 per cent suggested that work units had a responsibility to provide medical insurance, 96.6 per cent thought they should be responsible for pensions, and 91.8 per cent thought they ought to arrange their workers'
housing. In addition to this, the supply of daily life requirements, mediation of
quarrels and arranging the schooling and employment of a member's children
was thought to be an important responsibility of the units by 86.7 per cent, 85.9
per cent and 82.3 per cent of respondents respectively. What was really strange
about the survey, however, was the fact that 45.1 per cent of those questioned
believed it was the responsibility of the work unit to take care of its employees'
divorce proceedings should the need arise! Little wonder, then, that people would
quip: the work unit dotes on its employees so much so that it hampers the individual's ability to grow.

Sun Liping, an associate professor at Beijing University's Sociology Department, thinks that there is an inevitable historical stage in the very early period of
the process of industrialisation that requires the work unit system. This enables
the state to mobilise human and material resources and to concentrate them in
key places. From the late Qing Dynasty onwards, China's finances were in a pitiful state and social resources were rapidly being dispersed. Because China was like
'a sheet of loose sand', no lead was given to industrialisation and, consequently,
the process was extremely slow and society was in fear of complete chaos.

Much later, however, and under the influence of a new form of market economy, the work unit system has increasingly been shown to be too inflexible. One
aspect of this inflexibility is that it limits the possibility of growth. The work unit
is not independent but relies on the State to allocate money, finances and materials. It does not fear losses because these are subsidised by the State. With market
economics, there are laws to distinguish the superior from the inferior and the
successful from those to be deleted. Despite this, however, the work unit is 'not
dead'. Another aspect of inflexibility relates to the way that an individual's own

possibilities are contingent upon the work unit. This leads to a whole range of things such as a lack of independence on the part of unit members. It also leads to a growth of too much egalitarianism and no financial incentives being offered for work undertaken. In relation to 'go slows' or workers lacking discipline, little can be done within the work unit for, ordinarily, the unit leaders lack the authority to dismiss personnel.

## The Psychological Pressure on Work Unit Personnel

There is little doubt that reform will be of benefit to the entire nation and all its citizens. Nevertheless, when one examines concrete items of systemic reform such as labour utilisation, wages, housing and state-supplied medical care etc., it is also obvious that some people will miss out on certain benefits. Many of those who are employed in the work unit system will, in the process of reform, be forced to pay a certain cost. While people generally support reform, they simultaneously worry about personal gains and losses and have significant doubts and even conflicting feelings about the reform process.

Wu Zhongmin, a professor of sociology in Shandong University, has analysed this problem and suggested that economic reform has so far failed to really carry out measures to change the 'complete dependence on the work unit' and also the 'complete equality with regards to the distribution of resources to all work units, regardless of the different demands of each work unit'. The rather hazy notion of public ownership has been transformed into work unit ownership. To ensure that their workers' benefits are given quickly and money given to benefit them, the work unit has used a variety of means to offer bonuses and material benefits, squeezing the money out by allowing equipment depreciation and drawing from technology transformation funds. There is no desire to abandon vested interests in the strategy known as 'policy above' and 'counter-attack on policy from below'. The 'counter-attack on policy from below' is essential to let work units carry on as normal. Professor Wu warned that: 'at present, employees' insurance and welfare funds are a percentage of their total wage, the average income level of employees is at its highest point since liberation. We need to think about regulating this kind of abnormal benefit structure. It is quite possible that within the work unit though, any such strategy to bring about change will encounter a certain kind of "colony of resistance."'

To avoid this kind of resistance, work units should be slowly disbanded. The Party and government need to bring into play their political skills and do the necessary ideological work. The bottom line is, however, a new organisational form needs to be created.

## The Significance of the Modern Enterprise System

From a technical perspective, large numbers of work units in China are well endowed with modern equipment and form part of the large-scale socialised production process. As a result of a tightly closed organisational form, however, work units tend to be inward looking and not very socially orientated. The goal of the Third Plenum of the Fourteenth Central Committee of the Chinese Communist Party was to initiate the reform of public ownership so as to establish a modern enterprise system. One aspect of this reform was to create good relations between enterprises and the State and realise a legal separation of ownership. The other aspect of this reform was to smooth out relations between enterprises and workers. On the last point, Professor Li Hanlin of the Sociology Research Unit within the Academy of Social Sciences has some interesting ideas to offer about the reform process:

1.  In the contemporary work unit, the relations between the unit and its workers can be governed by a labour contract. The granting of a right of movement to workers will also enable the work unit to adopt best practice and become a superior organisation. This reform is needed in order to gradually establish the labour market.

2.  The enterprise is clearly designed to operate only as a site of production and not as a welfare institution. Therefore, the non-production-orientated function of the contemporary work unit should be separated off and returned to the social sphere. In recent years, the work unit has increasingly operated as though it were a society. In the past, providing accommodation for workers relied upon state investment. These days, work units build their own accommodation with funds that principally emanate from the unit itself. In some work units, on average, one worker bears the cost of the pension of one or two retired employees. Work units cannot possibly bear the costs of such a heavy burden and they are financially crippled as a result.

3.  In the contemporary enterprise system, enterprises are principally responsible for the production activity of their employees. They play little or no part in their after-work activities which are governed by society. In order to appropriately adjust to this gap created by the withdrawal of the work unit from this arena, it is important to put in place a comprehensive system of social management. We need to modernise our social control and management methods. That is to say, the State, operating through the work unit, must gradually transform the methods by which employees are managed and give up the State monopoly over the productive forces. In this way, State control will operate through the legal controls over citizens but ethical regulation will be a social matter.

A key issue here, however, is how to kill off the work unit system and eliminate all the irrational social burdens which are borne by enterprises. Naturally, the reform of the enterprise system is an unavoidable task. The enterprise reforms must be genuine. A superficial reform would be worse than useless. As the sociologist Lu Feng pointed out: 'If the enterprise is still of an old form with the status of members frozen and profits being shared in common, then this is really little different from the old work unit.' (See also Part I, 2.)

## Those without Work Units

After economic reform took hold, changes swept through the work unit and led to many 'people without work units'. Outside the traditional (work unit) system, these people still managed to make a living with much ease and grace. Professor Li Hanlin explained that because of the collapse of the monopoly once enjoyed by the work unit over social resources, a fair proportion of the resources and opportunities ended up flowing into civil society and this, in turn, produced many 'spaces of free activity'. From the rusticated youths sent down to the countryside, who have subsequently returned and set up stalls and opened snack bars in the city, through to the rows and rows of 'high-tech' companies that line the streets of a suburb like Zhongguancun, from the 'three types of capitalised enterprises'[2] through to the large-scale private companies and famous individual cultural workers, many have broken away from their original work unit and re-established themselves with a definite independent status. Despite the fact that many private companies are still really subsidiaries of State companies, it should be pointed out that they are no longer simply sub-sections of their work unit owner. In fact, they have significantly decreased their reliance upon their work unit owner and, in the cut and thrust of the market economy, their ability and market-orientated consciousness has enabled them to stand independently and bear the brunt of the market forces on their own.

Nevertheless, over a very long period of time, many people who have left the work unit system have found the going very tough, very lonely and the outlook bleak. One former cadre from a very large enterprise named Xiao Zhang set up a business soon after his retirement. Nevertheless, he always seemed to be spending time chatting with his former colleagues back at the work unit. It was only in this way that he could maintain his 'sense of belonging'. And then there are those people who are really unhappy with their work units but, when it comes to facing the possibility of transfer, realise the benefits of it. Things such as housing, cadre status and public health care would be lost if they moved into the private sector and this sends a shiver down their spine. Of significance is the emergence, in recent years, of a special Chinese characteristic 'one family, two systems' (*yijia liangzhi*). Either the husband or wife leaves their unit in order to make money. The other partner continues to work in the work unit and continues to enjoy all sorts of State benefits. One even finds some of the more famous 'individual writers' joking about it, saying that although they themselves don't have a work unit to rely on, they can always get their wife's work unit medical form when they are sick. Even though the salary is very low in the work unit, it is at least stable. Outside the work unit one is 'at sea', and even though the opportunities are great, it is not easy to make a killing. 'One family, two systems' has a cooperative function that aptly expresses and reflects the contradictory state of mind of the

---

2  That is, joint venture capital, state capital and private capital.

present Chinese under conditions of both market economics and the plan. On the one hand, they want to make lots of money and yet, on the other, they also want stability. It is as though they want to have their cake and eat it too.

## 'ONE FAMILY, TWO SYSTEMS'
### An Interview with HU LIANPIN

Hu Lianpin's story offers an interesting variant on the 'one family, two systems' model. Unlike many of the cases explored in the literature, the principal benefit she derives from this arrangement is relational, not material. The symbolic capital she derives from this arrangement via her husband's position and status in the Public Security Bureau is the key to her success and is far more significant than any material amenities his work unit provides, although the unit does take care of this facet of their lives also. Indeed, it could be argued that this case demonstrates the way in which this system is not restricted to one class but is flexible enough to cover a range of classes and conditions. Here is an edited version of an interview I undertook with her on 21 January 1995.

*MD: I am interested in the 'one family, two systems' model and I understand your family has divided up the family labour in this way. Can you tell me a little about your own history?*

**Hu**: I was originally an associate professor at the China Political Science and Law Cadre Management Institute. I subsequently left that position and became a lawyer in a private practice along with two friends. My husband works in the Public Security Bureau where he is a section head. We have a son who is now eight years old. Neither my husband nor I are natives of Beijing. We both come from the south and only came to Beijing when we were accepted into universities here.

*Can you explain the reasons behind your decision to 'go to sea'—leave your safe State job and go into business?*

It was quite an easy decision but it wasn't simply the money. I was actually a very good teacher at the Institute. The problem is that in China today, those who choose to remain on the scholarly path will face the prospect of being poor their entire lives. That is not a problem, in itself, but it has increasingly begun to affect the psychological state of a lot of scholars. They feel undervalued. Society obviously plays a crucial role in influencing one's perceptions of oneself. Through social interaction we are given 'face' and respect, we are seen to be in demand, are given power and gain relaxation. These days, if you have money the rest tends to follow. Money has become the symbol of success. In the past, while I was a teacher I was pretty poor, but I really didn't mind because I felt I had a respected social role and a respected social position. Increasingly though, I began to realise that this was not the case. As a teacher I neither had money nor respect. What was the point in remaining a teacher? In addition to this, things were not all that rosy in my department either. I had this on-going conflict with some colleagues and that made my time there pretty miserable. I thought, what was the point of this struggle which was really for nought? I really could do with the money so I thought why not leave and become a lawyer? And this is exactly what I did.

*Before leaving the institution, didn't you think about the consequent loss of amenities like the free housing and medical care the State organ offered you?*
No, not at all. After all, my husband still worked in a State organ and they had supplied the most precious of things to us anyway: a flat. So that aspect was not really much of a consideration. It is really hard to think what aspect of the Institute I was worried about when I left my old work unit. Frankly speaking, I was simply scared about the security. As a lawyer, I was simply worried I would not make a good fist of the partnership and I would not make any money. I was pretty confident though because my area of expertise was company law and I had taught that for quite a while. This was an area in hot demand in private enterprise and I had freelanced in this area before so I already had a number of contacts. Also, it has to be said that my husband's connections have helped a lot.

*You have been in private practice now for nearly a year. Are you making much more than you did as a teacher?*
Oh yes. I am making an amount many times over my university wage.

*Your husband is a middle-level and reasonably successful official in the Ministry of Public Security. Has his position within the Ministry aided you in your work?*
Oh yes! My husband can give me enormous help because we are in related areas and he meets lots of people and has lots of friends through his work. Because of his extensive friendship and colleague network I can get a lot of help to further cases I am working on. I can also find out and chase some cases that are coming up and may be worth quite a lot of money to me. In addition to this, I can also avoid a lot of problems in conducting my own investigations. Because of my husband's friends and position, I don't get hassled in the way others might. Put simply, if a person knows who I am related to, then they are unlikely to give me too much trouble but are instead likely to show me respect and allow me to get on with my job.

*So you are pretty happy with your change of career?*
Most definitely. I make much more money and that was a crucial factor in my decision so I have at least attained that end. I find a lot of other teachers at universities are envious but are still too timid to follow my lead. I guess that makes me feel good also!

# 4

# CHANGING LANDSCAPES, CHANGING MENTALITIES

'I have nothing to say, only show'.[1] This was Walter Benjamin's working design for the 'arcades project'; an enquiry into the embryonic, so called ur-forms of the European mode of consumption. I could begin this chapter with a similar motto, for this part of the work is made up mostly of pictorial juxtapositions. What the pictures 'describe' is the emergence, in embryonic form, of a new economy of vision taking hold in China. Modernisation and memory are played with through mimetic ingenuity. Gone, it seems, are the attempts to remember the past in the 'new'. This form of remembrance was once popular and exemplified by the 'water tower' pagoda built by the side of the 'unnamed lake' in Beijing University. Here, a modern water storage tower is concealed within a traditional pagoda form. Gone too, is the slow process of expansion and transformation of the compound household form into the socialist work unit. Time and space have eroded this particular need and recent architecture reflects the desire to capture the new rather than encode the traditional.

The wonderful world of architectural mimesis where, as Bruno Latour points out, desire 'adorns objects with a value that is not their own'[2] seems to fall prey to the bulldozer's blade in the China of economic reform. In place of the slow process of mimetic transformation of space, there is architectural amputation exemplified by the new sign of this surgery of the landscape, the ubiquitous circled character 拆 chai, meaning to 'tear down'. Found on the side of old buildings, houses, shops and other functional but decrepit structures, it is more than the mark of death, it is a sign that flags permanent erasure. The result is that the cities of China become the cities of chai. Urban spaces are transformed into construction sites and the remaining walled compound enclosures become relics of both a classical and socialist tradition that is, quite literally, being ripped asunder and suppressed. This 'flash of an eye' pace of change in China is shocking to the eye and to human sensibilities and has caused anxiety in lives to the point whereby other ways of remembering are employed to unconsciously soothe troubled brows. Mimesis makes its return in new ways at this point.

In this process of acquiring for the new, a means to usher out the old, the 'magic' of mimesis, as Taussig[3] so aptly describes it, proves useful. Mimesis forms a

---

1  Walter Benjamin, Gesammelte Schriften, Volume 5 (eds Rolf Tiedemann and Hermann Schweppen-hauser) Suhrkamp Verlag, Frankfurt am Main, 574, quoted in Susan Buck-Morss, *The Dialectics of Seeing: Walter Benjamin and the Arcades Project* (Cambridge Massachusetts: The MIT Press, 1991), 73.
2  Bruno Latour, *We Have Never Been Modern* [Trans. Catherine Porter] (Cambridge Massachusetts: Harvard University Press, 1993), 45.
3  See Taussig, *Mimesis and Alterity*.

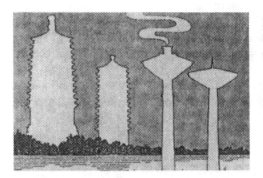

The external appearance of the water tower built by the side of the 'Nameless Lake' in Beijing University in the 1920s (second from left) mimics the form of the 800-year-old 'heavenly pagoda' which is also in Beijing (left). Its function, however, is identical to the more recent and functional towers illustrated to the right.

The ubiquitous nature of the character *chai* (meaning to 'tear down') in every Chinese city is not only an indication of the pace of change in China but the way, before our very eyes, the cities of China are physically eliminating their own past structural forms as they rush to embrace the new.

bridge from the past to the future, securing for the economic reform process the possibility of reconfiguring the old according to a new 'economy of the eye'. In this new economy of the eye, the first task is destruction. Shopping centres are transformed from factory-style distribution points into enchanting, seductive feasts for the eye and the wallet. In the process, everything is made 'for sale'. Mimesis works its magic by transforming everything from nation to revolution into a commodity form that can be desired and sold. Classical depictions of the nation, captured in palace architecture that locate the emperor in the epicentre, give way to theme parks that make the ticket buyer the focus of activity. The form of these parks alone seems to yell, 'buy a ticket and join the nation!' The changing space of the city becomes the changing face of nation. The physical ordering of city life taps into deeper psychological changes taking place. Even the socialist revolution is enchanted and seduced. In 1995, in Mao's home village of Shaoshan, a massive new theme park of the revolution opened, enabling one to walk through history and through class struggle for the price of an entry ticket. Outside the park, Mao is the logo on every product. The great helmsman had become the great gimmick demonstrating, once again, the power of consumption to mimetically reconfigure the world as market opportunity.

Yet the power of the new which has forced itself on China so violently and so rapidly has given rise to a nervousness and fear that even the seductive powers of consumption cannot fully erase. Chinese cities are richer but far less stable places these days and it is in Xu Hanmin's article on changes in residency that this nervous, almost resentful view of city life comes to the fore. As city space has become more difficult to obtain because marketisation has forced up prices, new high-rise accommodation replaces the sealed compound housing structure of the era of the work unit. The 'unity' of life and work encouraged by the former struc-ture and by the Party has given way to radical separation. As the high-rise build-ings emerge, the social solidarity of the work units crumbles. Welcome to the alienated world of estrangement where the only way out is to buy into a consumer fantasy. As Xu's article suggests, the move from 'work unit person' to 'social person' is proving to be a social problem. There is no liberation in this move for Xu Hanmin—all he sees are increased social problems. It is with these problems that the changing landscape of economic reform begins to demonstrate its darker and less stable side.

## HIGH RISK, HIGH RISE: CHANGES IN WORK UNIT ACCOMMODATION AND THE PROBLEM OF CRIME[4]

### XU HANMIN

High-rise apartments need daily surveillance and this is a new problem in the history of public security management. It is a problem that has developed rather quickly for there are high rises in most places and in all cities. This is a new build-ing style that is very different from the old single-storey standard accommodation of the past. This change in style has brought with it changes in lifestyle, as well as changes in relations between people. This, in turn, means that those charged with public security management (the police) are faced with a series of new challenges. Clearly, some new security methods appropriate to high-rise apartment structures are needed. To develop these methods, though, we must begin by seeking truth from facts.

### From Single-storey Multi-family Complexes to the Independent Family Residence

Neighbours sharing the same courtyard are affected by similar conditions and share many common concerns. Hence, they see each other regularly and grow to know each other intimately. When they move to individual apartments in differ-ent buildings and on different floors the situation changes. Each family has sepa-rate rooms, water, electricity, toilet facilities, washrooms, etc. and these are only for the individual family's use. So the original intimate social relations that were built up in the multi-family blocks disintegrates in a multi-storeyed apartment building space.

In the single-storeyed multi-family residences, it can be said that each family's secret is revealed for their lives are like open books. As residents come and go,

---

4    Xu Hanmin, *Forty Years of People's Public Security* (Beijing: Police Officer Educational Publishing House, 1992), 128–33. [徐汉民,《人民治安 40 年》.] Xu Hanmin is a professor at the Police Officers' Academy in Beijing.

they all see one another and it is even said that their conversation can be heard between the walls and their manners known. Everything is heard and everything is there to see. This quite often leads to these places operating as sites of mutual control. But when they move into the multi-storeyed apartment buildings, things change. Each family's life becomes a private affair. The comings and goings of people, as well as their activities, become difficult for others to know. Why is it that so much of the uncultivated, unhealthy and sometimes even obscene materials and activities, all of which are prohibited, can be discovered and are even popular in these large apartment buildings?

This has a lot to do with the way family lifestyles have become private affairs. It has a lot to do with the fact that other people have no way to keep an eye on them. Also, those with a love of money will use the opportunities created in such apartment blocks to carry out their nefarious activities ... As a result of economic reform, a lot of people are moving from the countryside to the city to trade and, among these people, there are those with criminal intentions. They use false identity cards, make use of friendship networks, and often reside in these types of apartment blocks. This form of residency makes the job of the police all that much more difficult and complicated.

## Implementing Comprehensive Management that Covers All

We need to shift from a superficial management form to one that covers all aspects of life. This is the viewpoint developing among those who manage the security of these multi-storey apartments. Using criminological theory, and with the cooperation of the masses, a number of methods—ranging from patrols to apartment management entrance guards etc.— are being implemented. From the experiences in a number of places it can be said that such work must involve:

1.  The inclusion of mass participation in the area of security work. Most importantly, the police should rely upon local Party and governmental leaders to organise the masses into protective groups, and use such models as the 'civilised streets' system, whereby low crime rate areas are given this honorific title. Most importantly, regularly, deeply and on a large-scale, carry out legal propaganda work among the residents.
2.  Building mass self-security organisations. Bring them into play in an area to protect the security of the multi-storey apartment blocks. Start from existing practice and work on what is objectively needed and possible. Some places have built up their security committees, small security teams, security offices, or joint security brigades. Others have implemented a system of building leaders, or used specialist shift workers to watch over the building. In buildings where work units have many residents, get these work units to participate. There are literally a million and one ways to improve things.

Nevertheless, all these must build on experience and the best solution is specialist organisations or personnel. To bring these into effect though, you need to watch out for the following things:

2.1 Talk over the various options with the local security committees and work out a strategy that is not in conflict with theirs.

2.2 In order to improve the quality of security, the police should carry out some training of these personnel.

2.3 Every month, offer security personnel bonuses or fines.

2.4 The station should watch over, check and supervise all this work.

3. Many things affect social order. Changes in the weather, criminal habits, and developments in a particular area can all have an effect. Hence, when a police station or the police of a particular area start thinking about security, they need to begin by examining the specific circumstances they face. If they want to help the people of these areas, they must encourage them to help themselves by forming their own mass organisations, organisational patrols, as well as other forms of defensive activity. For example, in areas where there are many cases of crime, or at times when crime cases are high, a police patrol system should be introduced. Patrol routes and patrol times should be regulated so that they 'block up all the holes'. They must coordinate each patrol team with all other patrols. They will, thereby, make this whole system of patrols work in unison. It is important to quickly organise linkages between one building compound and another. If this is done and the work is carried out in unison then one building security group can help another … If this is done the criminals do not stand a chance.

4. Get to the truth of the matter with regard to anti-social activities. Find out where the trouble is, find out the building entrance number and the apartment number and then arrange social help and education for those who need it.[5] If the family is in a position to help with this work, then they should be employed and their roles fully brought into play. In most cases, though, the families of anti-social elements are of little use. Hence, three to five responsible people need to be enlisted and they should form a small social help and education team to carry out this work. Here, work must centre on those anti-social elements whose activities could harm society and threaten people. These are the most important ones to get to. For example, there are those who have committed crimes or are anti-social, but still have not satisfactorily reformed after release from reform through labour or after returning from reform through education. They are still regarded as 'not

---

5 According to Shao Daosheng, 'social help and education refers to mobilising sectors of society to educate youth who have committed minor offences in order to help them correct their mistakes and to encourage them to embark on a path of healthy development. Social help and education is neither an administrative sanction nor criminal punishment, but is a form of political and ideological education of youth.' For further details see Shao Daosheng, *Considerations on the Sociology of Youth Crime in China* (Beijing: Social Science Literature Press, 1987), 196–209. [邵道生，'社会帮教'，《中国青少年犯罪的社会学思考》。]

good people' and they could once again begin to threaten the common folk. Such people are still under legal restrictions and should be kept under surveillance, checked, educated and reformed by those responsible for such work.

5.  Public security in the high-rise apartments should be carried out by everyone other than those who are still subject to regulations requiring them to be kept under surveillance. By bringing others into the picture and getting every household involved in this work, things can be turned around.

6.  In line with the spirit of making whoever is in charge responsible, we need to implement a method whereby work units that own these high-rise apartments get involved in the security work. If each work unit leader and organisation were to stress this work to their individual workers and staff as part of their own management work, then the results could be very good indeed. The police station, the neighbourhood committee and the security committees need to have a close working relationship with the work unit concerned and they need to be able to help each other, keep each other informed of any suspicious activities and so forth.

These are just some of the ideas worth thinking about in constructing plans to police the high-rise apartments, but it can be said that the policing of these areas needs to be scientific, comprehensive and based on practice. It is worth keeping these things in mind while continuing to explore the options available.

## COMPOUNDS OLD AND NEW

The work unit (pictures to the left) and the compound household (pictures to the right).
The pictures in the second row show the gates leading into the respective compounds.
The work unit administration and office building (last row) is a far cry from the traditional
compound household, a site of family affairs and family residences, all of which face the
courtyard or 'Well of Heaven'.

## WORK UNITS AND HIGH RISE

Old-style work unit residences forged a community bond between work unit members. Neighbours were co-workers and together, behind the high brick walls of the unit, they forged a sense of community.

New-style high-rise apartments have become a ubiquitous feature of urban life since economic reform. The massive rise in the cost of land which had been formally allocated to units pushed prices and buildings upward. This resulted in the dissolution of the agnatic bonds tying work unit employees together. Life is now dispersed as work and home are separated.

## GOING SHOPPING

### Remnants of the Proletarian Dream: Factory-style Consumption in the Maoist Palaces of Purchase

Unadorned and austere entrances, interiors designed along factory lines, Maoism mimicked the dream of the proletarian revolution and created shopping space like factory space. Neon strip lighting, surly and monotonously attired staff, and a shabby make-shift display of items for sale—these characterised proletarian consumption. The desire to buy is not the desire of the eye but based purely on the slogan of need that can then be translated as, 'no need to display'.

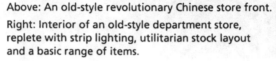

Above: An old-style revolutionary Chinese store front.

Right: Interior of an old-style department store, replete with strip lighting, utilitarian stock layout and a basic range of items.

## New Visions, New Desires

In the new shopping arcades of China, it is the gaze that is central. These brightly adorned glass, mirror and chrome monuments to the capitalism of the gaze are also designed to enchant and enhance. One enters the shopping centre as though entering a dream. Everything is made desirable and everything is for sale. This is a far cry from the factory-style shopping arcades of the Maoist era.

Above: Inside the shopping pleasure dome.

Left: The new shopping centre in Xidan district, Beijing.

## BUYING NATION: IMPERIAL AND COMMODIFIED RENDITIONS OF NATIONHOOD

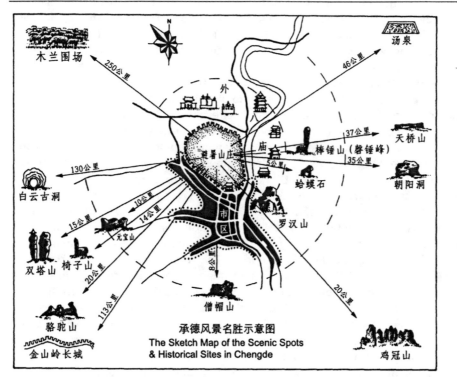

承德风景名胜示意图
The Sketch Map of the Scenic Spots
& Historical Sites in Chengde

Empire and nation: this Jehal Palace (the Mountain Resort) depicts a site built in 1792 as a summer retreat for the Qing Emperor. Yet it also came to constitute a symbol of the unified Chinese nation as the map and the following quotation from it make clear: 'While the construction of the Mountain Resort was underway, a number of temples, known as the Eight Outer Temples, were built. The Mountain Resort, semicircled by the Eight Outer Temples, symbolises the various nationalities rallying around the court. It is a testimonial to the consolidation and development of China as a unified country of multiple nationalities.' From 'A Sketch Map of the Scenic Spots and Historical Sites in Chengde' (Shijiazhuang: Hebei People's Press).

Commodification and nation: for the price of a ticket, one can partake in the celebration and reification of nation. This newly opened 'tourist site' offers 'life-sized replicas constructed by the people from minority areas and who themselves are minorities'. Once the Emperor retreated from the

capital and contemplated 'his' empire in miniature. Now the capital reifies its desire to be the capital of all its ethnic and cultural parts. This theme park of nation in Beijing now has a 'sister reference point' in Mao's home town of Shaoshan, which has recently completed a 'revolutionary theme park'. Whether it's revolutionary or national, it always takes a commodity form.

## MAPPING MAO: FROM CULT TO COMMODITY

Every revolutionary event in Chinese Communist Party history is mythologised in the chart by Zhang Da of Mao badges and the revolutionary struggles they commemorate.[6] The route the revolution took becomes Mao's life journey as the badges move from commemorating His birth in Shaoshan through to His consecration in Tiananmen Square. His revolutionary life is the life of the revolution and the rebirth of China. The Mao badge became the technology through which revolutionary stories were remembered, retold and etched onto the mind. It is a very different story from the one being told in China these days. The revolution that currently takes place in China is one that sees the commodity form taking centre stage.

Nowhere is the story of the commodity more compellingly told than in Mao's home village, Shaoshan. As a pseudo-religious site of the nation throughout the Cultural Revolution, it constantly had between 1 to 2 million visitors annually. Mao's death and the shift to economic reform saw the number of visitors drop precipitously: from a high of 2.9 million in 1966 to just 233,300 in 1980, the fall in numbers was a litmus test of the Maoist revolution. That decline in interest in Mao and Shaoshan was arrested only by the 're-invention' of the revolutionary heritage of the village as a theme for tourism. This culminated in the construction in 1994 of a massive 200,000-square-metre 'Mao theme park' costing close to 50 million *yuan* ($US6 million), and built directly opposite the home in which he (now a small 'h') was born.[7] With the 'fun' put back into the revolution, tourists returned. In 1994, an estimated 1.2 million people[8] made the journey to Shaoshan, but they came not to worship Mao but to consume him. Shaoshan became the harbinger of a new 'revolutionary' tourist industry and this theme park to Mao stood at the centre of this new form of 'revolutionary enterprise'.

## FROM MAO MAP TO TOURIST TRAP

Zhang Da's 'Map of Mao Badges' illustrates the way in which each revolutionary moment of the late Chairman's life was commemorated by being miniaturised into a 'portable' Mao badge to be pinned to the hearts of the devoted. As the following chapter on the Mao fetish will show, such devotion could not be bought and such 'signs' of it could not be sold.

The theme park is different. It quite literally sells the Revolution. Like the badge, the Mao Zedong Memorial Park 'miniaturises', but it then re-organises Mao's 'revolutionary footsteps' into an easily travelled route for tourists. Indeed, the original name for this park was 'The Route of Mao Zedong Scenic Park'. Where

6   Zhang Da's artwork as reproduced in *Contemporary Cultural Relic*, 12 (1992). 〔《当代文物》。〕

7   Long Jianyu and Gao Jucun (eds), *Grasping the Beauty of Shaoshan* (Chongqing: South-West Normal University Press, 1996), 240–41. 〔龙剑宇，高菊村（编著）《韶山揽胜》。〕

8   Bi Yuxiao (ed.), *Selected Works of Poems, Paintings and Calligraphy in Mao Zedong's Memorial Park of Shaoshan* (Changsha: Yuelu Publishing House, 1996), 15. 〔碧玉萧（主编），《韶山毛泽东纪念园诗书画选集》。〕

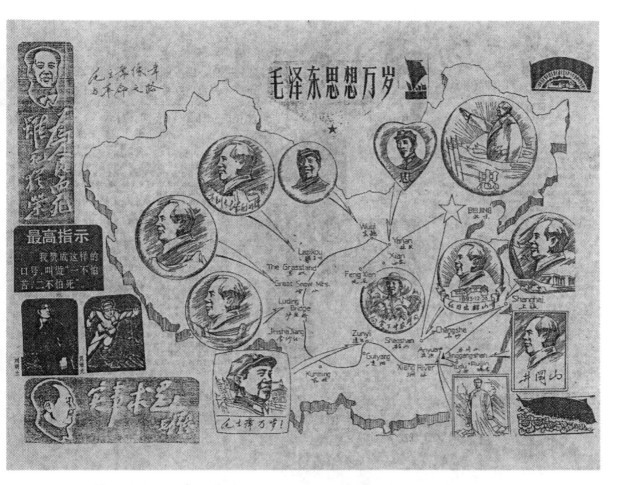

Zhang Da's map of Mao badges.

the badges of the Cultural Revolution wed the urge to remember Mao to the theme of revolutionary transformation of self and class struggle, the theme park ties Mao to a different fetish: the urge to consume. Part 'stations of the cross', part side-show, this attempt to make revolution the 'theme' of a scenic park elides questions of struggle, transformation and commitment. Instead, it shows the Communist Party tactically employing consumption to promote its politics in an enterprise that almost leads to vaudeville. Indeed the whole idea behind the project seems to suggest this wedding as the preface to the park's publicity brochure explains: 'Through visiting the Park, people can both learn and play. They are likely to experience the revolutionary process in China for themselves by walking down the revolutionary road and "reading" of the life and form of the revolution in this history book without words.' At an estimated cost of around $US6 million, it is an expensive 'volume', yet one is left wondering what it is Chinese are actually being taught.

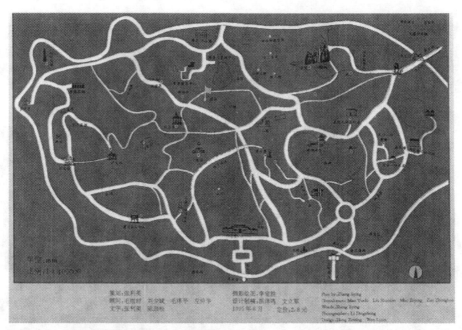

Map of the Mao Zedong Memorial Park. This 'theme park of the Revolution' plots the path of the Revolution as it winds its way to power. The Revolution, like nation, is in this way offered 'for sale'.

Entry ticket to the park.

The Yan'an Cave Dwellings of Mao and other Party leaders from 1943–45 are simulated in the park. Unlike Yan'an itself, the caves are used as souvenir shops and a cardboard image of Mao sits outside his dwelling, awaiting tourists who pay to have their photographs taken with him.

The 'long march' through the park mimics Mao's long march to power. One stop along the way was the Zunyi meeting hall where, in 1935, and in the middle of the Long March, the Party met and effectively put Mao in charge. Long marches can be thirsty work, so in this simulacrum of the Long March one can not only buy Zunyi commemorative souvenirs but also refreshments.

## ★ MAO BADGES ENTER THE MARKET

By way of introducing Part V, it is worth highlighting the changing landscape of the Mao badge as it is reconfigured as commodity in the new era of the market. Pure Mao is from a catalogue of Mao badges compiled by Wang Anting. For Wang, the badge is priceless and Mao avoids the market and is reified as icon. Each badge is chronicled in detail and each description offers the reader a way to 'know' their Mao badge, if not their Mao.

Yet there is now another side to the Mao badge collector's personality and that other side is given prominence in another publication produced, rather appropriately, by the China Economic Press. In this publication, which more or less replicates the format of Wang Anting's volume, one crucial addition is made to each

Pure Mao.

鋁質．直徑 56mm．做工細致，交
通部爲慶祝 1970 年國慶而制．參
考估價：20 元

鋁質．直徑 50mm，沈
陽制．背面刻有分三
列的各種字體 9 個
"忠"字．參考估價：
50 元

鋁質．直徑 32mm．南京制．此款
式很快流行于全國．以後面有"毛
主席萬歲．萬歲．萬萬歲"者爲
上．參考估價：20 元

Mao priced: the estimated price of each badge is located at the end of each badge description. The middle one costs 50 *yuan*, the others 20 *yuan* each.

photograph and description of the Mao badge: the estimated market price of the badge. Mao enters the market and, as he does, souvenirs and mementos of him gain a monetary value. One no longer 'requests' the badge, it is subject to barter and sale. The estimated price at the bottom of each description of the badge constitutes a veritable guide for buyer and seller alike. It trains both in what to expect and, in so doing, reinforces the Chinese version of what the Monopoly board game calls the 'art of civilised trading' (see page 279 for details on the Chinese version of Monopoly). The Mao market may be momentary, it may falter, but while it lasts, it helps to demonstrate the power of consumption to transform even the most iconographic of symbols into simply another commodity available for purchase. The magical economy of enchantment fades as the monetary reading of the badge eclipses all other readings. Mao is once again valuable, but now he has a price on his head!

PART **V**

# STORIES OF THE FETISH: TALES OF CHAIRMAN MAO

Michel de Certeau once remarked that in eighteenth-century France, dominant culture represented 'the voice of the people' as being filled with sweetness and innocence.[1] 'The people', wrote de Certeau, 'may not speak, but they can sing'[2] and, if one were to look over the marketplace of contemporary China, we would find that, apart from the marginal and marginalised niche market of heavy metal and rock, it is the sickly sweet songs of Canto-pop that fill the airwaves. If we were to look back over the Maoist past, however, we would find that the people sang to the rhythm of a different drum. This was less the sweet, soothing music of today and more a clarion call to arms. The 'East is Red' and other such songs of that era *demanded* to be sung. Not to sing or to sing out of tune was, like the refusal to wear the Mao badge, or chant the slogan, or dance the 'devotion dance', a cause for rebuke. The people-as-one under the leadership of the 'Other'[3] (Mao) was both a dream of the Cultural Revolution, but also something of a normative expectation. Yang Dongping's article on revolutionary culture (Part III, 1) has already told this side of the story. It plotted the changes in language as a more robust militaristic and rural inflection became the norm within the Chinese vernacular. It told the story of the 'collectivisation' of language and the transformation of the individual's name. It suggested a complete social transformation—a cultural revolution. Yet beneath this sea of red banners, or the ocean of Mao badges, there is some cause for doubting this unity. The multiplicity of identities, of ways of seeing, remained intact and disrupted this myth of a 'people-as-one'. Indeed, what becomes obvious from the readings in this part of *Streetlife China*, is that the very devices used to try to enforce this oneness of identity produced both division and a fetishisation of form. An example of this is the fate of, and fights surrounding, the Mao badge. As Wang Anting's short history of the badge explains, the Mao badge began life as a medal and, therefore, the 'rarity' of the early forms flagged its value. By the time of the Cultural Revolution in 1966, this rarity was replaced by ubiquity. The Mao badge was ever-present. In this period it was, as suggested earlier, designed to instil the idea of Mao as sun, as guide, as leader. Nevertheless, it ended its life, all too often, as a point of conflict, competition and differentiation. The desire to produce endless Mao badges, with different depictions of Mao, different background settings, different commemorative

---

1   Michel de Certeau, *Heterologies: Discourse on the Other* [Trans. Brian Massumi] (Minneapolis: University of Minnesota Press, 1993), 124.
2   de Certeau, 122.
3   See Claude Lefort, *The Political Forms of Modern Society: Bureaucracy, Democracy, Totalitarianism* [Edited and introduced by John B. Thompson] (Cambridge: Polity Press, 1986).

Mao badge with an
estimated price of 90 *yuan*.

motifs and different words, could well be calibrated with the twists and turns of
the Cultural Revolution itself, but it could also be seen as a way of designating,
under the aegis of Mao, a multiplicity of identities and claims.

Hence the army, who are thought to have produced something like 25 per cent
of all Mao badges, would offer depictions which placed their claims for recognition under the sun-god Mao to the fore. Similarly, each of the revolutionary
committees that sprang up after 1967 at Mao's behest felt compelled to produce
Mao badges to commemorate their formation. These were distributed in a variety
of ways (see Liu Xin's article in this section) but most often, they were given out to
each work unit within the committee's jurisdiction and used by them as an
emblem of that particular committee. Each of the red rebel factions, Red Guard
factions and red rebel groups felt the need to produce their own form of group
identity around the production of a Mao badge. Most work units that had the
resources to do so (and a great many that didn't) felt similarly inclined. Every move
the Chairman made, from a visit to a particular region to a gift of mangoes he
passed on to workers, was dutifully chronicled in an endless stream of news items
that took the form of the ubiquitous red and gold Mao badge. Mao badges also
became points of conflict: the badges were the flags and emblems of competing
Red Guard groups and, as such, were the single most visible symbol of heterogeneity and conflict. Yet, quite apart from this, the very act of producing the image
of Mao was fraught with difficulty.

Pictures of Mao, lifted and re-sited on the Mao badge, required delicate nego-
tiation. At times, when the picture of Mao used on the badge faced right, not left,
the simple act of transcription onto the badge could lead to a political challenge:
is this not to question the Chairman's own stated assessment that the East wind
prevails over the West? Badges fired wrongly in the kiln, burnt or otherwise
damaged, could lead to charges of counter-revolution. Indeed, such was the
political sensitivity around the badge that the decline of the porcelain badge, in
particular, can be attributed to its fragility. Should such a badge fall and break in
a public place, it could lead to serious charges being laid—was this an act of deliberate and calculated insult? Before 1969, something like 4.8 billion Mao badges
were produced with over 100,000 different motifs. The country's airline industry
ground to a halt as the aluminium needed to produce aeroplanes was diverted

and devoted to the production of Mao badges. The country entered a period not of 'the people-as-one' under the gaze of a supreme 'Other', as the myth-makers of the Cultural Revolution might suggest, but a period of heterogeneous excess. It was an excess well illustrated by the fetishistic collection of the image of Mao by some of the Chairman's most zealous followers. It is this fetishistic excess that the interview with Wang Anting, the badge master, and the stories of Yang Xinlong and Zhou Jihou capture. It is a form that is aptly captured in the writing on the badge outlined in this section.

Yet more recent times have revealed another side to this fetishisation of Mao, and this comes in the figure of the artist Zhang Hongtu. Caught in a more recent Mao craze (the 1993–94 commemoration of his 100th birthday), Zhang had cause to reflect upon an earlier one (the Cultural Revolution). Indeed, the whole of his 'Mao Series' of artworks was a cathartic attempt to come to terms with this once ever-present figure. (See Part III, 2 for a sample of Zhang's work.) It is through Zhang's art that we begin to catch a glimpse of another process of fetishisation that is much more relevant to contemporary post-economic reform China. Zhang's artwork is but an extreme and subversive redefinition of Mao as commodity. His image is, once again, everywhere. Today, however, it always comes with a price tag prominently attached (as the diagram of the Mao badge depicted in the last section revealed). There is, in fact, a Mao for everyone. His face is on lighters, on watches and even on holograms. Rich devotees can buy solid gold MasterCards with Mao embossed on the surface. Poorer fans can buy the double-sided photo portraits that adorn many a small cab. Mao sells, but what he sells today is the very new idea of everything being for sale. Thus, when Zhang called his Mao portrait series 'Material Mao', he was much more prescient than even he could have imagined. The reference point, here, however, is the pop star Madonna, not the revolutionary Mao. It is both a reference point and starting point for a new China, with a new desiring gaze. It is a China where, increasingly, everything is for sale. This is the China that Da Yang examines in the final article in this section. While not purely about Mao, her article is included for it ties the Mao craze into the wider question of the commercialisation of cultural artefacts. She argues that, far from mourning the death of culture, one must rejoice in commercialism for this is a 'universal trend'. Not for her the pessimism of Adorno suggesting that all culture declines with consumerism. Hers is very much a celebration of commercialism and a tribute to economic reform.

# THE BADGE AS BIOGRAPHY

Hagiography, according to Nadel,[1] is the precursor to true biography. This precursive form began life in the West as part of a process for the edification of saints. For de Certeau,[2] it is more than this. Hagiography is historiography's 'temptation and betrayal'. It differs from biography in that it is about 'actions' not 'words' and, for de Certeau, these actions always lead back to 'place': 'the Life of the Saint is a life in a place, a founding place, that later is a liturgical site ceaselessly returned to.'[3] In fact, de Certeau goes on to conclude: 'The very itinerary of writing leads to the vision of the place: to read is to go and see.'

Like the saints, Mao's life in the hagiographic depiction on the badge is dominated by place. The 'sacred sites' are plotted as emblems on a badge, which, together, plot a 'revolutionary life'. We follow the birth–life–death chronology of most biographic forms. In Jinggang Mountain we have the birth of the new revolution, in Yan'an, we discover the everyday revolutionary life that will one day dominate all of China, and with Tiananmen Square, we have the culmination of the revolution, not in death, but in victory and everlasting life. All this under the glowing gaze of Mao who, like the sun, brings forth life and the possibility of renewal.

Zhang Da's Map of the Mao Badge (Part IV, 4), is 'summarised' in this emblematic rendition. Yet the badge differs because it offers a strange form of biography that eludes words. The Mao badge of the Cultural Revolution subverts the logic of biography in so far as the life depicted requires no telling. Actions, not words, speak in these pictographs. Biographies work from 'the proper name', categorising and detailing a life that is thereby unified. With the Mao badge there is no need for words, no need for names.

The face and the place (as reminders of actions) speak for themselves. Mao's face tells all. The badge prompts memory. In the recurrent chants of 'long live Chairman Mao' that echoed throughout the period of Cultural Revolution, the 'Mao myth' was burned into the unconscious of all Chinese so that this face and these sites can tell only one story—a story of revolution and liberation, of struggle and the moral way. The badge becomes a central component of the biography of each and every person who wears it. Mao's story becomes their story. Hagiography and biography are fused.

---

1   Nadel, *Biography: Fiction, Fact and Form* (New York: St Martin's Press, 1988), 6.
2   See Michel de Certeau, *The Writing of History* [Trans. Steven Randall] (New York: Columbia University Press, 1988).
3   de Certeau, 1988, 281.

Top: Mao the Sun God; Mao, the giver of light and revolution. Under the radiance of this sun and this face, the 'potlach' of the socialist system beams down. Without Mao the revolutionary way is dark. With Mao, the way becomes clear and his light guides.

Left: Jinggang Mountain where Mao Zedong began the revolutionary Soviet that would effectively lead to a new type of socialism—a socialism with peasant characteristics. From there we travel clockwise under the beaming light of Mao to Yan'an.

Middle: The rostrum in front of Tiananmen square where Mao stood in 1949 and proclaimed the founding of the People's Republic of China. This symbolises the fruition of the Long March which began in Jinggang Mountain in the south of the country and took the Communists to the far north-west (Yan'an). Tiananmen was the final resting place for the Long March, for it symbolised the ascension of the communists to power. All this revolutionary action under the radiant gaze and light offered by Mao.

Right: Yan'an: after the Long March the Red Army fled north to this barren and desolate region. Under Mao at Yan'an, they rebuilt their forces and their image.

## INTRODUCTION TO THE MAO BADGE (1)[4]

**WANG ANTING**

### The Pre-liberation History of the Badge

The earliest Mao Zedong badges appeared in the Yan'an period. In 1945, on the eve of the Seventh Party Congress, in order to produce a memento for those attending the Party Congress, a comrade from the Lu Xun Art College of Yan'an

---

4   Wang Anting (ed.), *A Collection of Illustrative Plates of Mao Zedong Badges* (Beijing: Chinese Bookstores Publishing House, 1993). [王安廷（主编），《毛泽东像章图谱》。]

produced a commemorative Mao Badge. In the later period of the war of liberation (1945–49), limited edition Mao Zedong badges were produced by different liberated areas. For example, the north-east liberated zone produced Mao Zedong badges and gave them as awards to those designated model workers. After liberation, the Party and the government, in order to celebrate key events, pressed a series of Mao badges.[5] In the early 1950s, in Shanghai and some other places, they even pressed a 22-carat-gold Mao Zedong badge.

The period of Cultural Revolution was one in which the fad for badges came into its own and went out of control. This started fairly simply, but as the Mao craze and personality cult took hold, the badge became a potent symbol of the times. As the number of wearers increased, so too did the styles, shapes and sizes. From the uppermost leaders in the Party, army and government through to the most ordinary of people, everyone wore the badge.

No one really knows how many badges there were. Some suggest hundreds of millions, others 2.3 billion. Either way, it is clear that it was the biggest ever commemorative badge production for any politician or ideologue, both in terms of the variety produced, and in terms of sheer numbers.

## INTRODUCTION TO THE MAO BADGE (2)[6]
### ZHOU JIHOU

### The Badge as Historical Record

In part, the history of the rise and decline of the Mao Zedong badge is the history of the early part of the Cultural Revolution. From the characters on the badge, the pictures etched onto it, as well as the date of its production, its purpose, the background to its production, what the badge image implied and the characteristics it had, we are offered some deep traces of the extraordinary period and the specific historical phase. Thus, the badges naturally form an historical record upon which to write on this period.

### The First Badges of the Cultural Revolution

The first Cultural Revolution Mao badge came out in the middle of July 1966 from the Shanghai United Badge Factory. This badge was 1.2 cm in size and red on gold. On the back was written 'serial number one'. By the end of July the factory had produced 32,000 badges of this type. By August, they had modified the design and were able to produce 175,000 badges. By September, they

---

5   The text goes on to point out that volunteers fighting the US in Korea were given Mao badges, as were those sent to Tibet.

6   Zhou Jihou, *The Mystery of the Mao Badge—The Ninth Wonder of the World* (Beijing: Beiyue Literature Publishing House, 1993), 35ff. [周继厚,《毛泽东像章之谜－世界第九大奇观》.]

increased production even more, reaching a production figure of 1.3 million badges. In fact, on 5 September alone, they got close to producing 50,000 badges.

In the summer break, Shanghai students went home and took their badges with them. Word of the badges spread. Shortly afterwards, the Beijing Red Flag Badge Factory also began to produce a small round badge of Mao.

Most of the badges produced were round and did not exceed 3 cm in diameter. Most retailed for about five to eight Chinese cents (*fen*) and could be bought at the New China Bookshop. The majority of consumers of the Mao badge were young people. Early on, there were also very definite limits placed on the production and sale of these items. This, however, began to change as demand led to limitless production.

What really spread the popularity of the badge were the revolutionary exchanges. After these, the badges became ubiquitous across the nation. In the process of carrying out revolutionary exchanges, Red Guards wanted small mementos of their visits. While these mementos took many forms, the ideal form was to 'request' (请) a badge.[7] To prove one's revolutionary zeal, badges would be divided among friends and colleagues upon a person's return to college or home. A gift of a badge was more precious and more welcome than fine wine. So, whenever Red Guards ventured into an area, the Mao badges became extremely hard to get. In order to keep up with the Red Guards' voracious appetites for badges, all sorts, shapes and sizes of Mao badges were produced and the prices were kept extremely low. Hence villagers could offer the Red Guards badges in a variety of forms cheaply, and thereby enabled them to be given as gifts.

## STORIES OF EXCESS: MAO AS GIFT, MAO AS CURSE[8]
### ZHOU JIHOU

### The Wedding Gift

Every generation has different gifts to offer during marriage celebrations. In the 1980s it was fashionable to give the traditional 'red envelope' within which there could be as little as 10 *yuan* (Chinese dollars) or as much as a few hundred. In the 1970s the most common gift was something useful and cheap like pots, bowls, wooden ladles or basins. In the 1960s, especially the late 1960s, the marriage gift, like everything else, was thoroughly suffused with the need to 'revolutionise' things and it had a heavy political coating. Guests gave a newly married couple presents like *Mao Zedong's Selected Works*, Mao's *Little Red Book* or Mao Zedong badges. For a short period, the entire nation was in something of a turmoil and this was very well reflected in the popular television series *Yearning*. In the series,

---

7   See also Liu Xin and Zhou Jihou, 'Buying Mao'.
8   Zhou Jihou, *The Mystery of the Mao Badge*, 97–100.

the characters Song Dacheng and Yue Mei's room had a Mao badge hung over a red cloth, which aroused memories with deep feelings and uncontrolled sadness in the viewers.

In February 1968, in a factory in Canton, a couple of young workers had a marriage ceremony. Party and work unit leaders, as well as comrades, relatives and friends came to pay their respects and congratulate them. Each brought presents and all of the presents were of a distinctly 'red' nature. But there were so many of this type that it caused the young couple to be less than honoured and other couples to be less than admiring.

Finally, at night, the party came to an end and the guests departed. The newly-weds still did not feel like going to bed, so they began to unwrap and examine the various presents they had received.[9] They very carefully examined and made an inventory of the treasures that had been bestowed upon them. These 'treasures' consisted of 24 sets of *Mao Zedong's Selected Works*, 32 volumes of the *Little Red Book*, and 167 Mao badges.

Making such an inventory made them very sleepy. In their six-square-metre bridal chamber they sat on their bed and the husband said to his new partner very quietly: 'Oh no, such a huge pile of books and badges. If we wanted to eat them we couldn't, if we wanted to sell them we couldn't, if we wanted to lose them we wouldn't dare and if we wanted to store them in this flat we couldn't because there isn't enough room! What the hell are we going to do with them?' In hushed tones, his wife advised him: 'Don't ever say things like this in public.' Pacing at the foot of the bed they pondered on the problem for ages. Then, finally, the husband exclaimed, 'I've got it!' He excitedly explained his idea to his wife: 'Look, in our factory don't Wang and Zhang intend to marry in a few days from now? Well, let's just rewrap the presents and pass them on to them. What about that for an idea!' And so it was that in a little over a week at their wedding reception, Wang and Zhang ended up being the recipients of their own pile of 'revolutionary presents'.

## Burying Mao

Weddings were not the only time that Mao badges could be given as presents. In expressing one's grief at the loss of someone, or to express one's profound regret at any wrong committed, one often found the Mao badge being used as a commemorative item.

Wang Wenjiang in his work *I do not repent* disclosed the following. In 1968 he was 'sent down' to the Jiangxi province Wu Mountain copper mine. While there, the son of the mine doctor named Ao Mei drowned. The doctor was grief stricken. She took her son and dressed him in his favourite clothes, put his favourite Mao badge on his chest and then placed him in a coffin and buried

---

9  It is customary in China to wait until the guest has departed before unwrapping presents. To unwrap them in front of the giver is regarded as ungracious.

him. Some time later, a well-meaning neighbour was telling people of the fate of the child and, in the process, told of the Mao badge the mother had placed on the child's body. She carelessly told the story and it was listened to with great interest. A couple of the young fellows listening to this were without scruples and used it to talk of 'the class struggle taking on new directions'. In order to promote themselves within their work unit they wrote a highly sensitive report to the clinic in which the mother of the dead child worked. The clinic, upon formally learning of the event, acted immediately. Workers were sent to the gravesite and the body exhumed. There, on the corpse of the dead child, they found the child's favourite Mao badge. With righteous indignation they exclaimed: 'How dare she bury the precious Chairman Mao badge in a grave. Such malice is inexplicable!' The poor pitiful doctor Mei was unable to explain herself and unable to wipe away the stain of these events. She attempted to kill herself by throwing herself into the Yellow River but failed. Then came the struggle sessions at the mine site where she was dragged out and 'struggled against' as a 'monster and demon' and this she remained for the many years that followed. Without a mother's care, the exhumed body of the child was simply lightly covered over with yellow earth and left to rot.

## Swallowing Mao

According to reports, there was a certain unit in Shanghai run by a Red Guard 'heavy' who would attack the opposite faction and take prisoners. While imprisoned, the inmates were tortured. Not only were they beaten, but they were refused water or food in an attempt to starve them. One inmate, who found this unendurable, felt he had nothing to lose and decided to commit suicide, but all his laces and his belt had been taken. Suddenly he noticed a glint off the Mao badge on his chest. He quickly took it off, put it in his mouth and tried to swallow it. By chance, his captors noticed what he had done and rushed in. Using both hands, they forced open his mouth and made him spit out the badge. It was only because of this that he was saved.

## Breaking Mao

The porcelain Mao badge is really rare these days and there are a number of reasons for this. First of all, political and environmental conditions conspired against them. Not every factory was able to produce porcelain badges. In addition, the period of their production was extremely short. Not long after the Cultural Revolution began, the aluminium badge began production. They were very popular throughout 1967. In this period, no one had really thought about using porcelain to produce badges. Moreover, even if one did have the idea, they must also have been very apprehensive about it both because of the porcelain material itself, and the process of its production, namely, kiln burning. Just the idea of producing Mao badges out of porcelain brought one thing to everybody's mind: burning the image of Mao. Hence the question: can one really burn the 'precious badge'? But there was no other way! Until the beginning of 1968, no badges were produced. Then a number of rather brave people broke the taboo— large-scale porcelain-producing factories within Jiangxi and Hunan became renowned for the volume and quality of their badges. But this period was not to last very long.

On 12 June 1969, the Central Committee issued the document 'Certain questions to pay attention to concerning the propagation of Chairman Mao's image' within which was stated, quite emphatically, that 'It is prohibited for people to reproduce Chairman Mao's image on porcelain.' The porcelain badge ceased production after this. The period of porcelain badge production lasted about a year. Another reason why they were not produced was that they were 'unsafe' for the wearer. Such badges, if they fell, could easily be damaged or broken. There were untold numbers of people across the nation who suffered a terrible fate because their porcelain Mao badges fell and were broken. Perhaps the similarity of the stories of these unfortunate people leads us to be less than surprised by the fate they suffered. Over the years, I have actually tracked down one example of a very lucky fellow whose story is worth putting down on paper.

In-between the tall buildings that envelop Shanghai's Nanjing Street are throngs of merchants. It is a bustling area, renowned throughout the country, and it bristles with activity and people all year round. One day in March 1968, a soldier from the People's Liberation Army was wandering down Nanjing Street on his way to the Daguangming Cinema wearing on his chest a porcelain Mao badge. He didn't pay attention to the crowds that were bumping into him and they finally knocked his Mao badge to the ground. After he picked up the broken remnants he turned pale with fright and became flustered. The people on both sides of him surged forward and glared at him. Under their gaze, the soldier felt he had committed some heinous crime, but he came up with a brainwave to extricate himself from the mess.

'Bang!' Down he went on his knees, then, holding the badge up in his hands, he began to weep tears of remorse. Through his tears he began to chant incessantly, 'I have committed a crime ... I have committed a terrible crime ...'

The surrounding crowd still did not leave the scene. So he abruptly stood up and ripped open the front of his Mao suit, and, gritting his teeth, dug the broken parts of the badge into his chest. Red blood flowed onto the pavement. The observing crowd stood agape and aghast at what had happened. Then he turned to the crowd and from the depths of his chest yelled out: 'Revolutionary comrades, I have committed a crime, for which I really should be given a thousand deaths. To atone for my crime, let me punish myself before you for I will remember the crime I have committed today for an eternity!'

He finished speaking, turned toward the crowd of onlookers, and bowed three times. He then donned his army cap, cut through the crowd, and walked away in a vigorous marching style, putting on a gallant expression as he went.

## BUYING MAO: THEN AND NOW
### LIU XIN AND ZHOU JIHOU

### Acquiring the Mao badge during the Cultural Revolution[10] (Liu Xin)

There were principally three means by which one could acquire the Mao badge. First, the work unit or the organisation to which the person was attached would freely issue their members with badges. Second, individuals could purchase the badges themselves. The price paid was usually somewhere between twenty and forty Chinese cents and they would usually be bought from the work unit propaganda department. Sometimes shops would also offer a supply. Finally, people would exchange badges among themselves. Many people became avid collectors and went through relatives and friends to collect and exchange badges other than those from their own work unit, province or city.

### The Language of Acquisition[11] (Zhou Jihou)

As one person reported during the Cultural Revolution, 'Buying Mao badges in those days was really something … tons of people. Queues would run 24 hours a day and, when you finally did get to the counter, you were only allowed to have one. In order to buy a really significant Mao badge, I dare say a number of people even queued up for 24 hours … But in those days you could not use the word 'buy'. To say you wanted to 'buy a badge' (买像章) was to display a low level of consciousness. Instead you had to 'request a badge' (请像章).'

### Marketing Mao during the Cultural Revolution[12] (Zhou Jihou)

From May through to November 1967, in a backstreet running off Beijing's Wangfujing Street One Hundred Goods Store was a small bookstore that specialised in Mao badges. It was there that you could see Mao badges from across the country. Every day people would queue and wait to get a chance to 'request' a badge … The most expensive badges they sold were twelve Chinese cents each. It was rare for anyone to buy only one badge. Mostly people bought three, four or up to ten or twenty.

At the same time, there developed a badge swap and exchange market.

In Beijing, the market was set up close to Qianmen district. The badge market enabled people to swap any double copies of badges they had for others. It also enabled them to pick up badges they did not have from numerous others on offer. In this way, they could replace those they had in multiples or thought of as

---

10 Liu Xin (ed.), *A Treasured Collection of Mao Zedong Badges* (Beijing: China Economic Publishing House, 1993), Afterword, np. [刘鑫 （主编），《毛泽东像章珍品集》.]
11 Zhou Jihou, *The Mystery of the Mao Badge*, 40–1.
12 Zhou, 47–8.

inferior. There were quite a few instances where money also changed hands ... At this place, all kinds of Mao badges from across the nation were available, including many special, rare or treasured examples. Here one could find wooden, stone, copper, shellfish and porcelain Mao badges. There were also badges commemorating special events for which they had been specially minted. There were Mao badges that glowed in the dark, were of a 3D design, or were made of bamboo or some other special substance.

The city of Kunming also had a badge swap market. It was located in the city area right next to the Red Flag Movie Theatre. Huge numbers of people would gather here and many went simply to watch what was going on. The swap market was a crowded and place of great chaos, and was not a good place for children. Reselling for a profit was not the only thing going on there and, as a result, it became a focal area for police surveillance. However, it was invariably left to the Red Guards to clear these places up.

Shanghai, too, had a badge market and it was of a similar nature. Shanghai people called the Mao badges the 'treasured badges' and quite a few people stole aluminium sheeting, strips or barrels and reforged them into Mao badges which they then took down to the swap market to make a little money. The Shanghai Public Security Bureau regarded such activities as lacking in 'devotion' and they countered them by organising militia teams and taking 'revolutionary action'. One night, the police sent a number of plain-clothes officers down to the market to mingle in the crowds and, although these police confiscated badges, they were far more humane in their treatment of the traders than the Red Guards were.

### Stealing Badges isn't Stealing[13] (Zhou Jihou)

[I]n those days of cultural revolution social order was quite stable and criminal cases were fairly rare. Nevertheless, 'thieves' were pretty numerous (although these so-called thieves did not steal money or belongings and, therefore, it is clear they were not thieves in the conventional sense). More often than not, thieves at this time were youths who would 'souvenir' Mao badges or military caps in the busy crowded streets of various public places ... As Lu Xun once remarked, 'for the lover of books, to take a book cannot be described as theft.' So, too, one can now say of the lover of the Mao badge that theft of the Mao badge by the lover of the badge is not stealing.

### Marketing Mao Today[14] (Zhou Jihou)

At the beginning of 1992 throughout the streets and lanes of all the big cities, in all the markets and busy shopping areas, the only sound around seemed to be the

---

13 Zhou, 102–3.
14 Zhou, 232–34.

music of the the 'Liuyang River', Mao's birth place, the 'Washing Song' and 'The Bumper Harvest Song' … Quite a few people on the street stopped to listen, and a number of middle-aged people seemed pleasantly surprised by the rhythm, and started to join in the singing. The songs came from a cassette recording entitled 'The Red Sun—New Rhythms to a Compilation of Odes to Mao Zedong', made by Shanghai's China Record Company. The success of this tape led to others. 'Cherishing the Memory of You—Coming Down from the Altar in Praise of Mao Zedong', 'Sounds From the Past' and 'The Radiance of the Path' followed. Tunes that were once very popular proved to be popular again and became the 'hot new items' for sale. The sight of consumers rushing out to buy 'Red Sun' produced a quite unprecedented spectacle.

In the newspaper *Chinese Women* came a report on 17 December 1991 that stated: 'Recently, in the countryside around Changsha, tens of thousands of people have been struggling to buy picture portraits of Chairman Mao at the markets. One late arrival to the scene was a young woman carrying a small baby. She looked around at those people at the front of the queue and begged them to buy a poster of Chairman Mao for her. Her husband was away working and her mother-in-law had a cherished desire to have a picture of Mao. In Shuangqi village, there was even one old man in his seventies in the queue. He was known locally as "old man Yusi". After he bought his picture portrait of Chairman Mao, he held it firmly in both hands and exclaimed: "Chairman Mao, the Communist Party, socialism, these things are our symbols of stability. For those of us who are old, Chairman Mao, the Communist Party, and socialism offered us old people's homes, for those of us who were sick, they arranged hospitals, for infants, they built kindergartens. With good deeds like this, who could ignore them!" From statistics that are available about this phenomenon, one can note that in Changsha county alone there are around 230,000 peasant households and around 99.5 per cent of those have 'requested' that Mao's portrait come into their homes.' It is reported that, quite apart from the popularity of 'requesting' that Chairman Mao portraits come into their homes, a number of provinces, cities and areas have hung portraits of Mao during important conferences.

From the perspective of daily life, one really does gain the deep impression that when 'one leaves the house, one is likely to bump into Chairman Mao'. On New Year's Day in 1993, in big, medium and small cities across the land, in vehicles of all varieties, the spirit of hanging Chairman Mao's portrait in the car is gaining in popularity. Wherever one looks, in the magazines and newspapers of this land, one will always come across commentary and editorials featuring 'special reports', 'special perspectives' and probes into the causes of this phenomenon. There have been television reports on the same theme.

From the statistical material available we can gain some understanding of the extent and breadth of this craze: on the afternoon of 22 March 1992 on the busy street of South Fending in Xi'an city at the old city market intersection, there were 214 vehicles stuck in the traffic and, of these, 193 had the Mao portrait hanging in their windows. From 1.40 p.m. through to 3.40 p.m., from the inter-section through to the railway station, 326 taxis passed by and, of those, 204 had Mao portraits. On 28 March, I personally stood at the side of the busy Huangshu Freeway in Guiyang and counted 100 vehicles, of which 68 had the Mao portrait in their vehicle.

## AN INTRODUCTION TO WANG ANTING: CHINA'S 'BADGE MASTER'[15]

### ZHOU JIHOU

Those wishing to experience something of the feel for the 'Cultural Revolution' should take a trip to Chengdu city in China's Sichuan province. There, at number 23 Five Fortune Street, is a very small old house in a very ordinary, small laneway. Yet despite this, here is a house that has even made it into the *Guinness Book of Records*. The reason for this is because the famous Chinese Wang Anting lives here, at his 'Very Small Museum'. Wang is getting on, he is hard of hearing and his eyes aren't as good as they once were. His family is also quite poor. In recent years in particular, he is finding it hard to get around and cannot work. He is totally reliant upon his wife, who has to bath, shave, feed and clothe him. From this invalid position, he has still managed to open up an 'Individual Cultural Traders' Very Small Museum'.

In the first month of 1989, after a dream revelation, Wang Anting set forth to open up a private museum. His premise was simple: irrespective of whatever else they may mean, Mao Zedong badges represent a definite historical period. To this end, he went to business, cultural and taxation departments to apply for a licence to open his house as the site of an 'individual cultural trader'. After this, he gathered together all his badges, and even though his house was only 20 square metres, he redesigned it so that it became a 'Very Small Museum'. Once that was done, he opened it up for business.

On 11 March of that year, the *Sichuan Daily* announced the opening of China's first Mao badge exhibition, with an article introducing Wang Anting and his badge collection. This article was entitled 'An exhibition of tens of thousands of Mao badges', and it announced the achievements of Wang in opening this private exhibition. Later on, Wang Anting's exhibition would be profiled in the *Chengdu Evening News*, *The Sichuan Youth News* and the Shanghai paper *China Youth News*. This transformed the activity of collecting the Mao badges from an 'underground' activity into a highly visible, public one, drawing both praise and support. From this beginning, the collecting of Mao badges and research into the badges developed.

---

15 Zhou Jihou, *The Mystery of the Mao Badge*, 245ff.

This situation continued until 26 December 1990. At this time, Wang Anting's 'Very Small Museum' established the nation's civil badge collectors group, which was called 'The Chinese Mao Zedong badge collectors and research preparatory committee'. After its establishment, many other areas throughout the country began to organise similar groups to collect and research the Mao badge.

## ★ INTERVIEWS WITH THE 'BADGE MASTERS' WANG ANTING AND DANG MIAO

Mr Tang or Dang Miao (a pseudonym he has adopted since joining Wang Anting, literally meaning 'Party seedling') as he is now known, was the first person I met when I visited Wang Anting's 'Very Small Museum'. He introduced himself and took me around, showing me the collection and pointing out interesting badges and mementos. As he did this, he explained how he came to be with the Badge Master. Dang Miao used to be a small trader before he joined Wang Anting. He used to sell a lot of different things but, when the Mao craze hit, he started to stock up on Mao badges. One day, a university student saw his Mao badges for sale on his stand and told him of Wang Anting's collection. Dang Miao decided he should visit this person and see if he was interested in parting with any of his badges. When he met Wang Anting, Dang Miao was so touched by his dedication that he decided to join him in his cultural enterprise. Financially, it has not been

Above: This cake was bought to celebrate the formation of the 'Sichuan International Communist Alliance Headquarters'. Dang Miao is General Secretary. At the top it reads: 'Long live the spirit of the world alliance!' Below are two Mao badges and sunflowers.

Left: With a statue of Chairman Mao in the background 'Dang Miao' stands with two red candles which are placed in the museum and burnt to commemorate the death of Communist revolutionary heroes.

beneficial. When he was a free trader he used to make about 700 *yuan* per month ($US84). Since joining Wang Anting he makes very little, only about 200 *yuan* per month ($US24). There are other rewards, however.

The museum itself holds one of the world's largest collections of Mao badges. There are over 57,000 Mao badges with 17,000 different types. In addition to the badges, they have also founded a Mao Zedong research centre with over 1300 members worldwide. The research centre has members in over twenty countries, including the US, France and Japan.

Dang Miao pointed to a range of badges and explained their meaning. The badges that display three red banners under the figure of Chairman Mao are meant to signify the Great Leap Forward; the Party's Main Line and the People's Communes. When badges display nine stars around the face of the Chairman, it signifies that the badge commemorates the Party's Ninth Congress. When badges have the character for 'adore' written three times on them, all of which are found on a sunflower's face, the meaning is that one must adore Chairman Mao as a great leader, adore his revolutionary road and adore his Thought. The sunflower is displayed as open under the face of Chairman Mao, indicating that Mao is the sun, bringing light to the people's lives. Wherever he is, flowers open. There is often a chrysanthemum branch on a badge under the Chairman's face. This is partly because Mao particularly liked chrysanthemums because they flowered in winter. For Mao, the chrysanthemum was a metaphor for a good Party member and the tree stood as a motto for all Party members: blossom in times of adversity.

Wang Anting is 62 years old. At the time of the Revolution, Wang was only sixteen. He used to be a carpenter, but when he was 50 years old he could no longer work because of illness. It was in May 1951 that he first began collecting Mao badges. He bought the first one in Chengdu's Rangfangai market area. From then on he started to build up his badge collection and other Mao paraphernalia. He has two very full rooms where he displays his collections, but there is an additional two tons of material in his loft that is not on display.  These things were all collected from the Cultural Revolution era. The exhibition has been in operation for about five years.

**MD**: *Why did you decide to start the exhibition?*
**Wang**: About five years ago I had a vision. In that vision Mao came to me and said: 'Old Wang, Old Wang, you have had my badges locked up in these boxes now for quite some time, let them out and let the world once again see my face for I fear I am being forgotten.' Then, on the very next day, I read a newspaper report that in Shanghai, a private person organised an exhibition of precious stones. From that I decided that it was in this way I could honour my promise to Chairman Mao.

The sign in front of the museum which advertises the fact that it is also a Mao badge research centre.

The main entrance to the museum. Above the door, in bold red characters is written: 'Wang Anting's Very Small Museum'. In fact, it is a very small house which Wang has converted into a shrine of remembrance to Mao.

*What about government support?*

**Wang:** 'When I had decided to set up the private museum, I went off to the various government ministries to get permission and support. I went to the tax department and the cultural department but, instead of support, all I ended up getting was a lot of trouble and many hassles. Despite this, I still felt the need to continue with my plans. So I continued to work toward the opening of the exhibition. It was in this way that I ended up being the person to open up the first ever Mao Zedong badge exhibition.

After it opened, lots of people came to see it and, although I charged an entrance fee, I decided not to charge students, the old or the crippled. People from the US, France, Germany and Australia have all been to have a look. Also, Sichuan Television has featured it in a report. The government, however, offered no subsidies and no support although, in the end, they did give us help to repair the wall in the second room. They also gave me this wheelchair. Generally though, money comes from the donations of the people who visit. From this money I have now been able to put together a newsletter. My newsletter is called *Contemporary Cultural Relic*. I run off about two thousand copies of every

Wang next to his bed in the middle of the main display room of the museum. There isn't enough room for Wang's family and the Mao paraphernalia, so they must make room.

edition. I think of *Contemporary Cultural Relic* as being like an 'underground newspaper' that the CCP used to get its message across in pre-revolutionary days. **Dang**: He has only ever had two years of education yet he is able to assume the editorship of this newsletter and he writes all the slogans about Chairman Mao himself.'

*What is the point of the newsletter?*
**Wang**: Through the exhibition and the newsletter I hope to spread the word of Mao Zedong to the young people who do not know about it and have not heard of him. In this way, I am also able to commemorate the 20,000-odd people who died for the revolution.

Wang Anting: 'Every edition, I produce about two to three thousand copies of the magazine. I even send it to the Central Committee, but they never respond!'

*What did you do in the Cultural Revolution?*
**Wang**: I was the leader of a small red rebel group.

*What do you think of the economic reform programme?*
**Wang**: It was okay, but inflation now is far too high.

*What do you think about the current Party position on Chairman Mao?*
**Wang**: They are wrong. The current Party assessment of Chairman Mao is simply wrong. Mao was not 70 per cent right, 30 per cent wrong as they suggest. Mao was a person of such greatness that he made very few errors. Everybody blames Mao for the Cultural Revolution, but it was aimed at getting rid of revisionists and corruption within Party ranks. Unfortunately, at the lower levels, mistakes were made and these were all later attributed to Mao and so you have this '70 per cent right' assessment.

When I asked Wang if any of his collection of posters were for sale he said no. He said the only thing he would consider 'trading' was a framed picture of three letters written by Chairman Mao before the Revolution. These letters, written in the Nationalist period before the Communists seized power, have been discovered by Wang. He is hoping to use these original and historically valuable letters as collateral for a 2000-square-metre exhibition hall and a school for the very poor. Anyone who supplies these two things will be given the three letters to display.

## THE STORY OF YAN XINLONG[16]
### ZHOU JIHOU

In June 1992, I was invited to attend the 100th birthday anniversary activities commemorating Comrade Mao Zedong. These were being held in Mao Zedong's home village of Shaoshan. It was there that I was lucky enough to meet Yan Xinlong. At that time we had just entered 'the ancestral temple of the Mao clan' where a Mao Zedong badge exhibition was being held.

In my mind, I had always imagined Yan to be a much older character with a wealth of experience and a range of skills that had long been built on. To my surprise, Yan Xinlong turned out to be only 27 years of age. To put it another way, as the Cultural Revolution rolled out over the landscape and swept up all before it, he was still a baby. Yet, despite this, he is, today, a Mao badge collector with over 40,000 Mao badges and would have to be the collector with the most Mao badges in the whole of China.

Maybe it was because our ages were not all that different, or because of our family backgrounds, or perhaps it was the fact that our personal histories were not all that dissimilar that we immediately became the best of friends. We were

16  Zhou Jihou, *The Mystery of the Mao Badge*, 253–55.

both staying in a small garret in 'the ancestral temple of the Mao clan'. In reality, we had a merry and very long chat, talking all night without sleep. Through this, I became aware of the background and reasons for him becoming a Mao badge collector.

Yan Xinlong's father, Yan Yuhuai, was an old cadre. When he was fourteen, he ran away from his home in Shanxi's Wutai county and went to Yan'an, where he joined the Eighth Route army. As part of the Eighth Route Army that later became known as the People's Liberation Army, Yan Senior followed battles from one end of the country to the other. After liberation, he was transferred to the Space Ministry where he became a leading cadre in a research institution. He is now aged and has already retired.

Under his father's uplifting influence and education, Yan Xinlong, from a very early age, gained a very deep feeling for Mao Zedong. This was despite the fact that his own father suffered attacks during the Cultural Revolution. Despite this, his father never wavered in his own appraisal of Mao and raised and educated his son accordingly.

In 1981, Yan Xinlong was only seventeen and had just returned from his period in the countryside. He intended to fulfil his desire to attend a university of the PLA and follow in his father's footsteps.

The instructor of the new recruits for that year was also an avid Mao student and gave them lessons on Mao's works, starting with 'Serve the People' and 'Oppose Liberalism'.

One time, when Yan returned home with *Mao Zedong's Selected Works* in his arms, he discovered his father's collection of over 1000 Mao badges. When he discovered these beautiful items, he immediately kept hold of the badges more tightly and said, 'Dad, give me these!' Yan Yuhuai had been making revolution with Mao for a couple of decades and had a profound impression of him. He had seen him on many occasions. He saw the keenness and happiness in his son's face and was happy to give him the badges. From then on, Yan Junior started collecting Mao badges.

In the process of collecting the badges, his father gave him many lectures concerning the joys and sorrows of stories around the various badges. His father also told him about the Cultural Revolution, when most of the badges were produced. Indeed, today, we have no statistics on just how many badges were produced in this period. These stories and accounts only tended to excite Yan Xinlong's interest in the badges even more and he became the greatest of all the collectors of Mao badges.

From 1985 onwards, he spent his entire wage, coupled with the extra money he earned helping out a free trader friend, to support his badge-collecting habit. He gave nothing to his family apart from that which was absolutely necessary to support their daily life. Every penny went toward buying his treasured badges. In addition, he would quite often ask his father for money to help him buy the ones he particularly desired.

Yan's father and younger brother were also in attendance at the exhibition at Shaoshan. In fact, his younger brother said to me: 'Getting to Shaoshan to arrange this exhibition wasn't easy. My brother's wife is about to give birth and there is only my mother at home to look after her. We really don't know whether she has given birth or not. It's okay though, because my brother managed to get out of the job of washing the nappies.' He then continued: 'Even before he was married he was like that though. In fact, he rarely ever took his wife out to parks or to see the movies when they were courting. Do you know what he did with his time? He spent it all with those badges, collecting them, arranging them, putting them together, he would while away the night like that. My sister-in-law, father and mother really got a bit sick of it.' From his younger brother, I learned an awful lot about Yan and about the relationship he has with his wife.

## MY STORY[17]
### ZHOU JIHOU

In 1964, I was only three years old and, while still in my parents' arms, I was forced to go with them to the countryside. I was very sentimentally attached to Beijing and had a very deep feeling for all things from Beijing. My parents, though, were transferred from the Beijing detachment to become members of a Guizhou detachment and so we ended up in a distant outlying tableland in a small county city called Bijie in Guizhou province.

For a kid from Beijing to end up in the south of the country in a small rural mountain area was a very strange experience for here there were trees, leaves, small birds and insects, so it was a very beautiful place in its way. Hence, the leaves, the flowers, the beautiful crickets, these things all became precious to me and I would collect them all and put them in my very own 'treasure chest'.

By the time the Cultural Revolution hit, I had already begun primary school. By this time, too, my treasure chest was already getting too big and could not fit anything else in it. I had collected all sorts of stuff, from stamps, cigarette packets, matches, old coins, sweets, comics—even toys and posters came to be part of my treasure trove.

The full wind of the Cultural Revolution hit our sleepy little mountain retreat and I noticed that everyone had started wearing various types of Mao badges. In my heart, I thought of these badges as sacred and beautiful objects. I really had a strong desire to own my own. But at that time it was impossible. My father was being severely criticised as a 'capitalist roader' and would suffer criticism sessions daily, while my mother was sent to work in a canteen as a cleaner. At this time, who could even think about, let alone fulfil, these youthful desires.

---

17 Zhou Jihou, *The Mystery of the Mao Badge*, 282–83.

In the spring of 1968, a relative from our old home in Jiangjin, Sichuan province, came to visit. On his chest he wore a beautiful glowing badge. It was red, glass covered and it had the figure of chairman Mao covered with phosphorus so that it would glow in the dark. This particularly beautiful and rare badge fascinated me and I could not take my eyes off it. When my relative left, I followed along the way until he finally decided to give me this most treasured thing. I would wear this rare Shaoshan manufactured badge wherever I went, and was very proud of it. Later, I was wearing the badge and playing with some friends in a place not far from home at a time soon after rain. We were using the mud to build up a dam when suddenly, someone started throwing mud at the dam.

'Zhou Xiaoqing,[18] pass over your red scarf and your badge to us. You son of a bitch, you are one of the five black elements,[19] how dare you wear that badge!'

I raised my head and looked around and there, in front of me, was a teacher with a number of 'little red rebels', all of whom aggressively surrounded me. Their mood became really foul when I refused to submit to their demands. I would have fought to the death to protect my badge, but they came at me and carried out their 'revolutionary action'. I was pushed into the mud and they forcibly snatched my red scarf and glowing badge.

I was wet from head to foot, covered in mud, and sick to the stomach with a sense of outrage. As I walked along the road to my home, I cried and cried for my heart was heavy. When I finally got home, I told my mother and father about what had happened, but what were they to do? They could hardly help themselves. They could, of course, console their child who felt a sense of grief, but what could they do apart from heave a sigh of anguish and regret? The only thing they could offer was a sense of 'comfort'. My mother's kind face consoled me in my hour of need.

After I had been beaten, I made an inner vow: I would definitely collect the badges of Mao Zedong and, what is more, I would have more than anyone else. I took this wish very much to heart and, bit by bit, I began this endless process of collection.

---

18  Zhou Xiaoqing was my original name. Later on, my father changed it saying: 'Because you love those Mao badges so much and in the hope that you will inherit my own profound feeling for Chairman Mao Zedong and therefore pass it on to the next generation, I will re-name you Zhou Jihou.' Zhou is my surname, Ji is an abbreviation of *jicheng* meaning to inherit and *hou* is an abbreviation of *shenhou* meaning profound.

19  The five black elements are landlords, rich peasants, counter-revolutionaries, rightists, and bad elements.

## THE BLACK HOLE OF MAO ZEDONG: THE ART OF ZHANG HONGTU[20]

### CAO ZHANGQING

When the Mao craze hit China people were, once again, speechless. Mao's portrait was put on porcelain, embroidery, T-shirts and in taxis. Even the Mao badge made a big splash on the market. It is said that the person who holds the record for the greatest number of badges is a person from Sichuan province. It is said he has collected something like 18,000 badges. This year has just witnessed the one hundredth anniversary of Mao's birth and the Chinese Communist Party authorities have really pushed this craze along as a result. With the support of the Party's General Secretary, Jiang Zemin, millions of Chinese dollars have been thrown into Mao's home village of Shaoshan in Hunan province where ten major long-term engineering projects to celebrate Mao are underway. These include such things as an enormous twelve-metre-high statue of the Chairman and, in the surrounding hills, the carving of 100 stone tablets with Mao's poems on them.

At the same time as all this was going on, on the other side of the Pacific in the United States, an artist who was originally from the mainland was himself deeply immersed in his own unique form of Mao craze. His name is Zhang Hongtu and he has a second-storey studio in Hope Street, Brooklyn, New York. His studio is very quiet and quite cool and it is also very big. On the walls and in every corner, the place is full of his creations from a series he has named 'The Material Mao Series'. Zhang's paintings are really very different from those of the masses for he doesn't want to add things to the canvas but to take things away—he cuts out the head section from Mao portraits and, in the black holes left, he leaves people to simply imagine the form of Mao's head.

He chiselled out pieces on concrete boards, thus forming a 'Concrete Mao'. He had sawn out the middle of sheet metal plates, thereby creating an 'Iron Mao' and, in addition to these, he also produced a 'Wire Mesh Mao', a 'Plywood Mao', 'Corn Husk Mao', 'Hessian Mao' 'Woollen Mao', 'Grass Mao' … indeed an entire 'Material Mao' world.

The artist said: 'This blank spot isn't just a geometrical shape nor is it simply to give the painting a new concept of space. Here is a real hole and, at the same time, it is an idol worshipped historically and in reality by the people. In working through this blank form, it leads one to query the significance of the form itself. It leads the viewer of the space to drift into thoughts somewhere between existence and non-existence.'

Zhang Hongtu's 'Black Hole Art' reminds one of the traditional Chinese Taoist concept of 'nothingness'. It is reminiscent of the use of 'blank space' in

20  Cao Zhangqing, 'The Black Hole of Mao Zedong: Visiting the States and Seeing the New Images of Mao by the Artist Zhang Hongtu', in *The King of the Devils of Chaos, Mao Zedong* (Taibei: Huixiong Publishing House, n.d.), 208–13. [ 曹长青，'毛泽东的黑洞 – 旅美画家张宏图的毛像新作'，《混世魔王毛泽东》。]

traditional Chinese art or of the classical poems that could 'without a single character, fully express their meaning' in great style. This type of intermingling of 'presence/absence' also leads one to recall Sartre's work, *Being and Nothingness*, which expresses itself in the extremely complex philosophic notions of 'self as existence' and 'self in existence'.

From the perspective of reality, this type of black hole hints at the figure of Mao as a type of idol with a power to spiritually influence in an invisible way. But in mainland China, this Mao craze really only expresses the surface level of things and the whole matter goes much deeper. This is true for every mainland Chinese, but it is especially so for the intelligentsia who have still not been able to completely throw off their Mao thought and their 'Mao speak'. Nowhere is this more in evidence than in relation to those people who throw down the gauntlet to Mao's Communist Party, for they are still strongly displaying the inertia of a commitment to Mao culture. In other words, they are using Mao's methods to oppose Mao, and although this type of 'method' is expressed in many differing situations, it is an unconscious commitment to it none the less.

One of the early paintings of Zhang Hongtu in his 'Mao Image Series' was greatly utilised by many magazines. This was a painting of the student leader Wuer Kaixi holding a microphone when addressing the crowds in Tiananmen Square with Mao behind him. Whether it was Tiananmen Square or the overseas democracy movement, what surely must be a cause of regret is the fact that all believe that, under this portrait of Mao, they could gain enlightenment. In other words, people still don't have a way of moving beyond the framework of Mao Thought.

## Mao's Last Supper and the Acupunctural Chart

Zhang Hongtu's portraits of Mao began at about the time of the student movement in 1989. It was at that time that three youths from the province of Hunan threw eggs at the huge portrait of Mao that hangs over the Tiananmen Square gate. For this, they were immediately turned over to the police by the demonstrating students and later they received hefty sentences. This, in turn, produced the impulse to make art. It led Zhang to recall 'the first time I "did" Mao, I felt really uncomfortable, as though I was committing some sort of heinous crime'. Mao has been dead for close to twenty years and Zhang has been in the US for close to ten, so what accounts for this lingering fear, this sense of a crime, this feeling of disrespect? It really is as though Mao was a kind of idol, a type of spirit force, a latent and terrible power.

On the question of why he chose his 'Black Hole' artform, Zhang explains: 'If you concentrate on a red object long enough, if you really just keep staring at it until your eyes are tired and only then turn your head and look at something else, what you discover is that a kind of green shadow object of the same shape remains in your mind's eye. The time I lived in China, no matter where you looked, all you could see was the image of Mao. It was his "positive" (阳) frontal form that was constantly on view. But this type of eye-strained image we have of him today, this is a view of his back side, his "negative" (阴) side.

'When I make my art, it is this kind of psychological change of perspective that I am attempting to materially capture in my paintings.'

In fact, it was an American artist who pointed out that the portrait of Mao on display over the Tiananmen Square gate represented this positive view of Mao (阳毛), while Zhang Hongtu's 'Mao Series' captures the 'negative Mao' (阴毛). Negative Mao is for real and he's a frightening figure.

But Zhang Hongtu's painting style isn't one-dimensional. In fact, it is more akin to a spaghetti crossing in a multilayered freeway because it raises so many ideas that it leaves the observer's head spinning with possibilities.

One student from mainland China went to Zhang's studio and 'saw' his piece 'Chairman Mao Lives in the People's Hearts Forever'; others viewed it and could only see a black hole—Mao culture really has had a profound effect. Within the 'Material Mao' artworks, the structural antagonism between the materiality of the art piece and the spirituality of the Mao image is palpable.

One early topic Zhang covered in his Mao art was 'The Last Supper' and this piece was the subject of some controversy. In this piece, Zhang used Leonardo da Vinci's painting of the same name as his base. Unlike the original painting, however, Jesus and all of the twelve disciples became the figures upon which Mao appears in different postures, and different guises. The table is covered by a red table cloth on which is placed a very contemporary object, the microphone stand, while, at the side of Mao's leg by his foot is a spittoon. On the back wall there are articles of Mao's stuck up while outside, through the window, one can vaguely see the Great Wall.

There are at least three hidden levels to this piece of art. Firstly, Mao's revolution is represented as a cult movement wherein Mao becomes a Communist religious figure like Jesus. Secondly, Mao becomes something of a spirit in so far as each of the figures to the side are all Mao Zedong and this helps show that, within all of us, there is a little of Mao Zedong present and it is this fact that makes Mao like a fish within water, and able to draw up a social blueprint for all Chinese. In the original scene depicted in da Vinci's portrait, Jesus says: 'One among you will betray me' but the Judas within Zhang Hongtu's painting is still Mao Zedong. In his view, it isn't external forces that defeated Maoism but the betrayal of Mao by Mao himself. The rational elements within Maoist thought are betrayed by the bastard elements.

This particular portrait was to be shown in a Washington exhibition in 1989 but the organisers, fearing Church objections, temporarily withdrew it and this action created quite a storm.[21]

---

21 This painting was excluded from an exhibition organised by the Congressional Human Rights Foundation and Senator Edward Kennedy held in June 1990 in Washington on the grounds that it was offensive to religion. Zhang's response: 'Eight years ago, I moved to the United States from China in order to have freedom to paint. Should I now move from the United States?' Geremie Barmé and Linda Jaivin, *New Ghosts, Old Dreams* (New York: Times Books, 1992), 409.

A little while ago Zhang Hongtu completed 'The Mao Acupunctural Chart' where thoughtfulness passes over into humour. In this portrait, both the front and back of Mao are covered with acupunctural points which are written as oppressive 'stimulation points' for revolution, power, and struggle. Earlier on, Zhang also produced 'Mao and the Goddess of Democracy' and this, too, is quite humorous for in this picture Mao looks at the Goddess of Democracy erected in Tiananmen Square and, from the thought balloons emanating from his head come the words 'arh, women!'

Zhang Hongtu is 49 years old this year and, like many his age, worshipping Mao came during the Cultural Revolution when hundreds of thousands of them religiously left their homes for Mao's. Zhang left his home in Canton and went on revolutionary exchanges to Mao's birthplace of Shaoshan in Hunan province. He was also sent off to the countryside. This was because he had 'relations with the outside world' and so he was subject to 'internal control' and he suffered for many years. Zhang painted Mao portraits to come to terms with his fateful experience, to forget about life and to raise his spirits. It was a way of painstakingly avoiding opposing things or fighting things. The way Zhang figured it, Mao's authoritative influence extended over his everyday fate for so long that to 'do Mao', to take charge of Mao's image, was a way of gaining self-liberation. It was impossible for him to do anything else because he could not avoid reflecting on his fate.

## CHINESE CULTURE DRAWN INTO THE MARKET[22]
**DA YANG**

### Two Waves, Surprising but not Dangerous

The economic development of socialism brought on by reform and the open-door policies, also brought with it a fairly large 'subsidiary' product, namely, trendy overseas cultural products which could all be labelled as effects of 'commercialisation'. From the beginning of the 1980s, pop songs, ballroom dancing, disco, rock 'n roll, video games, right through to the bikini and fashion models all rolled into mainland China and led to a series of hot crazes. At the same time, it also produced a series of surprises and some pretty strong disagreements. In the end, however, those who fought against the trend ended up waking up to the fact that all these things were surprising but not dangerous, and they really would be of use to us Chinese.

In the process, the fact that there was now a Chinese cultural market meant that those with symbolic cultural capital moved from being a hidden facet of society to something to be celebrated. They shifted from being something that

22 Da Yang, 'Chinese culture drawn into the market', *Women's Studies*, 3 (1993), 4–9. [达扬，'中国文化卷入市场'，《女性研究》.]

wobbled when they first walked to a thing that now moves with more strident steps. The notion of a cultural market has now strongly penetrated the consciousness of government offices, enterprises and the masses.

The effect of increasing levels of regulation was to force a general decline in this cultural market, but because those with cultural capital had experience and could work their way around such regulation and develop new opportunities, in the end, it developed even more deeply. By the end of 1991, it slowly became obvious that yet another cycle of the cultural craze was upon us. But this time around, it was ghosts from China's past that emerged as the objects of desire. In this period, it was our most venerable of cultural icons: the poems, the ancient books and writings, and the most famous of memories of our most venerated national leaders which fuelled this trend and led to the expansion of the market.

A close observation of the ebb and flow of culture reveals that contemporary Chinese culture has become a genuinely creative force. It is one in which market forces are the only 'hidden hand' and it is a process of change in which every Chinese participates.

### *The Hope of the Great Wall*: the Deepening of Despair

*The Hope of the Great Wall* was a television series which didn't really catch people's imaginations and didn't 'rate'.

The idea behind this show was for one of the characters, Jiao Jianchen, to travel the countryside and find the popular folk star Wang Xianglong. In the first show, he failed to find his star. For the audience who sat in front of their television sets during this search, the feeling was one of disappointment. Along the way, however, the show depicted the honest, natural and simple folk of China's countryside who were themselves a reflection of the Great Wall in their timeless character and the greatness of their ideals. In a survey of viewers of the show, some of the scholars of literature who were watching said: 'When I saw them (that is, the peasants who lived by the foot of the Great Wall) and then compared their life with mine, I thought to myself that their life was probably better. They have blue skies, prairies, cows and sheep, while all we've got is noisy cities and electrical appliances.' One student said: 'We have so many good people in this country, why on earth do so many of us feel dissatisfied and want to go abroad?' But the vast majority of the city residents, workers, and staff who viewed the show pointed out: 'What the hell was that all about!' The more you watched it the more it became a muddle.

The object of the series was to enable people to come to some understanding of popular culture and strengthen the sense of national self-confidence. The plan and the result, however, seem to have ended up going in opposite directions. There is a reason behind this. Between 1986 and 1989 there was, of course, the 'cultural craze' and, no matter whether one praised or damned traditional culture, all of the viewpoints shared one common aspect: they excessively praised themselves as being part of the 'cultural élite', picking up certain aspects of society to praise or damn with deep emotion and strong feeling. The narrative techniques deployed in the production of *The Hope of the Great Wall* had many advantages and its cultural level was fairly high, but the problem was that it reflected the aesthetic views and interests of those with cultural capital but avoided the commodity society. The avoidance of this was closely tied with the desire to promote and develop national culture. But the end result was that the whole thing became divorced from the feelings, rhythm and language of the ordinary people as well as from the ordinary social psychology. This really was the most important reason behind this 'superior cultural product' losing its mass appeal. From this, we can say it is a sad conclusion to such a sterling effort.

## The Craze over the 'East is Red'

A recent edition of the *Shanghai Art and Literature Newspaper* reported that the tape of the 'East is Red' has, in little over two months, sold something like 3.5 million copies and the market still displays great demand for this product.

In the Spring Festival period, a number of publishing houses printed poster portraits of Mao Zedong. Some 3.4 million posters were printed and sold on the market. That was three years ago and by 1993 something like 11 million posters of the Chairman have been printed. This information came from the *Xinwen Publishing Reports.*

It was in 1992 that the leader craze began to really hot up extraordinarily. The sales people from these companies remarked, 'The market in this area is so big we cannot see the end of it, we can produce 100,000 or even 200,000 and it is like a drop in the ocean.' From those who have gone through the horror of the Cultural Revolution such renewed interest in Mao is to place him in the position of a God. Moreover, the new rhythmic version of the 'East is Red' is thought by some to be too flippant and, as a result, some said: 'the somewhat ironic nature of this version makes the contemporary people sing these songs without much regard for their solemness'. There are others who say: 'This "East is Red" craze proves that we have failed to really fully eradicate all aspects of the Cultural Revolution and also proves that the media, the art and literature circles must really think about getting rid of the whole thing.'

In reality, the media outlets should actually encourage a more critical stance toward leadership. Within the country, most of our newspapers have been in the forefront of promoting objective reporting around this newly emerging 'craze'. Some members of the press say that the craze over Mao Zedong focuses on the way these feelings embody the view that the great man has been brought down to earth after being treated as a God for so long. As a result of this, he has come to be truly and more objectively loved by the Chinese people. Still other newspapers report that it is the form of the song rather than its content which is now important. People now listen to the melody and don't really notice the words. They concentrate on whether or not it is pretty, relaxing and happy, filled with humour or even has a bit of an ironic twist in it. All of this, I think, really does demonstrate that the open door and reform period is very broad and well established.

This reporting and commentary on the Mao Zedong craze has actually resulted in a deepening of research into Mao and also into the psychology of socialism. This, then, is a pretty impressive harvest. Moreover, the actual process of reporting the Mao Zedong craze has revealed some even more important information: only when the press have learned to utilise the market without avoiding or trying to confront it will they realise 'leadership' and have the reader's trust. Then they can develop their own leadership skills.

At the same time, it is easy to see that the market is gradually coming to have an influence over news and social spirit and this is getting deeper and more widespread. We can actually say that a very deep cause of this production of the Mao craze has to do with socio-psychological choices, although the direct cause of this craze was actually the market. Qi Anqing, a novelist who has turned his hand to company management, sees things rather clearly: 'The whole thing, the posters of Mao, the redubbed version of the "East is Red", all of it is really business people grasping opportunities and demands brought on by the psychology of the consumers.' For example, this demand comes from middle-aged people who cannot forget the past, older people who hear about the past and remember happier days, and from the very young, fresh-faced people who have become thoroughly delighted by it all. This new consumer demand has led to very quick and big production, and sale, of these items and it also offers some very real incentives to business people. Mao pictures for the car and the rhythmic version of the 'East is Red' are not really designed as purely artistic products but are instead designed as art products for trade. *The Hope of the Great Wall* also adopted a popular television series format but it was unable to obey the demands of trade and, therefore, naturally failed to become a hit.

## Stories from the Editorial Room

The leading arts critic Yu Qiuyu once praised the cultural level of the television serial *Stories from the Editorial Room* and said that it surpassed *Yearning* (Kewang).[23] What he didn't mention was that the key factor in the success of the former was its greater level of commercialism.

Very early on, the Hundred Dragon Mineral Water Receptacle Company approached them about doing an advertisement. The head of production, Liu Shatou responded with 'For the purity of our artistic product, we will never consider any such endorsements. But ...' In the end, there wasn't really all that much consideration given to purity, and the company obtained the services of the actors Ge You and Lü Liping to make a television advertisement. At the start, both were pretty reluctant and responded that it was all beneath them. Finally, they made the thing and it turned out like a comic opera and became as popular

---

23 Both serials were highly successful.

as the series itself. Many people couldn't tell the advertisement from the programme. In many American movies they place commercial trademarks in strategic places during various scenes and the companies must pay a fee—this really could be described as the second stage of deepening the process of commercialisation. Finally we will get to the stage, no doubt, when there is little other than the promotional blurbs.

Meanwhile, every episode of *Stories* was reviewed in terms of its morality, ethical nature and effect on social order and was found to be thoroughly acceptable. Within the structure of each episode there were, however, some pretty incisive exchanges between characters. The result was that the viewing public had a very enjoyable time listening to such dialogue because it gave vent to their own strong desire to say such things in real life. Hence, with this show, they got what they were after. The Beijing University art critic Zhang Yiwu summed it up briefly as being 'a clash between story and dialogue, an opposition between desire and the law'. He then went on to suggest that this televised type of clash and opposition was one of the growing strengths of the mass medium and that, because of it, television was fast becoming a very influential medium. The demands upon the television industry were twofold. Shows must be in accordance, or in support, of social ethics and social order, and secondly, they must operate as a channel through which the desires of the masses can be satisfied. *Stories* fulfilled both criteria.

The wedding of art and commerce is a universal trend in contemporary society. Very large companies promote themselves or strengthen the company image by investing in art, and at a time when governments are reducing the amount of subsidies to the artistic field, artists also turn to other means to try to promote their work. The time of the individual artist is now a thing of the past as, too, is the time of wealthy aristocratic patrons and state sponsorship. We are now entering a new stage. But in China we should note, we have not as yet fully reached this new stage and the artistic market really hasn't developed fully or in an all-round way. In these conditions of chaos caused by the incomplete development of the market mechanisms, many artists, directors, painters and musicians often become double victims, both of the market and of social norms. They may lose their personal characteristics as they try to please both masters. Their artistry is crushed in the squash and they may become the tragic losers of careless moves toward the market.

## MAO AND THE REVOLUTION ENTER THE MARKET

Commodification has produced a market for many things, including the revolutionary artefact. From Mao restaurants specialising in his favourite food, to the soundtrack of revolutionary favourites such as the 'East is Red', the revolution returns as product. Old revolutionary clocks with Cultural Revolution designs are again for sale, but this time, far from confirming 'the continuous revolution' is a second by second event, they confirm that everything is for sale. Time and its calculation have always been an important marker for revolutionary politics. In the French Revolution, on the first day of fighting, the revolutionaries fired on the clock towers throughout the city in a spontaneous gesture of independence from past calculations. Great revolutions always introduce new calendars.[24] Under Mao, every tick of the clock was also the wave of the Red Guard's arm holding a *Little Red Book*. Here was a representation of 'continuous revolution' in action. Now, it is a niche market product for revolutionary kitsch. The sale of these things, and the way Mao is now packaged, is confirmation of the subversive, corrosive power of the market. The appearance of revolutionary kitsch is a sign of the power of the market to envelop all within its fold.

The Cultural Revolution clock on sale again.

---

24  Walter Benjamin, *Illuminations* [Trans. Harry Zohn] (London: Fontana Press, 1992), 253.

Above: A Mao restaurant in Beijing.

Right: 'East is Red' double-cassette soundtrack, back on sale.

# PART VI

# MARKET
# TRAININGS

 TALES OF THE MARKET, TALES OF THE FETISH:
STORIES FROM THE STREET

> The street in the extended sense of the word is not only the arena of fleeting impres-
> sions and chance encounters but a place where the flow of life is bound to assert itself.
> Again one will have to think mainly of the city street with its ever-moving anonymous
> crowds. The kaleidoscopic sights mingle with unidentified shapes and fragmentary visual
> complexes and cancel each other out, thereby preventing the onlooker from following
> up any of the innumerable suggestions they offer. What appears to him are not so much
> sharp-contoured individuals engaged in this or that definable pursuit as loose throngs of
> sketchy, indeterminate figures. Each has a story, yet the story is not given. Instead, an
> incessant flow of possibilities and near-intangible meanings appears. This flow casts its
> spell over the *flâneur* or even creates him. The *flâneur* is intoxicated with life in the
> street—life eternally dissolving the patterns which it is about to form.[1]

'Tales of the market' are never-ending stories. They are stories of the street.
Stories that are as numerous as the consumers themselves. In some respects, this
volume is a tour book for the *flâneur*, a *flâneur* on a Chinese street. A *flâneur* that
the authorities might name *mangliu*. Through these pages, we have listened to
something of the gossip, heard something of the cadres' pronouncements, looked
momentarily at some of the more lurid things available on the sidestreets and
walked past at least one of the market crazes. While the sounds of the street may
be well and truly muffled in this volume, it is only through the market reform
process that even these hazy sounds can be heard. This is because the market has
ripped the social fabric of Chinese society to such a degree, that the land beneath
the cloth is more visible than ever before. It is visible in the shop display windows
that vie for custom no less than in the faces of the subaltern who walks the street
in search of work. While consumerism seems to push China in an identical direction to that already taken in the West, it is the shop window display and the eye
of the consumer that reveal aspects of the story of difference.

The suggestion that economic reform in China is the harbinger of a modern
individualised political subject is seductive but unconvincing. Take the most obvious 'sign' of Western consumer individualism, the fashion statement. In China,
especially among the middle-aged, fashion is quite often recoded to promote a
collectivist, not individualist, ethos. As though in recognition of the fact that we

---

1   Siegfried Kracauer, 'Once again the street' in *Theory of Film: The Redemption of Physical Reality* (New York
    and London: Oxford University Press, 1960), 72, quoted in Anthony Vidler, 'Agoraphobia: spatial
    estrangement in Georg Simmel and Siegfried Kracauer', *New German Critique*, 54 (1991), 31.

live in mass-producing and mass-consuming times, many consumers in China do not operate with the notion of individuality that underpins even the most mass-produced of fashion products in the West. For these Chinese, fashion is not constructed to mark out one's individuality, but to mark out one's success. Success is made verifiable through the notion of correct choice. Success means choosing a coat that everyone else is wearing for, to see others in the same coat, dress, trousers or shirt is not a sign of social disgrace, but a mark of wisdom and affluence. One has chosen wisely, for one has made 'the popular choice'. In this respect at least, fashion stands in for a wider, deeper and more unconscious sense of collective self. Not for these Chinese the transparent delusion of individuality that Western fashion victims entertain. The Chinese, in this one crucial respect, have never really changed out of their Mao suits. But then again, as some of the articles in this volume suggest, the Mao suit, like Maoism itself, may well be simply a more recent refashioning of much deeper, unconscious commitments to a notion of the collective whole.

If the notion of individuality does emerge in the Chinese marketplace, its most obvious location is not in the mind of the consumer but rather, in the eye of the trader. Even here, it is not the individual of the 'American dream' full of promise and bearing the gifts of freedom that is most apparent. In market streets in China, individuality comes in a more Foucauldian form for it is a body subject to the trader's gaze. In these backstreets, it is the traders who 'size up their marks' and, in so doing, reduce the individual consumer to the barest of forms. Individuality, for the trader, is a particular shirt size that needs accommodating, a distinctive skin colour that will suit a particular shade, or a hungry mouth that can be tempted from their chores by a whiff and a word about some local or imported delicacy. The body, in Chinese market streets, is fragmented and assessed such that each part can be catered for 'individually'.

Nor is it simply the trader's gaze that segments the body in this way. While traders divide up and fight over the right to cater for various parts of the consumer's body, the less visible but ever-present thieves of the street segment the body in a different way. For them, the task is to search individual subjects to determine points of vulnerability. They choose targets that are perceived as being 'ripe for the picking'. They scan the body to determine the location of the wallet or purse. It is through this sort of mapping exercise that individual bodies are made visible. It is on the basis of this mapping process that the language of the thief becomes audible: a wallet in the back pocket becomes 'a free-gift' (page 176), in the trouser pocket, 'a meal from the lower warehouse' (page 176), in the breast pocket an opportunity to breastfeed (page 175).

The traditional Chinese compound house has a 'heavenly well' at its centre. This is the courtyard in the middle of the compound where family members come together as one. At this point of connection, the traditional cosmological order and structure is reaffirmed and renewed. For the thief, the criminal, the *liumang*, 'moral order' has no 'location' for they are always 'outsiders'. Not for them the sedentary, compound structuring of life. Theirs is a life on the move. Heaven, for them, comes in the form of an 'easy mark'. Hence, the 'heavenly window' for the thief, is the 'perfect opportunity' created by those who foolishly place their wallets in their open shirt pockets. Each point on the body, each position that it adopts, every moment and each and every location gives forth a new word with new implications. Hence, under certain circumstances, the heavenly window becomes Shanggan Mountain, a risk not worth taking.[2] Theirs is the language of movement, of chance, of risk and, of opportunity. Yet it is also the language of jest, of fun and of play.

The Chinese police, building on the Maoist political campaign model, launch campaigns of their own against crime. The thief responds with mimetic humour, belittling the efforts of their enemy with campaigns of their own: hence the 'campaign to steal from the breast pocket'. China's burgeoning punk rock scene plays a similar tune. In Cui Jian's song, 'Beijing Story', a 'revolutionary campaign' is launched when he notices a woman he fancies! In the juxtaposition of these three statements on campaigning—one from the police, one from Cui Jian, and one from the thief—we come to see the sly, subversive potential of mimesis.

## Playing With Words (i): Police Campaigns

### From the police: internal police criticism of campaign-style policing

'Under the influence of China's political system, for nearly 40 years since the founding of the People's Republic of China in 1949, national public security goals and policies have been determined by a combination of factors … Party leaders urged the public security organs to serve the interests of various campaigns (mainly political ones), and to keep an eye out for serious deleterious effects certain types of crime, particularly counter-revolutionary crime, were believed to be having on public order. At the same time, the public security organs had to perform other services that, in one way or another, served the government's economic construction work … In the absence of clear guidance from any long term and stable policy and from guarantees from the administrative system, the public security department has, for a long time, adopted specialised struggles and campaign style policing as its work method … The short-sightedness of public security theory, then, is the direct outcome of this "campaign theory" (运动论) viewpoint of the past.'

—From Huang Jingping, Li Tianfu, and Wang Zhimin, 'The situation with regard to public security management', *Police Research*, 4 (1988), 42; 44. [黄京平, 李田夫, 王智民〈公安管理现状〉,《公安研究》.]

---

2  Shanggan Mountain was the site of an infamous battle in the Korean war which proved almost impossible to take. See 'Framing' (Part III, 2).

### From the punks: playing with the campaigns—'Beijing Story'

> Suddenly, I find a 'campaign' happening by my side,
> it's like a revolution, transforming my life,
> a loving girl comes before my eyes,
> it's like a raging storm blowing and slapping my face.

> —From Cui Jian, 'The Egg from the Red Flag'
> (Beijing East and West Art Producing Co. Ltd.,
> marketed by EMI (HK), 1994. [《红旗下的蛋》.]

### From the liumang: campaigns of subversion

里怀运动 (*Li huai yundong*): 'The Campaign to Steal From the Breast Pocket'. This is slang from Beijing and means that groups of thieves will work together like police and political activists during campaigns. In China, whenever major action is needed, there is an enthusiastic call to the campaign. Maoist politics were characterised by campaigns and, in the current period, it is police campaigns that predominate. The *liumang*'s response is a cynical play on this, yet it also keeps faith with the central tenet of the campaign, the enthusiastic act of doing. This time, however, it is turned to criminal ends.

—Liu Yanwu [Compiler], *A Compendium of Slang and Hidden Language* (Beijing: China People's University [internal publication], 1992). 〔刘延武，《隐语，黑话集释》，公安大学.〕

## Playing with Words (ii)

Similarly, traditional myths of injustice and righteousness are played with in Chen Jing's song 'Forced to go to Liang Mountain'. Liang Mountain was the home of a group of 108 just and upright rebels who were forced by an unscrupulous government to flee there in the classic Chinese novel the *Water Margin*. It has been a favourite metaphor of those oppressed for correcting social evils ever since. Little wonder that it, too, has become a phrase of both the juvenile offender and the rock hero. Juvenile offenders in the 1960s renamed the Guiyang Youth Detention Centre, which housed 108 inmates, Liang Mountain. The inmates saw themselves as rebels rather than criminals. Chen Jing's song suggests the same of rock 'n' roll heroes.

## *Forced to go to Liang Mountain*

Once upon a time, water formed a moat around Liang Mountain and on that
    mountain there lived a group of brave men.
The actions of these brave men stood for the just emperor and they stood
    together as sworn brothers, sweeping away the evils and difficulties of society.
Opposing oppression, opposing corrupt officials,
These men could not be fooled and they refused all amenities and attempts to
    enlist them.
The people think they are great, the officials are struck with terror.
In fact, these men were simply forced to go to Liang Mountain
Oh, oh, oh, … Liang Mountain, oh, oh, oh … brave men
Oh, oh, oh, … rebelling, oh, oh, oh, … Liang Mountain.

          —From Chen Jing, 'Red Scrunchy' [《红头绳》.]
          (Dadi Records Ltd, 1993).

Through these examples of language 'turning the tables' we see the way language,
bodies, places and times are reconfigured to offer the best opportunity, the most
chances and then, with these in hand, the most suitable tactics. These moves
rummage across most facets of the social landscape, covering key elements of life:
from money to sex, from the police to the prison. It is a world which, like the anti-
heroes in Brechtian theatre, is populated by 'often resourceful, humorous nobodies'
whose existence, or even position of resistance, should not be overly romanticised.

Here we need to draw lessons from the language of the thief. We need to
determine which forms of resistance are a 'gift from heaven' and which are
'messages from hell'. As their language all too easily demonstrates, determining
this involves being on the spot, being in the know, getting the timing right and
taking chances. Such is the nature of the tactical response that it cannot be known
in advance. What it does tell us is that the mode of consumption is not all-deter-
mining and all-knowing. It is simply a strategic field and, like all strategic fields, it
offers up its own points and possibilities of resistance. The trick is to get the timing
and the tactic right.

But is this not an over-enthusiastic endorsement of the subversive power of
consumption? After all, as both Walter Benjamin[3] and Theodor Adorno[4] point out,
one facet of this mode is to reduce the new to a status of being always-the-same.
Everything, including personal relations, is reduced to the status of a commodity.
Commodification literally trains us to see (gaze) in a certain way, to act and react in
a certain way, and to live with certain pre-conceived desires. In China, even a game
of 'Monopoly' is pressed into the service of training those desires.

---

3  Susan Buck-Morss, *The Dialectics of Seeing*, 293.
4  Theodor Adorno, *The Culture Industry*, 35.

国际型智力游戏棋

正业家

风靡世界　老少皆宜

The game of Monopoly, known in Chinese as 'Entrepreneur'.

Extract from the description of the game given on the back of the box:

> In the game of skill, 'Entrepreneur', the basic elements of the original American edition have been altered in accordance with our country's national situation. Parts of the rules have also been altered to make the game easier to learn, and therefore more popular.
>
> In 1987 and early 1990, we launched the first and second editions of the game and received widespread accolades from consumers. This is because it is a leisure item that can be enjoyed by young and old alike, but it has particular social benefits in that it fosters the intelligence of young students. Furthermore, it is not merely a game for whiling away the hours, for by playing this game, you will learn a little correct business knowledge and sharpen your judgement and bold enterprising spirit. The game also fosters a cultured and civilised business spirit, as well as the enterprising spirit of the 'Entrepreneur'. Because of this, its benefits to the market economy and society are incomparable.

Through consumption, our identities—who we are, what we stand for, who we were yesterday—and the sale of the product—which ones are being pushed, which are popular, which have moved from the advertisement to the fashion statement—are tied together in a metonymic unity that makes product and body inseparable. We wear the T-shirt and, in so doing, come to play the role of both advertising hoarding (for the T-shirt bears the logo of the company) and tattooed subject (for our identities are marked by how we look), yet we fail to recognise ourselves in either of these forms.

In recognising the legitimacy of at least part of this argument, we also begin to notice the power of consumption. We begin to see why this power, beyond commitment to any cause, beyond any simple notion of 'ideology', is so voracious, so all-encompassing and therefore so very powerful. It includes the power to transform us, which we accede to willingly and happily. We are trained, after all, into the idea that we need the image offered for sale. We are trained so well that we become a nation of 'sandwich board' people, tattooed for life with the slogan 'shop till you drop'. We become consumers and, in so doing, are ourselves consumed.

Herein lies the power of consumption and the reason why China's economic reform programme is careering chaotically down this never-ending trail. It is a programme buoyed by the thought that to consume is to be heading for a bright new positivist future. A future that the modernising dream of the Marxist past imagined but failed to deliver. Nevertheless, while recognising this power of consumption to supplement and promote Chinese government initiatives and dreams, one must simultaneously recognise that it is irreducible to such initiatives and dreams. Recognising that consumption goes beyond government policy forces us to reconsider the way we view the economic reform process in China.

The economic reform process in China, therefore, cannot be understood simply by examining the State's decision to shift from the production of capital to consumer goods, nor in the fact that it adopted an economic contract or responsibility system. While these have been important, what any analysis that focuses on these alone ignores is a theory of desire. It is because desire, like the *mangliu*, knows no home, that the market consumes government just as it does the consumer. There is nothing that indicates this consumption of government more clearly than the Mao paraphernalia craze of the last few years. Mao, the 'eternal' religious symbol of socialist China, is brought down to earth and reborn as 'commodity Mao'. Mao and revolutionary memorabilia become 'big sellers', as Da Yang pointed out, in a market that is implacably hostile to the socialist message. Nevertheless, Mao sells. Hence, along with all the other 'revolutionary' paraphernalia—from watches, things with Mao's face on them designed to dangle like dice from car mirrors, through to lighters that play the 'East is Red'— Mao's image is endlessly embossed on things. There are even Mao restaurants that specialise in serving Mao's favourite dishes.

The hype around this reborn Mao obviously eats away at some of the key tenets of Maoism (Mao as a consumer idol can do little else) but, somewhat less obviously, it also eats away at some of the key values being promoted by the Party and has been used even by critics of the reform process. It erodes the certainty of meaning that Mao was once thought to represent. His image is no longer the sole preserve of the Party. Consuming Mao leads to one hundred schools of consumption contending and, in this plurality of meaning around his image, come a variety of symbolic forms: Mao as sage, Mao as hero of the stable 1950s period, Mao as leader who would never have countenanced the economic reforms, Mao as young rebel leader against authority and not unlike the punk rock heroes of today.

Consumerism, therefore, transgresses the limits of any attempt to 'inlay' a dominant ideology. Consumption, then, can be a productive moment but the desire it unleashes is also quite unstable. It is, in this way, productive of its own points of resistance. It is at this stage that we begin to see cracks in the edifice of the all-encompassing, all-powerful rendition of consumption. In place of this, it becomes an (albeit limited) field of contestation. Firstly, this is because consumption, while geared purely toward purchase, is productive of desire and desire may not always lead to purchase. Consumption produces desire but it cannot police purchase, hence it is also productive of crime. Secondly, and in a similar manner, it is productive of a desire to own the reified objects of the gaze, but it cannot 'police' the reasons for those desires emerging. In other words, there is no 'right way' to consume.

A Mao lighter that, when opened, plays the 'East is Red'.

A Mao watchface.

Another face of Mao.

The failure of consumption to entirely account for all possible ways of consumption opens market forces to 'play' and recoding. The ways in which we limit or avoid costs, the way in which we play with images (take them on as a joke or 'ironically' etc.), becomes the tactical field opened up by the mode of consumption itself. We must, therefore, recognise that the general mode of consumption cannot account for every single act of consuming.

Nevertheless, consumption does attempt to direct our desires, so that even resistance works within its fold. In fact, it can do nothing else. This, however, does not make commodified resistance 'packaged', tame or lame. It simply makes it tactical and potentially effective. This point is best exemplified in the figure of a marginal character who is always on the lookout for new ways and new things 'to market', consume, subvert, rebel against or steal. People may be seduced, but the specificity of the gazing public who always come to the market place with different cultural and symbolic capital means that the market is also productive of certain degrees of heterogeneity that can be turned on consumption itself.

How this symbolic and cultural capital is unpacked on the street will vary with time and place. What makes the Chinese street an interesting place to 'loiter' and examine the various acts of consumption at the moment is the fragility of the process itself. It is all so very new. China is, in that flash-of-an-eye moment that Benjamin would no doubt have described as an ur-form[5] of consumerism. In one street, one literally sees different modes snuggling and struggling alongside one another. The transition process that is taking place in the cities of China today is occurring so rapidly that little can be said about it, for little can be explained. Indeed, it is probably best to simply end with Benjamin's maxim: I have nothing to say, only show'[6] and then, to quite literally, show the way consumerism has eroded the political edifice of socialist China. Nowhere is this erosion more in evidence than around the newly sexualised figure of women exemplified in the new form of the 'material girl'.

## Material Girls

In the Chinese Cultural Revolution, Julia Kristeva wrote in *About Chinese Women*,[7] women 'brandish pistols and paintbrushes [and] liberate themselves from their husbands and fathers under the portrait of Mao.' Under the planned command economy of that time, China produced capital not consumer goods and females were coded, like their male counterparts, as proletarians 'liberated' from gendered concerns and focused solely on the twin task of production and revolution. In government and Party rhetoric, gender was obliterated as material production saturated all forms of life and all concepts of desire. The first of the images reproduced on page 283 tells of this revolutionary fantasy. Female workers stripped of gender definition smile as they work in this fantasy world where

---

5   The ur-form was just like 'a leaf [that] lets unfold out of itself the abundant variety of the empirical plant world'. For Benjamin, it was the shopping arcades of early capitalism which were their ur-forms because they enabled 'the capitalist-industrial economic forms ... [to be] seen in a purer, embryonic stage ...' Quoted in Susan Buck Morss, *The Dialectics of Seeing*, 73.
6   Buck-Morss, 73.
7   From Julia Kristeva, *About Chinese Women* [Trans. Anita Barrows], (London: Marion Boyars, 1977), 16.

production is stripped of pain. Here was fantasy on a grand scale for it was not the private world of the fetishised body but the public world of the Party and production. In this dream-desire of proletarian purity, sexuality is repressed, emerging only in the contorted frame of material production and proletarian solidarity.

This image of Chinese women forms a rather neat counterpoint to the 'total' fantasies of the contemporary Chinese male as expressed in the calendars of recent years. These calendars tell of a double fantasy. Whereas the Party fantasy of the past reduced all desire to the single act of material production, the contemporary calendars tell of the proliferation of fantasies. Sex, though central, is not enough and it is left to the 'material girl' herself, Madonna, to tell us this as she stands suggestively in a perfect bourgeois lounge-room that becomes the second level of fantasy and desire. While the gaze in the former 'revolutionary' frame leads to a single conclusion, namely, that 'faster, better and more economic production' is the way forward, the multiple desires of the latter image lead to a very different conclusion. Anything can be obtainable through money. It is in this new economy of the eye, distracted first by the sexuality of the body in the foreground, but then seduced by the comforts to the rear, that epitomises the new desires of male China and the new technologies employed to engender them. Together these pictures tell of the march from the historical materialism of Mao to the consumer-based materialism of Madonna, and highlight the degree of change China has undergone.

From materialist girl to the material girl: the sexualisation of female iconography.

Sex is not the only example of this process of commodification. Indeed, many others have already been given from the 'Nationalities Theme Park' that re-codifies 'Chineseness' such that it is reaffirmed and celebrated for the price of a ticket, through to the Mao badge collection that forces Mao onto the market. These examples point to the power of consumption and to the tactics of sale. It is in these tactics that we are offered the possibility of other, more political moves being made.

Under consumption, the taboo, the hidden, the secret, gain value. It becomes a voyeur's market. From stories and details of the secret category of the 'special population'[8] through to a thinly veiled 'fictional work' on the crimes of Beijing's former mayor, Chen Xitong, 'culled' from highly confidential police files,[9] economic reform has put virtually everything on the market. In turning these pages and seeing the way consumption threatens the Communist Party, however, one should never lose sight of one other group that is 'under threat'. In China today, not everyone has the money to buy into consumption. In new China, to not consume is to remain 'poor and blank'. Subalternity means silence or at the very least a process of speaking in tongues. Their tactical language takes many forms; stealing, embezzling and ripping things off. These are but a few of the 'dialects' of subalternity and, if Chinese police reports are anything to go by, these have become the 'mother tongue' of an ever increasing number of speakers who are talking with louder and louder voices.

---

8  Compare the official but internal category of 'special population', given in Yu Lei's police manual (see Yu Lei, 'Special Population', Part II, 2) with the 'pulp literature' version given in Ge Fei's sensationalised work on second-class citizens (Part I, 3). Clearly, the latter work draws upon internal documents to elucidate its point.

9  The scandal surrounding Chen Xitong's corruption charge has been 'leaked' in novel form. The name of the novel is *Heaven's Rage* (*Tiannu*) and apart from the names used, all other details are said to be accurate and drawn from highly placed internal sources compiled by the prosecution.

# SELECT BIBLIOGRAPHY

Translations in this volume were undertaken by David Bray (DB), Sylvia Chan (SC), Tom Clarke (TC), Michael Dutton (MD), Li Shaorong (LSR), Li Tianfu (LTF), Sun Xiaoli (SXL), Xu Zhangrun (XZR) and Zhou Tao (ZT).

## Newspapers

*Beijing Daily Beijing ribao* 北京日报
*Economic Evening News Jingji wanbao* 经济晚报
*Legal Daily Fazhibao* 法制报
*New York Times*
*People's Public Security Newspaper Renmin gongan ribao* 人民公安日报
*People's Daily Renmin ribao* 人民日报
*Social News Shehuibao* 社会报
*Worker's Daily* Gongren ribao 工人日报

## Books, monographs and articles

Adorno, Theodor and Horkheimer, Max, *Dialectic of Enlightenment* [Trans. John Cumming], London: Verso, 1979.

Adorno, Theodor W., *The Culture Industry: Selected Essays on Mass Culture* [ed. J. M. Bernstein], London: Routledge, 1981.

Anderson, Benedict, *Imagined Communities: Reflections on the Origin and Spread of Nationalism*, London: Verso, 1983.

Barmé, Geremie, 'Soft porn, packaged dissent, and nationalism: notes on Chinese culture in the 1990s', *Current History*, 93: 584 (September 1994): 270–75.

Barmé, Geremie and Javin, Linda, *New Ghosts, Old Dreams*, New York: Times Books, 1992.

Bataille, Georges, *The Accursed Share: An Essay on General Economy, Volume One: Consumption* [Trans. Robert Hurley], New York: Zone Books, 1991.

Benjamin, Walter, *Illuminations* [Trans. Harry Zohn], London: Fontana Press, 1992.

Benjamin, Walter, *One Way Street and Other Writings* [Trans. Edmund Jephott and Kingsley Shorter], London: Verso, 1979.

Bhabha, Homi K., *The Location of Culture*, London: Routledge, 1994.

Bi Yuxiao (ed.), *Selected Works of Poems, Paintings and Calligraphy in Mao Zedong's Memorial Park of Shaoshan*, Changsha: Yuelu Publishing House, 1996.

Bogdanov, A. A., *A Short Course of Economic Science* [Trans J. Fineburg], London: Labour Publishing Company, 1923.

Bourdieu, Pierre, 'The thinkable and the unthinkable', *Times Literary Supplement* (15 October 1971), pp. 1255–56.

Buck-Morss, Susan, *The Dialectics of Seeing: Walter Benjamin and the Arcades Project*, Cambridge, Massachusetts: The MIT Press, 1991.

Buck-Morss, Susan, 'The flâneur, the sandwichman and the whore: the politics of loitering', *New German Critique*, 39 (1986): 99–142.

Cao Zhangqing, *The King of the Devils of Chaos, Mao Zedong*, Taibei: Huixiong Publishing House, n.d. [MD]

Chen Baoliang, *A History of Chinese Hooligans*, Beijing: Chinese Social Science Publishing House, 1993. [MD/XZR]

—, *A Chinese–English Dictionary*, Beijing: Beijing Foreign Languages Institute, 1978.

—, *A Collection of Rules, Regulations and Policies on the Comprehensive Handling of Social Order*, Beijing: Masses Press, 1992. [MD]

Da Yang, 'Chinese culture drawn into the market', *Women's Studies*, 3 (1993): 4–9 [MD]

de Certeau, Michel, *Heterologies: Discourse on the Other* [Trans. Brian Massumi], Minneapolis: University of Minnesota Press, 1993.

—, 'On the oppositional practices of everyday life', *Social Text*, 3 (1980).

—, *The Practice of Everyday Life* [Trans. Steven Randall], Berkeley: University of California Press, 1984.

—, *The Writing of History* [Trans. Tom Conley], New York: Columbia University Press, 1988.

Deng Yunxiang, *The Compound House of Beijing*, Beijing: People's Daily Press, 1990.

—, *Do you feel safe?*, Ministry of Public Security Research Unit document, Masses Press, 1991.

Emerson, Ralph Waldo, *Emerson's Essays*, Philadelphia: Spencer Press, 1936.

Fitzgerald, C. P., *The Birth of Communist China*, Middlesex: Penguin Books, 1964.

Foucault, Michel, 'The life of infamous men' [Trans. Paul Foss and Meaghan Morris], in Meaghan Morris and Paul Patton (eds), *Michel Foucault: Power, Truth, Strategy*, Sydney: Feral Publications, 1979.

Freud, Sigmund, *Jokes and Their Relation to the Unconscious* [Trans. James Strachey], Middlesex: Penguin, 1981.

Gao Jian, 'Tattoos—a revival', *Social News*, 690 [Mid Month Edition] (1993), 2–3. [MD/SXL]

Ge Fei, *Second-class Citizens: A Record of China's First 'Severe Strike' Campaign*, Chengdu: Chengdu Publishing House, 1992. [MD]

Gong Xikui, 'One perspective on the current household registration system in China', *Social Science* (Shanghai), no volume number, (1989) 32–40. [MD]

Gu Mengchao, [see Zhao Dongri].

Guha, Ranajit and Spivak, Gayatri Chakrovorty (eds), *Selected Subaltern Studies*, New York: Oxford University Press, 1988.

Harmon, Philippe, *Expositions: Literature and Architecture in Nineteenth-century France* [Trans. Katia Sainson-Frank and Lisa Maguire], Berkeley: University of California Press, 1992.

Hershatter, Gail, 'The subaltern talks back: reflections on subaltern theory and Chinese history', *Positions: East Asian Cultures Critique*, 1:1 (1993): 103–30.

He Xinghan, 'People of the work unit' in Shao Yanxiang and Lin Xianzhi (eds), *People and Prose*, Guangzhou: Huachen Publishing House, 1993. [XZR]

Huang Jingping, Li Tianfu, and Wang Zhimin, 'The situation with regard public security management', *Police Research*, 4 (1988): 42–6.

Jiang Fuyuan, 'A survey of criminal tattoos and how the situation should be rectified', *Special Teacher*, 27 (1989): 24–5. [MD]

Jin Ren, 'Homosexuals in Beijing', *Economic Evening News*, 23 April 1993. [SXL]

Kracauer, Siegfried, *Theory of Film: The Redemption of Physical Reality*, New York and London: Oxford University Press, 1960.

Kristeva, Julia, *About Chinese Women* [Trans. Anita Barrows], London: Marion Boyars, 1977.

Latour, Bruno, *We Have Never Been Modern* [Trans. Catherine Porter], Cambridge: Massachusetts: Harvard University Press, 1993.

Lefort, Claude, *The Political Forms of Modern Society: Bureaucracy, Democracy, Totalitarianism* (Edited and introduced by John B. Thompson), Cambridge: Polity Press, 1986.

Leuninger, *A Third Eye on China* [Translated into Chinese by Wang Shan], Xi'an: Shanxi People's Publishing House, 1994. [MD]

Li Yiyuan, 'Traditional [Chinese] cosmology and economic development', *21st Century*, 20, (1993): 146–58. [MD]

Liu Binyan, 'A comment on *A Third Eye on China*', *Beijing Spring*, 17 (1994): 23–32.

Liu Xin, *A Treasured Collection of Mao Zedong Badges*, Beijing: China Economic Publishing House, 1993. [MD]

Liu Yanwu, *A Compendium of Slang and Hidden Language*, Beijing: Chinese Public Security University Press, 1992. [MD/XZR]

Lu Feng, 'The *danwei*: a unique form of social organisation', *Chinese Social Sciences*, 1 (1989). [DB]

Lung Jianyu and Gao Jucun (eds), *Grasping the Beauty of Shaoshan*, Chongqing: South-West Normal University Press, 1996.

Luo Bing, 'A change in the Beijing atmosphere?', *Zheng Ming*, 203 (1994): 7–10. [MD]

Ma Zhenfeng, *Benevolence and Humanity: The Philosophic Thought of Confucius*, Beijing: China's Social Science Press, 1993. [XZR]

Marx, Karl, *Capital*, vol. 1 [Trans. Ben Fowkes], 3 vols, Middlesex: Penguin, 1976.

Marx, Karl, *Grundrisse* [Trans. Martin Nicholaus], Middlesex: Penguin, 1973.

Nadel, Ira Bruce, *Biography: Fiction, Fact and Form*, New York: St Martin's Press, 1984.

Prakash, Gyan, 'Writing post-orientalist histories of the third world: perspectives from Indian historiography', *Comparative Studies in Society and History*, (1990): 383–409.

—, 'A report from the Beijing City Public Security Bureau Beef Street Station', *People's Public Security Newspaper* (December 1993) [MD]

Rossi, Aldo, *The Architecture of the City* [Trans. Diane Ghirardo and Joan Ockman], Cambridge, Massachusetts: Opposition Books, The MIT Press, 1982.

Schein, Louisa, 'The consumption of color and the politics of white skin in post-Mao China,' *Social Text* (1995): 146–64.

Shao Daosheng, *Considerations on the Sociology of Youth Crime in China*, Beijing: Social Science Literature Press, 1987.

Shao Mingzheng, Wang Mingdi and Niu Qingshan (eds), *The Encyclopedia of Chinese Reform through Labour Laws* Beijing: Chinese People's Public Security University Press, 1993.

Spivak, Gayatri Chakravorty, 'Can the subaltern speak?', in Cary Nelson and Lawrence Grossberg (eds), *Marxism and the Interpretation of Culture* Urbana: University of Illinois Press, 1988, pp. 271–313.

—, 'A summary report on the successful completion of the tasks of cleaning-up, rectifying and making secure the Big Red Gate Area', an unpublished internal report of the PSB, Beijing: Beijing Public Security Bureau, 1996. [LSR]

Sun Xiaomei, 'A group of outsider women inside Beijing', *Women's Studies*, 3 (1993): 22–27. [MD]

Tao Li, *Developments in Legal Studies Research* [edited by the legal studies association of China] 6 (1992). [XZR]

Taussig, Michael, *Mimesis and Alterity*, New York: Routledge, 1993.

Vidler, Anthony, 'Agoraphobia: spatial estrangement in Georg Simmel and Siegfried Kracauer,' *New German Critique*, 54 (1991): 31–45.

Virilio, Paul, *The Lost Dimension* [Trans. Daniel Moshenburg], New York: Semiotext(e), Autonomedia, 1991.

Wang Anting [ed.], *A Collection of Illustrative Plates of Mao Zedong Badges*, Beijing: China Bookstores Publishing House, 1993. [MD]

Wang Shiren, 'The wisdom of the Chinese nation and the vitality of traditional architecture', in Gu Mengchao and Zhang Zaiyuan (eds), *Criticism, Analysis and Prospects in Chinese Architecture*, Tianjin: Tianjin Science and Technology Press, 1989, 138–142. [XZR].

Watson, Trevor, *Tremble and Obey*, Sydney: ABC Books, 1990.

Weber, Max, *Religions of China*, New York: Free Press, 1951.

Weber, Max, *The Protestant Ethic and the Spirit of Capitalism*, London: Counterpoint, Unwin, 1976.

— 'The Weikeng Public Security Committee of Beijing mobilises the masses in security surveillance and prevention work', in *Reports on the Experiences of the Work of the Social Order Committees*, Beijing: Masses Press, 1984, 5–8. [SC]

Wittgenstein, Ludwig, *Philosophical Investigations*, Oxford: Blackwell, 1953.

Xia Yong, *The Origins of Human Rights Conceptions*, Beijing: Chinese Political Science and Law Publishing House, 1992. [XZR/MD]

Xu Hanmin, *Forty Years of People's Public Security*, Beijing: Police Officers Educational Publishing House, 1992. [MD]

Xu Ping, *The Customs Attached to the Presentation of Gifts*, Beijing: Overseas Chinese Press, 1990. [MD/LSR]

Xu Yiqing and Zhang Hexian, *A History of Life Faiths: The World of the Tattoo*, Chengdu: Sichuan People's Publishing House, 1988.

Yang Dongping, *City Monsoon: The Spiritual Culture of Beijing and Shanghai*, Beijing: Eastern Publishing House, 1994. [MD/SXL/LSR]

Yang Wenzhong and Wang Gongfan, 'The influence of the floating population upon social order', *Police Research*, 2 (1989): 52–3. [LTF/MD]

—, *The Yearbook of Chinese Juvenile Delinquency Studies—1987*, Beijing: Spring and Autumn Press, 1988.

Yi Zhongtian, *Casually Talking Chinese*, Beijing: Hualing Publishing House, 1996.

Yu Lei *et al.*, *The Study of Public Security Administration*, Beijing: Masses Press, 1987. [MD]

Zeng Zhaofen, *Design and Style in Contemporary Chinese Architecture*, Tianjin: Tianjin Science and Technology Press, 1989. [MD]

Zhang Duanhui, *Heaven and Earth*, Lianjing Publishing House, nd.

Zhang Qingwu, *A Handbook on the Household Register*, Beijing: Masses Press, 1987. [MD]

Zhang Wenqing (ed.), *A Dictionary of Chinese Policing*, Shenyang: Shenyang Publishing House, 1990.

Zhao Dabin, Zhang Sen, Shen He, He Yong, and Cen Shengting (eds), *A Workbook for the Resident Identity Card*, Beijing: Police Officer Educational Press, 1991.

Zhao Dongri, 'My understanding about and prospects for Chinese architecture' in Gu Mengchao and Zhang Zaiyuan (eds), *Criticism, Analysis and Prospects in Chinese Architecture*, Tianjin: Tianjin Science and Technology Press, 1989. [XZR]

Zhao Xiaogang and Guo Zheng, 'The development of the city and crime', *Police Research*, 4 (1988): 31–7. [LTF/MD]

Zhou Daping, 'Levying a fee for residing in Beijing: reasons for the surge in Beijing's population', *Outlook*, 51 (1994): 8–9. [SXL/MD]

Zhou Jihou, *The Mystery of the Mao Badge—The Ninth Wonder of the World*, Beijing: Beiyue Art Publishing House, 1993. [MD]

Zhu Huaxin, 'From "a person of the work unit" to a "social person"— a psychological evolution under the impact of reform', *People's Daily*, 14 December 1993, p. 11.

# INDEX

accommodation *see* housing
acupunctural charts, 162–3, 172, **173–4**, 265
administration *see* government agencies
advertising, 268–9, 279; *See also* posters
agriculture *see* rural areas
AIDS, 73–4
alienation, 85, 150
ancestor-worship, 34–5
apartments, 224–7, 229
architecture, **193–5**
  clans and gifts, **204–7**
  culture, 169
  illegal buildings, 152, 155–6
  social relations, **203–4**
  tradition, 194, **196–7**, 203–6, 222–3;
    symbolic hierarchy, **207–8**
  *See also* compounds; high rise; office
    buildings; temples; urban
    design
army *see* military
art:
  culture, 169, 269
  framing, 172, 174
  Mao Zedong, 174, **262–5**
  rebellion in, 6, 162
  *See also* tattoos

badges *see* Mao badges
balance, **31–4**, 35, 39, 171
*bao* (recompense/revenge), **35–7**, 112
*baomu*, 10, 13, 79, 107, 130, **132–44**, 212
bar workers, 127
Barmé, Geremie, 5–6

Beef Street (Beijing) police station, 93, **103–7**, 112
beggars, 13, 112, **119–24**
Beijing:
  cultural influence, 162, 166
  floating population, 12, **89–92**, 144–7
  Forbidden City, 197–202
  government, 152, 154–7, 166
  Heavenly Temple, 198, 207
  homosexuals, 22, 62, **70–74**
  Mao craze, 245, 249–50, 271
  map, 153
  place names, 168
  Qianmen shopping district, 1–4, 153, 212
  residency fees, 99–103
  service persons, 130, **132–44**
  urban design, 193, **197–202**, 208, 211–13
  Zhejiang village, 78–80, **147–59**
  *See also* Tiananmen Square
benevolence, 19, 25–7, 30–31, 40–41
bicycle thefts, 110
biography, 93, 242–4
black societies *see* secret societies
body *see* human body
bourgeoisie, 23, 28, 48, 79, 132; *See also* professions
bribery *see* corruption
Buddhism *see* religion
building *see* architecture
business licences, 114, 146–7, 152–3

cadres *see* Communist Party
cafés *see* catering sector

calendar girls, 130–32, 283
Canton (Guangzhou), 183–4, 246, 265
capitalism:
  culture, 169
  shopping centres, 1, 3, 230, 282
  work units, 215, 219
  *See also* economic reform; private
    businesses
caste, 77–8, **81–6**
catering sector, 133–4, 138–9, 153; Mao
    restaurants, 269, 271, 280
ceremony *see* propriety (*li*)
*chai* ('tear down'), 222–3; *See also*
    demolition
chance (*jiyuan*), 38
change, **222–37**
char-ladies *see: baomu*
Chen Xitong, 284
Chengde, 208, 231
child-care, 149
children, 126–7, 140, 216; *See also*
    kidnapping; naming; population
    control laws
cities:
  administrative planning, 96, 98
  architecture *see* urban design
  household registration, 82, 98–9
  levies on immigrants *see* residency fees
  movement into *see* migration into
    cities
  place names, 168
  *See also* Beijing; city residents; urban
    design
city residents:
  household registration books, 95
  relations with immigrants, 79, 87,
    100–1, 132–4, 136–8, 142, 147,
    150–51, 266
  rights, 28, 54
  work units, 49
citizenship, 28–9
civil disputes, 107, 116
clans (lineage groups):

architecture, 194, 199, 203, **204–7**
traditional society, 28, 34–5, 45, 62
work units, 21, 45, **54–8**, 62, 214–15
*See also* families
class:
  architecture, 193, 195–6, 199
  emergence of, 3, 9, 13, 77–8, 85–6,
    130
  language, 165
  'one family, two systems', 220
  *See also* bourgeoisie; proletariat;
    subaltern classes
class struggle, 51, 162, 167, 223, 247
clean-up *see* social order
closed society, 169, 210, 223; *See also*
    open-door policy
clothing, 58, 175–8, 274
code of conduct (work units), 54–8
collectivism, 48, 57, 215, 239, 273
colours, 196–7, 202
commerce, 39, 199
commercialisation *see* consumption
commodification, 14, 278
  Communism, 164, 232–4, 251, 254,
    284
  dissent, 5–7
  Mao paraphernalia, 232–7, 241
  nationhood, 223, 231
  popular culture, 163–4
  residency, 99
  revolutionary culture, 132, 223, 231–4,
    269–72, 275, 280–84
  women's bodies, 130–32, 282–3
  *See also* consumption
communes, 44, 46, 48, 50, 57
Communist Party:
  Central Committee, 152, **154–6**, 157,
    166
  commodification, 164, 232–4, 251,
    254, 284
  compounds, 213
  history, xiv, 232, 243–4
  human rights, 19, 77

language, 161–2, **165–8**, 170, 273, 282–4
Maoism, 5, 256–9, 262–3
national minorities, 105
peasants, 86, 88
prostitution, 125
public security, 108–9, 147, 225, 275
residency fees, 102
work units, 44, 49, 51–4, 57–8, 194, 212, 217, 219, 224
Zhejiang village, 152–9
Communist Youth League, 44, 111
compounds (*siheyuan*):
cities as, 197, 199–202, 210
old and new, 223, **228**
security, 109–10
tradition, 193–4, 205–10, 274
work units, 203–4, **211–13**, 222
Zhejiang village, 150, 157–9
*See also* courtyards; walls
'comrade' (*tongzhi*), 45, 52, 167
conduct code (work units), 54–8
Confucianism:
architecture, 194, 196–7
social ethics, 19–20, 24–7, 29–31, 34, 36, 40–41, 45
Congresses, 44
'connections' (*guanxi*), 20, 34–5, 40, 56, 59, 215
consumption:
commercialisation of culture, 265–9
European and Chinese modes, 222, 273–4, 278–84
fetishised things, 131–2, 224, 232–3, 241, 245, 282–4; *See also* commodification
pluralism, 5
shopping, 1–4, 193, 223, **229–30**, 273–4
contractual obligations, 45–6, 51–2, 218
co-operatives, 48
corruption, 147, 149–50, 278, 284

cosmology:
architecture, 194, 204, 208
names, **169–71**
traditional, 18–20, **31–9**, 171, 274
counter-revolutionary elements, xiv, 98, 116, 240, 275–8
courtyards, 193, 202, 205, 209–12, 224, 228, 274; *See also* compounds
crime, 79–80, **87–8**, 89–90, 107, 141, 146
crime prevention (*sifang*), 94–5, 98, **108–10**, 115
criminals:
economic reform, 8, 68, 89, 91–2, 274–8, 281
gangs, 8, 90–91, 109, 150–52, 156, 163, 172, 180–86
high-rise apartments, 224–7
juveniles, 107, 110–11, 277
policing, 13, 66–9, 89–92, 106–11, 129
prostitution, 67, 125–7
slang, 163, 175–9, 274–8, 284
special population, 116, 121
special professions, 113–15
tattoos, 163, 172, 180–6, **187–90**
Zhejiang village, 150–52, 154, 156–7
*See also* detention centres
Cultural Revolution (1966–76):
clocks, 269–70, 272
culture, **168–9**; *See also* revolutionary culture
language, 161–2, 166–7, 170–71
Maoism, 48, 232–3, 239–42, 244–50, 252, 254, 258–61, 265–7
migration to cities, 11
public security, 108
women, 130–32, 282–3
cultural workers, 48–9, 213, 219
culture:
cities, 200, 212–13
commodification, 241, **265–9**

traditional and contemporary, 4, 19, 31, 39, 163–4, 169, 265–9
*See also* revolutionary culture

daily life, **31–9**, 212; *See also* work units
Dang Miao, 253–4, 256
de Certeau, Michel, 6–8, 239
death, 60–61, 246–7
demolition, 147, 152, 156–7, 159
Deng Xiaoping, xiv, 10, 86
denunciation, 97–8
department stores, 3, 230
destruction *see: chai*
detention centres, 116, **119–29**, 158, 187, 277; *See also* reform through education; reform through labour
deviance, 163, 180
dialect *see* language
'difficult households' (*kunnanhu*), 138, 140
discrimination, 142, 147, 150–51
diseases *see* health and medical services
dissidents, xii, xiv, 5–8, 13–14, 16–18, 87, 162, 263–4
divination, 33
divorce *see* marriage
dog control, 101
drifters *see: liumang*
drug use, 8, 150, 154, 156
duty and obligation, 26–30, 52

'East is Red' (song), 4–5, 239, 267–9, 271, 281
economic reform:
    architecture, 195, **222–5**, 229–30
    Chinese culture, 241, **265–9**
    consumptive mode, 4
    crime, 8, 68, 89, 91–2, 274–8, 281
    fetishes, **273–84**; Mao, 232–3, **235–7**, 239–41, 249–52, 258, 262, 284
    psychological effects, **215–20**
    residency and population flows, 78, 88–90, 93
    social effects, 8–13, 17, 77–80, 87–93, 101, 130–32, 140
    work units, 44, 47, 50, 57, **214–21**
    *See also* commodification; 'one family, two systems'; open-door policy
'economy of measurement', 20, 43
'economy of the gift' *see* gift-giving
education:
    migrant workers, 136, 140, 142, 144, 149
    peasants, 48
    tattoos, 186, 188
    work units, 216
    *See also* reform through education; universities
egalitarianism, 56, 77, 83–5, 132, 217
elections, 44
employers, 137–40
employment:
    detainees, 121, 123
    economic reform, 57, 217–21
    floating population, 89, 101, 103, 145
    juveniles, 110–11
    life-long tenure ('iron rice bowl'), 44, 46, 48, 51–2, 58, 216–17
    surplus labour, 12, 65, 135
    women, 80, 130, 133–4, 149; *See also: baomu*
engraving services, 113, 114
enterprise work units, 52, 217–18, 219
'Entrepreneur' (Monopoly), 237, **278–9**
environmental conditions *see* hygiene
equality, 56, 77, 83–5, 132, 217
ethics *see* morality
ethnic groups *see* nationalities
'exchange', 35–7, 56
extortion, 151–2

'face', 18, 21, 35, 56, **58–61**
fake products, 150
families:
    architecture, 194, 196, 206, 209–10, 212, 224–6, 228, 274

floating population, 120, 128, 132–8, 140–45, 147, 149, 151
 household registers, 77, 97–8
 language, 168–9
 Mao fetish, 256
 police and public security, 106–7, 109
 size, 133
 tattoos, 180
 traditional society, 28–9, 34, 36, 45, 91
 work units, 215
 *See also* clans; compounds; 'one family, two systems'
family planning, 144–5
family service personnel *see: baomu*
famine, 11
fashion, 273–4, 279
fatalism, 77
fate, 31–3, 38
*fengshui* (geomancy), 33
fetishes, 131, **237–84**; *See also* Mao badges
feudalism:
 architecture, 196, 200
 household registration, 84
 peasants, 77, 84
 tattoos, 190
 work units, 42, 45
five elements (*wuxing*), 33–4, 171
flats, 224–7, 229
'floating population' (*liudong renkou*), 21, 61–2, 86–7, 89–93, 98, 144, 149; *See also: liumang*; migration into cities; repatriation
food:
 balance and harmony, **33–4**, 171
 famine, 11
 Mao, 253, 269, 271, 280
 processing, 153
 work units, 43, 48, 58
 *See also* catering sector
Forbidden City (Beijing), 197–202
foreigners, 79, 86, 129, 131–2, 156, 169, 199; *See also* West

forgery, 113
fortune, 32–3
framing, 17, 162–3, **172–9**, 265
free market *see* economic reform
freedom, 24, 29, 84–5, 88, 125, 274; cities, 200
freedom of movement, 10–13, 45, 80, 218; *See also* migration into cities
funerals *see* death

gambling, 116, 151
Gang of Four *see* Cultural Revolution
gangs *see under* criminals
gates, 213, 228
gay community, 22, 62, **70–74**, 172
gender:
 Cultural Revolution, 282–3
 language differences, 167, 171, 175–8
 repression, 132
 *See also* women
geomancy (*fengshui*), 33
gift-giving:
 architecture, 204–7
 Confucianism, 20, 27, **39–41**
 Mao badges, 245–6
government agencies:
 architecture, 197, 199–200, 202, 211–12
 employment in, 220–21
 local, 81–3, 88–9, 92–3, 99–100, 102
 public security, 225
 rural areas, 88–9
 residency fees, 102–3
government strategies, 49, 51, 57, **77–80, 93–129**
 response to subaltern tactics, **130–59**
 *See also* household registration; resident identity cards
'great culture', 19, 31, 39
'great harmony' *see* harmony
Great Leap Forward, xiv, 11, 48, 170, 254
Great Wall, 197, 266
group consciousness, 56–60

Guangzhou (Canton), 183–4
*guanxi* (relational networks), 20, 34–5, 40, 56, 59, 215
guards *see* surveillance

hagiography (Mao), 242–3
harmony, 19–20, 23–7, **30–35**, 37–8, 210
health and medical services:
   balance, 34
   *baomu*, 137, 139–40
   culture, 169
   detainees, 122–3, 128–9
   education, 73–4
   tattoos, 186
   work units, 43, 216–17, 219, 221
   Zhejiang village, 149–50, 153
   *See also* acupunctural charts; hospitals; sexually transmitted diseases
heaven (natural systems), **32–3**, 210
heroic figures, 7–8, 17–18, 277–80
hierarchy:
   traditional architecture, 193–4, 196–7, 207–8
   work units, 47, 51
'high culture', 19, 31, 39
high rise, 223–7, 229
'high-tech' companies, 219
higher education *see* universities
history of China (timeline), xiv
HIV/AIDS, 73–4
homeless people, 61, 120–21, 123–4
homosexuals, 22, 62, **70–74**, 172
Hong Kong, xiv, 39, 98, 182
hoodlums and hooligans *see: liumang*
*The Hope of the Great Wall* (TV series), **266–7**, 268
hospitals, 79, 107, 128
hot–cold conceptualisation (*yin* and *yang*), 33–4, 171
hotel service industry, **113**, 114, 127, 132
household registration:
   *baomu*, 137–8

management system, 43, 69, 77–8, 95–7; files, **97–8**; reform, 7, 10–11, 93; *See also* resident identity cards
   peasant life, **81–5**, 88
   people without, 65; *See also: liumang*
   policing, 103, 105–6, 115, 147, 149
   population registration cards, 76, **98**, 102
   repatriation, 120–21, 123–4
   residency fees, 101–3, 145
   work units, 43
household service companies, 134–5
households *see* architecture; compounds; families
housekeepers *see: baomu*
housing:
   apartments, 224–7, 229
   maintenance, 107
   rental, 149, 154
   work units, 43–4, 52, 216–19, 221
   *See also* architecture
*huaiyuan* building, 205
Hui nationality, 103, 105
human body:
   charts, 172, 173–9
   economic reform, 274–5, 279–80
   slang, 163, 173–9, 274
   *See also* male body; tattoos; women's bodies
human relations *see* social relations
human rights, 8, 10, 13–14, **17–20**, 77, 79; Chinese tradition, **23–31**
humanism, 23–5
hygiene, 122, 149–50, 154, 210

identity cards *see* resident identity cards
ideology:
   *baomu*, 137, 140
   consumerism, 5, 280–84
   detainees, 120, 122
   language, 162, **165–71**
   police, 104

rural areas, 88
tattoos, 190
work units, 43–4, 46, 48–9, 217
imperial households, **196–202**, 207–10, 213, 232
income *see* wages
individualism, 29–30, 46–7, 51, 214, 273–4
individuals:
  balance and harmony, 32, **33–4**
  work units, 43
industrialisation, 45, 91, 216
information networks, 114–15; *See also* surveillance
interpersonal relations *see* social relations
'iron rice bowl' *see under* employment
Islam, 103, 105
itinerant workers *see: youmin*

Jehal Palace (the Mountain Resort), 231
*ji* (ceremonial sacrifice), 36
*jinbu* (striving for attainment), 33
*jiyuan* (chance), 38
joint state and private enterprises, 48, 219
junk dealers, 113–14
justice, 27, 29–30, 277
juvenile crime, 107, 110–11, 277

kidnapping, 150, 152
Korean War, xiv, 49, 170, 244, 275
Kristeva, Julia, 282
*kunnanhu* ('difficult households'), 138, 140

labour centres *see* reform through education; reform through labour
labour contracts *see* contractual obligations
land, 77, 84–5, 144–6
laneways, 212–13
language, **161–4**
  etymology, 21, 172
  reform, 161–2, 165–6

revolutionary, 161–2, **165–71**, 235, 239, 249, 261, 282
rural and urban areas, 136, 162, 167–8, 239
slang and vernacular, 162–3, 165, **172–9**, 274–8, 284
vocabulary, 166–7
*See also* naming; tattoos
law, 24–5, 28, 45; *See also* public security
lawlessness *see* crime
lawyers, 220–21
legal documentation *see* household registration; resident identity cards
legal rights and interests, 94–5
letters of introduction, 95, 140
liberation, 29, 265, 282
licences (business), 114, 146–7, 152–3
lineage groups *see* clans
Li Peng, 47, 154
*li* (propriety), 25–7, 30, 36, **40–41**
'literary front', 48–9
liumang:
  attitudes towards, 78–9
  crime and policing, 90, 98, 109, 116, 128–9, 146–56
  definition, 21–2, **62–5**
  history, 11
  human rights, 8, 13
  slang, **172–9**, 274–8
  tattoos, 181–5, 188, 190
  traditional society, 61
  *See also* beggars; *youmin* (vagrants)
living allowance fees, 77, 93, **99–103**
living standards, 87, 133, 138, 150–52
local-level government agencies, 81–3, 88–9, 92–3, 99–100, 102
Long March, 234, 243

Macao, 98
Madonna, 283
maids *see: baomu*
male body:
  thieves' slang, 175–7

*See also* tattoos

*mangliu*, 8–9, 78, 149–50, 273, 280

Mao badges:
  as biography, **242–5**
  collections and museums, 235–7, 241,
      249, **252–61**, 262
  commodification, 232–3, **235–7**,
      240–41, 249–52, 262, 284
  as gifts, 245–6
  history, 239–41, 243–50
  porcelain and aluminium, 240, 247–8,
      250

Mao craze (1990s):
  art, 174, **262–5**
  commodification, 4–5, 132, 223,
      231–7, 267–71, 280–82
  fetishisation, **239–41**; *See also* Mao
      badges

Mao restaurants and food, 253, 269, 271,
    280

Mao suits, 274

Mao Zedong:
  acupunctural chart, 174, 265
  maps, 232–4
  paraphernalia *see* Mao craze (1990s)
  personality cult, 232, 242–50
  portraits, 5, 240–41, 251–2, 262–5,
      267, 280–81

Mao Zedong Memorial Park *see* Shaoshan

Maoism:
  Cultural Revolution, 48, 162, 232–3,
      239–42, 244–52, 254, 258–61,
      265–7
  materialism, 229–30, 283
  peasants, 86
  policing, 93, 275–6

market economics *see* economic reform

markets, 1–4, 133, 147, 152–4, 249–51

marking *see* tattoos

marriage:
  architecture, 206–7, 210
  *baomu*, 137–8, 140–44
  gifts, 245–6

  homosexuals, 72
  language, 167
  tattoos, 187
  work units, 44, 216

Marxism:
  Chinese tradition, 19–20
  human rights, 23, 79
  language, 166, 168
  modernisation, 280
  proletariat, 10–13
  work units, 215

'mass consciousness', 56–60

'mass-line' policing, 93, **107–11**, 112,
    128, 147, 225–7

measurement, economy of, 20, 43

medicine *see* health and medical services

middle class *see* bourgeoisie

migration into cities:
  crime and policing, 87–8, **89–92**, 93,
      120, 130, 152, 154–6, 159, 225
  economic reform, **8–13**, 77–8, 86–7,
      225
  freedom of movement, 10–13, 45, 80,
      218
  household registration, 82–5
  Maoist era, 8, 11, 86
  residency rights and fees, 54, 77–8, 93,
      **98–103**, 147, 155, 158
  subaltern groups, 8–13, 78–80, 130,
      135, 138, 140, 144–6, 149–50

military:
  language, 162, 166–7, 170–71, 239
  Mao badges, 200
  prostitution, 125
  security forces, 87
  urban design, 199, 213

mimesis, 19–21, 203, **211–12**, 222–3,
    234, 275

Ministry of Public Security:
  household registration, 11–12, 81
  regulations: on beggars, 120–22; on
      prostitution, 125, 127–9; on
      special population, 115–16

minorities *see* nationalities
modernisation, 54, 222, 280
Monopoly (board game), 237, **278–9**
morality:
  architecture, 205, 274
  Confucian, 18–19, 24–7, 30, 34,
    40–41, 112
  education, 110–11
  work units, 57
movement, right of *see* freedom of
  movement
multiculturalism *see* nationalities
municipal government *see* local-level
  government agencies
museums (Mao badges), 252–8
music, 4–6, 163, 239, 251, 267–9, 271,
  275–8, 280–81
'mutuality' ('exchange'), 35–7, 56

naming:
  'proper name', 7, 242
  revolutionary culture, 161–2, **165–71**,
    235, 239, 261
  traditional, 34, 162, **171**, 207
nannies *see: baomu*
nationalism, 168–9, 223, 231; 'symbolic
  spaces', 193, 229
nationalities, 9, 103–5, 231; theme park,
  99, 284
natural systems (heaven), **32–3**, 210
neighbourhood committees *see* 'mass-line'
  policing
neighbourhood ties, 206–7
'networks' (*guanxi*), 20, 34–5, 40, 56, 59,
  215
nightclub workers, 127
nobility, 197
northern domination, 162, 166
numerical codes (resident identity cards),
  7–8, 93, 96
nursing, 130, **131–2**

obligation, 26–30, 52

office buildings, 212–13, 228
officials *see* government agencies
one-child policy, 144–5
'one family, two systems', 214–15, 219,
  **220–1**
open-door policy, 50, 89, 91, 140, 265;
  *See also* closed society; economic
  reform
outsiders, 8, 21–2, 28, **62–5**, 78, 147,
  151, 154–5; *See also:* beggars;
  floating population; homosexuals;
  *liumang*; prostitution; residency
  rights; second-class citizens;
  strangers; *youmin*
overseas Chinese, 98

painting *see* art
palaces, **196–202**, 207–10, 213, 232
patriarchy:
  architecture, 194, 196, 209–10
  naming, 162
  tradition, 28–9, 35, 46
  women, 79, 132
  work units, 21, 55
peasants *see* rural areas
penal system *see* detention centres; reform
  through education; reform through
  labour
penalties, 26, 116, 126–7; *See also* tattoos
pensions, 216, 218
people's communes, 44, 46, 48, 50, 57
People's Congresses, 44
personality cult (Mao), 232, 242–50; *See
  also* Mao craze
'petitioning to the law', 24
*pinyin* romanisation, 161, 165
place:
  architecture, 193
  meaning, 22
  names, 168, 170
  people without *see: liumang*
  'sacred sites', 242–3
  work units, 58–61

pluralism, 5
police:
    campaigns, 68, 130, 147–9, 275–7;
        Zhejiang village (Beijing), 147,
        149–52, 154–7, **158–9**
    corruption, 147, 149–51
    criminals and, 13, 66–9, 89–92,
        106–11, 129
    criminals' slang for, 179
    economic reform, 250, 281, 284
    government strategy, 3, 8
    high rise, **224–7**
    homosexuals and, 73
    household registration, 103, 105–6,
        115, 147, 149
    investigations, 97–8, 127
    peasant movement, 10, 79–80, 86–8,
        **89–92**
    population policing, 93, 98–100
    prostitution, 67, 125
    special professions, **114–15**
    student movement, 263
    transients, 12–14
    work units, 44
    *See also* 'mass-line' policing; public
        security units; special population
police stations, 109, 115, 227; Beef Street
    (Beijing), 93, **103–7**, 112
political culture, 49, 54, 87–90, 212, 273,
    275–6, 280, 282, 284; Mao badges,
    240, 245
political education *see* ideology
political language, 161–2, **165–71**
pop music *see* music
popular culture, 4, 31, 39, 163–4, **265–9**
population:
    age, 133
    flows *see* migration into cities
    statistics, 97
population control laws, 144–5
population registration cards, 76, **98**, 102
posters, 131–2, 258, 267
poverty, 144, 149, 248

pragmatism, 39
predestined relationships (*yuan*), 32, **38**
prisoners *see* criminals
privacy, 210, 225
private businesses, 48, 50, 219–21
'problem households' (*kunnanhu*), 138,
    140
production, 6, 44, 217–18, 280, 282–3
professions, 206–7, 220–21; *See also*
    lawyers
proletariat:
    culture, 169, 229
    emergence, 10–13, 130
    human rights, 23
    Marxism, 10–13, 23
    women, 282
propaganda, 49, 110, 157, 159, 225; *See
    also* posters
'proper name', 7, 242
propriety (*li*), 25–7, 30, 36, **40–41**
prostitution:
    human rights, 8
    migrant women, 79, 150
    policing, 67, 125
    regulations, 10, 13, 112, 119, **125–9**
    tattoos, 184
    urban design, 199
protocol *see* propriety (*li*)
psychology:
    socialism, 268
    tattoos, 186–7, **189–90**
    work units, **215–20**
public health care *see* health and medical
    services
public order *see* social order
public ownership, 48, 217–19
public security:
    compounds, 109–10
    deterioration, 68
    floating population, 91–2
    high rise, **224–7**
    policing, 92, 103, 250, 275; *See also*
        special population

work units, 44, 94–5
Zhejiang village, 150–52
public security units:
    employees, 118, 220
    household registration, 97–8
    prostitutes, 129
    resident identity cards, 94
    special professions, 114–15
    transient criminals, 89–90
    Weikeng Public Security Committee
        (Beijing), 93, **107–11**, 112
    Zhejiang village (Beijing), **152–9**
    *See also* 'mass-line' policing; Ministry of
        Public Security; police; special
        population
punishment *see* penalties
punk rock *see* music
puritanism, 132

Qianmen shopping district (Beijing),
    1–4, 153, 212

race *see* nationalities
rag trade, 149–51
reason (*yuan*), 32, **38**
recompense, reciprocation (*bao*), **35–7**,
    112
rectification *see* social order
Red Guards and rebels, 240, 245, 247,
    250, 258, 261
reform *see* economic reform; social reform
reform through education, 68–9, 90, 116,
    126, 187, 226
reform through labour, 45, 68–9, 116,
    128–9, 187, 226
registration cards *see under* household
    registration
regulations:
    beggars, prostitutes and undesirables,
        **118–29**
    cultural market, 266
    resident identity cards, 11, **94–7**
    service sector, 139

special population, 115–16
rehabilitation *see* detention centres
'relations' *see: guanxi*
religion, 24, 116, 280; *See also*
    Confucianism; Islam
architecture, 194, 196–7, 199; *See also*
    temples
rental accommodation, 149, 154
*renzhi* ('rule of man'), 25
repatriation:
    vagrant beggars, 120–24
    wages, 140–41, 143, 146
    Zhejiang villagers, 149
repayment, 'report' (*bao*), **35–7**, 112
repression, 17, 23, 278
residency fees, 77, 93, **99–103**
residency rights, 54, 77–8, 98–9, 147,
    155, 158
resident identity cards:
    introduction of, 7, 77, 93, 98
    numerical codes, 7–8, 93, 96
    regulations governing, 11, **94–7**
    work units, 43, 45, 214–15
restaurants *see* catering sector
retail sector *see* sales people; shopping
retribution, revenge (*bao*), **35–7**, 112
revolutionary culture, **168–9**
    architecture, 193
    commodification, 132, 223, 231–4,
        269–72, 275, 280–84
    history, 48–9, 53, 239–40, 244
    language *see under* language
    memorabilia, 4–5, 242–50, 253–61
    *See also* Cultural Revolution
righteousness, 27, 29, 277
rights, 24–5, 27–9, 52, 77; *See also*
    human rights; legal rights and
    interests; residency rights; *wenbao*
    (rights to subsistence)
rites *see* propriety (*li*)
roads and traffic, 152, 156
rock music *see* music
romanisation, 161, 165

rule of law/ rule by law, 24–5, 28, 45
'rule of man' (*renzhi*), 25
rural areas:
    architecture, 194–5, 197, 199–200,
        208–9
    caste and class, 77–80, **81–5**
    economy, 28, 57, 134–6, 219
    education, 48
    language *see under* language
    Maoism, 243, 251, 260
    migration from *see* migration into cities
    political authority, 88–9
    popular culture, 266
    revolution, 49, 53
    tattoos, 188
    work units, 54

'sacred sites', 242–3
sales people, 132, 138–9, 145–7
'saving face' *see* 'face'
scholarly ties, 206–7
script simplification, 161, **165–6**
second-class citizens, **65–9**, 80, 151; *See
    also* outsiders
second-hand and junk dealers, 113–14
secret societies, 67, 151–2, 180–5; *See also*
    criminals; triad groups
security *see* public security
sentencing *see* penalties
servants *see: baomu*
service workers, 127; *See also: baomu;*
    hotel service industry; sales people
'severe strike' (*yanda*), 68
sewerage, 210
sexuality, 22, 62, 131–2, 143, 189–90,
    278, 282–3; *See also* homosexuals;
    marriage; prostitution
sexually transmitted diseases, 73–4, 79,
    125, 127–9, 131–2, 150
Shanghai, 102–3, 150, 244–5, 247–8,
    250
Shaoshan, 223, 231–4, 258–60, 265

shopping, 3–4, 193, 223, **229–30**, 273;
    *See also* consumption; markets
*sifang* (crime prevention), 94–5, 98,
    **108–10**, 115
*siheyuan: see* compounds
slang *see* language
slogans, 239, 256, 280
social deviance, 163, 180
social intercourse *see* social relations
social order:
    architecture, 210, 226
    contemporary problems and policing,
        68, 91, 106, 109, 116, 125;
        Zhejiang village, 80, **152–9**
    Cultural Revolution, 250
    resident identity cards, 94–5
    tradition, 34
social organisation *see* cosmology; *guanxi*
    (relational networks); 'one family,
    two systems'; work units
'social persons', 215, **216–20**, 224
social reform, 30, 77–80, 165
social relations:
    architecture, 194, **203–13**, 224
    resident identity cards, 94–5
    traditional, 21; expressive actions,
        **35–8**; gift-giving, **40–41**;
        harmony, 29, **34–5**
    work units, 21, **56**, 59
social status *see* status
social welfare, 88, 124, 216, 218
socialism:
    building forms, 194–5, 203–4
    Chinese characteristics, 13
    economic reform, 3–4, 72–9, 130, 223,
        265, 282
    history, xiv, 48
    legal system, 110
    Maoism, 243, 251, 268, 280
    resident identity cards, 95
    work units, 42, 54, 215, 217, 222
songs *see* music
Soviet model, 54, 165–6, 169

spaces, 32, 193–4, **196–202**, 203–4, 210–11
special population (*zhongdian renkou*), 12, 69, 79, 112, **115–18**, 284
special professions (*tezhong hangye*), 79, **113–15**, 127, 132
stalls *see* markets
standards of living, 87, 133, 138, 150–52
state control, 56–7, 216, 218
state ownership, 48, 217–19
status:
    household registration, 82, 85
    outsiders, 78
    resident identity cards, 94, 98
    work units, 45, 52, 54, 56, 59, 218–20
stolen goods, 113
*Stories from the Editorial Room* (TV serial), 268–9
strangers, 9, 21, 112, 130
streetlife, 273, 282
students, 13–14, 186, 263; *See also* dissidents; universities
subaltern classes:
    consumerism, 273
    definition, 3
    human rights, 13–14
    regulations, 118
    tactics, 22, **77–80**, **130–59**, 284
    voices, 8–9, 14, 284
subjectivity *see* individualism
subsistence rights (*wenbao*), 14, 19
supermarkets, 133
surplus labour, 12, 65, 135
surveillance, 8, 10, 117, 224–7, 250; *See also* public security units
sweatshops, 149–51
symbolism (architecture), 193, **207–8**

taboos, 284
Taiwan, 33–4, 39, 98, 182
Taoism *see* religion
tattoos:
    criminals, 163, 172, 180–86, **187–90**

history, 163, **181**
    psychology, 180, **189–90**, 279
taxes, 145–7, 150
taxi station workers, 127
television, 245–6, 266–9
temples, 196, 198–9, 231
tenure of employment *see under* employment
*tezhong hangye: see* special professions
theme parks, 99, 223, 231–4, 284
Tiananmen Square (Beijing), 1, 91, 212, 243; demonstrations (1989), xiv, 16–17, 263–4
time, 32–3
*tongzhi* ('comrade'), 45, 52, 167
tourism (theme parks), 99, 223, 231–4, 284
tradition:
    architecture, 194, **196–7**, 203–6, 222–3
    culture, 19, 31, 39, 168–9
    human rights, **23–31**
    naming, 34, 162, **171**, 207
    work units, 21, 214–15
    *See also* Confucianism; popular culture
traffic, 152, 156
transformation, 39
transients *see: liumang*
triad groups, 8, 180, 182

unemployment, 8–12
United States:
    'American dream', 274
    art, 262–5
    employment compared, 46
    housing compared, 210
    Korean War, 49, 244
    naming, 170
    Revolution compared, 49
universities, 101–3, 220; *See also* students
urban design:
    Beijing, 193, **197–202**, 208, 211–13
    change, 222–30

cities as compounds, 197, 199–202, 210
Europe compared, 194, 196, 199
traditional, 194–7, 199–200
urban dwellers *see* city residents
urban life *see* cities
'user pays' (residency fees), 77, 93, **99–103**
utilitarianism, 39, 78

vagrants *see: youmin*
vertical migration *see* migration into cities
village governments *see* local-level government agencies

wages, 51–2, 57, 134, 138–43, 150, 216–17; repatriation, 140–41, 143, 146
walls, 194–5, 197, 199–200, 203–4, 210–13, 222, 229; *See also* Great Wall
Wang Anting, 239, 241, **252–8**
Weber, Max, 30
Weikeng Public Security Committee (Beijing), 93, **107–11**, 112
welfare, 88, 124, 216, 218
*wenbao* (rights to subsistence), 14, 19
West:
    attitudes towards China, 17–18; human rights, 23–9
    cities compared, 194, 196, 199
    influences, 23, 131–2, 183, 265
    mode of consumption compared, 222, 273–4, 278–84
    revolutions compared, 49
    *See also* United States
women:
    Cultural Revolution, 130–32, 282–3
    detention, 122, 124, 128–9
    employment, 80, 130, 133–4, 149; *See also: baomu*
    liberation, 282
    naming, 162

*See also* gender; nursing; prostitution; women's bodies
women's bodies:
    commodification, 130–32, 282–3
    tattoos, 184, 187, 189–90
    thieves' slang, 178
Women's Federation, 129, 134, 140
work cards, 94–5
work contracts *see* contractual obligations
work units:
    architecture, 193–4, 203–4, 212–13, 222, 224, 227–9
    authority, **56–8**
    code of conduct, **54–8**
    daily life, **42–61**
    detainees, 128
    'face' and 'place', **58–61**
    history, 3, 12, 48–50, **53–4**
    homosexuals, 73
    Mao badges, 240, 249
    people in, **42–53**, 214–18
    people outside, 21, 47, 59, 61–2, 78, 214–18, **219–21**; *See also* 'social persons'
    prostitution, 127
    security, 44, 94–5
    social organisation, 20–2, **53–8**, 215, 218
    *See also* enterprise work units; 'one family, two systems'
working class *see* proletariat
*wuxing* (five elements), 33–4, 171

Yan Xinlong, 241, **258–60**
*yanda* ('severe strike'), 68
*yin* and *yang*, 33–4, 171
*youmin* (vagrants):
    definition, 21, **63–5**
    economic reform, 78–9, 87
    Maoist era, 8
    Marxism, 10
    police response, 13, 79, 87, 112, 120–24

*See also: liumang*

young people:
  Communist Youth League, 44, 111
  crime, 107, 110–11, 277; re-education
    centres, 126
  Mao badges, 245
  tattoos, 183, 185–7
  *See also* students

*yuan* (predestined relationships), 32, **38**

Zhang Hongtu, 162–3, 172, **174**, 241,
  262–5
Zhejiang village (Beijing), 78–80,
  **147–59**
*zhongdian renkou: see* special population
Zhou Jihou, 241, **260–61**

discr...      z,
    14
discrim...          a         7–21
disease          f         101, 1
dissim...          fo
         l...         bou
dysp...          de...
us
t.

Printed in the United States
93853LV00003B/87-144/A